Elmer M Mason

Piedmont

7/21/59

DAY BEFORE YESTERDAY

DAY BEFORE YESTERDAY

The Reminiscences of

Mrs. Theodore Roosevelt, Jr.

DOUBLEDAY & COMPANY, INC.

GARDEN CITY, NEW YORK

1959

Library of Congress Catalog Card Number 59–8270

I am but a mirror
Having no virtue in myself.
It is my pride that he whom I reflect is distinguished.

ELIZABETH COATSWORTH

DAY BEFORE YESTERDAY

Chapter 1

"Where shall I begin, please your Majesty?"
he asked. "Begin at the beginning," the King
said very gravely, "and go on until you come to
the end: then stop."

LEWIS CARROLL

It was on the platform of the railroad station at New Haven, Connecticut, in October 1908 that I first saw Ted Roosevelt. He was twenty-one years old and I nineteen. I was not eager to meet the President's eldest son, whose name seemed always in the papers, as I thought he would be conceited and bumptious, but there was no avoiding it because we were both going to a weekend party at Mrs. Arthur M. Dodge's at Simsbury. Ted had come from Thompsonville, where he was working at the Hartford Carpet Company mill. There was time only for a brief introduction, as I was busy making sure my luggage had been transferred to the local train. In those days when you went on a house party you didn't go with a suitcase or two. You took a trunk, and if it didn't have a compartment for hats, you took a good-sized hatbox as well. I had both.

Although I had no idea of it at the time, this casual meeting was one of the most important events in my life, because Ted and I were married twenty months later.

I was born at 59 East Seventy-third Street, New York, a brownstone house that is still standing. My father was Henry Addison

Alexander, one of the handsomest men I ever saw, whose Scottish forebears came to this country in 1737. My great-grandfather, Archibald Alexander, was a Presbyterian minister and lived in Virginia. When a young man he was once seized with a severe chill while on a riding trip and stopped at the house of a friend, the Reverend James Waddel, who was famous as "The Blind Preacher." Dr. Waddel was in his study, being read to from the New Testament in Greek by his pretty daughter, Janetta. Archibald promptly fell in love. When he asked for her hand in marriage, her father said: "There is something I think I should tell you about Janetta's suitability as the wife of a clergyman. While her Latin is excellent and her Greek good, her Hebrew leaves much to be desired." In spite of this drawback they were married and were happy for many years. Archibald was president of Hampden-Sydney College and founded the Princeton Theological Seminary.

His son, Henry Martyn Alexander, my grandfather, married Susan Mary, daughter of the Reverend Matthew Brown, first president of Washington and fifth president of Jefferson College. The Browns were descended from John Brown, Scottish Covenanter, who was shot and killed in front of his farmhouse at Priesthill, Lanarkshire, Scotland, in 1685 by John Graham of Claverhouse, later Viscount Dundee, who, incidentally, was never called "Bonnie Dundee" until so named more than a hundred years later by Walter Scott.

The story of John Brown's execution is told in Macaulay's *History of England,* I believe quite inaccurately. Macaulay, always prejudiced against Claverhouse, is said to have got his material from an account written forty years afterward by a man who was not even there, the Reverend Thomas Wodrow. Macaulay uses some of his phrases, saying that John Brown "was for his singular piety called the Christian Carrier. He was versed in divine things and was blameless in life." The truth appears to be that Brown was a troublemaker. He was on the Porteous Roll of Criminals (Porteous was Public Prosecutor in Edinburgh) and had been in arms since Bothwell Bridge. He had weapons buried on his farm and treasonous papers hidden in his house. The story that Claverhouse did the shooting himself after his troops had refused to obey his order, and that it was done in front of John Brown's pregnant wife, who was holding a little child by the hand, is, in my opinion, pure fabrication.

My grandmother Alexander certainly inherited the blood of the Covenanters to a marked degree. She was an extraordinary old lady, who read her Bible from beginning to end every year of her life. She taught a large Bible class in New York and ruled her big family like a matriarch, never allowing them to dance, play cards, or go to the theater. No wine or liquor was ever served at her table; only hymns could be played on the piano on Sunday. I'm afraid some of the family reacted rather strongly in later years to this regime, but in spite of her strictness she had a keen sense of humor.

She and my grandfather spent the summers at Seabright, New Jersey, and built a small chapel on the beach where various evangelical ministers were invited to preach. Once when I was ten and was staying with my grandparents, the visiting minister said he would like to see the grandchildren. We assembled at tea. He looked around at us and said, "Fine! Fine! I am sure all these beautiful children have been raised in the fear of God. Now this little maiden"—turning to me—"can you repeat the books of the New Testament?" I knew all the books of the Bible and was halfway through the Shorter Catechism, but the unexpected question in front of people made my mind blank. I had been raised to fear God, but feared my grandmother much more. I began, "Matthew, Mark, Luke, and John——" and paused in anguish. Help came surprisingly from my grandmother herself, who said, "Saddle the cat and I'll get on. That's very nice. Thank you, dear. Now run away and play."

My mother, Grace Green, was born in New York. She had four ancestors on the *Mayflower*—John Tilley, his wife, their daughter Elizabeth, and her future husband John Howland. I used to think that no ship could possibly have held all the ancestors claimed by so many people, but a little research convinced me I was wrong. The descendants of the *Mayflower* passengers had enormous families, which fanned out in geometric progression to such an extent that almost anyone whose people came from New England can probably find such ancestors. I was astonished to find that both my mother and my mother-in-law, Mrs. Theodore Roosevelt, had four ancestors on the *Mayflower*, the same four. This I did not discover until after Ted's death, and I know he would have been amused to know I was almost the same degree of cousin to him that Franklin D. Roosevelt was.

Grace Green had over one hundred and twenty direct forebears in this country in the seventeenth century, who have been traced, thanks to the careful record of vital statistics kept in New England. Some of the men married women whose surnames are unknown. I wonder if these Christian names—Abigail, Mary, Elizabeth, Prudence, Mirabele—belonged to Indian girls baptized when they were married, and have been told this is very probable. These people settled mostly in Massachusetts and Connecticut. They seem to have been good citizens. Many were selectmen, magistrates, judges, and served in the militia. Some fought in the Indian wars. Two were colonial governors. In Hartford there is a monument erected in memory of eight of the original settlers. Six of them —Joseph Mygatt, Richard Seymour, John White, Samuel Stone, and Thomas Spencer—are my mother's ancestors. Another was Elizabeth Webster, wife of Jonathan Seymour, granddaughter of John Webster, Governor of the colony of Connecticut, and niece of Robert Treat, another Governor.

Some of Grace Green's forebears were pioneers in the West. Thomas Howe and his wife Clarissa, my mother's great-grandparents, journeyed with four children from Vermont to Ohio by ox sledge in 1817, the year after the famous "Eighteen Hundred and Froze to Death," also called "The Year without a Summer." Thomas and his cousins had bought a township in the Western Reserve. After settling in North Bloomfield, Clarissa got word that her mother had fallen ill in Williamstown, Vermont. Thomas was busy with his new acres, so she mounted a horse and rode back alone. The trip took three months. When the trail was rough and she had to walk her horse, she knitted socks to waste no time. Afterward she returned to her husband and children. Clarissa must have been a small woman, judging from her wedding ring, which I have.

One of their grandchildren was Albert Green, my mother's father. I remember him as a handsome man with thick white hair and black eyebrows, always willing to tell me stories of the early days. As a boy he was apprentice in a country general store and slept on the counter at night. For his supper he usually had two eggs cooked on the big stove in the center of the store. He would take a piece of heavy paper, bend up the edges, break the eggs on it, and put it on the stove. By the time the paper started to burn, the eggs were done.

Albert attracted the attention of Mr. Theron R. Butler of New York, who at the time was living in Columbus and was Secretary of State in Ohio. Mr. Butler offered him a job in New York. Albert ended by marrying his boss's daughter Mary and making a fortune in wholesale dry goods. Unluckily most of the fortune was embezzled after his death by a business associate who then committed suicide. Albert missed making another and larger fortune when he refused an opportunity to share in the oil business belonging to an acquaintance of his, John D. Rockefeller. He said oil came out of a hole in the ground; that sometimes you had it and sometimes you didn't. In any case, he preferred to invest in something he could see, like southern cotton mills.

Mary Butler was a pretty creature with chestnut hair and enormous brown eyes. She was educated in the 1850s at the Moravian Female Seminary at Bethlehem, Pennsylvania. According to its prospectus, "The Sessions commence on the second Monday in August and close on the last Thursday in June." The regular branches of instruction were "Spelling and Defining, Reading, Writing, English Grammar and Analysis, Arithmetic, Geography, Ancient and Modern History, Natural Philosophy, Chemistry, Mythology, Rhetoric, Geometry, Algebra, Book-keeping, Literature, Moral Science, Intellectual Philosophy, Logic and Natural History in its several branches, Geology, Mineralogy, Botany, &c." If a pupil took only these courses, the cost, including textbooks, "will not exceed Two Hundred Dollars" for a full session. Extra studies were provided at a small extra charge. These included "Ancient and Modern Languages, Drawing in Pencil and Crayon, Painting in Oil or Water Colors, Music on the Piano, Guitar and Melodeon, Vocal Music, and Ornamental Needlework in Worsted, Chenille &c." The prospectus goes on to say: "The correspondence of the students must all pass through the hands of the Principal or his wife, and is subject to their inspection if deemed necessary.

. . . To assist in forming correct habits of letter-writing, teachers revise the letters of the younger pupils . . . The young ladies are required to keep their own wardrobes in repair, and to spend some hours every week in plain needlework, which constitutes in the Junior Department a separate branch of regular instruction." Parents and guardians were requested "not to supply their daughters and wards with expensive or profuse ornaments" and were earnestly requested not to furnish them with too much spending money. The school, founded in 1785, felt no desire "to acquire a merely fashionable reputation," but used every effort "to cultivate correct personal and social habits, and to instill the principles of early piety." From all accounts this was most successful with Mary Butler, but I wonder how these rules would go down with modern teen-agers.

Theron R. Butler, Mary's father and my great-grandfather, was in the wholesale dry-goods business and for nineteen years was president of the Sixth Avenue Street Railways—in other words, the horsecars. He kept long working hours himself and took keen interest in the welfare of the men employed by his company, also in the health of the horses that drew the cars. He conducted a series of experiments to see if the Bible was wise in alloting one day out of seven for rest. He assigned a number of men and horses to rest every five, every six, every eight, and every nine days, and came to the conclusion that the Bible was right.

His franchise provided that nothing must be allowed to interfere with the free passage of his cars. When the Sixth Avenue Elevated was built he received a tempting offer to come in as an original stockholder. Disapproving of the project, he refused, saying he would fight it with his last dollar. This he very nearly did. He waited until the first posts were up and part of the track bed laid, then he had a double-decker car made just too high to go underneath. All had to be done over. I don't know what else he did to make things hard for the new company, but they defeated him in the end.

About 1860 he built a brownstone house at 433 Fifth Avenue, between Thirty-eighth and Thirty-ninth streets, for his second wife, Maria Miller, who was a little embarrassed at having it so far uptown. She was a cousin of General William Tecumseh

Sherman and outlived her husband by twenty-six years. As a child I often visited my step-great-grandmother, who told me she always addressed her husband as "Mr. Butler" and at the time of her marriage did not know his Christian name, taking for granted it was Theodore.

In the 1870s the Butler collection of paintings of the Barbizon school was famous. It included works by Corot, Millet, Rousseau, Diaz, Dupré, Troyon, Meissonier, and many others. When these were sold at auction in 1910 by the American Art Association in Mendelssohn Hall in New York, the sale attracted wide attention and was attended by dealers from England and France, unusual in those days.

Theron Butler had one child by Maria Miller, a daughter for whom I was named, Eleanor, Mrs. Henry M. Sanders. In 1893 she realized that woman suffrage was both desirable and inevitable but that women were as yet unprepared for this responsibility. Accordingly she gathered together a group of friends and founded the League for Political Education, now well known as Town Hall, recently taken over by New York University.

Chapter 2

One of those little prating girls,
Of whom fond parents tell such tedious stories.
DRYDEN

When I was three years old my parents were divorced. Mother and I went to California with my grandfather Green. While we were visiting friends there, Mother received a printed invitation with a deep black border, asking her to a hanging at the local jail. It was the first time in this town that a condemned man had stayed alive long enough to be executed by due process of law. The citizens made it a great occasion, with speeches and a brass band to play the "Funeral March." The prisoner, it was said, took deep interest in the preparations for the event. Mother did not attend.

We stayed two years in California, then were joined by Mother's sister, Alice Green, and went to Italy to spend the winter in Rome. They took me along wherever they went, and before the winter was over I had seen most of the churches and picture galleries. Although I was only just six, many of the places were familiar to me when I went back years later.

While we were in Rome we met Dr. Axel Munthe, later to become famous as the author of *The Story of San Michele*. Aunt Alice disliked him, but he was always ready to play with me and tell me stories, and Mother and I found him delightful. One night Mother and Aunt Alice had some friends to dinner. Afterward they were all in our sitting room at the Grand Hotel when a note was delivered to Mother from Dr. Munthe, asking her to meet him in the hall by the staircase. Aunt Alice was indignant. "This shows what kind of a man he is. Imagine his having the cheek to ask such a thing! Why on earth can't he come in and talk to you here? Tear it up and don't answer." Mother said she was sure he must have a reason for making the request, and left the room. Halfway up the wide staircase stood Dr. Munthe. "Don't come any closer. A little boy has diphtheria on the next floor. You must get your child out of the hotel at once. Her nurse can take her to my apartment. I shall be staying here for the next few days." At that time infection was believed to float through the air.

I was awakened and bundled off in a cab to Dr. Munthe's apartment near the Spanish Steps, where I stayed for a time, thoroughly enjoying myself playing with his various pets, including a most engaging monkey. The little boy died several days later.

Many years afterward I was to make friends with the woman who married him, Hilda Mellor. Her American mother, the wife of an Englishman, was an intimate friend of my mother's. They had a large place in Biarritz and frequently came to Paris. Hilda, who looked like the Venus de Milo, was interested only in studying and was out of sympathy with her mother's plans for her debut in Paris. On the night of her first ball Mrs. Mellor sent for a hairdresser. Hilda submitted, but sat engrossed in a book while the poor man frizzed her hair in the latest fashion. The effect of her dress, a white satin masterpiece by Worth, was not enhanced by the gray woolen stockings she had put on without noticing. Hilda fell deeply in love with Axel Munthe, who, saying frankly he was too old for her and was not made to be a good husband, went away. She then went into a decline until the doctors said she would die unless she could have her heart's desire. Her parents, who had opposed the match with all their might, sent Munthe an urgent message. He returned; they were married and had two sons. Since then I have never heard of her, nor have I been able to find more than the briefest mention of her in any of the books written about or referring to Dr. Munthe.

From Rome we went to Paris, where my parents were remarried and settled down in a house on a little square off the Avenue du Bois de Boulogne, now the Avenue Foch, where we lived for nearly six years. During this time I never stopped longing for the U.S.A. My family did not seem to mind being temporarily expatriated and were surprised when I gave a little tin box to a friend who was going home for a visit and begged him to bring it back to me full of "American soil."

Mother arranged for me to have an English governess in the morning and a French one in the afternoon. The former made me learn all the counties in England with their rivers and chief towns, study *Little Arthur's History of England*, and play scales on the piano. The latter was rather dull. I much preferred talking French to our chambermaid, Marie, an attractive girl who wore a Brittany cap of fluted organdy. One day she vanished and no one would tell me why. Years later I asked Mother about this and was told that a well-dressed, respectable-looking woman had rung the doorbell and asked to speak to Marie. After Marie answered the butler's summons, the woman whipped out a small revolver, shot her twice, wounding her severely, then left, saying, "This will teach you to leave my husband alone."

For two years I went to a small American school where the pupils were always addressed as Miss. When I was eleven I went as a day pupil to the Convent of the Assumption in the Rue de Lubeck. Having been raised a Presbyterian, I thought the Catholic customs glamorous, especially the services in the chapel, where we all wore long white veils, but at the same time I was a little worried as to how far I should go in doing what the others did. In the main hall was a life-size white marble statue of the Madonna and Child to which everyone curtsied when going by. This pricked my conscience a bit, and I told my parents about it. They said if it was the school custom perhaps I had better follow it. When I asked if this wasn't bowing down to graven images they were floored and made no reply, then or ever. I went on curtsying, but always with a slight feeling of guilt.

About this time the first automobiles were seen in Paris. Whenever one appeared, heralded by the terrific noise it made, people ran from every direction to watch it go by. These cars were painted in pastel colors, much like those of today. Besides an occasional automobile there was much to see on the Avenue du Bois. All sorts of carriages went by, from little cabs or fiacres to well-turned-out private victorias, landaus, dogcarts, phaetons, and coupés. My favorites were the Russian troikas, small open carriages drawn by three horses abreast, the one in the middle at a trot, the two at the sides at a canter with their heads turned away from the center. I liked to see the Parisian *nounous* or wet nurses, especially the more elegant ones, out for an airing with their charges. It was fun to watch an ultra-smart victoria with coachman, footman, and high-stepping horses in harness jingling with chains, stop while the footman assisted the *nounou* to alight with the baby and all her paraphernalia. He would set up her camp-chair in whatever spot she chose, moving it around until she was suited, make sure she had everything for her comfort, receive orders when to return for her, then jump up on the box as the carriage drove away. A *nounou* in a wealthy family wore an elaborate and costly costume. Wide ribbon of heavy silk grosgrain was pleated and sewed into a high round crown on top of her head, decorated with handsome gold filagree pins. The ends of the ribbon came down to the ground in the back. Her dress was of the finest silk under a long full cape of Kashmir wool. All was in matching color, usually pale pink or blue. These women were healthy peasants transplanted to a position of grandeur, where they ate nothing but the most delicate food and had everything their own way lest they be irritated and upset.

Also living in Paris at that time was John W. Alexander, the artist, who was married to my father's cousin, Elizabeth Alexander, and with them was their son James. Cousin John's first successful painting was a portrait of me aged nine with my doll. It was admitted to the Salon, then spent several years at various exhibitions all over Europe, winning a number of awards. In Berlin a representative of the Kaiser tried to buy it, but Mother refused to sell.

James, now a well-known scientist and mathematician, was just my age and we played together frequently. After we had all moved back to New York, James had a laboratory on the fourth floor of their house. One day when we were thirteen we amused ourselves by blowing soap bubbles full of gas and setting fire to them. James had attached a rubber tube to the illuminating-gas jet and put a cotton rag for a wick in a glass bottle full of alcohol. He would dip the end of the tube in a bowl of soapsuds and turn on the gas until a big bubble floated into the air. I would hold the lighted wick under it and it would burst most satisfactorily into flame. After we had done this for a time I felt the glass bottle crack and saw that the alcohol in it had caught fire. Before I could reach the table to put it down it broke, spilling blazing alcohol over the floor and my hand. We managed to stamp out the fire and moved a table to hide the large black patch it had made. Of course "they" must never hear of this. I had some trouble hiding my badly blistered hand and would have succeeded had I not come down with measles the next day. The trained nurse was horrified and refused to believe my story that I really had no idea how I had come by such a burn.

The whole house was put in quarantine for measles, with a warning sign nailed to the front door. No one but the doctor and nurse was allowed in my room. Before seeing me the doctor would wrap himself in a sheet, cover his head with a pillowcase with slits for his eyes, and wore white cotton socks over his shoes. All my dishes and bedclothes had to be boiled and my books put in the furnace after I was well. Times have indeed changed since 1901.

A Scotswoman named Jane had been my nurse since I was six weeks old. I never saw anyone who looked more thoroughly respectable, with her steel-rimmed spectacles, her gray hair combed back into a neat bun, and her little Victorian bonnet tied under her chin. For thirteen years Jane gave her age as "forty-two my last birthday." While we were still living in Paris, Jane's great friend was Agnes, a lady's-maid to Mrs. Beach Grant (whose daughter Adèle married the Earl of Essex), who lived in an apartment house on the other side of the Avenue du Bois de Boulogne. Sometimes we used to go to see Agnes, who often sat and sewed in the garden. I was always enthralled by their conversation, especially because they never wanted me to hear what they were saying and would tell me to run away and bounce my ball. Once I managed to get close behind them before they noticed me and heard, "And then she took the baby from the nurse and put it down the closet." To this day I wonder what else happened.

To Jane all foreigners were queer at best and thoroughly immoral. She disapproved of the French way of making Sunday a holiday and would never let me take a toy out on that day. To roll a hoop or whip a top was to break the Sabbath. Sometimes we passed boys playing marbles on the street. Jane would come to a majestic halt and say in English (she scorned learning a word of French), "Six days shalt thou labor, boys!" and walk on, her bonnet strings quivering with indignation.

Mother used to send me to Scotland with her during the summer for a change of air. We would take lodgings at little farmhouses in Aberdeenshire. I still remember the substantial food we had, bowls of finely ground oatmeal, Scotch broth almost solid with barley, oatcakes, bannocks, scones, and baps. I learned the Highland fling, and could do the sword dance from beginning to end, no mean athletic feat. I enjoyed sleeping on mattresses stuffed with chaff, learning how to care for chickens and how to milk cows. As no one thought of germs in those days, I used to fill my silver mug right from the cow, blow off the froth, and drink the warm milk.

Jane took pride in my blonde hair and encouraged its slight natural curl by rolling it on rags every night. She was always afraid I might get chicken lice in it from the hen house. Once when she suspected this she scrubbed and combed me for a couple of hours and forbade me to go into the hen house again. It made such an impression on me that I considered it one of the events of the summer.

Shortly after we returned to Paris after one of our summers in Scotland, the wife of a Scandinavian diplomat came to tea, bringing her two little daughters. I came down to our white-and-gold drawing room in my best black velvet dress with a *point de Venise* lace collar. The little girls hadn't much to say, and conversation lagged while I tried to think of something interesting. During a pause, when the grownups were watching us, I looked at their long hair, asked if they were often troubled with lice, and could not understand why everyone was so horrified and Mother was so annoyed.

In Aberdeen, Jane's home town, she had two sets of relatives who moved in different social circles and had little to do with one another. Her brother Willie, a brawny man with a curly black beard, was head blacksmith for the Aberdeen streetcar horses. As a special treat I would be taken to see him at his forge, pounding red-hot iron into horseshoes while an assistant worked a giant bellows. I never could see why it didn't hurt a horse to have a glowing-red shoe fitted sizzling to its hoof. Willie had two sons, both nice boys, but one had the added attraction of a withered leg he could twist around his neck. I much preferred this branch of Jane's family to her cousins, a well-to-do lawyer, his wife and grown children, who lived on Bon-accord Street. But what filled me with fearful joy was to be taken to see another Willie, Jane's cousin, "The Bookie Boy." He was seventeen, tall and shambling, and lived with his widowed mother in a little cottage across the tracks. Willie was daft and cared only for little pictures. We always took him some colored post cards. When he saw us coming he would hurry to meet us, calling: "Hev' ye a bookie? Hev' ye a bookie?" When given one he would shuffle into the house, hide it, and come back for another. He had little pictures tucked away all over the cottage and his mother never disturbed them.

As the years passed, Jane developed a weakness. She took to drink. At first Mother did not realize this, but I did and it vexed me. Once when we were ready to go for a walk Jane disappeared. I found her in the dining room drinking whiskey out of the bottle. She started when she saw me, put down the bottle, and said: "Ah, dearie, I wasna drinking oot o' it. I was just holdin' it oop to se if 'twas fu'." Sometimes at night she was so drunk that she would be actively sick and I would have to steer her to her bed. At such times she would wail: "I should ha' kenned better than to drink milk wi' cherries!"

I never told Mother anything of this, but she found out, lectured Jane, and received many promises that were never kept. The end came suddenly when I was thirteen and was having chicken pox. Jane was bringing up my breakfast and stumbled on the stairs. The crash of broken china brought Mother from her room to see cocoa dripping from step to step, scrambled eggs and marmalade all over the carpet, and Jane sitting in the middle of the mess, a foolish smile on her face. "Oo-aye, ma'am dearie," she said. "I caught me foot i' the tray!" Poor Jane left that afternoon.

In 1898, the year of the Spanish-American War, Mother and I

spent two months with Grandfather Green in Palm Beach, a quiet little place compared to what it is today. We stayed at the Palm Beach Inn, later made over into The Breakers. The famous actor, Joseph Jefferson, and his wife were there, and we all had a table together in the dining room. I loved to hear Mr. Jefferson's stories. One was about his son Willie, who telegraphed from college asking his father for fifty dollars. Mr. Jefferson wired back, "What for?" His son replied, "For Willie," and got the money.

I had been taken to see Joseph Jefferson in 1893 in a revival of *Rip Van Winkle*, his most famous role, but was so little that I can remember nothing except that I wore a yellow coat and bonnet and my new kid gloves were too tight.

When I was a child the popular theory was "wool next the skin." I wore gray double-breasted Jaeger "combinations" with long sleeves and legs, pajamas of the same with the additional protection of feet, woolen stockings, Jaeger binders (politely called "tummy bands"), and flannel petticoats, and was always too hot. Although Jane would say, "Ne'er cast a clout till May's oot," I generally wangled my way into summer things by the middle of May. This meant lighter-weight woolen underwear, pajamas without feet, and lisle stockings, but I had to wear flannel petticoats summer and winter until I finally rebelled when I was fourteen. After my marriage I was going to live in San Francisco, which my mother described as having a cold, damp climate. My trousseau came from Lucile, Lady Duff Gordon, a famous London and Paris couturière who had just opened a shop in New York with enchanting clothes. I remember her surprise when Mother insisted on having all my dresses either of wool or lined with pale pink albatross flannel.

Chapter 3

No dancing bear was so genteel.
COWPER

In 1900, when I was twelve years old, my mother divorced my
father for the second time. In those days divorce was rare among
"people one knew" and was viewed with disapproval no matter
where the fault lay, but the entire Alexander family rallied behind
my mother and arranged to have this demonstrated at once. On
the day the news of the divorce was carried in the papers my
cousin Susan—later Mrs. Peter Augustus Jay, daughter of my father's sister, Mrs. John J. McCook—and the family debutante of
the year before, called for my mother in the McCook carriage, an
open landau well known to New Yorkers with its fine horses, stout
coachman Mooney, and attendant footman. Susan said it might
be pleasant to take a little drive on such a lovely afternoon. Drive
they did, up and down Fifth Avenue for two hours at the fashionable time of day, until everyone in New York who mattered either
had seen them or would hear about them from friends.

After we had moved back to New York from Paris, Mother was
hunting for a house and happened to drive through West Forty-
fifth Street and saw a "For Rent" sign on Number 25. It was a
small brownstone house, and on the sidewalk in front of it were
three new enameled bathtubs waiting to be installed. She was attracted by the idea of nice new plumbing, went through the house

and leased it. It seemed odd that bolts were on the outside of the bedroom doors, but this was explained by the fact that the previous owner had been a "specialist in mental diseases" who treated patients on the premises.

A room on the third floor was set aside for Ernest Simpson, our Irish coachman, who had been employed for more than twenty-five years by my grandfather Green and lived with his family in East Orange. It was arranged for him to come to the city every day to drive Mother's carriage, and to sleep in the house in case she kept him out late at night. Ernest spent one night in that room and made no comment, but from then on he took a train home no matter how late the hour.

The room was then turned into a guest room. My aunt Mary, who lived in Port Chester, came to spend the night. About midnight she came to Mother's room, upset by something strange and indescribable, and spent the rest of the night on Mother's sofa. She never was willing to sleep in that room again. The next visitor was a girl from Boston, a friend of my own age. In the middle of the night she came into my room and woke me, saying, "There is something in that other room I don't like." By then I was dying to find out what the mystery was and changed rooms with her. I heard and saw nothing.

Soon after, Mother engaged a Frenchwoman, Louise Cupillard, as lady's-maid. Louise was to sleep in what was now known as the "ghost's room." Mother, out of patience with the whole thing, gave orders that no one was to tell her anything about it. No one did for several weeks. Then, thinking it would be all right, I asked her if she had ever noticed anything peculiar in her room. Louise laughed. "I certainly did," she said. "*C'était vraiment formidable.* But it's all right now."

"What was it?" I asked. "Tell me."

"Well, the first night I was here I locked my door. I always do in a strange place. It's a good thing to do anywhere. I was waked from a sound sleep by the door opening. Something with rustling skirts came in, walked over to my bed, leaned over me, and sighed. I don't like that sort of thing at all, and I needed my rest, so next day I did the necessary to stop it."

"What did you do?"

"Oh, the usual thing. There is only one precaution that works. Anyone can tell you that."

"*You* tell me!"

"It's simple. I went to Lewis and Conger on the corner of Sixth Avenue, and I bought the largest carving knife they had and asked them to put a razor edge on it. Then I laid it across the threshold of the door every night, with the sharp edge toward the hall. No spirit can cross anything like that, and I haven't been disturbed since."

I didn't know then that the Moi, jungle folk in the interior of Indo-China, when going on a journey are careful to leave thorns in the path behind them to prevent evil spirits from following them, or that in certain parts of Great Britain it is still believed that fairies cannot cross "cold iron."

Our cook and parlormaid, Elizabeth and Anna Malm, two sensible, unimaginative Swedish cousins who were with us for over thirty years, were aware of the ghost but paid no attention to it until we once went to the mountains for the summer, leaving them in the house as caretakers. One evening they tried to move a chest of drawers from the front room on the top floor to a room at the back. Halfway down the narrow passage, it stuck. They decided to leave it until morning and get the choreman to help. Anna told me about it later, saying they had been really frightened. Something had raged up and down the hall all night, making so much noise that neither had dared open her door. It seemed in a fury because the bureau was in its way. I was exasperated that all this could happen without my being able to see or hear any of it.

Our house was small, but we had the usual household that most of our friends seemed to have if they didn't have a butler and one or two footmen. We had a cook, kitchenmaid, parlormaid, housemaid, and lady's-maid, all Swedish but the last, who was French. In the morning the parlormaid and housemaid wore printed cotton dresses costing a dollar and a half. In the afternoon they wore black dresses at three dollars and a half, with white aprons and bibs. Their starched and pleated white muslin caps had long streamers down the back. They and the lady's-maid were paid twenty-five dollars a month, the cook thirty-five. If the kitchenmaid could speak English she got fifteen dollars; if not, twelve. We shared a choreman with some neighbors. He tended the furnace, shoveled coal, swept the sidewalk, carried up wood for the fires, and did odd jobs.

Many houses had speaking tubes from the upper floor to the kitchen. These had round openings into which you blew with all your might, causing a loud whistle to attract the attention of the cook. When she answered, you could talk together. Even after electric light was introduced to replace gas, bells were rung in old houses by pulling down a lever on the wall. A row of metal bells hung outside the kitchen. In order to determine in which room she was wanted, a maid had to look at them to see which bell was shaking. A great convenience, no longer seen, was a smaller lever pressed down to summon a Western Union messenger boy, who would come at once and do any errand required. Once before my father left us I was asked to bring some food to school for a poor family's Thanksgiving dinner. My mother suggested a turkey. That was all very well, but my father used to take me to school and positively refused to be seen carrying a turkey. We walked up Fifth Avenue preceded by a small messenger boy carrying an enormous turkey, its feet sticking out of the top of a paper bag.

Telephones were big wooden contraptions attached to the wall, usually only one in each house. In making a call you first turned a crank vigorously. This rang a bell and attracted the attention of the operator, whom you called "Central." You then gave the number before the exchange, which was named for a street, "4660 Thirty-eighth Street," or "572 Columbus Avenue."

Of course no traffic lights existed and no one-way streets. Horse cabs were plentiful, both hansoms and four-wheelers, and would come to your door when summoned. Buses, drawn by horses, ran only on Fifth Avenue. They were entered and left by a door in the middle of the back, opened and closed by the driver manipulating a strap from his seat high in front outside. Little coin receptacles were set in the window directly behind and below the driver, who would rap sternly on the glass if you didn't drop your nickel in promptly. If you needed change you slid back a pane in the window and reached out to the driver. The choicest seats in good weather were on top outside. Benches holding four were perched behind the driver, reached by little steps and handholds.

In 1907 theater tickets could be had a few hours in advance and cost $1.50, except for box seats at Buffalo Bill's Wild West Show, which were expensive and cost $3.30. The plays that year included *Cousin Kate* with Ethel Barrymore, *The Prince Chap* with Cyril Scott, *Little Johnny Jones* with George M. Cohan, *The Orchid* with Eddie Foy, *The Rose of the Rancho* with Frances Starr, and, best of all, *Salomy Jane* with Eleanor Robson, now Mrs. August Belmont.

The Junior League was founded in 1901 by Mary Harriman, daughter of E. H. Harriman, probably the most powerful railroad man of the day, and sister of Averell Harriman, recently Governor of New York. It consisted of perhaps twenty debutantes who had known one another since childhood and whose families had been friends for years. In sharp contrast to the almost professional spectaculars presented by the Junior League today, their annual plays in Carnegie Lyceum, a small auditorium above Carnegie Hall, were well done but of the utmost decorum and were never allowed to be mentioned in the newspapers.

News coverage was unlike that of today. Even the New York *Times* was different. As an indication of what interested people in those days, it carried news of New York politics in detail, but little of national affairs and very little foreign news. For some days it would have practically no news from Washington, then a long story about a dog someone had given my future father-in-law, headed: PETE, ENGLISH BULLDOG, JOINS PRESIDENT'S GUARD. A few days later another story appeared: PETE BITES TOURIST. The front page had local politics, murders, and sensational or trivial stories of various kinds. One item said that Gloria Gould, baby sister of Jay Gould, court tennis champion, had been sent with her attendants to a suite in a London hotel while her parents were in Paris. Another told of a woman having been beaten, robbed, and strangled with her own false hair. The clergyman of a fashionable church had left his wife and eloped with a seventeen-year-old parishioner. This was on the front page for days, giving every word said by prominent vestrymen and what the clergyman had replied. A tenor who had sung once at the Metropolitan became discouraged and cut out his tongue with a pair of scissors.

Foreign news, which nobody cared much about, was on page 4

or in a Special Cable Section on Sunday. In May 1907, for instance, this section contained a number of chatty social items, such as KING OF ITALY IN FAMILY ROW because his wife's relations were spending too much money; KING OF SAXONY'S ESTRANGED WIFE SEEKS FORGIVENESS, with many details; BRILLIANT SEASON START- ING IN LONDON, with a long list of people giving parties or seen at the races; SPRING COMES AT LAST IN PARIS, with a graphic description of the weather and names of people seen at the Ritz bar. Occasionally foreign politics would be mentioned: CLEMEN- CEAU HATED BY ALL PARTIES.

Advertisements in the papers were interesting. B. Altman was selling tan Russia leather pumps for $3.50. McCutcheon's had linen sheets for $4.50 a pair and matching pillowcases for $1.00 a pair. Hair mattresses, single-bed size, were at Lord & Taylor's for $10.00. At Gorham's, sterling-silver cheese scoops were $1.75. The best-quality Wilton velvet carpet was $1.15 a yard. Imported Chinese and East Indian rugs, nine by twelve, were advertised for $18.00. Upholstered armchairs sold for $9.00. You could get a hundred-piece dinner set of French Limoges china for $19.00. Best's was the Liliputian Bazaar with clothes only for children, and Woodbury advertised facials that would remove smallpox scars.

New York in the early 1900s seemed more like a country town than a big city. When we first came back from Paris I went to Miss Keller's School for boys and girls on West Fifty-fifth Street. We used to play prisoners' base in the vacant lot opposite, where the Gotham Hotel now stands. I was never allowed to go out of the house alone until I was eighteen, even when I went to Miss Spence's School for Girls only three blocks from where we lived. When two or three of us were together someone's maid walked discreetly behind us. Maids took us to dances and waited sleepily in dressing rooms until we were ready to go home.

We wore our long hair (I could sit on mine) down our backs, tied with a ribbon or in a braid, until we were about fifteen, then we wore the braid turned up, as my mother said, "like a horse's tail on a wet day." Two large bows were needed, one on top of the head, the other holding the turned-up braid at the neck. This was known as "a bob," and although ugly and unbecoming it was

31

cherished as a sign of advancing years. When we were seventeen our hair "went up" and was pinned high on our heads behind a pompadour as lofty as we could make it. At this stage we were allowed to lengthen our skirts to three inches from the ground, another eagerly awaited sign of being grown up.

When my class at Miss Spence's graduated in 1907 our average age was less than eighteen. With our elaborate hair-dos and the eighteen-inch train we were allowed to have on our dresses, we looked years older than the faculty at the same school today. Ridiculous as it may seem, I never did my own hair or put on shoes and stockings myself until after I was married. During the winter Monsieur Alleau, a French hairdresser with a mustache and tiny pointed beard known as an "imperial," used to come to the house every evening before dinner to do Mother's hair, which was even longer and thicker than mine.

Permanent waves had not been invented, and false hair was worn by everyone whose hair-do needed reinforcing. The use of switches or puffs pinned on the top of the head was said to be beneficial because it prevented damage to one's own hair from the too frequent use of curling tongs. To dye the hair was positively immoral. Colored liquid nail polish was unknown. If you wanted gleaming nails, you buffed them. Except for a very little surreptitious powder, we went around with shining morning faces, fresh from scrubbing with soap and water. All other make-up was taboo, and a girl using it was thought bad form by the others, who no doubt secretly envied her but whose parents had sharp eyes. When the Peter Pan collar, open to the base of the throat, came into fashion, replacing the high boned ones we were used to, my mother would not let me go out in the street without a scarf wound around my neck until after I was married.

People wore deep mourning if a member of the family died, the length of time depending on the closeness of the relationship. Widows wore heavy crepe veils reaching to the ground, front and back. After a time the front veil was removed. At the end of a year "half mourning" was correct: gray, purple, and black and white. Handkerchiefs had black hems, writing paper and visiting cards black edges of varying width. Although the postal tariff was two cents for a letter, some women used the purple three-cent stamps as

32

being more suitable than the red two-cent stamps. Several people I knew wore black underclothes. Coachmen and footmen were put into mourning livery. The custom extended to children. When I was eleven both my grandfathers died, and I wore black for six months. My grandmother Green died when my aunt Mary was born in 1872, and the poor baby's little dresses were trimmed with black bows for a year. Two small girls I knew had a bay pony, which was turned out to grass while a black one was provided for the period of mourning.

If we went to the theater before going to a ball, we would start out in a high-neck evening dress and a hat, going home to change in the middle of the evening. For this reason elaborate dresses were often made with two bodices, high and low. In the early 1900s hats were so enormous that often a notice would be flashed on the curtain in the theater: LADIES WILL KINDLY REMOVE THEIR HATS. If they didn't, half the audience might as well have stayed home. The year I came out every evening dress had a train. My mother had all mine lined with crinoline so that if stepped on they wouldn't be torn to pieces. It was considered bad form to hold them up, so while dancing one's partner had to be adept at kicking trains out of the way.

In summer we wore white blouses and ankle-length skirts of heavy white drill made by a tailor called Mrs. Dark, who once told me she had used three miles of drill in a single year. With these we wore white buckskin oxfords and silk stockings, the heavier the better, in red, blue, green, yellow, violet, or whatever color we preferred. These cost from five to seven dollars a pair, or even more if they were hand-embroidered. We also wore plaid stockings in gay colors. I still have two pairs which my children have always hung up at Christmas.

Our bathing suits, usually made of alpaca, had skirts below the knee and long sleeves. No one thought of going in the water without stockings; indeed, there was a regulation to that effect at Bailey's Beach in Newport. Most of us swam the breast stroke, our heads high above the water, because no rubber cap could ever keep our hair completely dry. As a result my children tell me I swim like a giraffe. I shall always remember Mrs. Emily Post at the Swimming Club in Bar Harbor in 1907. A real beauty, she was ravishing in a black crepe-de-Chine bathing suit worn over a long corset, with black silk stockings and a large black tulle hat trimmed with egrets. The costume was impractical, perhaps, but it certainly had great style.

Chapter 4

We have all the same number of forefathers.
SENECA

At Mrs. Dodge's house party in Simsbury everyone was asked to bring riding clothes as she had a stableful of horses and a paper chase had been arranged. I had spent two summers riding and camping with my mother in Yellowstone Park, a wilderness in those days, and was rather proud of my horsemanship. We had just returned. I was dying to talk about my adventures to anyone who would listen, but so far no one had been interested. Being shy and quite unable to tell a good story, I usually sat in silence while my friends described their summers at Bar Harbor, Newport, or Tuxedo.

The first night at Mrs. Dodge's I sat by Ted Roosevelt at dinner and was surprised and charmed to find him so agreeable. He knew the western country well and wanted to hear all about where we had gone and what we had done. Even at that age he was keenly interested in people and in different points of view and had a remarkable faculty of making one feel at one's best. After dinner we sat on the stairs and continued our talk while the others played games. Ted asked me to ride to the meet with him before the paper chase next day. When the evening was over I went to bed pleased with the world.

The next morning was crisp and cool, with bright sunshine. I dressed with care in a new riding habit: whipcord breeches under a long coat that hooked securely so that my knees would not show when I dismounted. Mother had thought it too extreme and wanted me to get a divided skirt to my ankles, but I had persuaded her to let me have it.

The horses were brought to the door. My Wyoming cow pony, while fleet and well gaited, and my McClellan saddle had in no way prepared me for a fresh eastern polo pony under a tiny English racing saddle. I could see Ted admiring my habit as he helped me to mount, and I flattered myself that I was appearing to advantage, when the pony bucked, whirled, and bolted for the stable. That saddle was nothing but an impediment and I would have been better off bareback. I lost both stirrups and hung on desperately. The pony stopped short at the stable door, nearly tossing me over his head. We were led back to the house by a surprised groom. I hardly dared look at Ted for fear he was laughing at me, but his face was set like a rock and he behaved as if nothing unusual had happened.

As we set out for the meet, several miles away, only one thought was in my mind: to avoid being dumped on the road. I had no purchase on the slippery leather and could ride only by balance. Ted tactfully suggested going slowly as it was such a beautiful day, but I could have done nothing else. Any attempt at a trot or canter would have meant my doom. That wretched pony would not walk, he would only jog-trot sideways. His mouth was made of iron. My hat was shaken off and, final and inexcusable humiliation, my hair fell down below my waist and flapped in the breeze, scattering hairpins. Ted recovered my hat, and while I frantically stuffed my hair under it, trying my best to make it secure, he held my bridle. All the while he kept talking to me pleasantly on various subjects, but misery kept me from answering him. Before we had gone a mile I realized I could not possibly go on the paper chase but would rather have died than confess it to the rest of the party.

"It's no use, Mr. Roosevelt," I said, "I just can't do it. What on earth am I to say?"

"Don't say anything," answered Ted. "You've a right to change your mind, haven't you? If you like, I'll tell the others you prefer not to go after all. Never make unnecessary explanations."

Mrs. Dodge and I watched the chase from an open touring car, catching brief glimpses of the riders tearing over the country at breakneck speed, but I didn't mind. Ted had made everything right. What was more, he never teased me about it or even mentioned the incident again.

The progenitor of the Roosevelt family in America was Klaes Martensen van Roosevelt, who came to New Amsterdam from Holland in 1644. He is thought to have been the son of Maerten Cornelissen Geldersman, who bought land including a farm called "Roosevelt" (Field of Roses) on the Dutch island of Tholen in 1649. Roosevelt was a place designation used to identify whoever owned this farm, and soon afterward Geldersman's name appears in the records as "Maerten Cornelissen Geldersman van Roosevelt." He seems to have run into hard times, for he had to make a new arrangement in 1652 with his creditors regarding payment for the farm, and the next year he was in jail at Tholen. He then went into bankruptcy and fled to the mainland, pursued by the bailiff of Poortvliet. To settle his debts his mother's house at Oud Vossemeer was confiscated, although his own farm was not sold until four years later. It may have been because of his father's circumstances that Klaes Martensen van Roosevelt left for America, where he founded a family of substance and distinction, numbering among his descendants two Presidents of the United States.

Seven generations of Roosevelts had been born on the island of Manhattan, including the first Theodore Roosevelt (1831–78), a prominent banker and philanthropist. In 1853 he married Martha Bulloch of Roswell, Georgia. Their son Theodore, twenty-sixth President of the United States, always said his father was the best man he ever knew. In addition to the first Theodore's many civic and charitable interests, he raised a fund to take care of the abandoned children roaming the streets of New York after the Civil War, sleeping in cellars of empty houses and living on whatever food they could steal or dig out of garbage cans. He had difficulty in this because many of the eminent men he asked for donations declared this evil was too deep-rooted to be cured and said New York would always have bands of wild children. In later years his descendants felt it was a pity that when his friend Alexander Graham Bell brought a new invention called a telephone to his office and connected it so that he could talk from his desk to a room down the hall, Mr. Roosevelt said that while it was indeed an interesting device it would never amount to more than a toy and he refused to invest in it.

Martha's great-grandfather, Archibald Bulloch, was the first revolutionary president of Georgia and signed the first constitution of that state. Three times in succession he was elected president of the Provincial Congress of Georgia and was delegate to the Continental Congress in Philadelphia in 1775, besides holding other offices.

Martha's two brothers were James Dunwody and Irvine. James was an admiral in the Confederate Navy and also a Confederate agent in England, where he arranged for the construction of the *Alabama*. Irvine was midshipman on this vessel and fired the last gun discharged from her batteries in her fight with the *Kearsage*. After the war both men lived in Liverpool, occasionally visiting their sister Martha in New York, but as they were among the Confederates not included in the amnesty, they were obliged to use assumed names.

Martha Bulloch Roosevelt was a woman of beauty, dignity, and courage. She was also an irrepressible mimic. One evening at a family party she started giving an imitation of "Old Bess in a fit." Her husband, who disliked seeing her lovely face distorted, remonstrated in vain, then picked her up, slung her over his shoulder, and carried her from the room. A story told by her cousin, Mrs. Samuel N. Clark, gives a good illustration of her courage. She and Mrs. Roosevelt were driving in a closed carriage in New York when the horses ran away and the coachman was thrown from the box. Mrs. Clark said:

> The thoroughly frightened team tore madly from street to street. Men repeatedly rushed out to stop them, but their attempts only served to increase the trouble, and the carriage lurched from side to side, running on two wheels part of the time.
>
> The horses kept on in the direction of the stables, the occupants fully expecting, at every corner, to be dashed to death.

38

During this most trying ordeal, Mrs. Roosevelt sat as calm as a statue, looking neither to the right nor the left, and saying not a word.

Dashing into the open stable, they crashed against the opposite wall, breaking the carriage pole and fatally injuring one of the horses.

A score of men came to their rescue. Someone opened the door and a half dozen asked if they were hurt. Mrs. Roosevelt stepped out, shook the bottom of her skirt slightly, and said to one of the stablemen in a very calm voice, "Will you hand me my cardcase, James?"

Theodore Roosevelt (1858–1919), the future President, married Alice Hathaway Lee from Boston in 1880. Four years later she died giving birth to a daughter, Alice, who was to marry Nicholas Longworth of Cincinnati, Congressman and later Speaker of the House. Nearly three years after his wife's death Theodore married Edith Kermit Carow of New York.

Edith came of French Huguenot stock on her father's side. The name was originally Quereau but was changed at the beginning of the nineteenth century by her grandfather, Isaac Quantin Carow, who was president of the New York Chamber of Commerce. On her mother's side she was descended from "The Great Divine," Jonathan Edwards. Her maternal great-grandfather, Benjamin Lee, was born in England in 1765 and was a midshipman in the British Navy. During the American Revolution he commanded a battery at the engagement between the sea forces of Admiral Rodney and those of the Count de Grasse off the island of Guadeloupe. He was commended for gallantry in this action, but his naval career was cut short when he had a controversy with his superior officer, who had countermanded a humane order regarding prisoners on his ship. He challenged this lieutenant to a duel, but instead found himself court-martialed and condemned to death for insubordination. His life was saved when his fellow officers drew up a petition for leniency which was taken to Admiral Rodney by another midshipman, Prince William Henry, Duke of Clarence, afterward King William IV. Benjamin Lee's sentence was commuted to dismissal from the Navy. When he left his ship

at Port Royal the whole fleet manned the yards and cheered him
—"an honor never before or since paid to a young officer." He sent
a second challenge to the lieutenant, wounded him in the duel
that followed, then came to America and entered the Merchant
Marine. He was nineteen years old.

As I have said, Edith Kermit Carow had four ancestors on the
Mayflower. The Kermit in her name was after her great-aunt's husband, Robert Kermit, a shipowner, who gave his wife a set of aqua-
marines as a wedding present: necklace, long earrings, bracelet,
and brooch. In order to have the set ready in time the jeweler
had to work on Sunday, horrifying their relatives. Many years ago
my mother-in-law gave me these sparkling drops of water set in
gold.

Ted's bringing up was completely different from mine. When
our engagement was announced, his aunt, Mrs. Douglas Robin-
son, remarked that we supplemented each other perfectly for this
reason. She said I had been raised subject to strict law and order,
while in the Roosevelt family these were subordinate to the development of the individual. This left us in utter doubt as to which,
if either, she approved.

I loved to have Ted tell me stories about his childhood at Sagamore Hill. I was an only child and had lived in orderly and precise
fashion in a small house meticulously run. Ted's account of his
life with his three brothers and two sisters—Kermit, Archie, Quentin, Alice, and Ethel—enthralled me. I never tired of hearing about
his family pets, which included at various times an eagle, a macaw,
a mountain lion, a bear, and a badger called Jonathan Edwards.
Emperor Menelik of Abyssinia had sent a present of a lion and a
zebra, which were given at once to the Washington zoo over the
children's frantic protests. Sagamore seemed at one time, oddly
enough, to have been infested with weasels, for Ted found one
under the family bathtub and another killed two flying squirrels
that slept in his room. There were always several dogs, and these
too slept with the children, in cold weather under the bedclothes.
All the children had guinea pigs and carried them around in their
blouses. Ted said they also took the guinea pigs to bed. When his
father was Governor of New York and the family was in Albany,
a menagerie of pets, rabbits, squirrels, guinea pigs, and a raccoon

was kept in the cellar of the Executive Mansion. No grownups seem to have noticed this during the winter, but one day in spring when Mrs. Roosevelt was having a reception the cellar windows were opened to give the animals some fresh air. The smell drifting in through the drawing-room windows astonished the guests; the cellar zoo was discovered, promptly reduced in numbers, and moved.

Behind the house at Sagamore Hill is a little cemetery with a boulder marked "Faithful Friends" where deceased pets are buried.

Before the days of automobiles the family had horses ranging from President Roosevelt's hunter to a Shetland pony for the youngest child. The rest rode anything they could put a saddle on. Ted said their riding parties looked like the Cumberbatch family in the Caldecott drawings. Once when they rode from the White House to Fort Meyer to see a review, their polyglot cavalcade thundering down the road so frightened the horse of a colonel of cavalry who had come to meet them that it ran away, to the delight of the children.

From an early age the Roosevelt children were encouraged to form the habit of reading and to develop intellectual curiosity. They were given access to the best in literature. Ted knew more poetry by heart than anyone I knew. His parents knew that education is not acquired from school alone and that it can be made attractive and interesting. To them history was living and exciting, and they made it so to their children. The study of natural history began with the children's pets. Outdoor recreation was an important part of their lives. Even the small ones took part in camping, hiking, fishing, rowing, swimming, and shooting. If they wanted to go places they saddled and rode a pony or they walked. They certainly were not pampered. As small children they would be thrown into deep water to force them to learn to swim. They were told that "sickness is always a shame and often is a crime," and in any case it was something to be fought against. In spite of this Spartan aspect of their bringing-up Ted had nothing but happy memories of his childhood and was sure that Sagamore was the most delightful and interesting house in the world.

He went to public and private schools wherever the family happened to be living—Oyster Bay, Albany, or Washington. While his father was Governor of New York, Ted attended the Albany Academy, where once the Boys' Junior Athletic Club was having a meeting at which the Governor was to speak. Ted's father told me about it years later.

"Ted was eleven, and I was not quite sure how he would behave at the meeting. As we walked down the street I was trying to think how I could tell him without hurting his feelings that he must not be fresh with me. Before I could speak he said, 'Please, Father, don't pay any attention to me or talk about me when we get there.' Then I realized that the responsibility of introducing one's father to a club in which one was a member rested just as heavily on the younger member of the family as it did on the elder."

Because of frequent changes of schools, when Ted reached Groton he was humiliated to find himself two years behind cousins and friends of his age. The course at Groton was six years, but after four years Ted left the school, covered the work of the next two years studying with a tutor, and entered Harvard a few days after his eighteenth birthday. He was in the class of 1909 but graduated in 1908 with a B.A. degree.

His college career was somewhat varied. Although he weighed only a hundred and thirty pounds, he played end on the freshman football team and later on the second-string eleven, until stopped by a badly broken nose and a broken ankle that was mistaken for a sprain and never fully recovered its strength.

During one language examination he was required to translate a Latin epic. Having done little studying, he was not too familiar with the work. Realizing that drastic measures were necessary, he wrote his translation in blank verse, with an explanatory note saying he had made certain changes from the original because of the meter. For this pious fraud he received an A. After a period of low marks he went off fishing. The dean wrote his father in March 1908: "Dear Mr. President, You may know where your son Ted is. We do not." A discussion of Ted's marks followed, revealing he had cut thirty-eight lectures since January 1 and was now on probation. President Roosevelt wrote Ted a letter, which unfortunately has not been preserved, saying he was a shame and a disgrace and would never amount to more than a twenty-five-dollar-a-week clerk. Ted came back from his fishing trip and settled down to work, received nothing but A or B+ for a specific period. He made the Dean's List on the same day he was taken off probation, and he graduated three months later.

Once he was arrested and nearly landed in jail. He and a couple of friends had gone to the theater in Boston and were running across the Common to catch a streetcar back to Cambridge when a man chased them. As there had been cases of robbery at night on the Common, Ted stopped and gave him what he later described as "a little push," but it turned out that the man was a plain-clothes policeman who claimed that his nose and a rib had been broken. Ted and his friends were taken to the station house but later released after they had made explanations.

Chapter 5

*I shall always remember the gentleness of
your manners, and the wild originality of your
countenance.*

CLARA CLAIRMONT

After graduating from Harvard, Ted was determined to get a job
without help from his family and to live without an allowance.
Robert P. Perkins, president of the Hartford Carpet Company and
fellow member of the Porcellian Club, offered him employment
in the carpet factory in Thompsonville, Connecticut. Starting at
seven in the morning, Ted worked ten hours a day for five days
and five hours on Saturday. He received seven dollars a week and
lived on it for two years, paying five dollars a week for board,
lodging, and laundry.

At first he had a hard time at the mill. The work was grueling.
He was pointed out as the son of the President of the United
States and was regarded with suspicion by everyone from the superintendent down. No one believed he would stick to a job like
that. Because of his father, the newspapers ran stories about him
and his job, giving his fellow workers the impression that the whole
thing might well be nothing but a publicity stunt. Some paper
published a photograph of him lighting a cigarette on his way to
work, and he was criticized by several clergymen and women's
organizations for setting an evil example to the youth of the nation. He made the mistake of accepting an appointment to the

staff of the Governor of Connecticut without stopping to think that this would mean more publicity, which he later regretted. In spite of it all, he went on with his work with the tenacity and singleness of purpose which were to be important qualities of his character.

After the first year it was easier. Because he worked as hard as anyone, the other mill hands began to accept him as one of themselves and came to like him. When we were married they took up a collection and presented him with a superb ship's clock. Twenty-four years later, when Ted was running for the governorship of New York, his opponent accused him of having pretended to work at making carpets while actually visiting the mill occasionally, rolling up in a costly limousine with a chauffeur. Ted's former landlady, Mrs. Robert F. King of Thompsonville, promptly went into action in his defense and gave an irate interview to the press. She said it was a shame to say such things; that she had known Ted all the time he was there and was prepared to testify, as were other citizens of Thompsonville, that he had worked full time and overtime and had had no limousine, nor, indeed, any car at all.

While in the factory Ted showed a peculiar and unexpected talent for wool-sorting. A company making carpets buys wool in quantity, and before buying raw wool it must be able to judge the quality accurately in order to know how much it will shrink and how much weight it will lose when washed. This is done by feel, smell, and taste and can make the difference between profit and loss. Ted seemed to have an innate ability for this (totally useless in later life!) for he soon qualified as an expert and got a raise.

After the house party at Mrs. Dodge's I did not see or hear from Ted until I went to Washington with my mother and a couple of girls for Ethel Roosevelt's coming-out dance at the White House in December 1908. I had a slight chip on my shoulder as I wondered if Ted would remember me, and was pleased when he did.

The dance was delightful. Mrs. Roosevelt and Ethel received in front of a large screen covered with green leaves, over which hung little bouquets of gay flowers, one for each girl at the party. Ted asked me what train I was taking back to New York next day, saying he would be on it too. I think it was my Scottish caution that kept me from mentioning this to the other girls when they teased me about having danced so often with Ted. I know I thanked my stars for it when he never appeared. A day or two later I had a letter from him saying he had duly taken the train I had told him and had twice walked the length of it. I had said Baltimore & Ohio instead of Pennsylvania.

After that Ted wrote me amusing letters, often illustrated with sketches of other people working at the mill. I answered them until I got one that I considered entirely too fresh. Instead of beginning "Dear Miss Alexander," as good manners required, it started "Dear Goldilocks." I tore it up and wrote no more until after I saw him at the Tuxedo Autumn Ball and had a chance to tell him I was annoyed. For this ball I tried an experiment and had my hair done in a new short-lived fashion called the "turban swirl," winding it around my head like a cap. It changed my appearance so much that Ted found it hard to recognize me. After cutting in twice on the wrong girls, he persuaded Suydam Cutting, whom I had known much longer than I had Ted, to walk around the ballroom with him and point me out.

During his second year at Thompsonville, Ted used to come to New York to see me whenever he had the price of a railroad ticket. This meant traveling all Saturday afternoon, reaching New York at eight in the evening, then leaving at half-past ten on Sunday night and sitting up in a day coach until he arrived at Thompsonville in time to go to work at seven on Monday morning. Several times the newspapers had said he was going to marry various people, including a popular young actress he had met once and the daughter of the Chinese Minister, whom he had never met. We knew that if we were to avoid rumors of our engagement before it existed we must be very careful. We used to take long walks along Riverside Drive and around Grant's Tomb, often in the snow, where chances were small of our meeting anyone we knew. Sometimes we had tea in a little inconspicuous restaurant in spite of the disapproval of my mother, who said emphatically that this was not done without a chaperone—true, indeed, in those days. In fact, I doubt if I ever did anything that made me feel quite so daring as having tea in a restaurant *alone with a man!* We never mentioned each other's name to anybody, and succeeded in keeping the secret so well that when our engagement was announced it was a complete surprise to all our friends.

Mother, of course, knew all about it from the start. She liked Ted but was inclined to be influenced by her Wall Street friends, to whom his father's name was anathema, and was not at all sure she wanted me to marry him. My step-great-grandmother, Mrs. Theron R. Butler, always a staunch supporter of Ted's father, came to the rescue. "My dear, what on earth do you expect for the child? I must say *I* should be extremely gratified." Later Mother spoke of it to my aunt Netty, Mrs. John J. McCook, whose wedding bouquet had been given her in 1876 by Ted's grandfather and grandmother Roosevelt, and whose opinion Mother valued highly. Her reply, "Go home and thank God on your knees!" drove the last doubt from Mother's mind.

Ted's father was in Africa on his famous shooting trip for the American Museum of Natural History, while Mrs. Roosevelt and Ethel were at Oyster Bay. Although our families had known each other for three generations, the only close relatives of Ted's that I knew were his two sisters, Alice and Ethel. I had seen Alice for the first time when I was staying at Seabright, where my cousin Martha McCook was having a house party to which Alice came. I was twelve years old then and regarded everybody over seventeen with admiration and awe, particularly Alice, who radiated a glamour all her own. Seizing my chance one evening before she came in to dress for dinner, I went to her room, where her gay rose-color dress was laid out on the bed and all her glittering gadgets on the dressing table, examined everything, and escaped just in time when I saw her coming across the lawn.

When Ethel asked me to Oyster Bay for a weekend in the autumn of 1909 I wrote Ted I was going, and he at once wired his mother that he would be there at that time. Ethel wrote him they were so glad he was coming, that unfortunately she had invited a girl for the weekend but could easily put her off if he thought it would be tiresome to have a stranger around when he got home so seldom. Ted answered that he didn't mind in the least and to let "the girl" come as planned.

Feeling even more shy than usual, on the Friday I took the Thirty-fourth Street ferry to Long Island City and boarded a train which, with a change at Jamaica, went to Oyster Bay. If we were to be married, I did want his family to like me, but I had little self-confidence and was sure everything would go wrong. When I reached Oyster Bay there was no one to meet me. For ten endless minutes I waited, wondering if I had taken the wrong train, maybe on the wrong day. What if they had forgotten I was coming? I couldn't telephone, as I didn't know their private number. When at last Ethel appeared, driving her horse Fidelity in a little trap, I sighed with relief. I had done nothing dreadful so far, but when we arrived at Sagamore Hill and Mrs. Roosevelt, after greeting me kindly, looked at me and said, "White kid gloves in the country? Dear me!" it threw me into a state of panic that lasted until Ted got there next evening.

My mother announced our engagement in February 1910 and was appalled by the flood of publicity that followed. She considered it in the worst possible taste and rather held Ted responsible for his father's "notoriety." Reporters came to our house in droves. It was not so bad when Ted was there to talk to them, but the day after he returned to Thompsonville a group of feature writers came from the evening papers. I had no idea what to do with them, so one of my aunts, with kindest intentions but with no experience in such matters, volunteered to see them for me. The result was a number of embarrassing stories quoting me in all sorts of silly ways. My friends sympathized, commiserated, and jeered. It was a most uncomfortable time.

Every day brought hundreds of messages wishing us well. I remember one from Cassidy, an old man who had been my grandfather Green's gardener. He wrote my mother that he had always thought I would marry the "King of Europe" or the "Prince of Whales" because I deserved the best. Agnes, a former Swedish maid, came to see us in great excitement. "Oh, miss! Oh, miss! Wasn't you lucky to get that young gentleman!" My mother bristled. "Indeed, Agnes, I think Mr. Roosevelt is the lucky one." Agnes paid no attention and went right on: "Wasn't you lucky! Oh, miss!"

Meanwhile former President Theodore Roosevelt—or Colonel, as he preferred to be called—on his way home from Africa, was joined by Mrs. Roosevelt and his daughters, Alice Longworth and Ethel. While in Europe he was appointed special representative to the funeral of King Edward VII. In London he made an address at the Guildhall. What he said about British policy in Egypt made a sensation. In effect he declared they should rule or get out. Many people both in the United States and abroad, including some members of the House of Commons, denounced it as a flagrant indiscretion, saying it was extremely bad taste to criticize his British hosts and tell them what they should do. Few people knew he had consulted Lord Cromer, the great authority on Egypt, Sir Edward Grey, Secretary of State for Foreign Affairs, and Arthur J. Balfour, leader of His Majesty's Loyal Opposition. In addition, he had talked about it for nearly an hour with King George V and had gone over his speech word by word with Sir Arthur Lee and Sir Cecil Spring-Rice, later Ambassador to the United States. They had not only approved but had urged him to bring these matters to public attention. Afterward he had letters of congratulation and thanks from Lord Curzon, Lord Roberts, Sir Francis Wingate, Rudyard Kipling, and many others.

Colonel Roosevelt and his party arrived in New York on June 18, 1910. Mother, Ted, and I were among those who went down the bay to meet them. Every craft in the harbor, decked with banners and blowing whistles, was taking part in the welcome to the former President. The boat carrying members of the press had a huge sign "Pres Bot," a take-off on his suggestion for simplified spelling. When we landed at the Battery there were great crowds, tumultuous cheering, speeches, and a parade of horse-drawn carriages, marchers, and five hundred Rough Riders who had come to New York from all over the country.

After the parade we gathered for lunch at 433 Fifth Avenue, the house built by my great-grandfather Butler, and later we made the trip by ferry and train to Oyster Bay.

Chapter 6

Marriage is a thing you've got to give your
whole mind to.

HENRIK IBSEN

On June 20, 1910, Ted and I were married at the Fifth Avenue
Presbyterian Church. Dr. Henry M. Sanders, a Baptist, husband
of the great-aunt for whom I was named, performed the ceremony,
assisted by the Reverend Gordon Russell, an old friend of Ted's,
a Methodist. We used the Episcopal service. I have no memory of
why we did not include the pastor of the church and fear the
omission may have hurt his feelings, for I discovered years afterward that no record of the marriage appears in the church annals.

I cannot remember a hotter day. The church was filled to the
doors. Crowds in the street were kept in line by policemen in the
heavy blue woolen uniforms and gray helmets of the day. At the
last moment we found that the Rough Riders were still in the city.
A block of five hundred seats in the gallery was reserved for them,
and of course they came to the reception afterward, where they
took most of the little boxes of wedding cake. The wedding reception was given by my uncle and aunt, Mr. and Mrs. Charles B.
Alexander, at their house at 4 West Fifty-eighth Street, and was
truly gala. Lewis, the colored steward from the Porcellian Club,
was there to pour champagne and was, as I recall, the last person
to say good-by to us as we rushed off in a shower of rice.

Ted had made up his mind that in spite of everything we would have no more undeserved publicity. His plan was ingenious but it backfired. We drove uptown at full speed in an automobile while the traffic police kept anyone from following, took the ferry at 125th Street, and went to Philadelphia, registering at a small hotel as "Mr. and Mrs. Winthrop Rogers." Next day we left for Chicago on our way to the West Coast, where after a month's holiday Ted was to work in the San Francisco office of the Hartford Carpet Company. In the station we bought papers and read with amusement the stories of "Roosevelt and Bride on Secret Honeymoon." In Chicago we again registered as Rogers at the Blackstone Hotel and went to our room to stay until our train left.

Fifteen minutes later someone knocked. When I opened the door a man said: "Mrs."—significant pause—"Rogers?"

Our little game was up. From that moment we were besieged. We arranged with the hotel office that if anyone from there wanted to speak to us the telephone operator would give a certain ring. Waiters would give a certain knock at the door. Otherwise we answered nothing. We made friends with a bellboy, who reported to us from time to time.

We thought the newsmen would get tired and go away, but they didn't. As the hour drew near when we would have to leave to catch our train, we wondered how we could get out of the hotel unnoticed. The bellboy said that reporters and cameramen were in the lobby, by the elevators and doors, but he thought he could outwit them. First he took down our suitcases, purposely unmarked with initials, and put them in a taxi; then he took us down in a freight elevator and out by a service door. By this time I would have been enjoying the excitement of having to escape like international spies if it hadn't been for Ted's anxiety and distress over the situation. The reporters saw us as we jumped into the taxi and they followed, but we had a head start and managed to get into our drawing room on the train, lock the door, and pull down the window shades before they arrived. After the train started we confided in the conductor, who helped by telling newsmen in Omaha that he had never heard of us.

This covered our trail until we reached the St. Francis Hotel in San Francisco, where we gave up "Rogers" as useless. The telephone operator called our room to say that several reporters were there to see Ted. He replied that he would be glad to see one representing the group, no more. John Francis Neylan, political writer of the *Bulletin*, was the one selected to come up. Later he became our good friend. Ted told him the publicity he had been getting as his father's son was not only embarrassing but calamitous from his point of view. He was not in politics but was beginning his business career. All he wanted was a chance to stand on his own feet without being made absurdly conspicuous. Whether Jack Neylan prevailed upon the others, I don't know, but the accounts in the newspapers next day were short and inoffensive. After that, real news held the public interest and we were left alone.

The disadvantages of being a great man's son far outweigh the advantages. Ted's truly remarkable career was to be cloaked inevitably and perpetually by the shadow of his father's fame. At twenty-five he was compared with his father at fifty and found wanting. He was always accused of imitating his father in speech, walk, and smile. If he had taken this seriously and tried to alter himself he would have been unbearably self-conscious.

Once a wise man, Charles Evans Hughes, said to me: "People will always say Ted is copying his father unless he does nothing but sit on the piazza and do crossword puzzles. Then the same people would attack him for being so different!"

Before Ted went back to work Stewart Edward White, the writer, and his wife Betty, old friends of Ted's, invited us to visit them at Carpinteria, near Santa Barbara, where they had a bungalow on the beach. I had not met them and was not inclined to visit anyone, but when we went to spend a day we ended by staying a couple of weeks. The Whites were good to us and left us alone to do what we wanted. We spent the days riding horses in the hills, canoeing in the lagoons, and surf-riding. It was a delightful interlude in a carefree world.

Stewart, one of the great shots of all time, trained me in target practice with a pistol. Betty taught me much about housekeeping and marriage in general. Some of her precepts I remember to this day: "Everyone gets cross sometimes, but don't be cross at the same time. Don't be a yes-woman. Tell Ted frankly when you disagree or disapprove, but don't tell other people. Never take him for granted. If you don't listen with sympathy and warmth whenever he tells you *anything* about himself, remember there are plenty of other women who will." This last I was to remember in later years when Ted, determined not to get stout, used to tell me every night exactly what he weighed before and after exercising.

When we returned to San Francisco tanned a deep brown, Ted started work. After a brief search we rented a small gray frame house with a little garden at 1942 Pacific Avenue, its back windows overlooking the Golden Gate. Soon all our possessions and wedding presents arrived from the East, and we settled down, as we thought, permanently. My mother sent us a quantity of furniture she had been collecting for years and could spare. To us that little house was a dream of perfection. We put window boxes wherever possible and filled them with dwarf heliotrope and pink geraniums. We planted the garden with roses, dahlias, various annuals, and all sorts of spring-flowering bulbs.

In those days help was no problem. Nearly all our young friends in the East had at least two or three maids, and some had a butler as well. We started with a Chinese houseboy, Ling Chen, who was supposed to do everything. Ted's father said he thought this exaggerated economy and hoped we were not trying to make a grandstand play. Ling was not very good at his job, and I was always cleaning and dusting. If I started to give him instructions not to his liking he would shovel coal or turn on both taps in the sink, making it impossible for him to hear what I said. Once when we were to have new potatoes with parsley for dinner, I went into the kitchen and found him chewing the parsley. When I protested in horror he explained it was the best way to get it finely cut. From then on we had no parsley in the house. He spoke a queer kind of pidgin English. When my little Boston terrier was sick Ling said, "He trow off from de face." "Also true," remarked Ted, "of many politicians."

Ling was a fair cook but preferred doing things his own way and did not hold with innovations. One day while shopping I found some *papillotes,* paper bags used by the French for cooking to retain juices and improve flavor. We were having our first dinner party, and I was anxious to have a particularly good meal. A large one of these would be perfect for the salmon. I explained carefully to Ling that he must grease the bag thoroughly inside and out, tie up its end securely, and put it in the oven. "Serve it bag and all just as it comes out of the oven. Never mind if the paper is scorched."

I was pleased with myself for having found the *papillotes*. It was so hard to think of anything unusual. Our friends would see that I was a clever housekeeper, with ingenuity and imagination, and Ted would be impressed.

The little party was going well. Ted, as host for the first time in his own house, was thoroughly enjoying himself at the head of his own table. The soup was excellent and very hot. Next would come the salmon, sure to be the sensation of the evening. It certainly was.

A pile of hot plates and the platter of fish were put in front of Ted to be served. There was a moment's silence at his end of the table, then a despairing cry.

"Bunny! What on earth do I do now?"

I looked around the centerpiece of flowers and saw, on my best silver platter, a large brown paper parcel securely tied with twine in hard knots. Ling had discarded the charred *papillote* for something tidier. My beautiful salmon was well cooked but was tepid and tasted of brown paper.

We kept Ling Chen for several months, largely because he looked so smart in his white Chinese clothes and felt slippers, and we were dismayed when the day after the Chinese revolution in 1911 he appeared in an electric-blue suit with padded shoulders, yellow shoes with bumpy toes, his queue gone and his hair sticking up in all directions. His place was taken by two Swedish maids, one of them Anna Malm, my mother's parlormaid, who had been with us since I was twelve and came out from New York. The other, Ella Grant, cooked for us and never quite approved of us. She used to tell me she knew how people should behave, as she had worked for the highest society in Spokane and had never seen people go to parties as seldom as we did. "And you with your beautiful dresses hanging in the closet! It's wicked waste, that's what it is. Don't you ever get tired of staying home so much? Don't you know anybody?"

It is good for a young couple to start life away from their families and have a chance to get used to each other and their new responsibilities by themselves. Families are too apt to overwhelm them with kind advice and affectionate criticism. We were fortunate in going to San Francisco, as it was so far and so different from where we had lived. To us, just out from the East, it combined achievement and culture with the interest and charm of a frontier town where anything could happen. Many of the generation next to those grand old pioneers, the forty-niners who had crossed the continent in search of gold, were still living. The Pacific Union Club, which Ted joined, an enormous brownstone structure on top of Nob Hill, had been built originally by James Flood for his daughter Jenny, who wanted a brownstone house like those in New York. Disregarding the native stone and marble of California, he had the material for his house brought around Cape Horn in sailing vessels.

We dined with Miss Jenny. I had read of such meals but had never eaten one. We had ten courses, including two roasts, one white meat, the other red, two kinds of fish, and a course of game, cooked to perfection by a French chef. After the fifth course we had Roman punch (water ice) in glasses, after which we again fell to. Of course no cocktails were allowed to desecrate the vintage wines served during the dinner.

For thirty years the political bureau of the Southern Pacific Railroad had dominated the government of the state of California. Just before the earthquake and fire of 1906 Abraham Ruef, a political boss, had taken over the government of San Francisco. While the city was in ruins the corruption of Ruef and his henchmen was so brazen that the city revolted; but its leading citizens were sharply divided when the grand jury indicted those who had paid bribes as well as those who had taken them. The result was the so-called Graft Prosecution, a reform movement that was a complete success.

President Theodore Roosevelt released from the federal government Francis J. Heney, prosecuting attorney, and William J. Burns, a detective, who, together with Hiram Johnson, finally sent Ruef to the penitentiary.

The Graft Prosecution had ended not long before we came to live in San Francisco, and the city was still divided into two hostile camps. As newcomers we were not expected to take sides and were practically the only people friendly with everyone. Naturally we had to be careful whom we asked to the house together, and several times we were startled when people calling on us would rise and leave in haughty silence when someone else came in.

The first time Hiram Johnson ran for the governorship of California was on the Republican ticket in 1910. He was ignored by the newspapers, which did not even print his speeches. He campaigned through the state in a little red car, covering an astonishing amount of ground. On the night of the primary election we went to his headquarters to show him we were in his corner. No one else was there but the Johnson family, a couple of their friends, and a few reporters. He won the primaries, tantamount in those days to winning the election. On the night of the final election we went again, and this time we could scarcely squeeze ourselves into the crowd of people climbing on the band wagon.

In the spring of 1911 Ted's father and mother, with his sister Ethel and his brother Quentin, came to spend ten days with us. Ethel stayed with friends, the others at our house. Colonel Roosevelt made six lectures at the University of California. It seemed to me that everybody in San Francisco wanted to see him. We had as many people as our dining room would hold every day at lunch and dinner. A stream of callers came in the mornings, afternoons, and evenings. It was the first test of my housekeeping. I planned menus well in advance with all sorts of California specialties, my favorites of which were sand dabs, crabs, and tiny oysters.

My father-in-law hated the telephone and thought it a modern gadget that could well be done without. After leaving the White House he had ordered the telephone removed from Sagamore Hill, saying it was nothing but a nuisance. If messages had to be sent they could be taken by a boy on a pony as they always had been. It was only because of protests by the children that it was allowed to remain. During this family visit to us Dr. Benjamin I. Wheeler, president of the University of California, rang up and asked to speak to Colonel Roosevelt. When I told him, he said, "Yes, dear, yes, I'll go." Ten minutes later I passed the telephone and saw the receiver off the hook. I ran frantically upstairs and found my father-in-law in his room with the door shut, reading a book. "Father! Poor Dr. Wheeler is still waiting for you. Didn't you ever speak to him?" He put down his book and looked at me. "Darling, I like Dr. Wheeler, but I do dislike telephoning. I thought if I went quietly away he would get tired of waiting and perhaps come to see me."

Our first child, named Grace Green after my mother, was born in San Francisco. In those days no one thought of going to a hospital and turning a family event into an operation. Before she arrived Ted used to come home to lunch almost every day so that I would not be lonely, as I was not feeling well and was in no mood to try to make new friends. He was enchanted by the baby and used to hurry home from the office to hold her on his lap for half an hour before her bedtime. He had a knack with tiny babies. Gracie, according to the fashion of the day, wore dresses about a yard long. When he picked her up he would first wind his right hand in the skirt, then slip his left under her head and shoulders. All our babies seemed to feel safe in his arms and loved to have him hold them.

Chapter 7

Love does not consist in gazing at each other,
but in looking outward together in the same
direction.

ANTOINE DE SAINT-EXUPÉRY

Ted took an active interest in politics, believing this was the duty of every citizen under our system of self-government. He wanted to go into public service, but before doing so he hoped to make and lay by enough money to have an income. As he had no profession to fall back on when and if out of office, he did not want to be dependent on the salary from a political position for the support of his family. Although he enjoyed the carpet business, he felt it did not hold much promise of his making money soon. In 1912 he was offered a position in investment banking with the New York firm of Bertron Griscom & Company. He accepted it, thinking it would enable him to realize his wish while he was still young.

In New York we rented a house at 165 East Seventy-fourth Street. It was not half as attractive as the one in San Francisco, but Ted always loved any house we had and thought it beautiful. Twenty-seven years later, when we were grandparents and at last could build one of our own at Oyster Bay, he was convinced it was the most wonderful house in the world, surpassing even Sagamore Hill, up to then his ideal.

At this time Ted was a bond salesman with odds against him. It was 1912, the year his father was running for President against

58

William Howard Taft and Woodrow Wilson and was the most hated man in Wall Street. Often the hatred seemed to include his relatives. Ted would go into the office of some man to try to sell bonds, only to have the man snap: "I never expected to see the son of your father here. Kindly make your call brief." Sometimes people were even more pointedly insulting. It was hard to bear, but Ted learned to keep his temper and incidentally learned the business.

He always threw himself vigorously into the task at hand. I never knew him to turn aside from something he had undertaken, even if it meant following a cold trail for years in the face of criticism and often ridicule as well. When I became exasperated he would laugh at me and quote poetry, perhaps a verse from Arthur Guiterman:

> "When Hercules ensnared the grim
>   Wild boar of Erymanthus,
> They did not pin one rose on him,
>   Nor yet one polyanthus.
>
> "This 'feat,'" they said, "is not the least
>   Amazing or surprising;
> Besides, he only caught the beast
>   To get some advertising.

* * * * * * * * * * *

> "For some are born to set things right,
>   While some are built for sneering;
> And he that likes to work and fight
>   Must never mind the jeering."

All through Ted's life he regarded waking hours as working hours, usually taking time off only to get hard physical exercise in the shortest possible time, such as squash rackets. After a long day at the office he frequently spent the evening talking over business problems with some members of the firm who could give information or advice. He seldom wanted to go to the theater or the movies. His chief pleasure and relaxation was an evening at home, a dozen books on the floor around his easy chair.

59

Two of the main reasons for this intensity of effort which lasted throughout his life were, I believe, a strong feeling that he must prove worthy of his father, whom he adored, and a deep love of country. His business career was nothing but the means to an end, and his desire was to get it over and done with as fast as possible. Personal ambition meant little. Often he could have advanced himself or taken an easier way at the expense of the public good, but did not do so. In later life he would travel as much as eighteen thousand miles in a presidential campaign, with all the dreary drudgery it entailed, speaking for a candidate whose election he thought would benefit the country, knowing well that the candidate, if elected, would give him neither credit nor recognition for his efforts. His patriotism, a quality considered as almost subversive by certain theorists in the Brave New World, burned like a flame—and eventually consumed him.

In the summer of 1912 we and our baby Gracie spent a couple of months at Sagamore Hill. It was the first time I had been there when the entire family was at home. Before twenty-four hours passed I realized that nothing in my bringing up as an only child had in any way prepared me for the frenzied activity into which I was plunged. Something was going on every minute of the day. The house was always full of people. Conferences went on all day. The telephone never stopped ringing. In the evenings my father-in-law received the newspapermen. At first I thought everyone would be tired when the day was over and would go to bed early, but I soon found out that nothing of the kind could be expected. The Roosevelt family enjoyed life too much to waste time sleeping. Every night they stayed downstairs until nearly midnight; then, talking at the top of their voices, they trooped up the wide uncarpeted stairs and went to their rooms. For a brief moment all was still, but just as I was going off to sleep for the second time they remembered things they had forgotten to tell one another and ran shouting through the halls. I tried going to bed with cotton in my ears, but it never did any good.

The first night I said to myself, "Here it is nearly one o'clock. No one is likely to wake up before eight at the earliest." Eight? By six the younger ones were up, and by seven I was the only one who was not joyously beginning the day. By the end of the summer I had gained invaluable experience. Like Kim, I had acquired the "true Oriental indifference to mere noise" and had learned to sleep under almost any conditions. It was excellent training, but while it went on I lost twenty-six pounds and have never regained them.

One day Colonel Roosevelt announced he would take the day off and we would all go on a picnic. Everyone was enthusiastic. I liked picnics. I liked picnic food—lettuce sandwiches in waxed paper, chicken salad, and other nice things. It would be pleasant on such a blistering day to have lunch outdoors in the cool shade of a big tree not too far away. Before we were well under way I realized with a pang that this was not going to be that sort of picnic. Our provisions were plentiful, but consisted of a large basket of clams, another of thick ham sandwiches, and a demijohn of water.

Friends and cousins had been notified, and by ten o'clock a dozen people had gathered. Carrying the supplies, we headed for the beach, walking the half mile through the woods as fast as we could put one foot before the other. At first I could see no reason for such haste and was inclined to walk slowly and at least try to keep cool. Then I understood. The mosquitoes in those woods seemed as big as bats and swarmed about us in clouds. Soon I was running ahead of everybody.

On the beach were five rowboats, two of which had comfortable chairs in the stern. I waited, thinking someone would suggest that I sit in one of those chairs, but I had the wrong idea. I should have run ahead, seized one, and held it against all comers. By the time everyone else was settled there was nowhere for me but a small space between the basket of clams and the demijohn of water in the flat-bottomed boat manned by Ted and his cousin George.

Under the blazing sun we rowed and rowed. There was no breeze. The Sound was as calm as glass. By and by I began pointing out places where we might stop, but they were declared unsuitable and far less attractive than the place to which we were bound. Two hours later we landed on a beach precisely like the one we had started from except that it was farther from home.

61

The boats were drawn up on the sand, and we settled ourselves at the water's edge, unable to go near the trees because of poison ivy. The provisions were spread out and a kettle filled to make tea. The thought of hot tea was depressing enough, but it was worse to see the roaring fire built over the clams. When they were judged ready Colonel Roosevelt selected one, opened it, sprinkled it with salt and pepper, and handed it to me. It was large, with a long black neck. I managed to get it all into my mouth, burning myself quite badly. Although gritty with sand, it was delicious at first, but that soon wore off and it became a piece of old rubber hose. I felt, to paraphrase Father William:

> The muscular strength that it gave to my jaw
> Will last me the rest of my life.

I looked around at the others eating clams and wondered how they did it. Finally I slipped it under a log, but not deftly enough to escape Colonel Roosevelt's eye.

"You aren't as persistent as Archie," he observed. "The first time he was old enough to eat a clam on a picnic he chewed for a time, then ate three sandwiches, some cookies, and an orange. Later he asked what he should do with the poor little dead clam. It was still in his mouth!"

As we packed up to go home a head wind started to blow. It had taken us two hours to get there; it took four to get back. Faces and necks were sunburned, hands were blistered. My father-in-law had a difficult time reaching shore, as the boat in which he was rowing Mrs. Roosevelt was leaking badly.

This was called "one of the best picnics we ever had," and everyone else was delighted with it.

Once when some friends were lunching at Sagamore my father-in-law asked me to tell the story of an adventure my mother and I had had in Yellowstone Park four years before. We were on horseback, as no automobiles were allowed in the Park at that time, and we were spending a few days at Old Faithful Inn. One morning we set out at six to ride to Shoshone Lake, a wilderness in those days reached only by a narrow trail. We planned to do some fishing and arranged for a boy to bring us our lunch at noon.

After riding and fishing until one o'clock we were hungry. The boy with our lunch never appeared. Seeing smoke rising above the trees beside the water a hundred yards away, we rode toward it, picking our way over the deadfall at the edge of the lake, and came upon two rough-looking men with a small tent and a pack horse. Tim, our guide, went ahead and told them he had two ladies who would be grateful for a cup of coffee. The men were rather surly, but they got out their coffeepot while we dismounted and sat down by the fire.

While the water was coming to a boil we talked with them. They gradually became less sullen, and when they heard we had not eaten for over seven hours they fed us from their scanty provisions. They produced something resembling sawdust, poured hot water on it, stirred it until it swelled to three times its original bulk, and gave us generous helpings on tin plates. It had a strange, unappetizing taste, but we ate every bit not to hurt their feelings. When the coffee was ready one of them got out a box of sugar. Mother and I said hastily that we never took sugar, but he replied, "Oh, we got plenty," and shoveled two heaping spoonfuls into each cup.

By this time we were friends and had been told their names, Red and Fred. Then—rather tactlessly, I am afraid—we asked where they were from and where they were going. After a moment's hesitation Red answered that they had entered the Park from the south over an old trail and so had not registered at a soldier station as people were supposed to do. They had had "a little U.P. trouble," and the sheriff in Jackson's Hole had been after them. They planned to gold-mine in the Park, illegal on government lands, and told us they hoped we would not mention having seen them or they would be fined for not registering. Mother assured them we would not tell on them after their kindness to us, and asked where their mining equipment was. After another short hesitation Fred reached into the tent and brought out a round metal pan. Mother looked at it and asked how they used it. He demonstrated by giving it quick short jerks from side to side, saying you put sand and water in it and if any gold was there it would sink to the bottom. There was something odd about this. When panning for gold a slow rotary motion must be used to separate

63

gold from sand and to collect it in the bottom of a pan. We listened and made no comment.

After thanking them warmly we rode back to Old Faithful Inn. On the way Tim remarked that "U.P." stood for Union Pacific, and wondered if they had held up a train or only a ticket office.

Shortly afterward Mother and I left the Park for a trip to Butte, Montana, returning a week later. While in Butte we read in the paper that seventeen stagecoaches in the Park had been held up by one man and the passengers robbed of over two thousand dollars. In those days tourists traveled by stagecoaches, which usually set out from the inns ten or fifteen minutes apart, with a soldier as guard riding at the head of the procession.

When we returned Tim was full of excitement. He had been driving the first coach in the line of eighteen leaving Old Faithful one morning and had reached a sharp bend in the road about ten miles farther on, when who should step out from the bushes but Red! He called Tim by name and waved good-by as the stage and the guard went on out of sight, then held up the remaining seventeen, forcing a passenger, by means of a sawed-off shotgun, to hold a sack into which the others threw their money and valuables. Fred and Red were never caught.

When I finished telling the story one of the guests was smiling. He said he had been in Yellowstone Park a short time ago and knew all about this episode. Every stage driver was using it to entertain his passengers. "But," he said, "you forgot part of it."

"I can't imagine what," I answered.

"You didn't say that when you left the men after they gave you lunch you wanted to repay them but didn't like to offer them money. Instead you gave them your book of excellent trout flies. Also, your mother's diamond rings flashed in the sun as she was eating. With far less trouble to themselves they could have taken them and her diamond and emerald brooch she always pinned on for safekeeping while traveling, and they probably would have made as much as they got from the stagecoaches. It's a good part of the story!"

Another visitor at Sagamore Hill was Alexander Moore, later Ambassador to Spain, who came with his wife, the famous actress Lillian Russell, a silver-gilt blonde in a black picture hat. As we sat on the piazza after lunch I was sewing on a little white corduroy coat I was making for Gracie and was having trouble putting in the sleeves. Mrs. Moore watched me for a time and then said, "Give me that," and deftly showed me an easy way to manage the gathers. Somehow I never would have associated Lillian Russell with the making of baby clothes.

Whitelaw Reid, United States Ambassador to Britain, died in London in 1912. His body was brought back to this country on a British cruiser, and his funeral was held at the Cathedral of St. John the Divine in New York.

I went to the funeral with my father-in-law, who had appointed Mr. Reid to the court of St. James's. We sat a couple of pews behind President Taft, whose relations with Colonel Roosevelt were, to say the least, not too cordial. At the end of the service, before the coffin was carried out, Mr. Taft rose with his retinue of aides and secret-service men, went down the aisle, making as much noise on the stone floor as a troop of cavalry, and drove away.

Afterward I asked Ted's father if it was customary for a President at a funeral to leave the church ahead of the coffin. He replied, "No, dear, no. It is not customary, but in this case Mr. Taft probably thought there should be precedence even between corpses!"

Our oldest son Teddy was born in June 1914 and was followed in sixteen months by Cornelius Van Schaack, named for his great-great-grandfather. We referred to them as the old baby and the new baby. It was fun having them so near in age.

The year Teddy was born, Axel Lemberg, formerly in the Swedish Merchant Marine, became my mother's chauffeur and remained in our employ for thirty-five years. I never knew a man who could turn his hand to everything better than Axel could. He taught Ted and me to drive, always refusing to admit that Ted was inclined to drive like his father and tended to be a menace on the road, but he agreed that I had better be the one at the wheel.

In 1914 Ted accepted a partnership in the Philadelphia firm of Montgomery, Clothier and Tyler, investment bankers. George Tyler was a cousin of Ted's through his mother, and Bob Montgomery had married George's sister Hope. The plan, delayed for a few weeks by the outbreak of war in Europe, was to open a branch office in New York.

Ted was happy in this business connection and made money from the start. We wanted to save every penny so that Ted could achieve his purpose of going into public life with an independent income. To this end we considered his earnings as principal, not income. He put every cent back into the firm, then borrowed from the firm for our living expenses. The psychological effect was good, as we always had the feeling we were running into debt and spent as little as possible. In 1915 Ted's share of the firm's profits amounted to over a hundred and fifty thousand dollars, but we did not even have a car. He practiced all sorts of economies, large and small, wearing his ready-made suits until they shone, his shoes until they developed holes, smoking the cheapest tobacco, taking few if any holidays, but at Christmas that year he broke all our strictest rules and gave me a pair of magnificent emerald-and-diamond earrings.

Chapter 8

War was a fiend that stopped our clocks
Although we met him grim and gay.
SIEGFRIED SASSOON

After World War I broke out in Europe, and especially after the invasion of Belgium, we were convinced that the plain duty of the United States was to join the Allies. All of us shouted for war. We felt it was a case of right versus wrong and that it was cowardly to be neutral. We despised President Wilson for his "Peace without Victory," without in any way realizing his wisdom. If he could have had his wish at that time I wonder if many of the world's future troubles might not have been averted.

In the summer of 1914 an incident occurred that my father-in-law described to me sometime later. I asked if he would please dictate an account of it for me to keep. Instead of dictating he wrote it down in his own hand.

SAGAMORE HILL
March 20th, 1917

Dearest Eleanor,

What happened was as follows:

Within a week of the outbreak of war, and after the first assault on Liége, a German whose name I have forgotten, but I think a count, and bearing letters from both the German Embassy and from the head of one of the great German steamship lines on which I had travelled, came to me at Progressive Headquarters, 42nd Street and Madison Avenue. Bowing, he stated that he was the bearer of a message from his Imperial Majesty; that his Majesty wished me to know that he always kept in mind the great pleasure it had given him to receive me as a guest in Berlin and at the palace at Potsdam, and to entertain me, and that he felt assured he could count on my sympathetic understanding of Germany's position and action.

I bowed, looked him straight in the eye, and answered in substance and nearly in words:

"Pray thank his Imperial Majesty from me for his very courteous message; and inform him that I was deeply conscious of the honors done me in Germany, and that I shall never forget the way in which his Majesty the Emperor received me in Berlin, *nor the way in which his Majesty King Albert of Belgium received me in Brussels.*"

He looked me straight in the eye without changing countenance, clicked his heels together, bowed—whereat I bowed in return—and left the room without speaking another word; nor did I speak another word.

Affectionately
(signed) Father

To Mrs. Theodore Roosevelt, Jr.

As the war went on in Europe people were beginning to worry about our condition of military unpreparedness. Compared to those of other nations, our forces and equipment were utterly futile. Secretary of State William Jennings Bryan said there was no reason to be alarmed, because in case of trouble a million men would spring to arms between sunrise and sunset. That they would be untrained and unarmed didn't seem to matter.

Many people gladly joined in the monster Preparedness Parade organized in 1916 by Charles Sherrill in New York. It was the greatest parade New York had ever seen, starting at nine in the morning and marching until late at night up Fifth Avenue from Twenty-third Street to Fifty-ninth. Hundreds of organized groups and thousands of individuals took part. Encouraged by Ted, I went to Mr. Sherrill, offered to organize a battalion of twelve hundred women, and worked hard for a couple of weeks getting people to sign up. The feeling for preparedness was so strong that many women marched who had never been in a parade before, like my mother-in-law and Mrs. Robert Bacon, wife of the former Secretary of State. We had to have a banner because all other groups had and, as we belonged to no particular organization, we designed our own. It was large and white and said in letters of gold: INDEPENDENT PATRIOTIC WOMEN OF AMERICA. We were to march at eight o'clock in the evening, after dusk, and to wear white dresses and carry lanterns.

Soon after seven o'clock I went down to our assembly point on West Twenty-second Street where the women were beginning to arrive. The parade was an hour behind its schedule, and we thought we had plenty of time. Just as we were unpacking our lanterns an aide came with a message from Mr. Sherrill, the grand marshal, saying that several groups had dropped out unexpectedly, the mayor and other city officials were waiting in the reviewing stand in Madison Square, and we must march at once. I tried to argue that we were not ready, but it was no use. The aide started our band down the street and we had to fall in like a flock of sheep. I walked alone directly behind the band, wearing a broad blue ribbon with "Marshal" in gold letters across my front. Behind me came Mrs. J. Borden Harriman, many years later U. S. Minister to Norway, carrying our banner. She had been chosen for this because she was a tall, handsome woman, strong enough to bear its weight. Behind us came the battalion, arranging themselves into rows as they went along.

We passed the reviewing stand and kept on up Fifth Avenue. I have never seen so many people. They jammed the sidewalks, hung out of windows, looked down from roofs. We reached the Public Library, where people were crowded on the wide steps, sitting on the balustrade and even perched on the stone lions. Directly opposite was the Union League Club, which had its own private grandstand filled with men we knew. I felt rather self-conscious at this point and was going along with my chin up, looking neither to the right nor to the left as the band played

"Columbia, the Gem of the Ocean," when suddenly Ted ran out from the sidewalk and grabbed me by the arm.

"For heaven's sake, stop!" he shouted. "You've lost your battalion!"

I looked back over what seemed miles and miles of empty asphalt with little white figures in the distance. The police had halted the parade at Thirty-fourth Street to let the cross-town traffic go through, and from there Daisy Harriman and I had marched alone behind the band under the banner: INDEPENDENT PATRIOTIC WOMEN OF AMERICA. Just the two of us. Men in the Union League Club stand were doubled up with laughter.

There was nothing to do but stand still, overcome with embarrassment, until the parade caught up with us. It was five years before I saw anything funny about it.

After the sinking of the *Lusitania* a group of young business and professional men met to consider the situation. Deploring the laissez-faire attitude of our government, they sent the following telegram to the President:

> May 10, 1915
> The undersigned citizens of New York express their conviction that national interest and honor imperatively require adequate measures both to secure reparation for past violations by Germany of American rights, and sure guarantees against future violations. We further express the conviction that the considered judgment of the nation will firmly support the government in any measures, however serious, to secure full reparation and guarantees.

The message was signed Robert L. Bacon, Arthur C. Blagden, Crawford Blagden, Philip A. Carroll, Grenville Clark, J. Lloyd Derby, Richard Derby, Hamilton Fish, Jr., George S. Hornblower, Devereux Milburn, John G. Milburn, Jr., A. Perry Osborn, Theodore Roosevelt, Jr., Elihu Root, Jr., Cornelius W. Wickersham.

These fifteen men held a meeting of about fifty, which included friends and acquaintances who felt as they did, followed by another meeting of a hundred at which a committee of three, Philip A. Carroll, Grenville Clark, and Ted, were appointed to prepare a plan of action. The country was gradually drifting into war, and these men realized that they, as well as the whole country, were without military training. Accordingly the small committee asked Major General Leonard Wood, formerly Chief of Staff, then commanding the Department of the East, if he would hold a camp for citizens who wanted military training. This would follow the lines of the student camps he had established in 1913 and 1914. The committee thought they could enroll a hundred men to attend. General Wood agreed to do this even if only twenty-five men came to it. The group then started a campaign of personal solicitation in New York and other cities. The response was so great that when the first "Businessmen's Camp" opened in August 1915 at Plattsburg, New York, more than a thousand had enrolled. The first camp was immediately followed by a second, almost as large.

In this way the Plattsburg camps were born. They furnished the system by which the great mass of junior officers were chosen and trained for the National Army of draftees, yet they started entirely because of private endeavor, without any backing whatsoever by the government.

The spirit of those first Plattsburg camps was that of a crusade. Men sought knowledge to enable them to fight for their country if need be, and they were there for that purpose only. No movies or other entertainment was required. Evenings were spent studying textbooks or military problems. Among those attending the first camp were Robert Bacon, at that time U. S. Ambassador to France; John Purroy Mitchel, Mayor of New York; George Wharton Pepper, later Senator from Pennsylvania; Arthur Woods, New York City Police Commissioner; Dudley Field Malone, Collector of Customs of the Port of New York; Bishop Perry of Rhode Island; and professors, lawyers, artists, farmers, bankers, journalists, and businessmen of every kind.

Ted was so anxious to concentrate on the work that he let me come to Plattsburg for only one weekend during the first camp. He and his brothers Archie and Quentin attended the camps from the beginning. Ted and Archie finished the course in 1916 with commissions of major and first lieutenant in the Officers' Reserve Corps. Quentin went into aviation and started training at the flying school at Mineola on Long Island.

71

When war was declared in April 1917, Ted and Archie were ordered to Plattsburg as reserve officers on active duty. Their one wish was to go overseas with the first contingent of United States troops. To this end, and for the only time I can remember, Ted asked his father's help. General John J. Pershing was to command the American Expeditionary Forces and he was Colonel Roosevelt's old friend. Following is an extract from the letter that was written:

My dear General Pershing,

. . . I write you now to request that my two sons, Theodore Roosevelt, Jr., aged 27, and Archibald B. Roosevelt, aged 23, both of Harvard, be allowed to enlist as privates with you, to go over with the first troops. The former is a Major and the latter a Captain in the Officers' Reserve Corps. They are at Plattsburg for their third summer.

My own belief is that competent men of their rank and standing can gain very little from a third summer at Plattsburg, and that they should be utilized as officers, even if only as Second Lieutenants. But they are keenly desirous to see service; and if they serve under you at the front and are not killed, they will be far better able to instruct the draft army next fall or next winter, or whenever they are sent home, than they will be after spending the summer at Plattsburg.

The President has announced that only regular officers are to go with you; and if this is to be the invariable rule, then I apply on behalf of my sons that they may serve under you as enlisted men, to go to the front with the first troops sent over.

Trusting to hear that this request has been granted, and with great respect, I am,

Very sincerely yours,
(signed) Theodore Roosevelt

May 17, 1917

When this letter appeared in the papers sometime later, we noticed that Colonel Roosevelt had made two small errors. He had taken two years off Ted's age and had promoted Archie a grade.

General Pershing's answer was favorable. Meanwhile Ted was leaving nothing to chance. He wanted to be sure that he and

Archie would be able to sail for France immediately after their orders came and would not have to wait possibly for weeks before getting on a ship. General J. Franklin Bell, commandant at Governors Island, was in charge of embarkation. He was an old acquaintance of mine and had given me a Whitman saddle as a wedding present. Ted asked me to see General Bell and arrange about his sailing.

"He'll do it for you if you approach him properly," said Ted. "Drop over to Governors Island and see him. Don't tell him right out that you want something; be diplomatic and lead up to it gradually."

I decided my best course would be to go and call on Mrs. Bell, whom I had never met. I went over on the ferry and found the General's quarters. Mrs. Bell was at home, asked me to sit down, and gave me tea. I asked where the General was and if I could see him. Mrs. Bell said he was somewhere around and would probably be in shortly. I knew I would have to stay until he appeared, as I couldn't think of another excuse to come over again casually. An hour passed, then two hours. Poor Mrs. Bell must have thought it very odd for me to stay so long and she smothered a yawn which I caught. We sat and gaped at each other, finding conversation difficult. I began to wonder if I could last it out, but I *had* to see the General. Suddenly there was a shout from outside.

"I want my overcoat!" Mrs. Bell sprang up and so did I. The General and his aide, a young captain, were running across the lawn.

"I've got to catch the ferry!" he shouted. "Hurry up with my coat!" Here was my last chance. "Is there a ferry now?" I said. "Oh, I must be going. Good-by, Mrs. Bell!"

We tore down to the dock and barely caught the boat. I had less than fifteen minutes to be diplomatic and was out of breath.

"General," I began, "Ted is at Plattsburg. He expects to get orders for overseas. He hopes so much that he will be able to sail as soon as his orders come through."

The General looked at me severely from under lowered brows. "And so he has sent you to fix things up with me, has he?"

"Yes, he has," I said. There was nothing else to say. A pause. Now, I thought, I've ruined everything.

73

"I like that spirit. All right, I'll see that he gets off on the first ship leaving after he gets his orders."

The relief was so great that I burst out laughing. So did the General. So did the General's aide, Captain George C. Marshall.

Shortly afterward orders came for Ted and Archie to go to France, and four days later, on June 20, 1917, thanks to General Bell, they sailed. Neither could speak more than a poor smattering of French, and as soon as they got on board the *Chicago* they arranged to take lessons from a French fellow passenger. When they landed they could speak fairly well and could understand each other without trouble, but no Frenchmen could understand either of them.

I went down to see Ted off and sat with him for a while on deck, determined to be gay and not show him what I was feeling. Finally this became difficult and I left. It was our seventh wedding anniversary.

That afternoon Ted's sister Alice and I drove to Sagamore Hill. Lord Northcliffe, the British publisher, was there at dinner. Soon after we left the table Colonel Roosevelt was told that a newspaperman wanted to speak to him on the telephone. Lord Northcliffe said, "How in the world do you suppose they found out that I am here? I told no one I was coming. I didn't even give the address to the chauffeur until we had left the hotel for fear the doorman might overhear." My father-in-law, on his way to the telephone, said mildly, "Perhaps it is only someone who wants to talk to me," but Lord Northcliffe shook his head. "Of course it's their job, these reporters. I employ them myself. But this is really a nuisance!" When Colonel Roosevelt returned a few minutes later he said it was a newspaperman who had seen Ted and Archie sail and thought their father might like to hear about them.

My father-in-law asked Lord Northcliffe if he thought it would be possible to get Kermit a commission in the British Army. Kermit felt very sad at seeing his brothers go and hated being left behind, but as he had started the course at Plattsburg only a few weeks before he was not yet qualified for a commission in our Army. Lord Northcliffe said he would take the matter up with Lord Derby, British Secretary of State for War, and felt sure there would be no difficulty about it.

74

Marshal Joffre, on a visit to this country, had said that if Colonel Roosevelt could come to France and march down the Champs Elysées, if only with a fife and drum corps, the effect on French morale would be electric. My father-in-law had offered to raise a division of infantry to be commanded by Regular Army officers and had the whole organization worked out on paper with the names of thousands of volunteers, but he was refused permission by the administration. He wrote to Ted in France:

Like Artemus Ward I am straining every nerve to get my wife's relations to the front. (My sons are my wife's relations, aren't they?) Quentin has his commission and hopes to sail in ten days. Lord Derby, thanks to Lord Northcliffe, has offered Kermit a staff position with the British General in Mesopotamia and he'll be sailing immediately.

(signed) Your loving father
THE SLACKER MALGRÉ LUI

Chapter 9

*Sailor Gare, as the French say. That's some
old pirate they blame everything on here.*
EDWARD STREETER

I was determined to go to France myself to do some sort of war work in order to be on the same side of the Atlantic as Ted. It would be a terrible wrench to leave my three children, but Ted might need me more than they. Gracie was five years old, Teddy three, and Cornelius a year and a half. They were small enough to be left with my mother. If they had been ten years older I could not have gone. Ted had agreed with this plan but told me positively that I must wait to hear from him. "I don't want you leaping off into space until I've had a chance to look things over. I'll cable you when to come." He both cabled and wrote me that he didn't like the look of things and I must not come until later. Then I heard by the grapevine that a regulation was soon to be passed forbidding soldiers' wives from going to France. Either I must go at once or I could never go. The Y.M.C.A. was to be in charge of recreational work for the American Expeditionary Forces in France. I went to see Mr. William Sloane, chairman of the National War Work Council of the Y.M.C.A., offered my services as a full-time volunteer worker overseas, and sailed five days later, July 24, 1917, on the *Espagne*, beating the regulation by three weeks.

Ted's father had declared emphatically that no women in the

family were to follow their husbands to France. This is the only time I can remember his giving a direct order to any of us. We greatly valued his good opinion and always did our best to live up to what he expected of us, but in this case I had to disregard his wishes. We were sitting on the piazza at Sagamore one evening after Ted had left when I mustered courage to tell him my plans. After a pause he said, "Darling, I see you have made up your mind. I don't know of anything I can do to help you, but if you can think of something you must let me know."

Soon afterward I knew he had forgiven me when he was told by newspapermen that President Wilson's son-in-law was going to France in the Y.M.C.A. With a gleam in his eye he replied, "How very nice. We are sending our *daughter-in-law* to France in the Y.M.C.A.!"

I cabled Ted I was sailing, unable to explain why I had ignored his instructions, and wondered how angry he would be at me. A week after reaching Paris I had a telegram from him: SIMPLY DE-LIGHTED YOU ARE HERE FELT SURE YOU WOULD COME ALL ALONG. Although we were only a few hours apart during the training period, I did not see him for two months. Theoretically he was entitled to a week's leave every four months, but in the year that followed he took only five days in all before he was wounded. I could not work in a canteen in his area, as the Army had forbidden the Y.M.C.A. to station a wife near her husband. The editor of a French magazine offered me an assignment to go to Bar-le-Duc, not far from Ted, and write the impressions of an American woman in France at war. I agonized over this temptation for days, then refused. The regulation prohibiting soldiers' wives from coming over had been passed since I left, but nobody would know that. They might think I managed to get there by pull and naturally would resent it. This could not fail to hurt Ted, the last thing I wanted to do. I tried to be patient running a canteen in the Y garden on Avenue Montaigne in the daytime and teaching elementary French to a class of twenty-five soldiers in the evening.

My aunt, Mrs. Hoffman, formerly Alice Green, had a large house with a garden on the corner of the Avenue du Bois de Boulogne (now Avenue Foch) and the Rue de Villejust (now Rue Paul Valéry). She wrote me that I might live in it and make it a center for those of the family in France. Augusta Girardin, her maid for seventeen years, was caretaker and lived there with her husband, who drove a taxi, and their little boy. My aunt said I must have five maids and a laundress to run the house properly. Of course this was impossible as I never could have afforded so many. Augusta said she could keep the house clean and manage perfectly with one good one. The trouble with them was that they all cut their bread too thin. When I asked what earthly difference this could possibly make she replied, "Butter is scarce." Finally she asked if we could engage Anaïs, a girl who had worked several years for my aunt until, as Augusta put it, "she had a little accident and has a little child." Anaïs was hired and I moved in immediately.

The house was extremely comfortable in summer, but in the unusually cold, damp winter of 1917–18 it was anything but comfortable. We had no coal for the furnace. A little stove in the front hall had a stovepipe going up through the curves of the spiral staircase which gave the illusion of warmth on the second floor. We had fuel for an occasional wood fire. At night I slept in woolen pajamas with feet and a hood, and mittens. We had hot running water only twice a week, but Augusta brought me a big pitcherful every morning and night. We raised chickens, ducks, rabbits, and geese and planted beans in the garden, with lettuces under the rosebushes. Augusta said, "If Mrs. Hoffman does not know, she will not mind."

Ted was in command of the 1st Battalion, 26th Infantry, 1st Division, in training in Demange-aux-Eaux. Marshal Joffre, during his visit to the United States, had requested that a combat division be sent at once to France as visual evidence of our purpose to participate actively in the war. The 1st Division, Regular Army troops, had been chosen and recruited to war strength with whatever men could best be spared from other units. Naturally the other units could best spare the men they wished to be rid of, including those in the guardhouse, who incidentally often make some of the best combat troops. It was a tough outfit and it became a superb fighting machine, of which General Pershing was to say in his Final Report: "Due to the magnificent dash and power displayed on the field of Soissons by our First and Second Divisions the tide of war was definitely turned in favor of the Allies."

In this division Ted had to hold his own with Regular Army officers whose career was the Army. His appointment to command a battalion in which there were a couple of captains several years his senior caused much comment. People said he was given this post because Pershing was his father's friend. Ted was twenty-nine, young in those days for a major. Because of all this he was more closely watched and criticized than the average officer.

He had his own methods of dealing with the men of his command. He maintained the strictest discipline for the good of all and, when necessary, used severe punishments, but in every case possible avoided having an offense put on a soldier's record. Once on maneuvers he noticed some men stepping along rather too nimbly under their full field equipment. He had their packs examined, found them full of straw, and told the rest of the platoon, to their delight, to replace the straw with rocks for the rest of the day. Another time the battalion band were excused from maneuvers to practice. Instead of doing so they went off and sat by a fire out of the cold rain. When discovered, they were made to climb a tall pine tree and do their practicing from there. These punishments were unpleasant for the culprits and made them ridiculous to the other men, but as they were not court-martialed for disobedience no stain was left on their records.

During the training period Ted organized competitions of all sorts. In one the men were called empty-handed from their billets. Then, at the word of command, they would race back and return with full equipment. The quickest platoon in each company was excused from reveille next morning. The quickest in the battalion was given something more substantial. As time went on the spirit of the command became remarkable. Each platoon thought itself better than any other, each company was convinced it was the best, and everyone *knew* the battalion itself was unequaled. The officers grew so enthusiastic that in November 1917, when the first weekend leave was granted, they all refused it until the period of special training was over.

No means of recreation for the troops existed at Demange. Ted wired me:

SEND AT ONCE TWELVE BARRELS SOFT DRINKS TEN POUNDS PIPE TOBACCO PHONOGRAPH AND RECORDS COMPLETE BASEBALL OUTFIT TWELVE PAIRS BOXING GLOVES TWELVE SOCCER BALLS SIX BASKETBALLS EIGHT FIFES EIGHT DRUMS AND STICKS GOOD SADDLE HORSE SADDLE AND BRIDLE MUCH LOVE Ted.

I had just arrived in Paris and knew little about where to buy anything. As the wire had come *sans origine*, I first had to locate Ted, then find the things he wanted and get them to him. No railway express existed in the war zone. I made friends with the man in charge of supplies at the Y.M.C.A., and persuaded him to let me have the boxing gloves, the various balls, and the first baseball outfit to reach France. These and the barrels of soft drinks he put on a Y truck which was going in the general direction of Demange-aux-Eaux. When those in authority heard about it they put their foot down, saying the Y.M.C.A. was there to serve the American Expeditionary Forces, not merely the 1st Battalion, 26th Infantry. Nothing more was to be sent to that unit.

From then on I was shameless and begged anyone I knew to take things to Ted. Colonel Count Aldebert de Chambrun, chief liaison officer on General Pershing's staff, who had married my brother-in-law Nicholas Longworth's sister, took the phonograph and several boxes of records. Cobina Wright, who was going up to sing to the troops, took the fifes, which had been tested to make sure they were all on the same key. No drums could be bought until Major Frank R. McCoy, who had been aide to my father-in-law in the White House and was a close friend, wangled some from the French and sent them directly to Ted. He also found an excellent saddle and bridle, but the "good saddle horse" was baffling. Finally a friend of Augusta's turned up who knew a man whose cousin worked in a racing stable. A little mare, Tamara, whose sire was Verdun, was not suitable for racing and could be bought for a reasonable sum. I asked Frank to try her in the Bois de Boulogne, and when he approved of her I hired a man to take her up to Ted. After the war Ted brought her home and, when she died, had her buried at Sagamore in the pets' cemetery beside

Little Texas, the horse his father rode in the Spanish-American War.

Meanwhile Ted was trying to get still more sports equipment. He thought there must be a store like Abercrombie and Fitch in the city of Bar-le-Duc, and he went there to look for it. After going about for a time he stopped an elderly couple on the street and asked in his most painstaking French if they would be kind enough to direct him to a *maison de sport*. They thought for a moment, then consulted each other. The old man made a suggestion, but his wife disapproved and recommended something else. After much conversation they agreed on an address, which Ted carefully wrote down. When he got there he was surprised to find it by no means the kind of establishment he had in mind!

After that he decided it was easier to have me send him what was needed rather than to try himself. Soon afterward he wrote me for six trumpets for the battalion band and eight extra drumheads. Fortunately the Provost Marshal General and his aide were coming to dinner. As we ate the delectable meal prepared by Augusta, I confided to them that I was having trouble getting things to Ted. The General offered at once to send the trumpets and drumheads and told his aide to see to it. Another time when General George B. Duncan, 1st Brigade commander, came to tea and asked if he could do anything for me, I told him Ted and Archie badly needed woolen underwear, sweaters, and socks. He said he would be delighted to deliver them and left the house with two large boxes.

By September, Ted's little canteen had been taken over by the Y.M.C.A. to my great relief, but he was always wanting other things. Once he wrote that payday was coming, the first in many weeks. Nothing could be bought in the little village where the battalion was billeted. He wanted a quantity of "small attractive articles" the men could buy and send home as presents; otherwise they might be tempted to spend too much on cognac and *pinard*. A congressman I met took up a batch of necklaces woven of tiny beads in gay colors by the French wounded. They were so popular that hundreds more had to be ordered and were taken to Ted by Major Robert Bacon, an old family friend who was on General

Pershing's staff. Another time he sent for a bass drum, but I don't remember how I got that to him.

Archie was commanding a company under Ted, to the disapproval of their father, who wrote them both advising against it. In spite of this they went on together until Archie was severely wounded months later. Always willing to admit when he had been wrong, Colonel Roosevelt wrote Ted in January 1918: "Your judgment as to Archie's coming into your battalion has been completely justified."

As the training period went on Ted received two commendations from the Inspector General of the American Expeditionary Forces, Major General André Brewster. The second of these was in a report praising Ted and criticizing the other two battalion commanders in the regiment, both regular officers.

On December 11, 1917, Brigadier General B. B. Buck, commanding the 2nd Brigade of the 1st Division, offered to make Ted brigade adjutant. Ted refused the staff position, preferring to remain with troops. On January 28, 1918, Brigadier General George B. Duncan, commanding the 1st Brigade, former Colonel of the 26th Infantry and noted for rigorous discipline, recommended Ted for promotion to lieutenant colonel and transfer to a vacancy in the 18th Infantry, saying in part:

> For six months I have had under observation the work of Major Theodore Roosevelt, Jr. He commanded a battalion in my regiment, the 26th Infantry, directly under me.
>
> I consider Major Roosevelt an officer of unusual ability. He is most conscientious in the performance of every duty, never falters, has an excellent command of men, and is today probably the best battalion commander in the 1st Division—I know he is superior to any on the 1st Brigade.

This was indeed an interesting comment by a Regular Army officer on a reserve officer serving with regulars.

According to a telegram to General Pershing from Major General J. G. Harbord, Deputy Chief of Staff, A.E.F., dated March 26, 1918, Ted was again recommended for promotion, this time by Major General Robert L. Bullard, commanding the 1st Division, and received further praise from the Inspector General:

> With reference to list of promotions General Brewster states that in all his inspections Major Roosevelt is the best major he has seen. He is recommended by Division and Brigade commanders to actual vacancy. Other members of board felt that promoting Roosevelt might injure him and that he had not been long enough in the service.

A few months later General Duncan became commander of the 77th Division and on May 31, 1918, again recommended Ted for promotion and transfer to his division. All these recommendations were turned down by General Staff Headquarters.

Quentin came over in August 1917 and began training at the flying school at Issoudun. Being an aviator, he had more time off than the others and came to Paris for weekends from time to time. Like all our soldiers, he and his brothers longed for home above all else, and our house was the best available substitute. Although no one but Quentin could get there except on the rarest occasions or until they were wounded, so many of the family were in France that I had a procession of visitors. Ted, Archie, Quentin, later Kermit, my brother-in-law Dr. Richard Derby, his brother Lloyd, Ted's cousins George, Philip, and Nicholas Roosevelt, and my uncle by marriage, Dr. John A. Hartwell, later president of the New York Academy of Medicine, all turned up from time to time. Usually I was away at work when they came, but Augusta's routine was always the same. No matter what time of day it was, she would bring a tray loaded with food and ask if there was anything to be mended. Often we had little in the house in the way of choice food, but she seemed always able to produce a savory meal. Archie said all she needed to make the best soup in the world was a handful of grass and a bone.

One evening I was invited to dinner by the de Chambruns to meet General Pershing. They lived on the left bank of the Seine, a long way from our house, but Augusta's husband promised to take me there in his taxi in time for dinner at eight. By twenty minutes to eight I was ready to start when word came that, much to the regret of Augusta's husband, his taxi was *en panne* and would not run. Anaïs went out to hail another while I waited, watching the clock. Fifteen minutes later she returned to say no taxis were on the streets. To go by Métro, making three necessary changes, would have taken almost an hour, for trains were few during the war. I telephoned to say I was delayed and begged the de Chambruns to sit down without me, while Augusta joined Anaïs in the search for a cab. The telephone rang. It was Captain Boyd, General Pershing's aide, to say the General's car would come to fetch me. Just then Anaïs returned with a rather dilapidated fiacre drawn by a weary horse. I gave the driver a couple of francs and sent him away. The telephone rang again. This time Captain Boyd said he had been unable to catch the General's car. It was then after half-past eight. I was frantic. I ran down the street, hailing every car I saw, and finally one stopped. The driver was a kind man who took me where I wanted to go. I arrived an hour late.

They were all very kind to me, saying it didn't matter in the least, and to make me feel better asked me about my job, finding it funny that I was with the Y.M.C.A. General Pershing asked how close he could get to the canteen in the Y garden while I was on duty and if he would be able to see me for the crowd. I had recovered sufficiently to suggest a second-story window in the next house. Colonel de Chambrun said he didn't know about American soldiers, but he knew any number of French ones who would be delighted to study French under me. As I wrote my mother at the time, "they were very silly and loved their own jokes." We were getting along beautifully and I was thoroughly enjoying myself when suddenly a thought struck the General. He turned to me, his face set like the Day of Judgment, and barked, "How do you happen to be here anyhow? No wives are allowed to come overseas. Where are your children? Your place is with them, not here. I think you ought to be sent home!"

It was as if the angel Gabriel had blown his horn at me. Everyone stopped talking to listen. I was startled and murmured something about having come over before restrictions because I wanted to be near Ted and had left my children with my mother, but he didn't listen. It took more nerve than I had to wrangle with the

Commander in Chief of the American Expeditionary Forces. He seemed to disapprove of me completely, and I went home feeling as if I had been spanked. I wrote Ted about it to the last detail.

A couple of weeks later Ted happened to see General Pershing, whom he had known for years, and spoke to him with lightness of touch and far more courage than I had.

"My goodness, sir, but you're in bad with my wife! What on earth did you do to her at the de Chambruns'?"

When I met the General again he took both my hands and said, "I'm afraid I must have hurt your feelings that night at dinner, but really I didn't mean to. I know about the work you're doing, and it's good. Can we be friends again?"

Even so, I was in constant dread that the few soldiers' wives in France might be rounded up and sent home, and for that reason I was careful never to break a rule or do anything that might attract undue attention, hoping to get by. After the war General Pershing gave me a citation for work in the Army Leave Areas run by the Y.M.C.A.

In August 1917 the Y asked me to design a uniform for its women. I chose a gray whipcord jacket and skirt. The jacket had capacious pockets and a powder-blue collar with the Y.M.C.A. insignia embroidered in scarlet silk. The blue hat had a small brim and the same insignia. Instead of an overcoat we copied an Italian officer's cape which Prince d'Udine had given to Cobina Wright. We had it made in dark gray-green blanket cloth with a blue collar to match that on the jacket. Long and circular, it proved far better than an overcoat, as we could roll up in it when sleeping in camp or on unheated trains. The uniform was successful except when some of the girls, unused to discipline, persisted in adding lace collars, strings of beads, and hats trimmed with flowers.

At the end of September 1917, two months after I reached Paris, Ted came down for two days, tanned and looking as if he were made of steel. We spent the first day driving around in a little fiacre, buying some things Ted needed, going for a moment to Y.M.C.A. headquarters where I showed Ted off to everybody, wandering along the quays to poke about in the old bookstalls, and sitting for an hour or so at a little table in front of the Café de la Paix, watching the crowd go by. Next day was Sunday, and in the morning we visited Notre Dame, then strolled along the Avenue du Bois to see the people in their Sunday best. One of the other majors from the 26th Infantry came to lunch, which we had in the garden. Afterward we walked down the Champs Elysées, stopping to watch the little guignols and the children on the merry-go-rounds. Later we wandered around the Faubourg St. Germain, looking at the old houses. The two days passed like a flash.

Chapter 10

In godless times one must be gay.
It is a duty.
FRANZ KAFKA

My French class grew so much that I had to have it in two sittings: one for those who knew not a word of French and one for
those who knew a little. One of my pupils was Sergeant George E.
Adamson, General Pershing's secretary, who held his post until
the General died in 1948, eventually becoming Colonel.

I was sorry to leave the class and the canteen in the Y garden
when the Y.M.C.A. assigned me to organize the volunteers at the
Hotel Richmond in Paris, which they had taken over for an officers' club. My instructions were "to make it like home." I had no
regular Y girls but managed to get some American women who
were living in Paris. We served lunch and dinner in the dining
room and made quite a function of afternoon tea in the lobby, with
an attractive tea table surrounded by easy chairs, and a phonograph playing good records. The officers were either stationed in
Paris or there on weekend passes, usually very young and home-
sick. We saw that their mending was done and helped them buy
presents to send home. This last developed into a real shopping
service as they passed the word along to others. Soon we were
sending lace collars, handkerchiefs, purses, and scarfs all over the
United States.

The capacity of the hotel was sixty, but soon after we got started we averaged ninety at dinner. Thanksgiving and Christmas were our busiest times. The cook was a fiend, but I managed to persuade her to prepare traditional menus, while Augusta and I made mince pies.

At Christmas time we had a little celebration of the kind held in most Y.M.C.A. posts in France. On Christmas Eve we decorated a tree, all the officers taking part. On Christmas afternoon we had a party for fifty small boys from Les Enfants de la Frontière who otherwise would have had no celebration at all. They marched in two by two, the oldest boys of ten each holding a little one by the hand, led by a Sister with the smallest of all, a mite of three who looked like my Cornelius. He finished me completely by holding out his arms to me and from then on spent most of the time in my lap. We had invited them to come at a quarter to four, having planned Punch and Judy for four o'clock, but they arrived at three. For a moment we were afraid it might be difficult while they waited, but they behaved like lambs, sitting in the rows of chairs we had for them, enthralled while they listened to the victrola. When the show began they watched it in awed silence, then gradually started to squeak and at the end broke out in a hullabaloo of shouts: *"A bas Polichinelle!"* When the show was over, their eyes grew round at the sight of sandwiches made with white bread and jam, which we gave them with large cups of cocoa. After they could hold no more they lined up for the presents. The officers had provided most of these because, as they said, Christmas was not Christmas unless you bought things for children. Each child was given two toys, an orange, and a bag of candy. The officers handed these out and, if anything, had a better time than the children. The Sisters then marshaled them to sing some little Christmas songs to us, after which they marched out, red-cheeked and chattering like magpies. When the littlest one said good-by, he saluted the officers.

That evening we had a hundred and twenty-six at dinner, with turkey and all the fixings. We had tables all through the lobby, and even so had to have two sittings and were forced to turn away forty-seven. I wrote place cards for the hundred and two who had made reservations, some of them three weeks ahead. This was invariably a difficult matter, as there were always people who reserved seats and didn't come, and always some who lived in the hotel and forgot to say they were coming yet expected to be taken care of, and literally dozens who came hoping they could get the reserved seats two minutes after the doors were opened. After everyone was seated friends would find one another and want to change. I was always kept on my toes trying to keep everyone contented.

Another time we had a gala evening entertainment arranged by my friend, Madame Baldini, formerly of La Scala. The program included a leading soprano of the Opéra Comique who sang arias from *Lakmé* and *Manon;* a first-prize winner of the conservatory at Rome who played selections on the piano from Debussy; an excellent baritone who sang the Prologue from *Pagliacci;* a noted violinist who played Chopin nocturnes; and another soprano, who sang music-hall songs in English, playing her own accompaniments. I don't believe they ever had such an enthusiastic audience. The place was packed; everyone applauded and shouted so much that every number had to be repeated.

In the middle of the performance there was a slight disturbance at the door, and in flounced an irate lady in an ermine coat. Baldini hastily drew her back into the hall. I was sitting by the door and could hear the newcomer whispering angrily, *"Non! Non!* Non! *Je ne chanterai pas. Je n'ai jamais été traitée ainsi!"* She had been invited to come by the pianist, a nice little mousy man who had forgotten to tell anyone, so she had not been mentioned in the newspaper notices and had not been sent for. The unfortunate pianist was afraid to face her and tried to hide behind a potted palm. While Baldini went after him I tried to soothe the prima donna as best I could, until he finally gathered courage to come and apologize. She persisted in her refusal to sing but sat through the rest of the performance, then told me she would arrange a better one at which she *would* sing. As I remember it, she never did.

Just before Christmas I had a note from Quentin saying he had a "touch of pneumonia." I went to Issoudun, where he was at the flying school, and found him in bed in a long narrow barracks inadequately heated by a stove at one end. It was bitterly cold and damp. The Army doctor said Quentin was to have three weeks' sick leave and should come back to Paris with me, then go to the Riviera.

That evening I went over to the American Red Cross canteen. A long line of soldiers, each with a large clean handkerchief folded lengthwise, was passing by the director, Miss Irene Givenwilson, who sat stirring something in a large bowl. Each man stopped while she spooned a kind of batter onto his handkerchief, then walked on, tying it around his neck. When I asked about it she said it was a mustard-plaster mixture. They all had sore throats.

I spent the night with the Red Cross girls in their hut, which had a large room with four beds and a big stove in the middle. Miss Givenwilson was English and knew how to make things comfortable even in a board shack. One girl distributed hot-water bags. Another passed around bowls of hot milk dashed with rum after we got into bed. When first call sounded in the morning the stove was lit by a German prisoner, who put large tin ewers of water on top to heat. By the time we heard reveille the room was warm and the water hot. We all had coffee before getting up. These girls were living far better than most of our Y girls under similar conditions.

Quentin and I went back to Paris. Two days later he left for Marseille, only to come right back. He found nothing but snow and rain on the Riviera and said he preferred Paris, where at least he could have family, even if only one in-law. He recovered rapidly. We went to the theater once or twice, and whenever I could take time off we went shopping or sightseeing. We went to La Belle Jardinière, one of the largest department stores, to get some knitted things for Ted and Archie. A nice little elderly Frenchman and his wife watched us buying sweaters. When we finished and started off to get some gloves Quentin, in passing the little old lady, slipped on the polished floor and did several agile and intricate dance steps to avoid falling on top of her. He came up facing her and ended by taking off his hat and making her a low bow. Everybody—saleswomen and customers, including the little couple—stopped whatever they were doing and laughed. Much embarrassed, Quentin hurried after me to the glove counter.

Anyone forced to be away from home knows what a comfort letters can be. My mother wrote me every day, describing all the children said and did. Ted's father wrote him every week and wrote me almost as often, always in longhand. One of his letters told of a visit to Sagamore Hill made by Gracie, Teddy, and Cornelius (Sonny).

October 27th, 1917

Teddy's memory was much clearer about the pigs than about me; he greeted me affably, but then inquired of a delighted bystander, "What is that man's name?" At supper, in pure friendliness and from a desire to encourage closer intimacy, he put the question to me direct, in a deep voice. Gracie explained that I was Grandfather, adding that he had two Grandmothers who were twins. . . . This afternoon I took the three to that haven of delight, the pig-pen. I trundled Sonny in his baby carriage. . . . We fed the pigs with elderly apples; then we came to a small rick of hay down which I had to slide each in turn until I finally rebelled, then halted so each could have a drink of water. . . .

In August 1917 the Chief Secretary of the A.E.F.-Y.M.C.A. in France had offered to prepare plans providing leave centers for the troops if General Pershing so desired. The need was clear. British and French soldiers could go home for the week's leave they were supposed to have every four months, military conditions permitting, but our men could not. Until after the Armistice our enlisted men were not allowed to go to Paris on leave for fear they might get into trouble. Accordingly, orders were issued by the Army in January 1918 authorizing the first Leave Area, which was in Savoy and included the towns of Aix-les-Bains, Chambéry, and a tiny resort called Challes-les-Eaux. Immediately after this I was one of a group of two women and ten men sent to Aix, a famous spa, to organize the first Leave Area under the admirable direction of Franklin S. Edmonds of Philadelphia. The following May I was put in charge of the Y women in all such centers. By December, when I went home, we had ten Leave Areas which included twenty-three towns. Almost as many more were established later, to take care of the men awaiting demobilization.

91

The Savoy Leave Area was to have four thousand soldiers at a time, with about six hundred arriving and leaving every day. Our orders were to make it so attractive that the men would not mind missing Paris, a tough job indeed. To this end we rented the Casino, or Grand Cercle, in Aix. It was a magnificent building with a theater, an elaborate bar where we had the canteen, and other vast rooms for various activities. In addition we leased a large field consisting of parts of eleven farms to be used for athletics. As leave was for seven days, we planned a program that had different events each morning, afternoon, and evening, then began again. Outdoors we had baseball, football, volleyball, tennis, golf, sightseeing tours on bicycles, boating on the lake, fishing, hiking to places of interest, and picnics. Indoors there were professional and amateur theatrical performances, movies, religious services on Sundays, concerts, billiards, card tournaments, ping-pong, and dances. Unlimited hot baths, swimming, and water games were to be had at the Etablissement des Bain at Aix, available also for the men at Chambéry, ten miles away by train.

Chambéry, although a smaller proposition, was in some ways harder to prepare than Aix. There was no casino, and at first large houses seemed unavailable. After much searching we finally found one suitable for a soldiers' club. It was attractive and had a large garden but needed many things. We had to install new plumbing, gas pipes, electric fixtures, canteen counters, fire grates, dozens of shelves and a few cupboards, furniture, curtains, and slip covers. The whole house had to be painted inside. Edith Stedman from Boston, my invaluable assistant, and I put on the last coat just in time for the opening of the club. As it would have taken too long to order from Paris the hundreds of cups and plates we needed, we went to Lyons to get them.

The casino at Challes-les-Eaux was in bad condition and needed redecorating, and as there was a labor shortage we had to let this go until later. We were told to have Aix and Chambéry ready in two weeks, and we did. During this time Edith and I attracted as much interest in the streets as if we had been Zulus. No one in the region had ever seen American women in uniform, and people were frankly curious. Children followed us, making candid comments. Sometimes I pretended to know no French, then would turn suddenly and join in the conversation. They would scatter like birds but returned when I held out some candy.

The French people co-operated with enthusiasm and could not have been more helpful. The mayors of Aix-les-Bains and Chambéry issued proclamations declaring that any merchant boosting prices would be prosecuted. Dr. Françon, a prominent physician in Aix, was head of a local committee which, among many other things, arranged for soldiers to be entertained in French homes. The nuns at the convent at Chambéry took some Y girls as boarders, the first time they had ever admitted non-Catholics. Edith and I stayed there from time to time. The chemist found us a cook, seamstresses to do mending for the troops, dishwashers, painters, carpenters, bicycles, and best of all a supply of milk. He put us in touch with a man whose cheese factory was going to be shut down. From him we got nearly five hundred quarts of milk a day.

All hotels at Aix and Chambéry were taken over for the soldiers, so we had to find lodgings for the twenty-odd Y girls who were to work in the Leave Area. This was a difficult task. It was of real importance to be comfortable, for we knew we would have to work at least nine hours a day and probably more at times. While the great majority of women in the Y.M.C.A. were conscientious, unselfish, thinking only of doing the best job they could, and ready to work until they dropped, there were always a few who were not content with clean comfortable quarters at reasonable prices, but demanded more. These were usually the shirkers who arrived late and left early, leaving part of their work to be done by someone else. Three of them said they could not be happy unless they had their own sitting room. Two others refused to stay at the really charming apartment of a French colonel's widow because, as they said, "She talks too much and is always wanting to know if there is something she can do for us. We don't want to be bothered." They turned up their noses at the little *pension* where Edith and I were because it didn't have private baths.

At first the soldiers resented bitterly being pushed around and not being allowed to go to Paris. They were fully prepared to hate Aix-les-Bains, which they called "Aches and Pains." In spite of this, our plans were successful. Before the war Aix had been the most fashionable of watering places, and many European royal families had been in the habit of going there "to take the cure." Soldiers delighted in sleeping in luxurious hotel suites once occupied by Queen Victoria, King Edward VII, Emperor Franz Josef, Empress Eugénie, King Alfonso of Spain, King Manoel of Portugal, and others.

The behavior of our men on leave was exemplary. Once the Mayor of Chambéry came to our headquarters to apologize because two of them had been drunk and disorderly and assured us he was going to fine the café owner who had served them too much. This was literally the only time I can remember any soldier giving trouble. They really enjoyed the entertainments we planned for them. My cousin, Martha McCook, later Mrs. Eliot Cross, who was head of the Women's Bureau of the A.E.F.-Y.M.C.A., was once stopped on the street by a soldier who said, "Ma'am, I promised myself I would never see your uniform without shaking hands. I've been down to Aix. If I was to say it was the finest week I've spent in France maybe you wouldn't be surprised. But when I say it was the finest week I've *ever* spent, maybe you will know how I feel about it!"

After the opening of Aix and Chambéry, Edith and I went over to Challes with samples of wallpaper. As we were staying at the convent, Edith suggested that we ask the Mother Superior and Soeur Constance Aimée to go with us. The two little old ladies were pink with excitement when we started off, Soeur Constance saying it was her first trip in an automobile, and the Mother Superior remarking it was her first visit to a casino. While I puttered about with wallpapers, Edith took them to the house we were planning to rent for our workers. They looked it over with lively interest and made all sorts of useful suggestions. As they were leaving the landlady offered each of them an apple from her own tree. Soeur Constance said she must have one for me, then shamelessly took the best four from the dish, hid them in her capacious pockets, and later gave them to me with pride. We had brought a small supply of candy which both enjoyed like children.

That spring my father-in-law wrote me from Sagamore Hill:

I hear of you continually, and really the admiration expressed for what the boys have done is no stronger than the tributes paid you for your administrative ability, judgment, tact, decision of character, unselfishness and ability to accomplish results. I doubt if I have ever known of such hearty and universal commendation being expressed for difficult work of a kind peculiarly apt to produce friction.

Of course I didn't deserve such praise, but I like to think that he exaggerated because he was fond of me.

In March 1918 Archie was badly wounded and received the Croix de Guerre. One kneecap was severely damaged and his left arm fractured and its main nerve cut. The doctors first thought they would have to amputate his leg, but they eventually were able to save it. It was doubtful if he ever would recover entirely, but recover he did, enough to command combat troops in the Pacific in World War II as colonel and to be wounded and decorated again.

Ted had telegraphed me about Archie and I took the night train to Paris to see if I could go to him at the hospital at Toul. At Y.M.C.A. headquarters both the Chief and Deputy Chief secretaries, Mr. Carter and Mr. Shipp, were out, so I went to a friend in the office, asked for a travel order to Toul, and got it just as Mr. Shipp came in. He told me that if I went I would be creating a precedent that other workers with relatives in the Army would want to follow. So far, he said, the Y had used me as an example of good behavior. There might be a case so serious that they would take a chance on breaking Army orders for me, but not this time. Although disappointed, I saw his point and gave back my travel permit.

Mrs. Whitelaw Reid, with characteristic kindness and thoughtfulness, asked me to lunch to meet General Bradley, Chief Surgeon of the A.E.F. We both begged him to have Archie transferred as soon as he could be moved to the new officers' hospital Mrs. Reid was equipping in Paris for the Army. The General was pleasant, friendly, sympathetic, and absolutely noncommittal. A day or two later a friend in the Provost Marshal's office told me he was pleased to report that Archie was scheduled to be moved to Mrs. Reid's hospital in a couple of weeks or so. It must be remembered that under the Democratic administration there was no possible way of my being able to influence anyone to do anything for these friends of mine in return for the favors they did for me.

On April 14, 1918, Ted's father wrote him:

I have written General March, the Chief of Staff, to find out whether Kermit can now be transferred to our army in France. He is very anxious for the transfer; the season for active operations in Mesopotamia is now closing. Lord Derby has cabled me that Kermit has "done excellently well with the light armored motor squadron in action twice."

My great-grandfather, Matthew Brown, and his daughter Susan, who married my grandfather, Henry M. Alexander.

Ted aged 2 with his father, 1889.

Myself aged 2 with my mother, 1890.

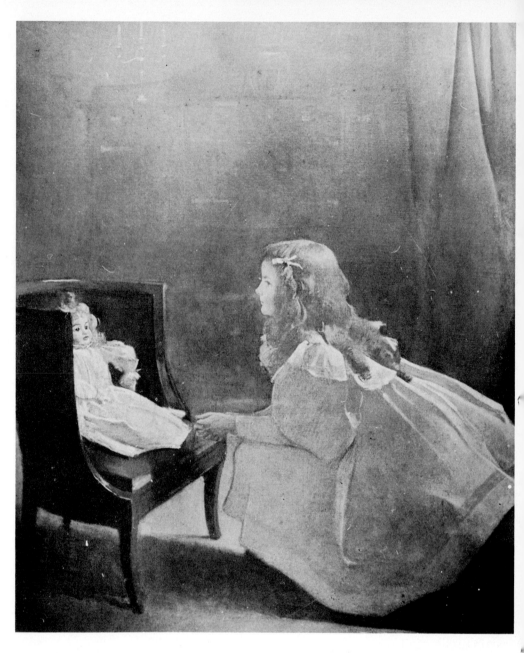

Myself aged 9, 1897. Portrait painted by John W. Alexander, a cousin by
marriage.

Ted at Albany Academy, 1900, with his dog Jack.

The Roosevelt children. Clockwise from left: Ted, Ethel, Alice, Quentin, Kermit, Archie, 1900.

Left to right: Ethel, Ted, Quentin, Mrs. Roosevelt, President Roosevelt, Kermit, Archie, Alice, Nicholas Longworth. On the White House Porch, 1908.

The Fifth Avenue bus, about 1902.

Chapter II

*For, when the trumpets sound at Armaged-
don, only those deserve undying praise who
stand where the danger is sorest.*
PRESIDENT THEODORE ROOSEVELT

At the end of May 1918 the third German offensive against the
French started on the Aisne and was all but successful. In Paris
we heard the guns clearly and at night saw flashes like summer
lightning in the north. By then I was working in the Y.M.C.A.
Paris office, assigning newly arrived women to the Leave Areas.

On June second, a Sunday and my day off, I was sitting writing
letters when the door opened and Ted walked in. I have never
seen anyone look so ghastly. His face was scorched and inflamed,
the whites of his eyes an angry red. He was thickly covered with
dust and shaken by a racking cough.

"Why are you still here?" he demanded. "Don't you know the
Germans are advancing on Paris? You must leave at once!"

He had been gassed some days before and had lost all his personal equipment. He had heard of the German successes, and the
moment his battalion had been relieved he came straight to Paris.
I did not know until later that he and his unit had taken part in a
battle that was first proof to the Allies and to the enemy that the
"half-trained, poorly disciplined American troops" could overcome
Germans steeled to combat by four years of warfare; a battle of
which General Pershing was to say in his Final Report: "The des-

perate efforts of the Germans gave the fighting at Cantigny a seeming tactical importance entirely out of proportion to the numbers involved."

More than twenty-five years later I had further details from General George C. Marshall, Chief of Staff, later Secretary of State, who had then been lieutenant colonel at 1st Division Headquarters. Ted had gone to his tent at three in the morning and asked for a pass to Paris to make sure I was safe. Colonel Marshall, waked out of a sound sleep, remonstrated.

"For heaven's sake, Roosevelt, go and get some rest! You've been gassed and you look like the very dickens. Your wife will be all right. She must have friends in Paris who will look after her. Go away and get some sleep!"

If he used stronger language he did not tell me.

"That's as may be," said Ted. "But I've got to be sure. You see, she's the only wife I've got!"

He ended by borrowing his regimental commander's car with permission but wrote his own pass. I knew nothing until I saw the papers three weeks later, but his conduct at Cantigny had been such that he probably could have got away with it if found out.

To relieve Ted's mind we called up a friend in the Provost Marshal's office who assured him he would see I got away if the Germans came. Ted had a hot bath and a change of clothes, a smart new uniform and boots which I had ready for him. It was a lovely summer night, and for the first time in two weeks there was no air raid. Quentin appeared, overjoyed to see Ted. It was the last time the two brothers were together.

I put on my prettiest Paris dress and we had dinner in the garden, where all the roses were in bloom. Ted collected books from all over the house and read aloud from Ironquill, Kipling, C. Fox Smith, and Alexander Pope. John Kieran once said Ted's knowledge of poetry was far greater than that of any man he ever knew.

After dinner we went to the hospital to see Archie. They talked of the battalion and of Archie's company. Archie wanted news of his friends. "How's so-and-so?" "Killed at Cantigny." "And so-and-so?" "They got him on a raid." "What about so-and-so?" "Both legs gone." When we left, Archie came to the door of the hospital and watched us until we were out of sight. I knew he never expected to see Ted again.

When we got home Ted told me he had not been able to lie down since being gassed, as he choked in that position. I propped him up with pillows, and he was able to sleep between spasms of coughing. Once he said to me: "What would you give to hear those good old back-yard cats we used to curse on Seventy-fourth Street?"

I would have given anything to keep him with me until he recovered, and begged him to stay and have medical treatment. All he had to do was to report himself ill, but he laughed at me. "Now that I know you're all right I'm fit as a fiddle." He left early next morning.

Three weeks later I picked up the Paris *Herald* and saw a headline: MAJOR ROOSEVELT CITED FOR BRAVERY. My hands shook so, I could hardly read the citation. "Displayed high courage and leadership . . . At Cantigny, although gassed in the lungs and gassed in the eyes to blindness refused to be evacuated . . . Retained command of his battalion through heavy bombardment." He was later awarded the Silver Star and Croix de Guerre for this and for a highly successful raid he organized and supervised a month afterward. The raid was considered so good that the French had copies of Ted's orders printed and distributed through their Army. Sixteen years later, in 1934, the *Infantry Journal* published an article called "Infantry in Battle, Simplicity," in which Ted's raid was described in detail. In 1939 this article was reprinted in the Army textbook *Infantry in Battle*. The raiding party consisted of six lieutenants, six sergeants, eleven corporals, thirty-six privates, and four stretcher-bearers. Thirty-three German prisoners were taken, as well as intelligence data. The company making the raid was composed of recruits who had had no military training of any kind until after their arrival in France five months before.

Meanwhile Ted's father wrote him about Kermit on June 1, 1918:

> He has received the British War Cross for gallantry in action in command of a light armored battery; he is to report to Pershing . . . it is a load off my mind to have him transferred.

The last five years have made me bitterly conscious of the shortcomings of our national character; but we Roosevelts are Americans, and can never think of being anything else, and wouldn't be anything else for any consideration on the face of the earth; a man with our way of looking at things can no more change his country than change his mother; and it is the business of each of us to play the part of a good American and try to make things as much better as possible.

Early in July, Archie's arm, which had been giving him pain for four months, was operated on again. Dr. Harvey Cushing, who watched the operation, told me that the severed nerve was so shrunken that there was a gap of some inches between the two ends. He said it probably would grow together now that it had been put in proper position, but it would be eight months or more before Archie could be sure of recovery.

A few days after Archie's operation Quentin brought down his first German plane and came to Paris to celebrate. He called for me at the Y.M.C.A. office, and we went on a search for wild strawberries and Normandy cream for Archie. The Café de la Régence sold us some in a china dish tied up with paper and string. I was carrying it as we walked along the Avenue de l'Opéra when the string broke and the package crashed to the pavement, oozing strawberries and cream in all directions. All we could do was walk hurriedly away. In the evening Quentin and I dined at Ciro's and went to the Grand Guignol. He left next morning, and I never saw him again. On July 14, 1918, he was shot down over Chaméry, far inside the German lines. Months later we learned that he had been buried by the Germans with full military honors, including a battalion of infantry at attention. He was not yet twenty-one.

My father-in-law wrote me that President Hadley of Yale, referring to Quentin, quoted from Napier's account of the storming of Badajoz in the Peninsular War: "None died that night with greater glory, yet many died and there was great glory."

On July 19, 1918, I was sitting upstairs reading when Augusta threw open the door, announced, "Major Roosevelt is here!" and vanished. I ran down and saw Ted being lifted out of an automobile at the front door. I tried to ask what had happened but could make no sound. Ted said cheerily: "I got wounded this morning, and here I am!" They carried him upstairs. He had been shot through the leg by a machine gun at Ploisy near Soissons and was wearing a tag saying GUNSHOT WOUND SEVERE tied to a button on his shirt.

"If only I could have got hold of a horse," he said. "I could have gone through the day at least. The fighting was so hot there were no ambulances around or they'd have taken me to a field hospital, but I came out on a Field Artillery limber and got away from them."

He had ridden for several hours in the sidecar of a motorcycle, dodging through traffic over shell-pitted roads until he ran across an old friend, Colonel Lawton, who lent his car for the rest of the way.

I wanted to get a doctor at once, but Ted refused, saying he had had first aid and anti-tetanus and needed no further medical attention of any kind. He would not even let me look at his wound but sat in a big easy chair with his foot up and bellowed: "I want a hot bath! Then I want my dinner! I haven't eaten anything since yesterday morning. I would like some black bean soup, broiled live lobster, steamed clams, wild duck and hominy, rare roast beef and browned potatoes, and buckweat cakes with maple syrup, but I'll settle for whatever French food you have in the house. You can start by bringing me a quart of champagne!"

Augusta and I were running around like chickens without heads. "We'll put water to heat on the stove," I said. "I can promise you a good dinner by the time you've had your bath. But a quart of champagne is too much. You can have a pint."

At that moment in walked our brother-in-law, Lieutenant Colonel Richard Derby, Chief Surgeon with the 2nd Division, who was in Paris recovering from what was called Flanders flu. He examined Ted's leg, which appeared paralyzed. A machine-gun bullet had gone right through it just above and behind the knee, leaving two nasty holes. Ted kept insisting that all he needed was a clean bandage and to be left alone.

"The wound is full of bits of cloth and dirt," said Dick. "It's in a bad place. That part of the leg is a bottleneck, with all the important tendons, nerves, and veins going through it. If it's not opened and thoroughly cleaned out right away it will get infected and you may lose your leg. We're going to the hospital now."

"At least let me have my dinner," Ted begged.

"You'll have nothing," said Dick. "Be thankful you've had a pint of champagne."

We took Ted in a taxi to Colonel Joseph Blake's hospital in the Rue Piccini across the Avenue du Bois. That night Colonel Blake operated, making a cut about eight inches long up the back of the leg. The main nerve had escaped serious injury, but Ted had no feeling in his heel for the rest of life. However, this never bothered him.

Dick watched the operation while Archie and I sat outside and waited. We both hoped, eagerly, frankly, and openly, that Ted's leg would be damaged enough to keep him out of combat forever. One of the medicos came to tell us the result. "When this has healed he'll be as good as new." I shall never forget the astonished look on his face when Archie said, "Gee, but that's tough," and I groaned assent. Ted was horrified when we told him about it later. "You'd have had me crippled for life, would you? You blackhearted rascals!"

The hospital was crowded with our wounded. Two days afterward Colonel Blake sent Ted back to our house, called him "sick in quarters," and let me take care of him. I had been with the Y for a year without leave, so I asked for a month off and got it.

After the battle of Soissons the 1st Division was withdrawn to rest billets. A day or two later half a dozen officers came to see Ted. He felt it ignominious to be found in bed for whatever reason and wanted to get up and dress at once. I prevented this and partly pacified him by making him put on a pair of pajamas of heavy white silk with his monogram worked in dark-blue on the pocket. I had bought them at the smartest men's shop on the Rue de la Paix and was saving them for his birthday. Then I ran downstairs for something extra-special for toasts. Two toasts were proposed by Ted according to custom. "Gentlemen, the Regiment!" and then, "The dead of the Regiment."

After this they settled down to talk. The casualties at Soissons had been terrific and included all the field officers of the 26th Infantry. The 1st Battalion, Ted's command, came out of the line under a second lieutenant. An officer from Corps was reported to have asked General Charles P. Summerall, commanding the 1st Division, if the division was capable of making another attack after such losses, and the General replied: "Sir, when the 1st Division has only two men left they will be echeloned in depth and attacking toward Berlin."

More officers appeared, until all remaining battalion officers and some from the regiment had been in. It was touching to see the respect and affection they had for Ted and to hear them say: "It's not the same without you. When are you coming back to us?"

The news of Ted's having been wounded reached his father soon after he heard of Quentin's death. In a letter written to both of us he said:

> For, when the trumpets sound at Armageddon, only those deserve undying praise who stand where the danger is sorest.

Colonel Blake dropped in to see us once or twice. When he took the stitches out of Ted's wound he said: "This is going to hurt, as I've got to poke about a bit. Steady now!"

I stood at the foot of the bed, holding up Ted's foot. Ted ground his teeth, clenched his hands, breathed heavily, and gave the impression of turning pale. When Colonel Blake had finished he said, "All over. You stood that like the soldier you are."

After seeing the Colonel to the front door I ran upstairs, my knees still shaking. "Ted darling, was it very bad?"

Ted burst into roars of laughter. "Don't tell me I fooled you too! Why, doggone it, my leg is completely numb. I never felt a thing he did. I didn't tell him so because I thought he would be extra careful if he thought he was hurting me. You have to know how to treat these doctors."

Chapter 12

And if I laugh at any mortal thing,
'Tis that I may not weep.
BYRON

Soon Ted was able to go out on crutches, his leg in a wire splint. Often we took drives in fiacres driven by *cochers,* elderly pirates in tall hats and capes of oilcloth. They were usually rather cross and disagreeable, but Ted could always get along with them, talking the most dubious French. Once Ted dropped me off at the dentist, saying he would be home about five o'clock, but it was nearly seven when he appeared. He had made friends with an old *cocher* who wanted to know about his wound and said the best thing for shrunken muscles was massage by an expert. He had a friend unexcelled at this art. Would Monsieur le Commandant care to try him?

They drove to a little restaurant in the Faubourg St. Denis, where an old man with a white beard was sitting at a table on the sidewalk, surrounded by a group of friends. The *cocher* pulled up with a flourish and an "E-eup!" to his horse and made a speech. He said he had with him an American officer of the highest rank and greatest distinction (of course he didn't know Ted's name), wounded while performing feats of unsurpassed gallantry while in the act of saving Paris, and incidentally France, from the Boches. This officer was, luckily for the Boches, obliged to remain in Paris until his shattered leg should heal, so he, the *cocher—*

"moi qui vous parle"—had done the obvious thing in the circumstances. He had brought the officer to that unequaled genius, his friend, so that for the glory of France and les Etats Unis and the discomfiture of the enemy, his friend could enable the officer to return more quickly to the front to inflict further and even more violent punishment upon the afore-mentioned Boches. The old man rose, took off his hat, and made a low bow, saying he had been waiting only for this opportunity and asked no greater honor than to do his poor best. He invited Ted to descend and for an hour gave him excellent massage on the muscles of his calf, with advice and comments from the rest of the group. After it was finished Ted stood drinks for the crowd, but the old man would accept no money.

Archie's left arm and shoulder were in a great plaster cast. He, Ted, and I used to wander around Paris, driving in fiacres, poking about in antique shops or bookstalls on the Left Bank, sitting at sidewalk cafés, and going to the theater. I had to stop wearing my Y.M.C.A. uniform when I went out with them, for they delighted in trying to embarrass me. If we took the Métro they would separate themselves from me and then ostentatiously pretend to pick me up, to the amusement of other passengers. Once when we were driving down the Champs Elysées they decided to be mental patients out for an airing, and their goings-on were indescribable. Ted cried out loud, "Boo-hoo-hoo! Ai-ai-ai-ai!" wiping his eyes with a large handkerchief. Archie clapped his hands on imaginary butterflies, tore them to pieces, and ate them. The grinning *cocher* sat sideways on the box to watch. Whenever they saw a chic Parisienne they waved at her frantically. After a moment of startled surprise she would wave back, thinking, I am sure, that all Americans were mad.

At the end of July 1918, Kermit turned up on his way to the Artillery School at Saumur, where he had been ordered after his transfer from the British Army. With him was his wife Belle, who had come from Spain, where her father was American Ambassador. We believed this might well be the last time we would all be together. Quentin, the youngest, was gone. No one knew how long the war would last. No one knew whose turn would come next.

We played around with the feverish high spirits felt only in the shadow of death.

On Sunday we all lunched at a Petit Durand restaurant not far from our house. Toward the end of the meal Kermit said that Belle was pale and needed some good red wine. Belle didn't want any. He tried in vain to persuade her, then took her by the back of the neck and tried to feed her from the bottle. At this she and I rose, saying we didn't like to be made conspicuous, and started for home. Ted whispered to Archie, "Let's show them what being conspicuous *is!*"

Before we had gone far we heard them coming behind us, singing "Hail, Hail, the Gang's All Here." First came Kermit, then Archie with his large plaster cast, and last Ted on crutches. Ted shouted, *"En avant, mes braves!"* and four wounded poilus fell behind them. It was a lovely day, and people were strolling on the avenue. They waved and beckoned, inviting everyone to join the procession. The French, always sympathetic to the wounded and ready to take part in anything gay, did so in droves. Soon everyone was singing "Madelon." A man came along with a pushcart and yelled: *"Vive l'Amérique!"* Kermit promptly climbed into the cart and rode along, waving his cap and shouting: *"Vive la France!"*

As we turned into the Rue de Villejust there must have been a hundred people following Belle and me as we walked with great dignity and crimson faces, pretending to notice nothing. Opposite our house was an ultra-respectable and exclusive apartment house with an elderly white-haired concierge. As the singing throng came marching down the street, heads came out of its windows. Belle and I fled through our front door. The gathering finally broke up after more songs, several speeches, and rousing cheers.

Next day Archie added the finishing touch when the white-haired concierge asked him politely but with a certain curiosity how Madame, his wife, was. Archie gave him a saucy wink and replied: "My wife? Oh, but she isn't my *wife*, you know!"

All this and more of the same caused speculation about us among our neighbors, but it was not until after the Armistice that I realized how far-reaching it was. Ted was in the Army of Occupation in Germany, Archie was back in the United States, and I was waiting for passage home to my children. One evening I had a small dinner party with the Count and Countess de Chambrun, Lord and Lady Hartington (later Duke and Duchess of Devonshire), General Hart, the American Provost Marshal, and two or three others. Everybody arrived on time except Lord Hartington, who had been detained and sent word not to wait for him. Half an hour later he arrived, chuckling. He had got into his car and told the chauffeur to go to 39 Rue de Villejust, only to have the man say there must be some mistake. This could not be the right address. Lord Hartington said there was no mistake. That is where they were dining, and her Ladyship had gone on ahead. The chauffeur was shocked. "But that's where a young American person lives—with several officers! And the way they carry on, my lord! The whole neighborhood is talking about it. Surely that's not where you and her Ladyship are going to dinner?"

The French custom of giving decorations immediately after they are won was by far the most satisfactory. Ted was given the Croix de Guerre immediately after Cantigny and Soissons, but it was nearly two years before he received the Distinguished Service Cross for which he was cited at the same time.

A letter from General Charles P. Summerall, commander of the 1st Division, who in Ted's opinion was the greatest troop leader developed in the war, gave him more satisfaction than all the citations he received. I quote a paragraph.

August 18, 1918

HEADQUARTERS FIRST DIVISION

Your services in this Division have been conspicuous for efficiency, energy and leadership. It would be difficult to convey to you my appreciation of the manner in which you led your battalion in the Soissons fight, and of the great assistance rendered by you in moving boldly ahead of the line, thereby greatly facilitating the general movement that followed on July 19. The Corps Commander was present when the report was received of your enterprise in gaining ground under the most difficult circumstances, and he shared with me the relief and confidence that your conduct inspired. I think no one who has been a member of this Division occupies a higher place than you in the esteem of your comrades, and you will receive a warm welcome whenever it shall be our good fortune to have you return to us.

I sent a copy of this letter to Ted's father, who wrote on September 13 that it was the finest tribute he remembered seeing a division commander pay to a battalion commander. He also wrote Ted:

You have made *the* great success of all our family in the war, for you have had the biggest and most responsible job, particularly delicate as you were a Major of the Regulars, and you have won really remarkable testimony to your success.

By the first of September Ted was growing restless and counted the days until he could return to combat, saying he disliked sitting around while others did his fighting for him. His wound had healed nicely, but his leg was still paralyzed in places and the muscles had shrunk. For this he was doing special exercises and having massage. The doctors maintained it would be at least two months before he could walk half a mile, and probably four before the full use of his leg would be restored, but he was determined to prove this nonsense. I hoped fervently that his disability would keep him out of the fighting indefinitely and urged him to stay in Paris until he could walk without two canes. He finally persuaded the medicos to certify him fit for limited duty, and he pestered everyone for some sort of assignment. What he wanted, of course, was to go back to the 26th Infantry, but that was out of the question. He was ordered to Langres both as instructor in the Army Line School and student at the General Staff College, and he left Paris on September 13, 1918, his thirty-first birthday, leaving one cane behind him.

Augusta told me later she had slipped a bottle of my aunt's priceless old brandy into his foot locker. She had fixed him some lunch, which included a whole roast chicken, sandwiches, and a bottle of champagne. He had tried to give her a present, but she refused to take it. When he insisted she said, with tears pouring down her face, she had not taken care of him for money but for *la gloire*.

Three days later his promotion to lieutenant colonel came through.

Believing Ted still in Paris, his father wrote a letter to both of us on October 20, 1918, telling us that he had been making speeches for the Liberty Loan and had stopped at Newport, Rhode Island. He said in part:

Grace Vanderbilt had convulsed Newport by announcing that as the wife of a Brigadier General she was entitled to take precedence of everybody except the Governor. When appealed to I explained that the situation was gravely complicated by her being also the mother of an enlisted man, a chauffeur; and that I thought the only solution was for her to sit in the Governor's lap during the early courses of dinner, but, as mother of a chauffeur, to eat her dessert in the kitchen.

Chapter 13

His men love him almost to idolatry.
BRIGADIER GENERAL FRANCIS C. MARSHALL

In addition to the Leave Areas in Savoy, the Y.M.C.A. established others in Auvergne, including La Bourboule and Mont Dore; and in Brittany, including Dinard, St. Malo, and Peramé.

When I wasn't in Paris interviewing the new Y girls as they arrived I was kept busy making inspection trips to these areas as a trouble-shooter. Train travel was uncomfortable at that time, with no proper sleeping cars and no dining cars. I always went by night to save time and because I could always sleep anywhere. If you were lucky you got a *couchette*, a bunk in a small compartment with three other people, usually men. There were no bedclothes, no pillows, and of course no reason to undress. Our uniform capes were most useful, as they were long and full enough to wrap around us from chin to feet, and kept us warm. If you weren't lucky you sat up all night.

When the Army asked the Y to establish twenty more Leave Areas as soon as possible, I was sent with four other Y people on a tour of southern and central France. We went in luxury in a big open Cadillac touring car belonging to Dr. J. H. Denison, a lame clergyman who had turned it over to the Y.M.C.A. with his services as driver. Our job was to select suitable places from a list given to us by the Paris office, preferably resort towns, and to make advance arrangements by renting casinos and inspecting possible hotel accommodations for the troops.

In October, Bulgaria capitulated, the first break in the ranks of enemy countries. It was barely possible that the war would end before Ted could get back to his regiment. His leg would not be well for another six weeks at best, but I knew Ted and prayed they would keep him at Langres.

Our tour ended with an inspection of Aix-les-Bains, now running with a staff of twenty-seven women and twenty-three men, and being used as a training school for the new workers. The Prince of Monaco had been there and was so pleased with the work being done that he offered Monaco for a Leave Area. He said we could have his palace while he would live on his yacht, and he promised to pass any required laws about saloons and so forth within twenty-four hours after we asked for them. When it was pointed out that as Monaco was a neutral country no American soldiers could go there, he said quite seriously he would declare war on Germany. This was not necessary, however, because Monaco was added to our list after the Armistice.

When we arrived at Aix I had a telegram from Ted: AM RE-PORTING TO OLD REGIMENT TODAY MUCH LOVE. Later I heard more about it from a friend at Langres. "Yes, Ted has left," he said. "He was doing all right here, getting a lot of useful knowledge and also teaching a lot of people. He should have had sense enough to stay put and not keep fretting like an idiot because he thought he was in a soft job. General Frank Parker is now commanding the 1st Division. He called Ted on the telephone and asked how his leg was. Of course Ted said it was entirely well, the liar. The General said his old regiment needed a commanding officer and Ted could have the job if he was able to come at once. Ted was off like a shot. He still walks with a cane and is certified for limited duty only, and now he's AWOL. I hope he gets court-martialed!"

For eleven days, until his orders caught up with him, Ted was technically absent without official leave while commanding the 26th Infantry in the last weeks of the Meuse-Argonne offensive. As General Douglas MacArthur and others have told me, he was

the first reserve officer to command a regiment of the Regular
Army in action.

On October 29, Kermit, who had finished the course at the Artillery School at Saumur, was assigned to the Field Artillery in
the 1st Division in time to see action with our Army during the
last two weeks of the Meuse-Argonne fighting.

In a letter to Ted's father dated November 11, 1918, Brigadier
General Francis C. Marshall, commanding the 2nd Brigade of the
1st Division, told of the last days of the war. He described the
26th Infantry's all-night march to attack Mouzon on the Meuse.
Fighting all next day, at 5 P.M. they were ordered to withdraw
and to march on Sedan, thirty kilometers away, which was to be
attacked at daylight. All this was in the rain, with cold food. He
wrote that the next day his brigade was advancing well when an
order came from Corps telling the 1st Division to retire and turn
over their gains to the Rainbow or 42nd Division. Again the brigade marched all night, to bivouac at La Besace. General Marshall went on to say:

> We marched and fought continuously from the late after-
> noon of November 5 until the early morning of November 8
> with reserve rations only, fought two battles and turned over
> our gains to other divisions.
>
> A little after noon on the 8th a very tired colonel of infantry
> with a happy contagious smile came limping up to my P.C.
> at La Besace, and reported his regiment in bivouac and him-
> self on the trail of chow. His automobile had broken down,
> he was worn, hungry and tired, it took two canes to carry him
> through, but he was proud and happy and anxious to get his
> men their food and their packs so they might be comfortable.
> When he had finished his report he said: "General, I'm afraid
> I will have to ask you for a horse. I doubt if I can walk back
> to camp."
>
> I don't wish to be fulsome, but I do wish to tell you that
> your son is a magnificent soldier, and that his men love him
> almost to idolatry, and that I consider it has been a privilege to
> see him at work and an honor to have commanded him.
>
> We have built up a wonderful fighting machine over here,

and the finest element in it is undoubtedly the 1st Division. It has never yielded a foot of ground it has taken. For every prisoner lost it has taken a hundred Germans. Its casualties are estimated as 200% of its authorized strength, and your son has earned, by sheer competition and grit, his promotion to lieutenant colonel and colonel in it.

You should be very proud.

On November 9 in Paris I received a message from Edward C. Carter, head of the A.E.F.-Y.M.C.A., saying that because I had worked hard for a year and a half without breaking rules or asking favors I was to have a reward. He and two or three others were leaving by car early next morning to establish a canteen at Dun-sur-Meuse, directly behind the front lines, and would take me with them. We set out at six o'clock. At midnight we reached Ippecourt, where we learned that an armistice would go into effect next morning at eleven.

From that moment my one idea was to reach Ted and tell him that as he was no longer in danger I would go home to the children, but I could not leave France without saying good-by to him. On November 11 we arrived in Bantheville, where only one house was left with a roof. Some soldiers said the 1st Division was not far away. I asked Mr. Carter if I might leave his party and search for Ted. The Y had a rule that no woman might stay alone in a town where there were no civilians, and of course there were none for miles around, but Mr. Carter agreed to waive this if a place could be found for me to sleep. One of the Y men attached to the 32nd Division, in whose territory we were, offered me a couple of blankets and a little tent used to store writing paper, chocolate, cigarettes, and other supplies. This was more than satisfactory, and Mr. Carter and the others went on and left me.

The Quartermaster Colonel of the 32nd Division asked me to lunch at his mess in the one house with a roof. We had blueberry pie. Rumor said the 32nd was moving out and the 1st moving into the town. I sat in a window all afternoon, watching for them to arrive. At dusk the Colonel of the 1st Engineers drove up, said the Division would not be along that night, and offered me his car and driver to go and look for Ted.

We drove for an hour on a road deep in mud through country fought over only the day before. Finally we reached the Bois de la Folie and saw many little fires twinkling among the trees.

"There they are, ma'am," said the driver. "It's the first time they've been allowed to make fires."

We went through three regiments and at last came to the 26th. I waited in the car while the driver went to see if he could find Ted.

A sergeant stopped to talk to me and told me the Division had just come to a halt after starting its march down from Sedan that morning.

"We could have taken Sedan easy," he said. "We were going strong until we got to Omicourt, where we met up with the French at a crossroad. A French General told Colonel Roosevelt to halt the regiment and let them through. The Colonel said his orders were to advance. The General said if he did we would get caught in the barrage he was going to put down. The Colonel got mad, ma'am, and said nothing would keep him from carrying out his orders. They say it was beautiful to hear him. Just then a runner came with new orders for the Colonel and we had to halt and let them frogs go by."

All this was true. The High Command had decided that the French deserved the honor of being the first to enter Sedan to wipe out the memory of 1870.

The driver found Ted almost at once, saluted with a grin, and said: "Sir, Mrs. Roosevelt is waiting for you down the road."

Ted slogged through the mud, still limping with his cane, and hugged the breath out of me. "How in the name of patience did you get here? Now I'm willing to believe the war's really over!"

Yes, the war was over. The world had been made safe for democracy and we could all go home and live happily ever after. At least we would never have to fight another war, nor would our children. People would have too much sense to fight wars. No doubt was in our minds.

We sat together in the car, silent with happiness. After a while Ted said I must meet his battalion commanders—Major Barnwell Rhett Legge, Major Rice Youell, and Major Lyman Frazier. We grasped hands in a circle, everybody talking at once. "The war's over! We'll be going home! *Home!* No more mud, no more sunny France! Think of sleeping in a real bed! Think of running water! My God, no more cooties!"

It was getting late and I had to go. They were all busy and I did not want to be in the way; besides, I had to return the car to the Colonel of Engineers. Meanwhile it had settled down in the deep mud and refused to budge. Ted put his head out of the window and called for a couple of runners to help. Major Legge said: "This is a battalion commander's job!" and the three of them pushed until we were free. Ted drove back to Bantheville to see me safely in my little tent. The Y men heard us arrive, guessed we were hungry, and brought us canned bully beef, bread, strawberry jam, and hot chocolate. Nothing ever tasted better. After supper Ted went back to his regiment.

Later I realized I had forgotten the name of the Colonel who had lent me his car. I was sorry indeed, as he had done me a very great favor and I wanted to thank him again. Twenty-three years afterward, at a party on Governors Island, a General approached me and said: "Mrs. Roosevelt, I haven't seen you since 1918 in France. Of course you wouldn't remember it, but I once lent you a car. It was in the Argonne and you were looking for your husband." Not remember it! I embraced him. It was Major General Francis Wilby, commanding the New England area, afterward superintendent of the U. S. Military Academy at West Point.

Early the following morning a soldier brought breakfast to my tent, coffee and a stack of hot cakes with syrup. I went out and helped the Y men prepare an immense container of hot chocolate, which we served at the side of the road to the men coming down. In the afternoon Ted arrived. I did not want to hang about and was making plans to go back to Paris. There were no railways in the area, so my only course was to hitchhike in Army vehicles. My uniform made this easy. Just as I was about to start, a message came from General Frank Parker. He was leaving late that afternoon for Paris on military business and would give me a lift. He added, bless his kind heart, that he was ordering Ted to come with us.

We left at five o'clock and reached our house at four next morning, November 13. We woke Augusta and told her we had not eaten since lunch the day before. In fifteen minutes she produced cold partridge and lobster salad—from where, I never knew—with champagne from my aunt's cellar. Next evening we drove with General Parker down the boulevards where the Armistice celebration was still going on. Crowds filled the streets. People jumped on the running board of the General's car. A girl put her head in at the window and kissed the driver. I can hear him now in embarrassed fury: "Quit that now! *Allez!*"

We had some shopping to do, as all Ted's belongings had been lost again, this time in the Argonne fighting. Early next morning Ted said good-by to me until we should meet four months later in New York.

The 1st Division was going into Germany as part of the Army of Occupation. On their way Ted and General Parker stopped at General Staff Headquarters in Chaumont. Here Ted ran into a peacetime acquaintance who had fought the war in the comparative ease and comfort of the staff. He drew Ted aside and said: "My dear fellow, you've been recommended several times for promotion; you've also been cited two or three times for the French Legion of Honor. Now I don't want you to feel we think you don't deserve these, old man. You've made a good record—I think I may say very good. I'm sorry—really sorry—that none of them could have gone through. It's just that we've been making a point of leaning over backward as far as you're concerned. People might say you'd been promoted or decorated because you're the son of your father, and might criticize us. We can't have that sort of thing now, can we? I'm sure you will understand our position and will agree."

They finally allowed Ted to receive the Legion of Honor, but not until after he had been recommended for it three times. He was also cited by General Summerall for his leadership against Mouzon on the Meuse and the subsequent operations against Sedan, entitling him to a Silver Star. General Parker recommended him for the Distinguished Service Medal in 1919, but nothing came of it until it was unexpectedly awarded to him in 1922. He thought this rather silly because the war had been over for so long. Also, he felt the medal had lost prestige because of the way it had been handed out to chairmen of municipal hospitality committees and such, and he refused it. Some years later he learned that according to Army regulations an award once made cannot be canceled, so he might as well take it.

Shortly after returning from France we were at a large luncheon given by our friends, the Belgian Ambassador to the United States and his wife, Baron and Baroness Cartier de Marchienne. Something was said while we were still at table that gave Ted a hint of a ceremony to come. Just as dessert was served he suddenly rose, apologized to Baroness Cartier for having an important engagement, beckoned to me, and left the dining room. We ran downstairs, pursued by Cartier, who caught us at the front door.

"Ted, how could you?" he said. "You've spoiled my surprise! My government has awarded you our Croix de Guerre, and I'm going to pin it on you and kiss you on both cheeks whether you like it or not." This he proceeded to do. "I'm sorry," said Ted. "Please forgive me. There were so many people there I just felt shy about it."

I waited for nearly a month before I could get passage home and arrived in time to spend Christmas 1918 with my children. It was a delight to be with them again. Gracie, aged seven, and Teddy, four and a half, remembered me and behaved as if I had never been away. Cornelius, who had been a year and a half when I left and was now three, had some difficulty getting adjusted. He greeted me warmly, having been thoroughly briefed by my mother, but then asked why that lady had taken her hat off in his house and how long she was going to stay. He insisted on beginning his evening prayer, "Our Father who art in France," and wanted to know if Ted would bring back any of the Germans he had killed to be stuffed. Gracie confided to me that she did hope I would make her brothers behave without her help. "I'm so tired of being an example!"

After Ted returned three months later Teddy was a bit suspicious of his father. Once when Ted said to me rather emphatically, "Oh no! You can't do that," Teddy turned red, clenched his fists, and said, "She's *my* mother and she can do anything she wants to!" Cornelius made friends with his father at once, following him around like a little dog, asking all kinds of questions and turning to me at intervals to say, "Father is nice!"

On my way from the steamer I stopped at Roosevelt Hospital to see my father-in-law, who was gravely ill. Soon after Christmas he was moved back to Oyster Bay, and I went to spend the day with him at Sagamore Hill. Colonel Roosevelt had received scores of letters from both friends and strangers about Ted and had written me, "It is of Ted that I continually hear, from his superiors and subordinates alike, and always in terms of unstinted admiration!"

"You know, Father," I said, "Ted has always worried for fear he would not be worthy of you." His answer touched me so much I wrote it down immediately afterward and then found he had written the same thing to Ted previously:

"Worthy of me? Darling, I'm so very proud of him. He has won high honor not only for his children but, like the Chinese, he has ennobled his ancestors. I walk with my head higher because of him. I have always taken satisfaction from the fact that when there was a war in 1898 I fought in it and did my best to get into this one. But my war was a bow-and-arrow affair compared to Ted's, and no one knows this better than I do."

How I wish he could have known that by the end of World War II Ted would have won every combat decoration awarded by the United States Ground Forces, including the Congressional Medal of Honor.

A week later my father-in-law died, mourned by the nation and the world.

Chapter 14

*. . . We associate ourselves together . . . to
consecrate and sanctify our comradeship by our
devotion to mutual helpfulness.*
PREAMBLE TO THE CONSTITUTION
OF THE AMERICAN LEGION

On February 15, 1919, twenty reserve and National Guard officers
of field rank were ordered to Paris by General Headquarters,
A.E.F., for the purpose of discussing the betterment of conditions
and development of contentment in the Army in France during
the necessarily slow demobilization of the troops. Ted invited
these officers to dinner at the Allied Officers' Club in Paris on
February 16. At this dinner the American Legion was born.

They formed themselves into a temporary committee with Ted
as chairman, Bennett C. Clark vice-chairman, and Eric Fisher
Wood secretary. Further meetings were held and subcommittees
appointed. A caucus was planned for March 15–17 in Paris. The
purpose of the new organization was primarily for the interests
of enlisted men, so many enlisted men must attend the caucus
as delegates. The difficulty was to get them to Paris. Regulations
were a barrier, as was the question of expense.

I quote from *The Story of the American Legion,* by George S.
Wheat: *

A dozen or more officer delegates brought with them as
orderlies an equal number of delegates from the ranks. Thus

*Published by Putnam, 1918.

enlisted personnel, by devious means, were ordered to Paris under one guise or another. One sergeant came under orders which stated he was the bearer of important documents. He carried a dispatch case wadded with waste paper. Another non-com had orders to report to Paris to obtain a supply of rat-poison. Several wagoners, farriers and buck privates acquired diseases of so peculiar a character that only Paris physicians could treat them.

The expense of the trip was gathered in diverse ways. In some divisions the officer delegates took up collections to defray the expense of enlisted delegates. In numerous instances enlisted men refused such assistance and took up their own collections. An enlisted man said that the "buddies" in his regiment had deliberately lost money to him in gambling games when he refused to be a delegate because he couldn't pay his own expenses. So by various means nearly two hundred enlisted delegates were in Paris by late afternoon on March 14.

One second lieutenant who attended has since confided that he sold his safety-razor and two five-pound boxes of fudge sent from home in order to get car-fare to Paris.

A few moments after the caucus convened a high-ranking officer moved that rank be forgotten while in the conference hall and should be resumed only when the delegates had regained the street. From then on generals argued with privates, sergeants with colonels, majors with corporals, and everyone talked with everyone else in complete equality.

The results of the caucus were that the name was chosen, a tentative constitution was adopted, and another caucus was planned to be held in the United States in May which would issue a call for a national convention in November.

Ted had left for home shortly before the Paris caucus in order to create a nationwide organization of the new American Legion in the United States. To do this huge job he gathered together what George Wheat called "a set of cheerful, competent optimists," including Richard Derby, William J. Donovan, Cornelius W. Wickersham, H. B. Beers, Franklin D'Olier, Henry Fairfield

Osborn, Jr., Grenville Clark, J. Leslie Kincaid, and Eric Fisher Wood. Early in April he issued the call to the caucus in St. Louis. By that time he and his "optimists" had formed a temporary organization in all states, Alaska, Hawaii, and the District of Columbia.

As Ted had announced after his return from France that he was resigning from his banking firm, severing all his business connections, including several directorships, and intended to go into politics at the first opportunity, there had been speculation in the press that this new organization might be used by him for his own advancement. For this reason it was essential for the good of the Legion that he hold no prominent position in its permanent setup.

The following news story about the St. Louis caucus appeared in the New York *Evening Mail* on May 11, 1919:

> The most amazing incident of the gathering so far undoubtedly has been the refusal of Lieut. Col. Theodore Roosevelt to accept the chairmanship of the organization pending the national convention in November.
>
> It took him an hour and a half to make his will prevail over the delegates who demanded he should be the leader of the new organization.
>
> He remained adamant, and in doing so put an end to the criticism which maintained that the foundation of the Amercan Legion was mostly a scheme designed to further his political ambitions.
>
> As a matter of fact Col. Roosevelt emerged from yesterday's extraordinary proceedings a national figure in his own right. There are plenty of delegates from states not usually Rooseveltian who are willing to credit him with having the genius of real leadership.
>
> There was no mistaking his hold on the gathering he called to order. It seemed an almost superhuman feat for a young man to refuse the honor tendered to him in such a manner. Delegate after delegate rose and called on him to reconsider his refusal to be nominated. But he never wavered.
>
> He was a curious mixture of sensitiveness and iron purpose as he paced from side to side of the stage while the shouting

delegates called, "We want Teddy!" The din would subside for a minute and he would advance to the front of the stage to try to further business. But like a great wave held in check to await a psychological moment, the torrent of admirative —and indeed affectionate—clamor would burst forth again.

The man who could turn so much popularity aside for the sake of a principle is destined to go far, in the opinion of the delegates here. They see not only in what he did the proof of character which is the foundation of statesmanship, but also the proof of intellectual qualities which in one naturally modest are not prone to reveal themselves cheaply.

To anyone who witnessed those dramatic scenes, when hard-muscled men who have gone through all the cynicism of war gave vent to an almost boyish hero-worship for so young a man, the conclusion is irresistible that he will go, barring accidents, as far as his ambition beckons him.

Ted had a hand in writing the preamble to the constitution adopted by the St. Louis caucus on May 10, 1919. I think it expresses well the aims and ideals of the American Legion.

For God and Country we associate ourselves together for the following purposes:
To uphold and defend the Constitution of the United States of America; to maintain law and order; to foster and perpetuate a one hundred percent Americanism; to preserve the memories and incidents of our association in the Great War; to inculcate a sense of individual obligation to the community, state and nation; to combat the autocracy of both the classes and the masses; to make right the master of might; to promote peace and good will on earth; to safeguard and transmit to posterity the principles of justice, freedom and democracy; to consecrate and sanctify our comradeship by our devotion to mutual helpfulness.

For the next couple of months Ted worked on preparations for the Legion's national convention in the autumn and started writing his first book, *Average Americans*, an account of his war experiences. Toward the end of August he went on a month's na-

122

tionwide tour to complete the Legion's organization, covering twenty-three major cities and working as hard as if he expected to hold high office. In the years to come he sometimes lost patience with the American Legion, believing it was mixing in politics, but it was always dear to his heart.

Nineteen-nineteen was a busy summer for us. In addition to the Legion work Ted spoke in several states for the Liberty Loan drive. In June, Harvard awarded honorary degrees of Master of Arts to ten of her graduates for war service, including Ted. They were asked to be present on Commencement Day and to wear their uniforms with whatever medals they had. Everyone did this except Admiral William S. Sims, commander of our naval forces overseas, who had evolved the system of convoys that protected our troops en route to Europe and who received the degree of Doctor of Laws. He came in his blue uniform without even a ribbon. I sat next to him at lunch after the ceremonies and taxed him with it, saying it really was the height of swank to be the only one without medals when he must have so many more than anyone else. His eyes flashed and he said, "I'll tell you why I wear no decorations. I have them, yes, from all the Allied governments, but I prefer not to wear them because although the war ended seven months ago I do not have a single one from the United States." This was an example of what was true at that time. Our armed forces had an elaborate system of punishments but probably the poorest system of rewards of any of the Allies.

Ted was nominated for the New York State Assembly from what was then the 2nd Assembly District in Nassau County, and on November 4, 1919, he was elected with the largest majority ever given to a candidate. I went with him on his campaign through the district but was unable to vote for him. On Election Day our youngest child was born at Oyster Bay and named Quentin after his young uncle who had fallen in battle over the German lines in France.

It had been agreed that the next boy born into the family should be given Quentin's name. Besides myself, Kermit's wife Belle and Archie's wife Grace were expecting babies. I felt I had known

Quentin better than my sisters-in-law had, as I had seen more of him, and I was determined to have the next Quentin mine. Grace's little daughter was born in July, but Belle's baby was due in November and mine not until January. Ted always declared that it was pure will power on my part that brought Quentin, who grew to be the tallest of our children, into the world two months ahead of time. We were spending the summer in a rented house in Oyster Bay and had planned to move back the following day to New York, where all the baby clothes were. My mother-in-law came from Sagamore Hill, bringing the baby clothes that had been worn by my father-in-law in 1858, and Quentin was dressed in the little old-fashioned "double gowns."

The day before Quentin was born Signorina Maria Nam, who was to play a great part in our lives, arrived from Italy to help me with the children. I was determined they should know at least one foreign language but had had difficulty finding anyone to teach them. Signorina was a friend of Ted's aunt Emily Carow, who lived in Italy. She had nursed at a military hospital during World War I and had been decorated several times. Her brother Cesare was on the staff of the Duke of Aosta and in World War II was a major general in command of troops in North Africa. We had never seen each other, nor had she ever taken care of children, but we were both willing to take a chance. The experiment was highly successful. She was young, handsome, with prematurely gray hair—"a ringer," as Alexander Woollcott said, "for Eleanora Duse"—and as lovely a person as I have ever known. She was admired by our friends and adored by our children and grandchildren. Signorina stayed with us for thirty years. After the children went off to boarding school she became my secretary and manager of the household, going with us to Puerto Rico and the Philippines.

About this time Constantino Balocca, who had been Ted's orderly during the war, also came to work for us. Italian by birth, he had had a good education before coming to this country but knew little of practical matters. In a few years he learned enough to be one of the best gardeners on Long Island as well as an excellent electrician, plumber, carpenter, painter, and motor mechanic. What was more, he taught our boys all he knew. He and his admirable and clever wife are indeed members of the family.

The first Assembly in which Ted was a member was remarkable because of its attempt to expel five members of the Socialist party elected from New York City. When serious charges were made against them Ted voted they should be tried, then studied the evidence carefully, concluded that nothing subversive had been proved, and voted with the small minority against expulsion. He made his first speech in the Assembly in their behalf, saying in part:

> We abhor the doctrines of the Socialist party. Many of us personally and through our families have suffered greatly from its actions and the actions of pacifists, for to them is attributed in large degree the unpreparedness of this country when war broke. Our actions, however, must have no reference to any except two things, justice and discretionary application. We must not let justifiable dislike force us to commit a crime against representative government. We must reseat these men and then, in our pleasure, take up and remedy by legislation such things in the party as may need correction.
>
> The Assembly, as sole judge of the qualifications of its members, has the right to expel anyone and its decision is final. As this power is subject to no external control it is doubly necessary for us to exercise it only with self-control, because the greater the power, the more dangerous the abuse.

After Ted finished, Thaddeus Sweet, Speaker of the Assembly, left his desk and made a speech from the floor, describing exactly how Ted's father would have felt about the matter and saying he would be aghast if he could see his son's actions. (How many people think they know just what Colonel Roosevelt would have done in any situation!) A week later Mr. Sweet was in New York and called Ted up, saying he was anxious to see him. When Ted asked him to Sunday lunch with the children and he came full of friendliness, I thought I should never understand politics.

Ted's vote was extremely unpopular not only in his own district but throughout the state. He received so many abusive letters that we thought his political career might be over before it began. The five Socialists, after being expelled, were triumphantly re-elected the following autumn, and this time were seated without any protest. The witch hunt was over.

At this time, and for years after, people anxious to find fault would declare that Ted would never be the man his father was. "What did he do in the Assembly?" they would ask. When they were asked in turn what his father had done when he was in the Assembly, they had no idea.

When Ted ran for a second term in 1920 he was called on by the Republican National Committee's Speakers' Bureau to campaign through the West for the national ticket, Harding and Coolidge. I went to see him off at the train. As we drove to the station Ted said, "By the way, I shan't have any time for my own campaign. You will have to fill all my speaking dates."

I was appalled. "Ted! I can't possibly do that. I never heard of such a thing!"

"Why, of course you can. You've got to! Constituents don't like to feel neglected. I shall probably lose if you don't. Get the dope from the Nassau County Committee and use all the local stuff you can. You know most of the people—after all, they're home folks—and you won't mind after you get started."

I made twenty-six speeches, or rather, as it was before the days of radio, I made the same speech with variations twenty-six times. Toward the end of the campaign two or three meetings were usually held on the same night in different parts of the district. A candidate, or in this case his substitute, would have to rush from one meeting to another and then keep talking until the next speaker appeared. Frederick Hicks was running for Congress, and he and I pirated each other's stories and jokes shamelessly. As soon as I got to a meeting I would ask if Representative Hicks had spoken yet. If not, I had first call on the stories. It always surprised me to see how a feeble joke would get a laugh from a friendly audience.

A German shepherd dog that had been picked up from the Germans and given me by General Parker went with me everywhere. He would lie at my feet on the platform and when I got up to speak would come forward with me. Once he became separated from me in a theater in Glen Cove and trotted forward down the center aisle, sniffing from right to left. When he caught sight of me on the stage he made a flying leap over the orchestra pit and received a great round of applause from the audience. My mother came with me for a few times and was amused and slightly ruffled by an item in a local paper: "Mrs. Roosevelt, Jr., is usually accompanied by her dog Caesar and her mother." She said if she didn't rate above a dog there wasn't much use in her coming at all.

Ted was elected by an enormous majority, running ahead in the district of everybody, including the national ticket. It was a Republican landslide.

On February 4, 1920, Ted introduced his first bill in the Assembly, an amendment to the stock corporation law:

> EMPLOYEE DIRECTORS. Stockholders of any corporation, except a moneyed corporation, may by by-laws provide for the election of any or all of its employees or one or more such employees as member or members of the board of directors of the corporation, and for the qualifications of such director or directors. All such elections to be by secret ballot.

When asked what he considered the most important problem facing the nation at that time, he replied it was without question the necessity of proper adjustments between capital and labor. He said the root of the matter was that for many reasons, most of them justifiable, the workingman looked for justice not to the country but to the union. "At the present time, in far too many instances, the employer wants to get as much as he can and pay as little as he can, while the employee wants to get as much as he can and give as little as he can. Inevitably they are antagonists, with no sense of partnership between them." To meet this situation he felt that many of our theories of business must be readjusted. We must work toward a condition where everyone engaged in business has some sort of direct interest in the success of that business. Ted believed that wherever possible some type of partnership relation should be worked out, to include not only profit sharing but also representation of labor in management. Labor should have a voice in conditions affecting it by representatives elected by employees to the board of directors of the company. Details of the arrangement are unimportant, provided that real representation is achieved. In this way knowledge of the company's affairs and economic aspect would be available to all, possibly preventing strikes and lockouts by anticipating them with righteous adjustments.

In working out such a partnership basis, Ted thought we should go as far as is consistent with orderly procedure and proper assimilation of new ideas. The closer the bond, the better the result. When industrial relationships of this kind are practiced, he urged, men engaged in an industry will tend to establish permanent homes near their work, possibly eliminating or at least cutting down the alarming tendency toward floating labor. With the establishment of permanent homes will come an increased incentive to save and buy property, and the best type of citizen, the home-owning family man, will be developed in greater numbers. Ted had no reason to foresee the enormous extent to which installment buying would grow, or that some interruption of wages could seriously and adversely affect those sectors of the national economy which today are dependent on installment buying.

Ted had criticism from both sides for his theories. Some industrialists brushed them aside as socialistic and impossible of realization. Others declared profit sharing was impracticable because labor would never be willing to share losses as well. Ted said labor should not be required to share losses because the worker has as his capital his health and physique. Each day he works he invests some of this capital. The matter of losses must be handled by adjustments in the share of profits. Businessmen also said that a year with no profits would cause great discontent, as the natural tendency of those living on a fixed wage is to spend it all, and they would regard the distribution of profits as part of a fixed wage. Ted argued that this would be true in the beginning and must be expected until the workers adjusted themselves and learned to save for a lean year. His idea of labor on boards of directors was called all wrong because of the "fundamental divergence of interests between capital and labor." Which brought the question right back to his first premise, that the interest of all is in the success of the business in which they are engaged.

Some labor leaders feared that by tying the men too closely to their jobs the power of the unions would be weakened. Ted denied this, saying, "Unions are essentially a part of our scheme of relationship. The working people need unions to protect them and to represent them, especially in collective bargaining, but certain mistakes made by the unions could be obviated because of the clearer comprehension of conditions that would result."

Naturally he was talking in general terms. What might be possible in a carpet company in Connecticut might not work in United States Steel. But his main argument did apply to everybody: that as long as labor and capital considered themselves opposing forces no satisfactory solution would be possible. "Unless you base your social and governmental reforms on human nature, they cannot be permanent."

In 1921 he spoke on these theories at the Pittsburgh Press Club and received letters of hearty approval from several labor unions, including Local 95 of the International Union of Steam and Operating Engineers, Interdepartmental Union 202 of the International Brotherhood of Electrical Workers, and the Hannibal Trades and Labor Assembly.

While it is interesting to note that many things advocated by Ted are today either law or common practice, he never foresaw the time when union leaders would fear the secret ballot, nor that some labor unions might come to be controlled by men not of a caliber to represent labor honorably. In Puerto Rico when he was Governor he created the Department of Labor in 1930 and brought into the Cabinet for the first time a representative of organized labor.

In 1922, at Herrin, Illinois, some fifty members of the Steam Shovelers Union, marching under a flag of truce, were fired on by nine hundred mine workers. Nineteen were killed outright, twenty more wounded. Full accounts were carried in the press, but not a man in public life mentioned the outrage except Ted, who was Assistant Secretary of the Navy at the time. In a speech made at the Elks' national convention at Atlantic City he said:

> A few weeks ago in southern Illinois as atrocious a massacre occurred as is contained in our annals. Men were brutally killed, and up to this time no shadow of conviction of the

murderers is in sight. A blot of this kind can be wiped out in only one manner, by due process of law. If we are to exist as a nation we must be law-abiding. On law depends our society. Destroy law, and we will be back in the days of slavery, rapine and pillage, when the strong oppress the weak, when interest triumphs over honor.

Fifteen years later this speech was quoted and editorialized in *The Iron Age*, a trade publication. The Premier of Ontario, Honorable Mitchell Hepburn, read it and made a statement, saying in effect what an excellent speech it was and how well it revealed the true courage and wisdom of a great man, Franklin D. Roosevelt! After realizing his mistake, he wrote Ted a letter of apology.

Chapter 15

'Tis not in mortals to command success,
But we'll do more, Sempronius; we'll deserve it.
ADDISON

Ted was appointed Assistant Secretary of the Navy (in those days there was only one) in March 1921. In Washington we had a hard time finding a furnished house we could afford to rent that was large enough to hold us all. Finally we found a big ugly one on Twenty-first Street which contained rather queer furniture. In the entrance hall hung a great chandelier, the figure of a girl made of brightly colored composition. She wore a white blouse, a blue skirt, and a red kerchief over her yellow hair. In one hand she held out a beer mug. No legs showed, but sweeping back from under her skirt were deer antlers tipped with red, white, and blue electric lights. We put her in the attic. A small room off the living room was full of brass bric-a-brac, including two in the shape of feet cut off at the ankles for ash trays. It might not have been so bad if they had been a pair, but they were both left feet. Huge paintings in elaborate gilt frames were on the walls. One was a life-size portrait of a monk shaving. Another was a man closely resembling French Ambassador Jusserand being given a drink by a nun in the snow. Ted's pet trick was to take strangers into this room and say, "Here is where my wife keeps her special treasures," until I packed up everything to join the chandelier in the attic.

Although we were to have bad trouble in Washington we enjoyed Ted's tour of duty there. We were young and life was fun. His work was absorbing. By Navy Department custom he had charge of certain matters, but because of necessary absences of the Secretary, Edwin Denby, Ted frequently had entire charge of the department for long periods.

The naval stations and yards at which vessels were built, equipped, supplied, and repaired were under his direction. Without efficient management in this field the Navy could not be kept on the sea. After careful study and investigation Ted worked out a plan giving all a uniform system of management. Each yard was placed in the charge of a commandant with complete authority and responsibility. Under each commandant was placed a yard manager, chosen from the commissioned personnel of the Navy, to be responsible to the commandant for building, repair, equipment, supplies, and the civilian personnel. This arrangement left the commandant free to better handle the military functions of the yard. A special officer of experience was appointed in the Navy Department to devote his whole time to Navy-yard problems, studying costs, checking the work of one yard against others in the interest of economy and efficiency, finding out which yard cost the least and which the most, and what good ideas in one could be useful in others.

Ted also won a debate with the Civil Service Commission in favor of giving preference to American citizens over aliens in the selection of Civil Service employees to be retained during reductions in force made necessary either by the cutting down of congressional appropriations or for reasons of economy. This was hailed by the press as a precedent to be followed in all other executive departments.

All Navy budgets were in Ted's charge. He had to be ready to go before congressional committees at any time to explain each item. It was he who disposed of the Navy's surplus war materials. A letter to President Coolidge dated March 7, 1924, from Charles H. Lipsett, publisher of *Sales* and *The Daily Metal Reporter*, gives information about this phase of Ted's work, saying in part:

As publisher of several trade publications, among which are two which are devoted primarily to assisting the Government in liquidating its war surplus, I have had an unusual opportunity of coming in close contact with Army and Navy officials, and of making an impartial study of their respective business abilities.

I have no hesitation in asserting that the achievements of Col. Roosevelt stand out in bold relief when compared to those of others . . .

I may also add that ever since Col. Roosevelt took over the supervision of the disposal of the Navy's surplus war material, the Navy's method of conducting these sales has met with the universal approval of businessmen, besides netting the Government an immense increase in revenue. The task of liquidating this surplus was an extremely difficult one, and in handling it the Navy's record is far superior to that of any other department.

It must be remembered that this country went through a period of depression after World War I, making it hard to dispose of surplus. *The Daily Metal Reporter* in its issue of September 23, 1948, makes an interesting comment about surplus after World War II:

There is every reason to believe that had the War Assets Administration utilized the same methods as were employed at the end of World War I, namely auction sales and sealed bids, the agency could have realized a much higher percentage of the cost than at the end of World War I, because in the years 1946 to 1948 the WAA was offering merchandise of every type in a seller's market when industry and the public were clamoring for machinery, tools, hardware, wearing apparel and what not. . . . Had the WAA taken full advantage of the prevailing market opportunities it could have disposed of a good portion of these surplus war materials at higher than cost prices. . . . If the auction method had been used, the thousands of warehouses would not have been bursting with surplus war materials that were rotting physically and deteriorating economically.

An entry in Ted's diary on January 2, 1923, is interesting in this connection: "I spent all morning today going over various surplus sales cases. In every instance I had to decide against friends, which is always an unpleasant proposition."

Another letter sheds light on Ted's work in the Navy Department. It was written to him by William Howard Gardiner of New York on January 23, 1923, and reads in part as follows:

Under the date of the 19th I received from Captain Harris Laning (Naval War College) a letter full of enthusiasm over the plans you put through for a Junior War College, for a Fleet School and for carrying the Naval War College to a higher level. . . . Then he says, "I think Mr. Roosevelt has done more for the Navy by taking up these questions than did his father by backing Admiral Sims on the gunnery question."

As Laning is especially interested in gunnery his statement is particularly noteworthy.

Lieutenant, later Admiral, William S. Sims was about the only man in the Navy who realized at the time of the Spanish-American War that our methods of training for markmanship were as obsolete as the old muzzle-loading guns themselves. President Theodore Roosevelt took up this matter and gave Sims the lead in organizing and introducing a new system. Because of this, astonishing progress was made by our fleet in gunnery. By 1908, gun for gun, the fleet was three times as effective in fighting efficiency as it had been in 1902. Captain Laning's statement was certainly complimentary to Ted.

Although we often had people to dinner we went out rarely, trying to avoid late hours, which would have interfered with Ted's work. We did not go to large purely social parties but usually saw small groups of intimate friends in the evening, almost always including Ted's sister Alice and her husband Nicholas Longworth, then Representative from Ohio. As most of our friends were either in the Cabinet or held other government posts, it was interesting to see how much important work was done during the talk at these little gatherings. Nick was an excellent amateur violinist and sometimes arranged musical evenings. We often played bridge or poker. The Longworths had a poker table which traveled from their house to ours, depending on where the party was. At first I did not play poker, as the stakes were rather too high for my ignorance of the game until Senator Charles Curtis of Kansas, later Vice-President of the United States, and one of the great poker players, offered to spend an evening teaching me. He said that while he could not guarantee I would win, in the long run I need not lose more than I could afford. After that I usually took part and found he was right.

I shall never forget a hand I watched one evening when the players were the Longworths, Charlie Curtis, Andrew Mellon, Secretary of the Treasury, John Weeks, Secretary of War, Albert Lasker, head of the Shipping Board, and Ted. It was a jack pot opened on the dealer's left by a pat full house. No one raised and everyone came in. The pat full naturally stood pat. Mr. Mellon drew a card. So did Charlie Curtis. I forget what the others did, but it didn't matter. The full house bet the limit, was raised by Mr. Mellon and again by Charlie. The rest couldn't throw in their hands fast enough. Even the pat full dropped. Mr. Mellon raised; Charlie raised. Mr. Mellon raised again, refusing to believe he was beaten. Charlie raised back. Mr. Mellon, remarking that he always had to pay for his experience, called and laid down four queens. Charlie had four kings and an ace.

At the end of the evening Mr. Mellon, a gentle, shy man, laid forty cents on the table. "That's all I have left," he said in a soft voice. Albert Lasker, who in addition to his government post was head of Lord and Thomas, one of the big public relations firms of the day, suddenly sat up straight. "Mr. Secretary! If you can contrive to be held up on your way home, I'll guarantee you space on the front page of every newspaper in the country tomorrow!"

After leaving Washington I did not play again until five years later when I went back for a weekend with Alice before starting for Indo-China to meet Ted after one of his scientific expeditions for the Field Museum. It was the spring of 1929, the year everyone had been making money by gambling in the stock market, which Ted had forbidden me to do. When asked to take a hand in a poker game I gaily accepted, feeling justified in taking a chance. The game, I thought, would be like the one we used to play, but it wasn't at all. The limit had been greatly raised. I was scared at the size of the stakes and played cautiously, remembering Charlie Curtis's wise advice. I kept about even until the last round, all jack pots, which defeated me because such high cards were necessary to open, the pot was sweetened each time and the limit raised. When we got to the last hand I was eighty dollars out and was much annoyed. This time it took three of a kind to open, with knaves wild. The pile of chips on the table was huge. Finally it was opened for the limit, by then two hundred dollars. I had three eights, with no sign of a knave, a ridiculous hand to bet on, but I threw away all common sense and put up two hundred dollars, shuddering. The opener drew two cards, and I had a hunch she was doing just what I was. One other player drew a card and promptly dropped. The opener bet the limit, and I called. She laid down three sevens. In that one pot I won enough to pay for my round-trip ticket to Saigon, and I gave up poker for good.

No administration had ever laid down hard-and-fast rules for Washington protocol. The Speaker of the House and the Chief Justice could not be invited to dinner together because it had never been established who came first. One evening in 1922 we dined at the British Embassy on the King's Birthday, the first official celebration of the event since peace had been signed with Germany. On the day of the dinner, when the seating arrangements were being made, it was found that the ranking guest was the German Ambassador. Charles Evans Hughes, Secretary of State, was appealed to. Were he and Mrs. Hughes free by any chance and would they help in a most embarrassing and awkward situation? They came, Mr. Hughes with a twinkle in his eye, and sat on the right of the host and hostess so that all was well.

When Ted's father was President his physician was Rear Admiral Presley M. Rixey, surgeon general of the Navy. He had been a close friend of the family for many years, but I met him and his wife for the first time when we came to Washington. One afternoon when I saw Mrs. Rixey at a tea party I tried to shake hands with her, but she turned away and burst into tears. I was baffled and asked her what on earth was wrong. Between sobs she said that she and the Admiral were deeply hurt because although I had been in Washington for over a month I had not done anything about them. They did not expect Ted and Alice to take time for such things, as they were busy and important people, but there was no excuse for me. Naturally I felt badly at having hurt their feelings and promised to try to make amends.

Sometime later when I was in the receiving line at a ball, Mrs. Rixey paused for a moment and said, "To show I have forgiven you I want you to pour at our housewarming in the country two weeks from next Tuesday at four o'clock." I accepted with enthusiasm and forgot all about it until I saw in the paper one morning that the housewarming had been the day before. Ice ran down my back as I wondered what I could possibly do. No ordinary excuse would serve. I knew they would take it as a deliberate slight. Ted did nothing but laugh at me for being such a goose. I ended by putting on my best clothes right after lunch and driving out to their house, forty minutes away. I dismissed the car, telling the chauffeur to come back for me at seven o'clock, rang the doorbell, and said I had come early to have a chat with them and see if I could help in any way before the party began. I actually got away with it. Their feelings were not hurt, thank goodness, and they felt sorry for me because I had come on the wrong day and missed the festivities.

It was customary for the Assistant Secretary to have an afternoon reception for Navy and Marine Corps officers and their wives stationed in or near Washington, about twelve hundred people. We had it in the spring to avoid the problem of hanging up overcoats. As we could not afford a caterer we had everything in the way of food made in the house. For two or three days before the party everyone coming in was greeted by delicious smells of baking. My mother used to come from New York, bringing a maid to help and several boxes of cakes made by her cook. We served tea and coffee and invited admirals' wives to pour. Once the weather changed overnight and became unseasonably hot. Our Swedish waitress, Anna, who had been with us since I was twelve, could make the most delectable pink lemonade combining all kinds of fruit, including rhubarb and cucumbers. I asked her to make a quantity of it as of course there was no question of serving anything alcoholic at an official party during Prohibition. Anna herself was a blue-ribbon teetotaler.

I did not taste the lemonade but saw that it was a success. People kept coming to me and saying, "That punch is *marvelous. Is there anything in it?*" "Oh no, indeed. Nothing but fruit juices."

Next day I told Anna that her lemonade had been the hit of the afternoon. She smiled. "It should have, madam."

"Why, was it different from usual?"

"Well," said Anna, "I thought as this was such an important party I'd do something special. I put in those two cases of flat champagne we had and some bottles of rum."

"*Anna!* How *could* you do such a thing!"

She laughed. "I knew if I asked you you'd have to say no. But if I just did it without saying anything you wouldn't mind!"

We were in Washington for three and a half years. When we moved there Gracie was ten years old, Teddy seven, Cornelius six, and Quentin two. Teddy and Cornelius were at the collecting age. Once I noticed a strange and fearful smell in Teddy's room and found in his desk a pile of old paper tops from milk bottles, which I lost no time in throwing out. When he came home from school he was sad and indignant because I had destroyed his collection. When I asked where he got "those horrid, smelly things," he answered, "Out of garbage cans on my way to school, and sometimes I had to dig deep for them and now you've thrown them away!"

Once when Ted had been away for a few days he brought each child a present when he returned. The one for Cornelius (Sonny) was a knife, very stiff to open and quite capable of cutting off a finger. I objected to this and suggested that Ted suppress it for a time and give Cornelius the present intended for Quentin. That was all right but left nothing for Quentin. "Cornelius has a little toy cannon," I said. "He's too old for toys like that. Let's ask him for it. He won't mind a bit, and you can give it to Quentin, who won't remember having seen it before." Little did I know! Quentin had had a secret passion for that cannon and drew it around all day by a string, saying, "Thank you, my good father, for giving me Sonny's cannon!"

Gracie kept a diary conscientiously. When the book was filled she gave it to her father for Christmas. On days when nothing special happened she would write "nothing." If this occurred frequently she would vary it by writing "nought." On March 21 she noted as follows: "Hurray! It is Spring. Henceforth I shall rite in ink to praise Spring. I have a very bad cold." She also prepared a weekly magazine for her brothers, called *The Sunday Visitor*. As editor she not only contributed the literary matter but transcribed it as well. It had a moral department, nature study, problems, conundrums, cartoons, weather forecasts, a picture section, and a continued story. The story was usually of a bloody and exciting nature, sometimes a "traggedy."

One day a little friend came to play with Gracie. I had been out and was coming in when I heard them in my room. Gracie was talking on the telephone. "Is this the Wardman Park drugstore? Will you please send me a dozen black powder puffs? . . . Yes, black . . . You don't have them? . . . No, no other color will do, I must have black ones. You see, I'm in mourning."

When she was twelve she conducted a little Sunday-school class for her three brothers and one or two friends. On Easter Sunday parents were invited. Gracie asked her pupils questions, which were answered successfully until she came to Quentin, aged four. "Who rode into Jerusalem on Palm Sunday?" Quentin considered. "Adam 'n' Eve?" "No, no! Remember you had it last week. Now *who* rode into Jerusalem on Palm Sunday?" Quentin thought hard and announced triumphantly, "Noah!"

We had a couple of children's parties in Washington that stand out in my memory. For one we had a man over from Baltimore with an old-fashioned Punch and Judy show, complete with Toby the dog. All went well until Mr. Punch began talking to Quentin, who was sitting in the front row of children. Quentin thought this out of place but stood it for a time, then said loudly, "You mind what you're doing. Don't pay attention to me!" Punch talked back to Quentin, who lost his temper and shouted, "You go to Baltimore where you belong!"

For the other party I tried to have something original, which was always risky. I hired a little hand organ from an old Italian I had seen in the street, then sent to New York for a bear's costume and persuaded Alice to wear it. I was to be a *contadina* wearing an Italian peasant's dress, playing the organ, and leading Alice as a dancing bear. I had trouble with her at the last minute because, while the bear's head was superb, the costume was too small and was skin-tight. She refused to be seen in it until I added a skirt and a shawl. The party with some twenty children was in full swing when we finally came downstairs. I played "Silver Threads among the Gold," the only tune I could get from the organ, while Alice did a little dance. Nothing was ever such a flop. The children stopped their games and observed us politely, without comment. In the middle of our act I caught sight of a solitary grownup watching our antics in bewilderment. It was Mrs. Wilbur, wife of the newly appointed Secretary of the Navy, whom neither Alice nor I had met, who had come to call.

A year or two later we went to the circus in Madison Square Garden. F. Darius Benham, a close friend of ours, who was doing public relations work for the circus and who was very fond of our children, arranged for some of the performers to come to our box as a surprise. First came the midgets, then the acrobats, including the peerless Lillian Leitzell in a magnificent ermine coat. Teddy and Cornelius, who were then ten and nine, disapproved highly. Circus performers in costume stayed in the ring, they didn't go around calling on people in the audience. We were being made conspicuous. Quentin, aged five, did not agree. During a pause in the performance twenty-odd clowns made their entrance and stopped in front of our box, waving and shouting, "Hello, Teddy! Hi there, Cornelius! How're things going, Quentin?" Teddy and Cornelius, covered with shame, tried to draw their heads inside their coat collars and didn't know which way to look. Not so Quentin. He rose to his feet, waved his arms, and addressing everybody in sight, he shouted, "See! See! They know me!" until his brothers forcibly sat him down.

We always made great occasions of birthdays. The children took pride in making presents for Ted and me, beginning with little pictures done with crayons, then useful wooden pen trays and such. Before Teddy left Groton he made me a beautiful writing desk and an oak bench to go before the fire in the library. Once Ted's birthday caught Quentin unawares. He looked sadly at the presents made by the other children and came to me. "Today's Father's birthday and I have no present for him. What can I do? Have I anything you think he would like?" I wanted the lesson in foresight not to be lost, so I looked over Quentin's treasures and selected a little carved-wood dwarf with a long beard. "You must get a nice piece of clean tissue paper and a ribbon," I told him, "and wrap it up yourself." Quentin did so. I pretended to be busy at the other end of the room, but I saw him take a last look at the toy and heard him whisper, "Good-by, little dwarf."

When it was given to Ted he admired it extravagantly and said he would love to have it but as he was going away shortly perhaps Quentin had better keep the little dwarf safe for him until sometime later.

Cornelius came home from school one day troubled about a mythology test. "Mother, who is the god of hearth and home?"

"Well, darling, I suppose Lares and Penates."

"Gee! I was afraid I was wrong. I put down Bacchus!"

On July 19, 1921, Ted handed me a letter he had written to me:

> I have decided to give you all my money. You have handled all our money affairs as far as spending is concerned ever since we were married. If I died, or if there was another war and I was lost, it would make it much simpler for you to have it all in your own right. You are the one primarily responsible for the most important undertaking we have, the children. It will therefore make me more comfortable to have our affairs arranged in this manner.
>
> I therefore give you all the moneys, stocks and securities that stand in my name at Montgomery & Co. and will notify them to this effect.

This meant I had to assume all responsibility for investments, about which I knew next to nothing. Walter Janney, an old and close friend and an ex-partner of Ted's, now senior partner in his own firm, took charge of our financial affairs and held all our securities. We owe him an incalculable debt of gratitude for what he did for us during the following years, for his unselfish help and wise guidance increased our capital to a great extent. He and I consulted about everything, and he taught me many things I did not know.

In 1920 I had bought a thousand shares of Sinclair Oil stock, considered a good buy at the time. In December 1921 Walter advised me to sell them at a loss of a couple of points and buy bonds which would pay an income that the stock did not.

The Conference for the Limitation of Armaments began in hope in November 1921 and ended in optimism in February 1922. Its aims were the reduction of naval armaments and settlement of affairs in the Far East. To this end President Harding invited the governments of the British Empire, France, Italy, and Japan to send delegates to Washington to confer on limitation of armaments, in connection with which the Far Eastern questions would be taken up. Belgium, China, the Netherlands, and Portugal were invited to take part in the Far Eastern discussions.

At the time France had the only really big army, but various signs indicated that a race in naval armaments was due to start at any time. Although there had been agitation in the Japanese press for peace and disarmament, her Diet had been voting seven to one for a formidable program of military preparedness. About fifty per cent of her budget was going for arms and munitions. She had extensive contracts for war materials in Europe. A considerable number of Japanese were emigrating from Hawaii because, it was said, of bad industrial conditions, but they were going to Japan, where conditions were as bad. Many Japanese were leaving California, ostensibly on tours to their land of origin, but selling their homes before going. All this looked dangerous.

The Conference opened dramatically. After greetings by the President, Charles Evans Hughes, Secretary of State and chief United States delegate, began to speak. No one had thought this first session would be anything more than addresses of welcome and exchanges of courtesies, but after a few minutes the delegates suddenly realized that this speech was nothing of the kind. The atmosphere in the hall grew tense as Mr. Hughes described specifically the drastic reduction in naval armaments the United States was prepared to make, and made definite proposals as to what the other nations should do. Foreign delegates were startled and whispered excitedly to their advisers. At certain propositions the galleries broke into applause. It was amid tumultuous cheering that Mr. Hughes finished laying the full American plan before the Conference for consideration.

The whole world was surprised. It was the first time in history that a matter of such importance had not been settled behind closed doors before being told to the people. Here was a novel kind of diplomacy, inviting public opinion all over the world to express itself, which it did with enthusiasm and unqualified approval. Mr. Hughes had felt that the success or failure of the Conference depended in large measure on the sentiment it aroused among the people of the countries concerned. For this reason he placed the American plan not simply before the foreign delegates but also before our people and all peoples at one and the same time. In order to be fair to all, he confined the circle of those who knew of the plan entirely to the Americans who were intimately concerned in its preparation.

Mr. Hughes was anxious to achieve real, not merely token, reduction. He had consulted members of the General Board of the Navy and got nowhere, because he wanted to cut so much and they so little. Finally he requested Secretary Denby to appoint a committee of three—Ted; Admiral Coontz, Chief of Naval Operations; and Rear Admiral William V. Pratt, member of the Navy General Board. This committee was to draw up a plan acceptable both to Mr. Hughes and to the General Board. Several plans were submitted before one was satisfactory. Mr. Hughes was pleased and took it home to put in his private safe. He wanted no one else to know he intended to read it at the opening of the Conference. Two days before this he told Ted he wanted fifty copies for distribution to the delegates, saying it was so important to prevent leakage that he did not want them done in his own office in the State Department, and he asked Ted to have them made in the Navy Department. Ted had them mimeographed by Admiral Pratt. No attempt was made to print any copies until the morning of the day when the plan was to be announced to the general public.

So strictly was the secret kept that no one on the outside knew anything about it. Ted did not even tell me he was working on a plan for Mr. Hughes. He did not mention the committee of three until afterward. When I told him Mrs. Hughes had asked me to

143

sit in her box during the Conference, all he said was, "Be sure not to miss the opening day. It's going to be interesting." It certainly was.

Although Ted had been less than seven months in the Navy Department, his knowledge of naval matters was such that he was chairman of the Subcommittee of Naval Experts consisting of Admiral of the Fleet Earl Beatty, First Sea Lord, and Rear Admiral Sir Ernle Chatfield, Assistant Chief of Naval Staff for the British Empire; Vice-Admiral de Bon for France; Vice-Admiral Alfredo Acton for Italy; and Admiral Baron Tomosaburo Kato for Japan. He was also on the Advisory Committee of twenty-one, but that was window dressing. A fellow member, Representative Stephen G. Porter, said this committee reminded him of a little boy who got a job as usher in a theater—he did nothing, got nothing, but saw the show.

Ted made the following comment in his diary on November 29, 1921:

> The good part about all these negotiations is that, though they are so vitally important, we are all of us having a good time. Hughes is enjoying his work to the full, and no one is losing his sense of proportion. There are no ponderously wise individuals in the American delegation. It is good to be alive and to be in the thick of things.

In a letter to George Harvey, United States Ambassador to Britain, Ted wrote on December 29, 1921:

> Mr. Hughes has very kindly asked me to draw up the treaty on the limitation of naval armaments. I have the rough draft finished. It has been through the hands of the lawyers once. This evening I am going over it in detail with Frank Brandegee [Senator from Connecticut]. I would like to get it as short as possible and written in everyday English. If Noah Webster gives a meaning to a word I don't want to have to say that in diplomacy it means something else.

Never had there been a limitation of armaments treaty of such magnitude. It was the first time in history that nations came to a concrete understanding as to their preparations for war. Signed by the United States, the British Empire, France, Italy, and Japan, the treaty established the tonnage ratio of 5–5–3 for the navies of the United States, Britain, and Japan, respectively. The United States would have a navy second to none and superior to those of all other nations except Britain, with whose it would be equal. The Conference for the Limitation of Armaments was a complete success and ended with most people convinced that a real step had been taken toward permanent peace. Unfortunately its work was to be undone in the next fifteen years by stalemates at other conferences and finally by the repudiation of the naval treaty by Japan.

In my files I have letters to Ted from Charles Evans Hughes and Elihu Root praising Ted's work and saying printed accounts of the conference proceedings cannot possibly show how great a part he played in making success possible.

By the terms of the naval treaty a number of our ships had to be scrapped. This came under Ted's jurisdiction. I quote again from Mr. Lipsett's letter to President Coolidge to which I referred earlier:

> You will doubtless recall that when it was decided to scrap these battleships the general opinion of the press and even of some of the high Naval officials was that it would be best to take these vessels out upon the high seas and sink them, for to try to sell them for scrapping purposes would be futile and would entail additional expense to the Government. Col. Roosevelt, however, was not discouraged by these dire predictions, but proceeded to lay his plans for their sale, and by the materialization of his plans the Treasury of the United States had been enriched by several million dollars.

While the Conference went on, many of the foreign delegates became our friends. We used to see them outside of working hours and away from the many official banquets, usually long and dull, that we all had to attend. After one especially gloomy function Ted and I asked a few of them to come around to the Longworths' house, to sit and gossip for a while before going to bed. We took General the Earl of Cavan, chief delegate from the British War Office, with us. The others said they would follow shortly. Alice expected us and opened the door herself, as the butler was out. I told her the rest would be along in a few moments, and she left the front door ajar for them so that we could all go upstairs to the sitting room. I did not realize that Lord Cavan had not heard this conversation, and when I saw him putting his overcoat with its sable lining and collar on a chair by the front door, I said it would be better not to leave it there. "Why not?" he asked. "It's such a handsome coat. I'm afraid it might be stolen," I replied.

"Oh, but I say, you know! It's most awfully good of you to warn me. Very, very kind indeed." He took his coat upstairs and practically sat on it for the rest of the evening. Some time afterward I found out that he had indeed wondered if Alice's was a house of thieves.

Chapter 16

. . . the bread of adversity, and the water of affliction . . .
ISAIAH 30:20

Soon after the Conference a wave of pacifism swept the country and was reflected in Congress. People declared that the Navy could be reduced still further. What did we need with great armaments, anyway? Another war was unthinkable. Why not cut taxes instead? In April 1922 a determined effort was made in the House to reduce Navy personnel from the eighty-six thousand men allowed by the treaty to sixty-seven thousand.

The debate on this bill was heated and lasted over two weeks. While it was going on, Ted spent every day at the House, giving facts and figures to representatives who wished to keep the Navy at treaty strength but who did not have the necessary technical knowledge. When the debate was over, the bill defeated and the Navy left intact, he went for a week's fishing in Pennsylvania, his first vacation in over a year.

While he was away it was announced in the papers that the Navy oil lands at Teapot Dome, Wyoming, had been leased to Harry F. Sinclair. Ted had not been consulted on these leases— his jurisdiction did not cover them—and he had not even known Sinclair was negotiating for them until he read the announcement on his way back to Washington. He arrived home as upset as I have ever seen him.

"My political career is over and done with," he said. "That land

147

has been leased to Sinclair and I didn't know about it. The Sinclair Oil Company stock has jumped ten points on the strength of the lease, and we own a thousand shares. I can never explain it. People will think my price is ten thousand dollars and will never believe the truth."

As soon as I could get a word in I said, "For heaven's sake, wait! It's all right. You gave me all your money, remember? I sold that stock last December, four months ago. I meant to tell you. We lost some money on it, but it helped with the taxes."

I shall never forget the look of relief on Ted's face. "Thank God, thank God! You don't happen to have the sales slip handy by another miracle, do you?"

"Certainly I have. It's right here in my desk." I have always kept that sales slip among my treasures.

The escape was too close for comfort, for in those days a profit made like that by a member of the Roosevelt family would have meant certain disgrace. We thought we would have no more trouble about oil, but this was not to be. The incident was premonitory of a period of indescribable distress that was to last for more than two years.

Ted had known Harry Sinclair before the war. His banking firm had helped finance the Sinclair Oil Company. Ted had been a director of this company until he severed all business connections during the war to go into politics. In 1919 he had asked Sinclair for a job for his younger brother Archie, who had been wounded and disabled and had a wife and children to support. It was natural to turn to an acquaintance at the head of a big company who was likely to have a position to offer. An editorial appearing later in the New York *Times* said in part:

> There was no earthly reason in 1919 or before that time for the most honorable man in American business to think of Mr. Sinclair as an unworthy associate, or to hesitate about acting with him or even acting for him.

Archie was employed and was occupied with the foreign business of the company. He had made several trips to the Near East on its behalf.

In 1921 the Navy's oil lands had been turned over to the Department of the Interior to be leased or otherwise developed according to the best interest of the service. There was a difference of opinion as to whether this should have been done. It was a complicated, technical question. As to the transfer, the Navy Department was not geared to arrange leases and sales, while the Interior Department was. As to the leases, it had always been the Navy's policy to keep its oil in the ground as far as possible, but in the case of Teapot Dome a board of geologists had reported that the oil was being illegally drained, without benefit to the Navy, by squatters drilling along the edges of the Navy reserve. Loss was being suffered not only from drainage but from reduction of gas pressure in the reserve area, affecting the amount of oil which could eventually be recovered. Therefore, it looked as if a lease, with proper provisions for the benefit of the Navy, would be wise.

To show Ted's connection with the transfer of the oil lands from the Navy Department to the Interior Department, I quote from a speech made in the House of Representatives on March 15, 1924, by John Jacob Rogers of Massachusetts:

> Colonel Theodore Roosevelt's connection with the oil leases was, briefly, as follows: Shortly after President Harding's induction into office Secretary Denby sent him, Roosevelt, a copy of a proposed Executive Order transferring the naval oil reserves to the Department of the Interior without recourse. At the same time a copy was sent to the Bureau of Engineering. After getting his copy of the order Colonel Roosevelt asked Admiral Griffin, who was then chief of that bureau, and who had naval oil matters under his particular care, to talk it over with him. Colonel Roosevelt knew very little of the matter for it was exceedingly intricate and complex and he had recently taken office. Admiral Griffin felt very strongly that this transfer to the Interior Department would be a mistake. After thinking the matter over Colonel Roosevelt decided he was probably right. His grounds for coming to that conclusion were that the Interior Department has as its general mission the development of the resources of the United States, whereas the oil lands belonging to the Navy

should not be developed except in case of real necessity; and that therefore there would be a conflict of ideas between the two departments. Colonel Roosevelt went to Secretary Denby and urged that the lands be not transferred to the Interior Department. Secretary Denby informed Colonel Roosevelt that his protest was made too late, because the transfer had already been agreed to by the President, Secretary Fall and Secretary Denby. After this Colonel Roosevelt went back and discussed the entire situation with Admiral Griffin and certain other officers. It occurred to Colonel Roosevelt that if he could get an amendment to the original order for transfer, making it necessary for the Interior Department to gain the consent of the Navy Department before any leasing or drilling was undertaken, the Navy could guard the oil lands against improper exploitation. In other words, the Navy would not lose its complete control over the details of ensuing transactions.

A number of amendments with this end in view were submitted to Colonel Roosevelt. He took them to Secretary Denby and discussed them with him. After considerable discussion Secretary Denby agreed to a modified form of one of them. Secretary Denby told Colonel Roosevelt to take it to Secretary Fall and that if Colonel Roosevelt could get Secretary Fall to agree to this amendment it would be all right with Secretary Denby. Colonel Roosevelt took the amendment to Secretary Fall, who agreed to it. Colonel Roosevelt then took it to the White House for signature.

I want you to mark carefully the language of the Roosevelt amendment:

"But no general policy as to drilling or reserving lands located in a naval reserve shall be changed or adopted except upon consultation and in co-operation with the Secretary or Acting Secretary of the Navy."

Now, gentlemen, see what that Roosevelt amendment did. That amendment reserved to the Navy complete supervision over the oil reserves. It was on account of this Roosevelt amendment that all of the leases under discussion by the Senate Committee at this time were countersigned by Secretary Denby. They could not have been validly executed without the affirmative sanction of the Navy Department.

At this exact point—and I ask you to note the sequence of events—Colonel Roosevelt's active participation in the entire matter ceased. It so happened that he was not consulted on any of the oil leases. Colonel Roosevelt did not know they were under contemplation until after they were signed. With reference to the Teapot Dome lease in particular, Colonel Roosevelt did not even know there was a plan on foot to lease Teapot Dome. Colonel Roosevelt did not even know that Sinclair was interested in any of the leases and heard of them only after they had been made known to the general public.

Ted had made the best possible protest against the transfer and had succeeded in pulling off a victory, but two years later when the scandal broke, people with better hindsight than common sense declared that even this connection with the matter had "smeared him with oil."

After the transfer of the oil reserves in 1921, Albert Fall, Secretary of the Interior, began to come in for a certain amount of speculative criticism. It did not occur to us that he had done or would do anything wrong. Certainly the Senate had foreseen no such possibility when they honored him by confirming his name first and separate from the rest of the Cabinet. We thought of him as the true type of old frontiersman, with his white hair and keen blue eyes. He had made the nominating speech for Ted's father at the 1916 Republican National Convention at a time when Republicans were still sore about the party split four years before, and although we had never happened to see anything of him, we had warm feelings for him. To show him we did not believe the vague gossip Alice invited him to family lunch on Thanksgiving Day. I remember being a little surprised when he came wearing a dinner jacket.

In 1922, after Teapot Dome had been turned over to Sinclair, it was found that more squatters were settling and drilling on the edges of the reserve, taking advantage of its now being in the hands of a private company. Secretary Fall told Ted that the government must live up to its contract and give the lessees undisputed possession. He said he had taken it up with the President, who felt that as it was the Navy's land the Navy should see to it rather than depend on local police. Would Ted send a few marines to settle the matter? It seemed a not unreasonable request, and Ted sent an officer and four men. Two years later he was bitterly attacked for so doing.

A Senate Investigating Committee headed by Thomas J. Walsh, Democrat of Montana, began in the summer of 1922 to examine the oil leases and to find out if corruption or conspiracy existed. As time went on it seemed to be getting nowhere. We still believed there was nothing wrong and thought the main question was whether the oil lands should have been leased or not.

In the summer of 1923 President Harding died—that kindly, ineffectual man whose friends took full advantage of his never being able to say no to them, yet most of whose Cabinet was the best in a decade and included such men as Charles Evans Hughes, Andrew W. Mellon, John W. Weeks, and Herbert Hoover. Ted wrote his mother on August 10, 1923:

> What strikes me as most pathetic is the sale made by the poor man of his paper for a good price, making him independent for the first time in his life; and the purchase of his grandfather's little farm, where he and his wife were going to spend the rest of their lives; where he could have had the pleasures he cared for—seeing his friends, playing his game of cards, his golf, and living in the sphere of activity which suited him and in which he belonged, instead of in the struggles, problems and difficulties of the world into which he came largely by chance.

By the beginning of 1924 the Senate's investigation of the oil matters seemed to have completely bogged down, when on January 17 Ted's brother Archie telephoned him from New York. "Of course I may be wrong," he said, "but I'm afraid there's been dirty work at the crossroads on this oil business. I don't want to talk on the telephone. When are you coming to New York?"

As it happened, Ted was going that very night to keep a speaking date. He returned with Archie two days later, arriving in Washington on Sunday morning, January 20, 1924. Archie said that G. D. Wahlberg, Sinclair's confidential secretary, had told him, Archie, that there was crooked business going on. Wahlberg said that at the time of the signing of the Teapot Dome lease Sinclair had sent Fall a check for sixty-eight thousand dollars. Wahlberg had seen the check.

Here was something definite, and it was appalling. The question was whether Archie should volunteer this information to the Senate committee or wait until he was subpoenaed, as he surely would be sooner or later. Advice was asked from several people, including Nick Longworth, Senator Frank Brandegee of Connecticut, and Senator William E. Borah of Idaho. The concensus was unanimous. When it is a question of harm to the United States, all other loyalties are secondary. Also, if Archie failed to come forward voluntarily, his own character and honesty might be impugned.

It was a terrible position for Archie, and a difficult decision to make. He was only thirty years old, disabled in the war, with his way to make in the world and a wife and children dependent on him. He well knew that if he came forward with this testimony he would not only lose his job but would lay himself open to criticism for having betrayed his employer, but he did not hesitate to follow the course he knew to be right.

Ted called up Senator Walsh that afternoon and arranged for Archie to appear before the Senate committee the following morning. We went to our house for the night and took Archie with us. Sleep was impossible, and we sat and talked. Ted suggested that if we could get Wahlberg to appear before the committee before anyone had a chance to intimidate him, he could substantiate Archie's testimony. Archie knew that Wahlberg lived somewhere on Riverside Drive in New York but did not know his exact address. We tried to get him by telephone, but he was not listed. It was hard to find anyone on a Sunday night.

Suddenly Ted had an idea. He called up William J. Burns, Director of the Bureau of Investigation, Department of Justice, and head of the Burns International Detective Agency, whom he knew. He told Burns he had a confidential matter in hand and needed help. Then he told Burns the whole story, stressing the importance of reaching Wahlberg that night in order to get him to take an early train next morning before he could be stopped. Burns said he could find Wahlberg in less than two hours.

We waited. At eleven o'clock Wahlberg telephoned. Archie talked to him first, asking if he would come to Washington to appear before the Senate committee and tell them about the check from Sinclair to Fall. Wahlberg was frightened, saying he could not do it as he would lose his job and had children to support. Ted then got on the wire and asked whether he could look his children in the face if he did not come forward with his evidence. "The committee is bound to send for you and will know you didn't volunteer to testify," Ted said. "It's your plain duty as an American citizen."

Wahlberg agreed to take an early train next morning. All was going well so far, but one more detail had to be considered. When Wahlberg failed to appear at his office next morning someone would be sure to find out where he had gone and might try to reach him on the train, probably at Baltimore. Archie's wife Grace had come down to join us. She knew Wahlberg. It was arranged that she should go to Baltimore, find him on the train, and sit with him until they got to Washington, then take a taxi with him directly to the Senate Office Building.

The committee room was crowded. Senator Walsh was presiding over the hearings. After Archie had testified, Wahlberg went on the stand. He was pale and his hands were shaking. Directly opposite him across the table sat Stanchfield, one of Sinclair's lawyers, who never moved his cold blue eyes from Wahlberg's face. Senator Walsh asked if Wahlberg had knowledge of the check sent by Sinclair to Secretary Fall. Wahlberg turned red, then gray. Stanchfield shifted his cigar to the corner of his mouth. There was a moment of breathless silence in the room. Walsh told us later that for fifteen seconds he thought Wahlberg was going to tell everything, but he shook his head. In a voice scarcely above a whisper he said:

"No, Senator. Mr. Roosevelt is mistaken. I never mentioned a check for sixty-eight thousand dollars. What I said was that Mr. Sinclair had sent Secretary Fall a present of six or eight cows and bulls."

Some newspaper ran a story called "The Euphonies of the Oil

Case," citing "sixty-eight thousand dollars" and "six or eight cows and bulls" as an example of smart trickery. We did not believe Wahlberg capable of thinking this up himself and felt certain he had received instructions from some mastermind. But how and when could this have been done?

We thought of two solutions but never knew which was the true one. Either Wahlberg himself had told his employers he found himself obliged to go to Washington, or else William J. Burns had done so. Burns, it will be remembered, was accused later of trailing Henry L. Daugherty's more vehement foes in the Senate and in 1928 was arrested in connection with the shadowing of jurors during Sinclair's trial. In any case, some genius thought up this defense between midnight and early that Monday morning.

A real witches' Sabbath then started in Washington. Frank A. Vanderlip arrived in Washington as head of an unofficial committee to investigate corruption. No one knew exactly who was on this committee or what it was supposed to be doing. All sorts of wild rumors flew about. People became slightly hysterical and went about looking hunted, saying their telephones were tapped. The Senate caught the general fever and on February 11, 1924, passed a resolution calling for the resignation of Secretary of the Navy Denby. They had convicted him without a trial, one of the worst instances of mob rule in American history. No man ever lived who was more honorable than Denby. Believing, with reason, that the leases of the oil lands were to the advantage of the Navy, he had countersigned them as a matter of course, with no idea that corruption was involved. President Coolidge immediately issued a statement in answer to the resolution, saying he refused to ask for Denby's resignation, but Denby did resign on March 10 and returned to Detroit, where the citizens, knowing well what sort of man he was, turned out by the thousands to meet him with a brass band. The unjustified smearing was too much for him, however, and he died a few years later.

After this no one knew where lightning would strike next. Ted went through hell. He was attacked and abused because he had been a director of the Sinclair Oil Company; because he had got a job for his brother with the company; because he had taken the Executive Order to President Harding (no one bothered about what this had been for); because he had sent marines to Teapot Dome. Although he knew all this was completely unjustified, the mere fact that his name had been assailed caused him gnawing anguish.

Archie was attacked for giving information about his employer, but not as bitterly as he would have been attacked by the same people had he withheld it until forced to testify by subpoena. Yet Archie's testimony was so valuable that, as Senator Walsh told us afterward, the Senate committee would not have reached first base without it.

Teapot Dome was not the only lease to be investigated. Others had been negotiated at the same time. One included a contract with W. L. Doheny of the Pan American Petroleum and Transport Company for the construction of tanks at Pearl Harbor to hold 1,500,000 barrels of oil, also docks, wharves, contrivances for loading and unloading, and the dredging of a channel to allow ships of considerable size to approach the tanks, all to be paid for in oil. I know little about these other leases and will mention only one incident in connection with them.

Secretary Fall and Mr. Doheny had been friends from the time they had worked together in mining camps in the Southwest. The first was believed to have almost no money but his salary as a Cabinet member. The second had been so successful in business that, as he told the Senate committee, a hundred thousand dollars was "a bagatelle" to him. Perhaps this is why Mr. Doheny gave his old friend that amount of money at this time, calling it a loan. A curious twist in the matter came when both old friends were tried in separate courts for giving and receiving a bribe. Mr. Doheny was acquitted while Mr. Fall was convicted for the same alleged bribe.

On the afternoon of March 14, while Ted was in Albany for a few days, I was on my way out of the house when my brother-in-law, Nick Longworth, telephoned and said: "Listen closely and answer as briefly as you can. I have only a moment. Exactly how much Sinclair stock did you have, when did you buy it, how much did you pay for it, when did you sell it, and for how much?" After I told him he hung up without saying good-by.

At that moment Representative William F. Stevenson of South Carolina was attacking Ted in the House, saying he should be forced to resign as Assistant Secretary of the Navy because his wife owned Sinclair stock at the time of the Teapot Dome lease. Nick wanted the accurate figures of the loss I had taken when I sold the stock several months before the lease was announced. Nick, John Jacob Rogers of Massachusetts, and J. N. Tincher of Kansas came to our defense. Next day the story was carried in every major newspaper in the country. If Nick had telephoned five minutes later, after I had gone out, the story would have had the attack and only a general denial by our friends. Still, it was very nasty indeed.

That evening Ted called me from Albany to say he was taking the night train back to Washington. I told him what had happened, and it made him so mad he didn't sleep a wink on the train. He arrived early next morning and refused breakfast, saying he was going to beat up Stevenson before doing anything else. I protested. This would do no good and would only mean more unpleasant publicity. Ted said no man could assail me in Congress or anywhere else and get away with it, and to bloody hell with the consequences.

I reached for the telephone and called Alice, waking her from a sound sleep.

"Sister? Ted is back. He's just leaving to go and beat up Stevenson." Alice caught on at once.

"Let me talk to him. . . . Ted? I hear you're going to beat up Stevenson. . . . Yes, of course he deserves it. . . . I know he's a rat. . . . By the way, he's a little elderly man and wears glasses. Remember to have him take them off before you hit him."

"Are you sure of that?" asked Ted, who did not know Stevenson.

"Positive."

"Oh, *damn*," said Ted. "Then I suppose I can't do it."

He sat down with a pencil and the back of a large brown paper envelope, and with everyone eating breakfast and talking and the children climbing all over him "to welcome Father home," he wrote a statement for the press that needed no correction before being given out. He described his former association with the Sinclair

Company, told how and why he had got a job for his brother, said I had sold my stock at a loss, and ended as follows:

Every crook should be punished regardless of politics or position. Equally crooked, however, with those who take bribes is he who, cloaking himself in Congressional immunity, willfully misrepresents facts in an endeavor to injure an innocent man. Regardless of politics, such a man should be held to strict account, and such a man is Congressman Stevenson of South Carolina. I call on all Americans, Democrat or Republican, who stand for honor, fair play and Americanism, to make it their business to drive from public life slanderers of this type.

After this statement was published Ted received almost two thousand letters from all over the country praising his stand. He had many from South Carolina begging him not to consider Stevenson typical of the citizens of that state. Only four letters were abusive.

To add to the general confusion at this time, Senator Dill of Washington put in his two cents' worth by introducing a resolution in the Senate on March 24 calling for Ted's resignation from the Navy Department because of the oil scandal. It was badly beaten and drew little attention. I remember an editorial from the Spokane *Review* that ended, "Someone should rise up and pickle Dill."

At this time Ted was running for delegate from New York to the Republican National Convention. The primaries were on April 1. Because of his denunciation of the Ku Klux Klan and his repudiation of their endorsement for Governor, a fight had been made against him in various parts of the state and to a certain extent on Long Island. He knew that a defeat at this particular moment would be bad, so he wrote to a number of people asking them to help get his friends to the polls. Just before primary day he had to go to Auburn, New York, to keep a speaking date and he asked me to telegraph anyone he might have left out. I wired everybody I could think of, including by mistake two or three of our Democratic friends, who were slightly startled at being asked to help in a Republican primary. Typical of their response was a telegram from Judge Townsend Scudder, a leading Democrat: CONFINED TO MY HOUSE WITH SICKNESS BUT WILL REACH PROPER PEOPLE AND DO MY UTMOST.

Ted was elected by a large and satisfying majority and was high man on the ticket for Nassau County. Promptly the press carried stories saying his hat was in the ring for Governor.

That summer the report of the Walsh committee exonerated Ted from any connection with the oil leases. By then all fair-minded people knew the truth, and there is no use trying to convince the other kind.

Chapter 17

The race is not to the swift, nor the battle to the strong, neither yet bread to the wise, nor yet riches to men of understanding, nor yet favour to men of skill; but time and chance happeneth to them all.

ECCLESIASTES 9:11

During 1923 there had been a lot of talk of Ted running for the governorship of New York the following year. One evening in the summer of 1924 when Senator James W. Wadsworth of New York was dining alone with us, Ted was called to the telephone. While he was gone Jim said to me, "I am sure you would like to see Ted nominated this fall. So would I. I believe he could make a superb run against Smith. But it isn't in the cards now. Eddie Machold is going to get it. He has done some splendid work for the party for years and the boys all love him. He is entitled to it."

Well, it was good to know definitely and not to keep wondering about something that was not going to happen.

Ted went to the state convention at Rochester as a delegate from Nassau County. I did not go with him as I was busy closing the house at Oyster Bay, opening the house in Washington, and attending to the children's school plans. The evening before the convention opened I dined with William J. Donovan, who told me it looked as if Machold was going to withdraw. "If he does it's a cinch Ted will get the nomination," he said. If that was so I wanted to be there, so I left at once for Rochester. Ted was nominated on the first ballot.

His sister Alice summed up the situation in a telegram: THEY HAVE CERTAINLY HANDED YOU A FIGHT.

As soon as the convention was over we took a train back to Washington. Ted resigned at once from his position as Assistant Secretary of the Navy, as he did not think it would be right to hold it and accept his salary while being away for over a month campaigning. He was going at once to Oyster Bay to make plans. I had to close the house in Washington, give up our lease (whether Ted won or lost, we would not need it any more), remove the children from the schools in which I had entered them, take them back to Oyster Bay, and reopen our house there which had just been put away for the winter.

Ted asked me how long this would take and how soon I could get to Oyster Bay. I considered. It was Saturday. "Well," I said, "perhaps I can do it by next Friday."

"Damn it, I want you with me," said Ted. "You'll do it by Wednesday!"

I made an appointment to say good-by to Mrs. Coolidge at five o'clock on Tuesday. All afternoon I had been packing china and lost track of the time. Suddenly I remembered and took my head out of a barrel full of excelsior to find it was quarter to five. I rushed upstairs, brushed off the worst of the dust, and hurried to the White House. I was shown at once into the Red Room, where Mrs. Coolidge was sitting, handsome and charming as she always was. As I came in she looked up and said, "Oh, Mrs. Roosevelt! Isn't it perfectly wonderful about Washington!"

"Washington?" I murmured vaguely.

"Yes," said Mrs. Coolidge. "Isn't it *too* exciting?"

What could she mean? George Washington? No. The state of Washington? Again, no. Washington, D.C.? More likely, but still baffling. I must have looked completely blank, for Mrs. Coolidge said, "Why, don't you read the papers?"

"I thought I did——" I began.

"Well then, don't you know that the Senators beat the Red Sox yesterday?"

I did not know what to do about moving our small supply of

pre-war liquor from Washington to Oyster Bay. To bring it down in the first place we had asked for and received a permit from the government prohibition headquarters in New York. We did not realize—nor, apparently, did they—that such a permit was entirely illegal, as the District of Columbia was dry and nothing was supposed to be brought into it except for the diplomatic corps. Anyhow, we had brought down our supply, and much of it was still left. Ted, feeling that prohibition was an iniquitous law which must be obeyed while it was law, told me to pour everything down the kitchen sink and have done with it. My Scottish thrift would not let me do any such thing. Unknown to Ted, who would have flayed me, I packed a bottle or two in every piece of our luggage and succeeded in salvaging all of it.

I have forgotten who came to our house in Oyster Bay to notify Ted officially that he was to run for Governor, but several hundred people were there. The enthusiasm culminated after the speeches were over, when the entire crowd headed by a brass band marched in the front door, through the house, out the back door, around the house, in again, through again, out again, and so on indefinitely, to the delight of the children.

Soon after this we left on a special train to tour the state for three weeks, traveling by day and stopping on a railway siding at night. The party consisted mainly of ourselves, some of the other candidates who went along from time to time, a couple of members of the Republican State Committee, who changed according to the district we were in, Ted's secretary, and two women speakers —only one of whom was needed. The Speakers' Bureau had invited them both by mistake and no one dared tell either of them her services were not required. Besides these were fifteen newspapermen whose editors had told them to stay on the train for a week. It was generally believed the campaign would be a walkover for Smith and not worth reporting for more than that. Smith himself was at French Lick and said he expected to stay there.

As Ted was young and strong the Speakers' Bureau had laid out a program for him such as no previous candidate for Governor had ever attempted. He was scheduled to make more than ten speeches a day. Actually he made a great many more than that, sometimes more than twenty. In some of the larger cities like

Buffalo, Binghamton, Syracuse, and Rochester, where he was supposed to make a major speech in the evening, he found such big overflow meetings that he had to make two or three. He made, in addition, many short talks from the end of the train to crowds that gathered unexpectedly along the route. At Mechanicville, for instance, five hundred people had waited an hour in the rain to see him. His tight schedule would not permit him to stop for more than a few minutes, yet he was sincerely touched by the waiting crowds and did not want them to feel slighted. To prevent this he sometimes was forced to use a ruse to end these talks. He would greet the crowd warmly and start on what was apparently to be a full-length speech. Five minutes later the train would begin to move. Ted would shout, "Wait! Wait! I haven't finished! Stop the train!" The train would gradually gather speed and carry him off. It was always an effective exit.

Of course there was an infinite amount of handshaking. Local leaders would board the train, bringing friends to meet the candidate and to chat with him until the next stop, when they would get off and others get on. He was kept talking all day long and all evening either by speeches or conversation. How he stood it, no one could understand, but he went on day after day, never losing his voice, his spontaneity, his charm, or his patience. I saw that he got three good hot meals every day by going into the dining car, ordering the food, then taking him by the arm and saying, "Now we eat." People usually left us alone until we had finished.

Record-breaking crowds turned out to hear him. According to the New York *Sun*, the meeting in Syracuse was the biggest political gathering in the city's history. At Binghamton the crowd pushing into the auditorium shattered the plate-glass doors. At Schenectady it took two burly policemen to get me into the theater. When I happened to put my hands on the back of someone in front of me, I was warned sharply to keep my arms straight down by my sides or they might be broken like matches by the pressure of the throng.

The false, vicious attacks made on Ted during the summer were now forgotten. We learned that Governor Smith and Mayor Walker of New York had told their supporters to "lay off the oil, boys. If you don't it will boomerang." From all we heard, no one mentioned oil except Ted's cousin, Mrs. Franklin D. Roosevelt, who had a truck built with a body like an enormous teapot labeled TEAPOT DOME in which she and her daughter toured the state making speeches for Ted's opponent.

Although none of the papers mentioned oil, the New York *World* and other papers carried on a cruel campaign against Ted. The *World* had a cartoon that showed him looking ridiculous in his father's Spanish-American War uniform, much too big for him. This infuriated the *Herald Tribune*, which declared angrily and emphatically that Ted's own war record was, to say the least, quite equal to his father's.

One by one the reporters received instructions to stay on with us. At the start none of them thought Ted had a chance of being elected and most of them were for Smith. As the trip went on, all but one of them told us they were so impressed by the fight Ted was making that they were going to vote for him. Later we learned that many of them had bet on him as well. The one exception told me he regretted he was so committed that loyalty forced him to vote against Ted.

When Smith decided that if he wanted to be re-elected he had better leave French Lick and do some campaigning himself, the newsmen cheered. Smith had an advisory board of strategy with some of the best political minds in the state. Ted had no help of any kind. The reporters constituted themselves his advisory council. Every Sunday when we all left the train for a rest, they would gather in our hotel room and spend hours sitting around on the floor, pooling ideas for the next week's speeches. It was a great personal tribute to Ted, and of course nothing could have been more helpful. They took the friendliest interest in everything. Ever since our tour began I had been wearing the same hat, a black velvet beret. It had been rained on several times and looked distinctly tired. I was going to buy a new one in Rochester, when the newsmen said in chorus, "Don't do it! Things are going all right. Don't change your hat! It might change your luck."

Once Ted got behind his schedule owing to several unexpected speeches. Realizing that crowds all along the line were waiting for him, he decided to make up some time by leaving the train and cutting across country by car. Three cars were produced, one for

Ted, the local committeemen, and myself, the others for the reporters. We drove over narrow, winding dirt roads at sixty-five miles an hour. I was terrified but could say nothing. At each stop the newsmen protested, saying we were all risking our lives. Finally I said, "Why must you be at every single meeting? Why don't you skip a couple of places and catch up with us later? There's no reason for *you* to risk your lives."

After a pause someone said, "If you should hit a telegraph pole going at that rate and we weren't there to cover the story, we'd be risking our jobs."

At a large open-air meeting leaflets urging his election were distributed to the crowd by the Ku Klux Klan. This gave Ted a chance to light into them with a sizzling attack. "At this time intolerance in many forms is strong in the country. . . . The word Americanism is soiled when used by a group for furthering intolerance. Such a group is the Ku Klux Klan. . . ."

Although all our reporters by now were predicting victory for Ted, saying he would "come down to the Bronx" with an unprecedented majority, he himself was not optimistic. He kept telling me that everything depended on the City of New York. He said his only chance lay in the possibility that the surprising success of his tour upstate might influence the voters of the Greater City to support him, but he refused to venture a guess about this until he had been there and got "the feel of things." He spent the last week before election campaigning in the city. After the second day there he told me he thought he was beaten.

He came down to the Bronx with the largest majority ever given to a candidate up to that time, carrying fifty-six out of the sixty-two counties of the state and losing only the five counties of New York City and Albany County, but this was not enough to win. The final vote was Smith 1,627,111; Roosevelt 1,518,522. Ted lost by 108,589 votes out of more than three million.

I have always believed that Ted was actually elected Governor of New York but was counted out by Tammany and by the trading of certain Republican leaders of the Old Guard in New York City. Ted never would agree, saying there was nothing to be done about it and that he hated whiners, but it seems to me so obvious. Lack of voting machines in the city made it easy to juggle figures. The returns from upstate came in before those in the city were reported, so that it could be seen how much of a lead must be overcome. *The New Yorker*, in September 1948, carried an interview with George J. Abrams, chief investigator for the Honest Ballot Association. In it he described the great reduction of election frauds in New York City in the last twenty years and is quoted as saying: "We figure that in any election held here [by 1948] there's an irreducible minimum of 75,000 fraudulent votes."

On this basis, in 1924 Tammany needed to change only about 54,000 to defeat Ted.

After the campaign we went off on our first long holiday in several years and spent two weeks in Louisiana with Governor John Parker. On the train we read the letters Ted had received after the election. I had not supposed a defeated candidate could get so many heart-warming letters, and I have kept them all.

Chapter 18

He crossed the great back bone of earth
He saw the snowy mountains rolled
  Like mighty billows; saw the gold
Of awful sunsets; felt the birth
  Of sudden dawn that burst the night
Like resurrection . . .
                          JOAQUIN MILLER

What to do next? That was Ted's problem at this time. He was out of politics, with small prospect of return for the present. He was too independent to be solid with the Republican organization, especially the Old Guard. He had great personal popularity and no way to make use of it. Friends walking down the street with him in New York were always astonished at the number of people who recognized him and stopped to talk. He did not want to go back into business, as he had made sufficient money which, properly invested, would give us a steady income, and he hoped to return to public service someday, so he decided to take what he called an "involuntary holiday."

For years he and his brother Kermit had wanted to take a shooting trip together. Now this was possible. They did not want to shoot merely for sport, so they planned an expedition along scientific lines. The Field Museum of Natural History in Chicago was interested in obtaining groups of the big mammals of Central Asia, particularly the *Ovis poli,* the great wild sheep discovered by

Marco Polo in the thirteenth century. When he had described it and its magnificent horns, no one believed him. No group existed in any museum in the world. The animal was so rare that for six hundred years it was considered as fabulous as the unicorn and the phoenix. Ted and Kermit were in no position to pay for an expedition of this kind, and James Simpson of Chicago, president of Marshall Field and Company, agreed to give financial support on behalf of the museum.

Weeks of preparation followed. Permits were needed from the British, the Chinese, and the Russians to cross the Himalayas north of India and to enter Chinese and Russian Turkestan. Everyone was helpful, especially the Chinese Minister Sze, later Ambassador, in Washington. He said that Turkestan was far from Peking, then the Chinese capital, and the reins of the government were lightly held. An impressive document was necessary to show to primitive people. In the attic of the Chinese Legation he found a form of credentials long abandoned, lettered in gold and trimmed with ribbons and seals. This was most useful, for even when people could not read they were awed by its splendor. A photograph of the Field Museum on another document was sometimes taken to be Ted's own house, with the result that they were often treated as royal princes.

Besides the masses of equipment needed, they had to take clothes to wear when calling on the ambans and begs, local officials in the back country. They would have lost face had they worn hunting clothes or even shirts and slacks. The garments easiest to pack were, they decided, dinner jackets and collapsible opera hats. These were so successful that some of the ambans tried to have them copied.

The story of the James Simpson-Roosevelts-Field Museum Asiatic Expedition has been told in a book written jointly by the two brothers, *East of the Sun and West of the Moon*, published in 1926 by Scribner. It describes their six-month journey, their hardships in the wilderness when twenty per cent of their baggage-carrying animals died, and their astonishing success in collecting not only eight *Ovis poli* but over seventy other large animals of twenty different species, and nearly two thousand specimens of small mammals, birds, and reptiles. The most important of these have been mounted and may be seen in the museum today.

They set out in May 1925 accompanied by George Cherrie, a noted naturalist, and C. Suydam Cutting, an old friend. It was arranged that Kermit's wife Belle and I should meet them after the tough part of the trip was over. We were to meet them in Srinagar, Kashmir, in November and have some months collecting specimens in India before returning home. Between us we had eight children to plan for. Belle was taking her four to England, where her mother was staying. I was leaving mine in Signorina's care, with a couple of grandmothers near at hand. They would be well looked after while I was away. Meanwhile I took them to our little house in Vermont, where I spent the summer practicing with my new .303 Mauser rifle and climbing hills to get into the best possible condition in view of the hard work ahead.

Bear could be seen from time to time in the vicinity and sometimes killed sheep on a neighboring farm. It would be good practice to shoot one. I consulted Axel, our chauffeur, who agreed to help, remarking that the last time he had gone hunting was in Australia, after kangaroo. We went several times at night to a hillside thickly covered with blueberry bushes, tethered out a lamb as additional bait, and spent long hours being eaten by black flies as we waited, hoping the berries or the lamb would attract a bear. Axel had a gun loaded with buckshot to reinforce my rifle if necessary. Only once did we have a chance. We had stationed ourselves on the hill a short time before the moon rose and almost immediately heard the snuffling and snorting of two bears stripping the bushes. They came nearer and nearer, until they were less than fifty feet away, then gradually moved off in the darkness. By the time the moon flooded the place with light they were gone. Next morning we went back and found their tracks. After that I practiced on a target.

I had never been to India, nor indeed taken any trip of this kind before, and had to learn by experience that the less I had with me the better. We needed bedding rolls with pillows, sheets, and blankets to use in camp and on Indian trains. Our friend, Lord Lee of Fareham, gave Belle and me pneumatic mattresses with a bicycle pump to blow them up. These made all the difference in our comfort. Whenever we camped and our bearer prepared our beds, interested bystanders would gather around to watch. With gracious condecension he would allow each one a turn at the pump until mattresses were inflated, like Tom Sawyer whitewashing the fence.

Besides this equipment I had my rifle in its leather case, a tin traveling box for my topee or sun helmet (people still believed you would die without one), a book bag, a dressing case, a hatbox, two huge suitcases, a typewriter, and a large canvas duffel bag. I needed clothes for travel, for hunting, for hot weather and cold, and took a far greater variety than I was ever going to use. We were going to stay with the Viceroy of India at Delhi and had to have formal evening dress. I took three lovely gowns with accessories which I never had a chance to wear. While we were en route Queen Alexandra died and the British Empire went into mourning for a month. As visitors at Viceregal Lodge were expected to comply, I wore either a mauve dress of Belle's or a sad-looking little black dress Signorina had run up for me at the last minute, made of material bought in Glen Cove. Into the suitcases and hatbox I managed to pack twenty-seven dresses, four coats, eight hats, nine pairs of shoes, and enough underclothes to last the trip even if most of them were beaten to pieces on the stony edges of riverbanks. The duffel bag held my hunting clothes, shirts, sweaters, mufflers, woolen socks, and a nutria coat of extreme elegance from Paris, lined with powder-blue Chinese silk hand-embroidered with little bouquets of flowers. At the last minute someone gave me three hospital-size cans of pulverized instant coffee. I crammed them into the duffel bag.

In 1925 the journey from New York to Kashmir took about a month, by sea to Cherbourg, by rail to Marseille, by sea to Bombay on Peninsular & Oriental ships sailing every fortnight, by rail to Rawalpindi, and by car from there on. As Ted and Kermit had told us six months before to meet them in Srinagar early in November and had sent us no further instructions, we had to choose our sailing dates by guess. We did not want to leave our children for longer than necessary, so we decided that if we were there on November 9 it would be about right. The earlier P & O ship would have got us there on October 26.

I crossed the Atlantic on the *Olympic* and spent at least two hours a day throwing the medicine ball, riding the mechanical animals in the gymnasium, and swimming in the pool. Belle and I met in Marseille and were joined by Duncan S. Ellsworth, an old friend who was going with us. We made a final effort to escape the endless journey by sea to Bombay by going to Alexandria, then to Damascus, across the desert by motor convoy to Baghdad, Basra, Karachi, and north from there by car, but we could not get permission from the authorities as there was trouble somewhere along the line. We had no choice but to take the P & O.

One day as we were sitting on deck I spoke of our itinerary to Colonel Markham-Carter, an Englishman who had spent fifteen years in the Civil Service in India and the Middle East. He said, "They were quite right not to let you go across the desert. Some nasty things have happened, you know. If your convoy had been captured—and they sometimes are—you would have been taken and sold as a slave." He looked at me thoughtfully. "You would have fetched over twelve pounds. That's about sixty dollars in your money."

"Colonel," I protested. "Can't you make me worth more than that?"

"Dear me," he replied, "twelve pounds is a very good price for a slave!"

Going through the Red Sea, we had a following breeze, making it almost unbearably hot. By the time we reached Aden, the city in the crater of an extinct volcano, I had caught a bad cold and would gladly have stayed in bed but was told our ship would take on coal. This meant general discomfort, with clouds of black dust and all portholes sealed, so I arose and tried to feel happy. The British Resident came for us in his launch and asked if we had been to Aden before. Belle and Duncan had, so they went off to the Residency to sit in the comparative cool of the veranda, while the Resident insisted on taking me to see the tanks built, it is said, by King Solomon of a concrete better than any we make today. They were arranged to catch the scanty rainfall and to provide a water supply for the people. I have never seen a place as arid and as desolate as Aden. No springs existed. Not a tree, not even a blade of grass could be seen. Water was in such short supply that a street urchin, given a penny, would run off to buy a cup of water.

We drove through the old part of town, passing cars driven by barefooted people and carts drawn by camels. Arriving at the tanks, which were built in series up a long hill, we climbed thousands of steps to the top. The heat was intense, the sun blinding. Between sneezes and sniffles I tried to tell the Resident at intervals during the climb that the tanks were indeed most impressive but one was very like another, wasn't it, and after seeing two I really didn't need to climb higher to see any more. He must be very tired, I said, of showing them, as he must have seen them so often. With sheer kindness he said the tanks were unique, nothing like them in the world, I might never be there again and must not leave without looking at every one of them. He didn't mind a bit how often he made the climb, for he felt every visitor should see them. Afterward he gave me some aspirin.

We docked in Bombay before daylight and immediately got a telegram from Ted and Kermit. They were already in Kashmir and told us to hurry. We had expected a few days' leeway in Bombay, but this changed everything. Perhaps we could still get to Srinagar before they did. If not, we would never hear the last of it. Fortunately the Viceroy had sent an agent to help us through customs without loss of time, most welcome because of formalities regarding our rifles. We hurried about doing necessary chores, canceling several engagements we had made, securing with difficulty accommodations on the train to Rawalpindi, and hiring two bearers, without whom travel was considered impossible. Duncan's turned out to be excellent. Belle's and mine was a mournful creature who did nothing but complain while we looked after ourselves. We left that afternoon after only a brief glimpse of Bombay, a fascinating city with buildings thickly covered with ornamentation in Indian, mock-baroque, and mid-Victorian styles. The streets were crowded with traffic—automobiles and all sorts of little carts drawn by bullocks of varieties unknown to me. It was like a zoo where all the animals worked except the sacred cows, who wandered down some of the streets, helping themselves freely at the vegetable stalls.

That night it was unexpectedly cold on the train. When I opened my duffel bag to get my fur coat I felt something sticky. I pushed my hands farther in, and it was very sticky. I pulled out the coat, bringing with it a cloud of acrid dust that nearly choked me and settled all over the compartment, turning to brown tar. Two of the coffee cans had come open. Everything in the bag was thickly coated with fine powder which had absorbed moisture from the damp air. Belle helped me shake my coat and all my hunting clothes out the window. A quantity of coffee still remained in the bottom of the bag. I turned it upside down out of the window as the train stopped briefly and heard something hit the ground with a thud. Grabbing my flashlight, I saw, as far away as if it had been on the moon, the only thing Ted had asked me to bring him: a toilet kit with a new razor, shaving soap, toothbrushes, toothpaste, talcum powder, nail scissors, everything he liked and needed. The train went on but stopped next day for forty-five minutes at Delhi, long enough for me to hurry out, find a drugstore, and buy fairly good substitutes for him. Most of my clothes survived, smelling of stale coffee during the whole trip, but my lovely nutria coat was never the same again.

The first night on the train I brushed my teeth, using water from the faucet in the little washroom. Next day while walking on a station platform during a stop I saw a man on the roof of the car filling the water tanks from what seemed to be a dead goat. It was indeed a goatskin with the hair still on it, the stomach sewed up, and the legs tied with string. From then on I was careful to use bottled water and once, when that was not available, ginger ale. This was the last time I was to see plumbing for several weeks. Except in hotels in big cities and at Viceregal Lodge, we poured water over ourselves from a tin dipper. Indians never wash so much as a finger in standing water, believing it to be unsanitary, and they think sitting in a bathtub is a dirty habit. If a shower is handy, that is best; if not, a tap will do or a dipper. There is a lot to be said for this.

We spent the night at Rawalpindi in a small hotel, our bearers sleeping on the floor outside our doors, according to custom. Next morning we were off at dawn to drive by car to Srinagar, accompanied by Captain Pym, who was a friend of Kermit's, and a driver. It was so cold we wore our warmest tweeds, sweaters, and fur coats. The sun rose over snowy mountains as we began to climb. Finally we reached seven thousand feet and started going down.

The road was cut in the side of the mountain and zigzagged in a series of pothooks, a hairpin turn by a precipice at the end of each. As we came to the turns, headed straight for the edge, our driver would give a hard twist to the wheel, turning the car at an acute angle. It was exciting when we met another car at a corner. Our driver always blew his horn, but many others did not and paid no attention to ours. The country was more and more beautiful as we went on. Far below we had glimpses of the Jhelum River, jade green against the pines.

All went well until afternoon, when we were delayed by a blowout and engine trouble. Automobiles were supposed to use the road only by day, bullock carts only by night. At sunset we were still fifteen miles from Srinagar. We were so anxious to get there before Ted and Kermit that we took a chance, risked a fine and kept on. Fortunately the road was comparatively flat from there to the city. We passed long lines of bullock carts, their drivers usually asleep while the animals made their own way, following the cart ahead, and we had to go slowly to avoid collisions. Several camel caravans went by, the sound of their bells lovely in the still air.

Suddenly we came to a car stopped beside the road. In the glare of our headlights were two figures in sheepskin coats, high boots, and heavy woolen caps, with great bushy beards. In one breath Belle and I shouted, "Stop! Stop! There they are!" Captain Pym thought we had both gone mad. "My dear ladies! Those are Pathans." Even Duncan was uncertain. We jumped from the car and ran to them. They were indeed Ted and Kermit, still in their hunting clothes. They hugged us and started scolding us. "Where on earth have you been? We've been waiting for you all day. Why didn't you take an earlier steamer, for goodness' sake? . . . You would have had to wait two weeks? So what? We got here this morning and you weren't here. Shame on you!"

We had traveled halfway round the world and, after vague instructions, had arrived at the appointed place on the same day they had. We thought we had done pretty well, but they always felt we should have come riding up into the hills to meet them.

They had had their pictures taken, for when they had called that afternoon on Sir John Wood, the British Resident, whom they

had met six months before, he had shouted for joy at their appearance and made them go straight to a photographer. That night
Belle and I sat them down at either end of the dining-room table
and spent the evening cutting off their beards. When we finished,
the table looked as if we had been making over a mattress. Ted's
beard was dark red.

Next day they unpacked their treasures. Ted had brought me a
sumptuous Chinese robe of scarlet satin from Yarkand. It was so
heavily embroidered, with a pattern of waves nearly eighteen
inches deep around the bottom of the full skirt and flowers and
birds in gay colors scattered over the top, that the satin could
scarcely be seen. The rather narrow sleeves were long and came
down far over the hands for warmth. Although it seemed a shame
to cut it, I had to have it altered after we got home, as it was so
enormous that I was lost in it.

Chapter 19

*But it was all pure delight—the wandering
road, climbing, dipping and sweeping about the
growing spurs; the flush of the morning laid
against the distant snows.*

RUDYARD KIPLING

We spent a month in Kashmir, our headquarters three houseboats tied together in the Jhelum River at Srinagar. One was for Ted, Kermit, Belle, and me, a smaller one was for Duncan, and a third was the cook-boat. Our staff consisted of Rahima Loon and his brother Khalil, who had been with Ted and Kermit as shikaris (guides) on their expedition, our two bearers, a khidmatgar (butler), a cook, and several coolies. Rahima was in charge of everything, but he and Khalil did no actual work except when we were hunting.

The Maharajah of Kashmir, his Highness Sir Hari Singh, gave us permission to kill two barasingha stags in his game preserve near Srinagar and to stay at his guest bungalow. We wanted a group of these for the museum, but even though there were too many does for the stags, according to the British forest officer, he refused to let us shoot a doe. This was the only instance of non-co-operation we met anywhere.

As we drove to the preserve we ran over and killed two dogs and a sheep. Our native driver seemed to take our protests in fun, but he was careful not to hit a cow. These were held sacred by the

176

Maharajah, a Hindu ruling over Moslems, and the penalty under the law for killing one was to be flayed alive.

Ted and Kermit decided that Belle and I should do the shooting here. It would be easy, they said, and good practice for us. Easy, indeed! It was the most difficult shooting I saw on the entire trip. They had not thought of the altitude because they had been hunting for months in really high country and had just crossed the Himalaya passes at eighteen thousand feet. The six thousand feet of elevation here meant nothing to them. On the other hand, Belle and I had come from sea level. Although slim, I am naturally short-winded, and it was hard for me to run uphill as fast as I could go and then shoot while gasping for breath.

We wore the native grass shoes, which lasted for one day's hunting. These were worn over a kind of sock made of heavy white felt, laced up in my case with bits of string. The sandals of twisted thongs of grass were made on our feet. Ted's had a strip between his big and second toes, but my toes were too small for that. The result of this omission was that in moments of excitement one of my sandals would come off and I would go tearing on without noticing it. However, a coolie would always seem to find it for me and tie it on again. These shoes were light and comfortable but slippery. Sometimes when running down a grassy hillside I would sit down unexpectedly and toboggan to the bottom.

The country was magnificent. I remember once stopping for sandwiches at noon on a hill overlooking a wide valley, the majesty of snow-covered mountains beyond. In the sky circled lammergeyers, giant vultures with a wingspread of eight to ten feet, obviously waiting for us to die.

Two days later, after Belle and I got our stags, we all returned to Srinagar and prepared to go into the mountains after bear and more barasingha.

We started early one morning. The houseboats were towed up the river by four coolies walking along the banks with towropes, while our boat coolies walked along the narrow strip of deck, digging long poles into the mud of the river bed, keeping time to their chant, "*La* Allah! *Il* Allah!" We sat on the roof playing bridge. Sometimes we passed little white temples gay with bright paintings and shining silver domes. Later I learned that the domes were covered with Standard Oil cans beaten flat.

We stopped for the night and reached Wular Lake next afternoon. There we got into small boats, each propelled by four men sitting in the stern, using heart-shaped paddles, and three hours later, at sunset, we landed near the village of Bandipur. Here we were to camp for the night after having a Kashmiri dinner at Rahima Loon's. Ponies were waiting for us and we rode to Rahima's house, white stucco with an outside staircase. We were shown into a pleasant room upstairs where a table was laid and a fire burning. The walls were rough plaster with niches for candles; the ceiling was dark, carved wood. On the floor were modern machine-made rugs, their strong aniline dyes evidently preferred to the soft colors of hand-woven local carpets. We were hungry as we sat down at the table, and the savory smell of cooking made us ravenous.

No women appeared, nor were they mentioned, but we heard their voices outside, hotly protesting something the men were saying. Afterward we found out what the trouble was. The feast was ready, but Rahima said we had had no afternoon tea. Sahibs had to have afternoon tea. The dinner could wait. It would be spoiled? Nonsense. It must not be spoiled. Also, no soup had been prepared. Sahibs began dinner with soup. In fact, they never began dinner without soup. Yes, of course, this was to be a Kashmiri dinner, and soup was not served at such, but when Kashmiris invited Sahibs to dinner, soup was necessary. Let there be soup!

A big pot of tea and some small dry biscuits were put on the table. We toyed with these, trying not to spoil our appetites for good things to come. Half an hour later Rahima came and asked if we were ready for dinner. We were indeed. Delicious soup with tiny green almonds floating in it was put on the table. The women had made it by diluting one of the sauces they had prepared. This was followed by a huge bowl of rice with sausages of lamb, chicken, and young goat. Next came another course of rice cooked in a different way, with great balls of curried mutton. Sweetmeats followed, and excellent coffee with a dash of salt to bring out the flavor. After we had finished, the two small sons of the house came in. Belle and I put a wrist watch with luminous hands on each. As we did so Rahima spoke to them. You did not need to know the language to understand, "Now what do you say to the ladies?"

After dinner we went to our camp, to find tents up and all in order. Next day we separated. Ted and I rode up into the hills, our equipment on pack ponies. We made temporary camp again that night, and next day we went on foot, our gear carried by coolies as the country was too steep for ponies. Often we crossed rushing streams on narrow bridges made of two slender logs with rocks on them. Ted could walk airily over these, but I always had to go on hands and knees, trying not to look at the swift water far below.

Our tents were finally pitched in a little pocket at an altitude of nearly nine thousand feet between snow-capped mountains. The sun reached us at ten in the morning from behind one mountain and disappeared behind another at one in the afternoon. By now it was late November, and cold. Our bedding rolls were comfortable, but I used my fur coat as well. Water froze in our tent at night.

This permanent camp was most luxurious. I had done a fair amount of camping in Wyoming but had never imagined such elaborate plans for comfort as we had here and throughout India. Ted said he thought Rahima was trying to make up for the hardships they had endured on the "roof of the world." We slept in a large tent lined with saffron-yellow cloth printed in bright Kashmiri designs. Behind it was a small tent that served as a bathroom. We had hot baths every night, the dipper kind, with water brought in the ubiquitous Standard Oil cans. Another tent was for dining, and a lean-to was for cooking on a charcoal brazier. The shikaris and coolies slept outdoors by a fire, wrapped in layer on layer of shawls and blankets. Remembering the "Come and get it or I'll throw it out" of my western trips, I rather expected the same kind of fare but realized my mistake the first evening. Dinner was announced in formal fashion by the khidmatgar. We had clear soup with vermicelli, chicken with a delectable sauce and mashed potatoes, then roast lamb with browned potatoes, carrots and creamed cauliflower. After this two more forks were laid down for each of us. I said in surprise, "What, more dinner?" The khidmatgar answered, equally surprised, "Yes, Lady Sahib, pudding and savory!" He and the rest had been trained by British sportsmen, who know better than anyone else how to make themselves comfortable in the wilderness at astonishingly low cost.

The first two days I stayed around the camp, writing letters and taking short climbs, while Ted went shooting. After he got an excellent barasingha and a seven-foot bear he said it was my turn. Rahima was anxious to have me shoot a bear and promised he would take me on an easy trail. It turned out to be straight up the side of the steepest hill. At first I was able to keep up fairly well, then my breath gave out. I never did believe in the theory of a second wind, anyhow. Ted looped his muffler through his belt and made me hang onto the ends. I went along like this for a time, getting more and more ashamed, and wishing I had never left home. I could not keep asking them to stop for me to rest every few minutes, and forced myself on until the hills began to turn dark and whirl around my head. It had to be on the steepest, narrowest part of the trail that I lay down and quietly fainted. Ted was scared to death, as I had never done anything like this before. Holding me by the shoulders while Rahima held my feet to prevent me from sliding off into space, he sent a coolie back to camp for his flask. I came to in a few minutes to find him chafing my hands as though I were an eighteenth-century heroine with the vapors and told him the proper thing was to burn some chicken feathers. He refused to let me go on, and we returned ignominiously down the mountain. Later we heard that the coolie had burst into camp and electrified everybody by announcing, "Lady Sahib dead! Sahib wants his whiskey."

We went out several times more but never had the luck even to see a bear. Rahima was greatly disappointed and kept shaking his head and saying, "If Lady Sahib not going sick that day I hope she shooting bear, please."

Fortunately I was never put to such a test again, as the rest of our shooting was done at lower altitudes.

At Bandipur we joined the others, returned to Srinagar, spent two busy days packing and saying good-by to friends, then motored back to Rawalpindi. Next day we drove to Mardan, a British Army cantonment in the North-West Frontier Province, where we had been invited to spend the night and dine at the officers' mess of Queen Victoria's Own Corps of Guides, and the 4th/12th Frontier Force Regiment (Sikhs). In 1846 the Guides had originated khaki to replace the time-honored scarlet of British uniforms and had once been commanded by Colonel Sir Samuel Browne, later lieutenant general, "one-armed hero of a hundred fights." He it was who designed the Sam Browne belt, adopted by regulations in World War I to be worn by all officers in the United States Army.

We were sixty at dinner at a long narrow table, down the center of which were a great number of historic silver pieces commemorating battles or famous members of the corps killed in action, as well as trophies won at polo, pig-sticking, tent-pegging, and shooting. On either side of the silver were tablecloths, narrow linen strips some fifty feet long running the entire length of the table. At the end of the meal, after all china, knives, and forks had been removed, came the "drawing of the cloth," which I had heard of but had never seen. Two khidmatgars stood at one end of the table, one for each linen strip. Moving their hands faster than the eye could follow, they flicked the long cloths off the polished table so that they lay in two neatly folded piles on the floor and were picked up and carried away. It was done in a matter of seconds and was a delight to watch. Decanters of port were then placed on the tables. After all glasses were charged came the toast to the King-Emperor, before which no smoking was permitted.

When we had arrived at the mess we heard bagpipes outside. At dinner Belle and I asked the Colonel if they were to come in and play. He said no, emphatically. Once this had been the custom, but it was abandoned when war broke out in 1914. We said we were sorry, as we loved the pipes, but he was obdurate. Then an officer across the table said he was sure they would "put on a jolly good show" if given a chance. The Colonel still refused, saying it would create a precedent for the future. I told him it need not, for we might never be there again. This made him laugh, and at last he consented.

The pipers were superb, all six of them Indian, piping as well as any Scots I had ever heard. They marched twice around the long table, then drew up behind our chairs. When they marched out everyone beat on the table. The Colonel was as pleased as a child. After we had eaten the next course he said, "The pipers were good, weren't they? Suppose we have them back!" Back they came, playing "The Black Bear," the march of the Black Watch. After dinner was over we danced. A couple of hours later the Colonel said to me, "You haven't heard our pipers with the drums. How would you like that?" This time we all fell in behind them and marched round and round the room. It was glorious. Just before the party ended at dawn the Colonel sent for them once more, but unluckily they had all gone to bed.

Chapter 20

*And when they came to the bazaars he must
stop and look at every shop: the sweetmeat
seller amid great pyramids of golden balls and
thickly bubbling pans, giving out a smell that is
the soul of India, the richness of boiling sugar
with smoke and buffalo milk and drifting dust
behind, a scent so heavy it seems a taste, unfor-
gettable, unforgotten . . .*

PHILIP WOODRUFF

Next morning Kermit and Belle went to Delhi, while Ted, Duncan, and I went to Peshawar, the walled frontier town. We wandered through the bazaars, the most interesting I had seen, and sat down in front of a shoe stall, where I tried on and bought some wonderful bright-colored leather slippers with turned-up toes and embroidered in gold and silver, while a curious crowd gathered to watch. From Peshawar we drove to the Khyber Pass on the frontier between India and Afghanistan. There had been some question about getting permission from the authorities for me to go. For three months no women had been allowed there because a couple of female smart alecks had pranced about and taken pictures of one another in a restricted area. Fortunately the ban had just been lifted.

The Khyber is probably the most historic pass in the world. Through it Alexander the Great, Genghis Khan, Tamerlane, Baber, and other great conquerors led their armies. For two thousand years, until Vasco da Gama discovered the sea route, the only road to India lay through the Khyber. We passed a camel caravan coming from the north in single file as it might have done in the days of Marco Polo.

The Pass is twenty miles long and fifteen feet wide at its narrowest defile. Farther on it becomes three miles wide, with several little villages in it. Each has a high mud wall and a tower. Sometimes two of them would declare war and shoot from their towers, rather an inconvenience to travelers on the road between. Two of them were on fighting terms that day, but we heard no firing.

We drove to the frontier of Afghanistan, where a large sign read: IT IS ABSOLUTELY FORBIDDEN TO CROSS THIS BORDER INTO AFGHANISTAN. Two soldiers, British and Afghan, were on guard. I said to Ted, "Someday let's come back and go all the way in." He replied, "I'm taking no chances with you. We might do it when you're old and ugly." Seven years later we did.

On our way back we stopped for lunch with some officers we knew at the British outpost, where no women were allowed to remain after sunset because of possible danger.

From Peshawar we made the long journey to Delhi by train. I never could read on an Indian train. There was too much to see from the window. At every station there were lively rhesus monkeys scampering about picking up bits of food tossed to them by passengers. I tried in vain to photograph them but could never get close enough. Ted offered to try and got out with my camera. He moved up carefully and quietly, snapped a delightful group of mother monkeys with babies on their backs, got back in the train, and handed me the camera. I saw that I had given it to him with no film in it, a fact I thought it wiser not to mention just then.

According to legend, Delhi has been a capital city from time immemorial. Its history is a tale of invasion, conquest, devastation, subversion, and civil war. Among its rulers have been Hindus, Moguls, Persians, Mahrattas, and British. Some of its grandest remains date from the dynasty of slave kings in the twelfth century. It has been rebuilt many times, and even when we were there a vast number of buildings, including a palace for the Viceroy, were going up under British supervision. Georges Clemenceau, who a short time before had been conducted through the new city without making a comment, finally replied when someone asked his opinion, "They are impressive, these beautiful new white buildings. I believe they will make as fine ruins as the ancient ones."

We arrived at six in the morning and went to the hotel, where we had a big porcelain bathtub with running water. I was so pleased with it that I didn't mind two lizards a foot long darting about on the walls. Kermit and Belle joined us, and in the afternoon we went to see Lady Blackett, the American wife of Sir Basil Blackett, member of the Governor General's Executive Council. When we arrived at their house Lady Blackett rushed out the front door and said that while Belle and I could come in Ted and Kermit must go away quickly. She was having a party for some Indian ladies in purdah (seclusion) who could not be seen, even for a moment, by men other than their husbands, fathers, or brothers. They had come in cars with curtained windows and had walked into the house between screens. As all this was new to me, I asked Lady Blackett why she had to bother with people isolated from the world, saying, "I don't suppose they amount to much, keeping apart from everything." Said Lady Blackett, "Don't make that mistake. You can't imagine what power these women have if you don't know India. Never underrate them. They keep in touch with all that goes on; they are highly intelligent and, through their men, have a tremendous influence on politics and everything else."

The best shop in Delhi belonged to an Austrian, Imre Schweiger. When Belle, Duncan, and I went to see it we thought it could have been Lurgan Sahib's in *Kim*. We spent a morning looking at jades, crystals, Mogul miniatures, embroideries and fabrics woven with pure gold and silver. Belle bought a crystal Buddha for her mother, I a golden sari for mine. Mr. Schweiger asked if we would care to see some jewels. Taking us into a small room, he opened an immense safe and took out two emerald necklaces, irregular stones large as pigeons' eggs, strung on green cord. All I could think of was Aladdin's cave. Belle and I sat and gazed at them, then put them on. At that instant Ted and Kermit came for us. Ted looked at me, asked Mr. Schweiger the price of the necklace I was wearing, then to my astonishment said we would let him know in the morning if we wanted it. We left the shop deep in conversation.

"Ted, how could we possibly afford such a thing?"

"Do you like it? Would you have fun wearing it?"

"Why, of course I would! Who wouldn't? But it would be completely out of scale for me to have jewels like that. We don't have enough money to think of such a thing."

"You look lovely in it. We are going to be young only once. That necklace would mean a lot more to you now than it would when you are seventy. It's a bargain, too. I thought it would be a lot more."

"But, Ted, it would mean spending principal. The money we've saved! We can't do that."

To Ted, saving money had meant, as I have already said, scrimping on himself in every possible way, including driving for years an old Model T Ford that was known in Oyster Bay as "the Colonel's historical relic."

"No, it won't mean spending principal," he said. "The price is exactly what *Cosmopolitan* is paying me for my articles on the expedition. I worked hard enough on these articles to be allowed to spend the money any way I like. I am going to get those emeralds for you. They'll be nice with your earrings."

The necklace was really mine and was a joy for twenty years. After Ted's death I gave it to Anne, my oldest son's wife. As he had said, we are young only once. Now it was her turn.

To carry out our plan of making a representative collection of Indian fauna for the museum, we arranged to spend several days in the Allapilli Forest, Central Provinces, with Sir Henry Farrington, Chief Forest Officer, who lent us his guest bungalow. We took with us Baptista, a Goanese naturalist from the Bombay Natural History Society, to trap small animals and take charge of skinning.

Unfortunately the hunting here was not good as far as big animals were concerned. We had not known it, but a devastating drought five years before had destroyed literally thousands of heads of game. It takes a long time for even a strictly preserved country to recover from such a disaster. However, we hoped to get a tiger or two and some deer and birds.

The tiger-shooting was done from machans, little wooden platforms woven with rope and tied high in trees. We sat on these while forty-odd native beaters moved in a line through the jungle, tapping with sticks to drive the game before them. The greatest care had to be taken to avoid merely wounding a tiger, as it then might injure a beater. For this reason I decided never to shoot unless an animal paused right in front of me, but although we had three such drives I never saw a tiger, nor did Ted. The only one we bagged here was shot by Kermit.

Although sitting alone in a tree for several hours might be considered tedious, it was nothing of the kind. All the smaller jungle creatures scampered by—little pigs or an occasional deer. None of these were shot lest the bigger game be scared off. Birds of bright colors flew over our heads. I nearly fell off the machan the first time I saw a peacock high in the air, its long tail floating behind.

On the days when there were no drives we went out after deer. Once Belle and I decided to do a little hunting on our own and asked our host if he would lend us an elephant. It was my first experience with one. It arrived at our bungalow, the mahout or keeper sitting on its head carrying an ankus, a metal hook with a spike at the end. This and verbal orders were his only means of control. The elephant knelt down; we climbed on its back by first stepping on a hind foot, then on the tail, which someone held in a loop, and pulling ourselves up by ropes that held a pad on its back. At first we felt rather insecure so far from the ground and clung to the ropes as we went along, but we soon got used to the motion and didn't hold on except when sliding down a bank or climbing. We dodged branches to avoid having our topees knocked off.

We rode through the jungle for a couple of hours, seeing no game at all. Once we passed through a little village with straw-thatched huts and small gardens fenced with bamboo. Without pausing in its stride our elephant reached over a fence with its trunk and deftly pulled up by the roots a tall bean plant laden with beans, munching them as he went along. The woman who owned the garden was frightened and dismayed. We had no money with us but made it up to her later.

On the way back I caught sight of a jackal running through a little clearing in the forest. Collecting for a museum means getting anything and everything, and up to now we had no jackal. It stopped about sixty yards away and looked back at us. Making a

sign to the mahout to stop, I fired and was lucky, for it dropped
dead with a bullet through its neck. I directed the mahout to take
us over to it. He obeyed, obviously thinking us demented, for the
sportsmen to whom he was accustomed considered jackals as ver-
min and would never have thought of shooting one. When we got
near the creature the elephant didn't like it at all and began going
round in circles. Elephants are as timid as rabbits and are afraid
of small animals. Finally the mahout got it to kneel. I slid down
over its tail and picked up the jackal by its legs. It had a horrid
smell and seemed to weigh a ton.

When I approached the elephant it kept shuffling around on its
knees to watch me, making rumbling noises. I was afraid it might
run away with Belle on its back or start swinging at me with its
trunk, so I maneuvered until I could come up to it from behind. I
was able to hand the jackal up over the elephant's tail to Belle,
who lay flat on her face and grasped it by the feet. It was so heavy
she could not haul it up without help. The mahout was no use—
he ignored us completely and sat in silence, watching the clouds
go by. Suddenly we were struck by the absurdity of the situation
and burst into helpless *fou-rire*. The rear end of the elephant was
fully occupied by the jackal, so I had to go around to the front
and clamber up over its trunk, holding onto the loose skin around
its eyes, with no one to give me a foot rest. I had been told this
was an approved method of mounting, but I didn't like it and was
sure the beast didn't either.

As the elephant rose to its feet and moved off, some natives appeared. I motioned to the mahout to stop so that I could get them to
hold the jackal until we got ourselves organized. Instead of merely
stopping, the elephant dropped to its knees, upsetting Belle's balance. She never let go of the jackal, but if I hadn't grabbed her with
the arm that wasn't holding our rifles she would have pitched off
headfirst. By then we were so weak from laughter that we had
trouble getting the animal back from the natives, who were walking off with it. They couldn't believe we wanted it and thought we
had given it to them to throw away. They questioned the mahout,
who broke silence for the first time and in loud and voluble Urdu,
which we couldn't understand, gave his opinion of our goings-on.
Our servants were more tactful when we returned and made as

much fuss over us as if we had brought back a tiger. Baptista said it was a good specimen for the museum, so we felt our afternoon had not been wasted.

Sometimes I went out by myself with a small-gauge collector's shotgun to get specimens of birds. I had reasonable luck and secured a parrot, a white heron, a crow-pheasant, two different kinds of woodpeckers, two large Brahmany kites, a dove, a great horned owl, a lark, a tit, and several more little dickeybirds whose names I don't remember. I shot the two kites as they circled overhead behind the bungalow. One fell right on the head of a little Indian boy who stood watching. From the way he took off, I think he may be running yet.

The native people were the most primitive I had seen. They wore only narrow strips of cloth, and the women were tattooed all over their faces. A favorite ornament seemed to be small brass earrings worn by the men, some of whom had holes punched from the top of the ear to the lobe, with as many as a dozen rings in one ear.

The veranda of our bungalow was always covered with various carcasses in the process of being skinned and cured. The smell was appalling. I used to spray around the dining room with my best French scent, but it did no good. By the end of our stay we had collected ninety-six specimens for the museum, including birds, reptiles, small mammals trapped by Baptista, several deer, Kermit's tiger, my jackal, and a rat that had eaten thirty-five rupees in notes in my table drawer.

Chapter 21

The day shall not be up so soon as I,
To try the fair adventure of tomorrow.
SHAKESPEARE

Our friends were envious when they heard we were going to Nepal
for tiger-shooting. It was forbidden country, where no one could
go without special permission, and this was rarely granted. We
were fortunate enough to receive an invitation from his Highness
the Maharajah to enter the country and to be asked by the British
envoy, Hugh Wilkinson, to spend a week at his camp in the Terai,
where the shooting was unexcelled. One train a day left Lucknow
for the railhead at Bikna Thori at seven in the morning, taking
twenty-four hours. We would be met by a car and an elephant for
our luggage.

The night before leaving Lucknow we went to a party, getting
back to the hotel at one in the morning. After the others were
asleep I suddenly realized that no one would wake us in time for
the train. Our bearers had already gone to the station with our
equipment; we had no alarm clock; I put no trust in the night
clerk. If we missed the train, we would lose one of our precious
seven days in Nepal. There was only one thing to do. I got up,
dressed, and played solitaire until it was time to wake the others.

We traveled all day and got out at six in the evening when the
train stopped to allow time for supper at a little station restaurant.
An Englishman heard us talking and said, "Going to Nepal? You

don't expect to reach Bikna Thori on this train, do you? Why, the railroad bridge over the river has been down for three years!" We dropped our forks and stared at him. He went on, "But there is another train from the other side, if you can get to it. It runs once a day about three in the morning. You will have to walk a couple of miles or so and then get yourselves over the river, but with luck you might make it. You had better wire ahead for coolies and a boat to meet you."

We sent three telegrams: one for coolies to meet us where our train stopped at the broken bridge, to carry our luggage; another for a boat to ferry us across the river; a third to the stationmaster on the other side requesting him to hold the train for us if at all possible.

A cold rain was falling when we alighted at midnight. No coolies were there. Ted and Kermit managed to persuade some passengers from the train to help us carry our equipment. It was three miles to the river's edge. We had four bedding rolls, five rifles, ammunition, Kermit's trunk, four suitcases, and several odd pieces. I remember struggling through damp sand with a bundle and my typewriter. We reached the river and found no boat. We stood and shouted until at last we heard a sleepy voice from the other side calling in Urdu, "It is night and very dark. Soon the sun will rise and we will come. God is great." Ted yelled back, declaring us to be children of the sun and moon and little brothers of the stars. The heavens would surely fall and indescribable vengeance follow unless a boat came at once. After an endless wait a barge appeared, manned by three oarsmen. We leaped aboard, throwing in our belongings and praying we would still be in time for the train. Halfway across we heard it leaving in the distance and realized that nothing short of a miracle could put us in Bikna Thori for at least twenty-four hours. We landed, deep in gloom.

After walking another half mile, our luggage growing heavier all the time, we reached the tiny station, its platform covered with sleeping forms wrapped in shawls. Belle and I undid our bedding rolls and lay down among them, while Ted and Kermit went off to see if they could hire a car. They found their way to the house of a British planter and, ignoring the fact that it was four o'clock in the morning, beat on the door and sent in their visiting cards.

The planter came out in a dressing gown and when he had heard their story said, "Oh, but I say, you know, nothing must make you lose a day's shooting in Nepal!" He dressed, drove them in his Ford to the station for Belle and me, and took us back to his house, saying all hope was not lost yet. He knew of another train going to Bikna Thori from a station some forty miles away and would drive us there after telephoning to have it held for us. We were anxious to leave at once, but he insisted on our having breakfast. Although food was indeed welcome, it meant delay.

When we arrived at the depot the stationmaster came out, full of apologies. He had indeed held the train for an hour, then had allowed it to leave, "but not before sending a boy to the top of the tallest telegraph pole to see if your honors were in sight." This was the end. All our efforts had been wasted. I was ready to cry from disappointment, fatigue, and lack of sleep when I heard him say, "I have been intending to send a goods train to Bikna Thori for some time. It is made up and might just as well go today as any other day. It has a small empty car at the end, and I could put some chairs in it. Would that be satisfactory?" Satisfactory, indeed! We could have hugged everybody.

We reached Bikna Thori that afternoon, only five or six hours behind our original schedule. Our equipment was loaded on the elephant while we got in the car and drove to Mr. Wilkinson's camp. It was on high ground by the river, with a stretch of forest behind it, wide plains beyond, and high mountains covered with snow in the distance. The camp was extensive and most comfortable. We had been told we would have fresh milk, cream, and butter, as Mr. Wilkinson had a model dairy. Having had none of these in India, we were eagerly looking forward to such luxury. At first I was suspicious, as the milk, cream, and butter were light blue, but the taste was delicious. The dairy cows were water buffalo.

The shooting party consisted of our host, two other Englishmen, and the four of us. During the season the Maharajah lent forty-five elephants to Mr. Wilkinson, to be used for the shooting. As we spent every day from morning to night on their backs, we became interested in their habits and the care required to keep them in good condition. Each had its own mahout. Every morning the mahouts took them out to forage for their food—grass,

Engagement picture, 1910.

Entering 4 West 58th Street for wedding reception, June 20, 1910.

Across the street from Fifth Avenue Presbyterian Church the day of the wedding.

PACH BROS.

My wedding picture, 1910.

Ted instructing in bay-
onet drill, Plattsburg,
New York, 1917.

Major General Frank
Parker, Ted and myself,
November 12, 1918, Ro-
magne, France.

MONTGOMERY & CO.
INCORPORATED
133 SO. FOURTH ST.
PHILADELPHIA

12/30/21

Mrs. Eleanor B. Roosevelt,
1601 21st Street,
Washington, D. C.

WE CONFIRM SALE FOR YOUR ACCOUNT AND RISK

AMOUNT	DESCRIPTION	PRICE	ACCRUED INTEREST OR DIVIDEND		COMMISSION	TAX	CREDITS
			MONTHS DAYS	AMOUNT			
800	Sinclair Cons. Oil Stock	21.			120.00	32.00	16648.00
200	do do	21 1/8			30.00	8.00	4187.00

Bot Cur Nov. 29, 1919. @ 24 7/8
600 shares @ 24 7/8
400 "   "   24 3/4
B & Co.

Payable

Deliverable

It is agreed between Broker and Customer:

1. That all transactions are subject to the rules and customs of the New York and Philadelphia Stock Exchanges and their Clearing Houses.

2. That all securities from time to time carried in the customer's marginal account, or deposited to protect the same, may be loaned by the broker, or pledged by him separately or together with other securities, either for the sum due thereon or for a greater sum, all without further notice to the customer.

Yours very truly,

MONTGOMERY & CO.
INCORPORATED
BY

The broker's slip showing the sale of my Sinclair Oil stock, with pencil memorandum of the price paid for it.

To show you how we spend the days, & why I have no time to knit!

Schedule sent by E to her mother.

FIRST WEEK

ROOSEVELT SPECIAL TRAIN
SCHEDULE

	STATION	TIME	STOPS
Monday	Lv. New York	11:45 A.M.	
October 6th	Ar. Yonkers	12.15 P.M.	25 Min.
New York	Lv. Yonkers	12:40 P.M.	
Central	Ar. Tarrytown	1:05 P.M.	15 Min.
	Lv. Tarrytown	1:20 P.M.	
	Ar. Ossining	1.30 P.M.	15 Min.
	Lv. Ossining	1:45 P.M.	
	Ar. Peekskill	2:12 P.M.	20 Min.
	Lv. Peekskill	2:32 P.M.	
	Ar. Cold Spring	2:52 P.M.	10 Min.
	Lv. Cold Spring	3:02 P.M.	
	Ar. Beacon	3:20 P.M.	45 Min.
	Lv. Beacon	4:05 P.M.	
	Ar. POUGHKEEPSIE	4:33 P.M.	
	(Night Meeting)		
Tuesday	Lv. Poughkeepsie	10:45 A.M.	
October 7th	Ar. Germantown	11:25 A.M.	10 Min.
New York	Lv. Germantown	11:35 A.M.	
Central	Ar. Hudson	11:50 A.M.	30 Min.
	Lv. Hudson	12:10 P.M.	
	Ar. Stuyvesant	12:25 P.M.	10 Min.
	Lv. Stuyvesant	12:35 P.M.	
	Ar. Castleton	1:10 P.M.	15 Min.
	Lv. Castleton	1:25 P.M.	
	Ar. Rensselaer	1:35 P.M.	60 Min.
	Lv. Rensselaer	2:35 P.M.	
	Ar. Albany (No Speech)	2:50 P.M.	
D & H	Lv. Albany (" ")	2:50 P.M.	
	Ar. Watervliet	3:01 P.M.	60 Min.
	Lv. Watervliet	4:01 P.M.	
	Ar. Green Island	4:05 P.M.	
	Lv. Green Island	4:20 P.M.	
	Ar. Cohoes	4:25 P.M.	60 Min.
	Lv. Cohoes	5:25 P.M.	
	Ar. West Waterford	5:28 P.M.	45 Min.
	Lv. West Waterford	6:13 P.M.	
	Ar. Mechanicville	6:35 PM	45 Min.
	Lv. Mechanicville	7:10 PM	
NYC	Schenectady (No Speech)	7:40 PM	
	Ar. Amsterdam (Night)	8:00 PM	
Wednesday	Lv. Schenectady	10:00 AM	
October 8th	Ar. Ballston	10:35 AM	15 Min.
D & H	Lv. Ballston	10:50 AM	
	Ar. Saratoga	11:00 AM	30 Min.
	Lv. Saratoga	11:30 AM	
	Ar. Ft. Edward	11:56 AM	19 Min.
	Lv. Ft. Edward	12:15 PM	
	Ar. Hudson Falls	12:23 PM	20 Min.
	Lv. Hudson Falls	12:43 PM	
	Ar. Glens Falls	12:50 P.M.	60 Min.
	Lv Glens Falls	1:50 PM	
	Ar. Ticonderoga	3:25 PM	15 Min.
	Lv. Ticonderoga	3:40 PM	
	Ar. Crown Point	4:04 PM	10 Min.
	Lv. Crown Point	4:14 PM	
	Ar. Port Henry	4:27 PM	20 Min.
	Lv. Port Henry	4:47 PM	

Schedule I sent to my mother.

美 國 芝 加 哥 大 博 物 院

執 照

敬院特遣前總統羅斯福長公子

蘇壯參將前往

貴國西部考察生物搜羅標本以

備陳列仰

貴處妥爲照料酌予協助不勝鳴

感

西歷一千九百二十五年三月元日

支加哥博物院院長戴維敬啓

THE GREAT MUSEUM OF CHICAGO U.S.A.

Certificate

Our Museum announces sending the eldest son of our former
President, Colonel Theodore Roosevelt, to the western part
of your country to investigate and collect some biological
specimens for display in our Museum. We hope that you will
accord him all hospitality and assistance.
With our thanks, March 1.1925.

(signed) DAVIES, Director.

The certificate given Ted by the Field Museum. A picture of the Museum
was added to impress the Chinese in the back country with the importance of the project. However, they misunderstood and thought the
building was the palace in which Ted and Kermit lived at home. As a
result they were treated like royal princes.

Ted, extreme right, with his *Ovis poli,* 1925.

Ted riding a yak, 1925.

branches, and leaves—and led them into a shallow part of the river and made them lie on their sides to be scrubbed, while they sluiced water over themselves from their trunks until they shone. Most of them were well accustomed to this kind of shooting and stood their ground well, but Ted and I were run away with twice before we got through. When this happens there is always the danger of being swept off by a tree.

Every night some fifty young bullocks were tied in various parts of the jungle as bait for tigers. In the morning the location of the kills, usually six or eight, would be reported. Mr. Wilkinson said that irate letters to the newspapers sometimes appeared, written by kindhearted British ladies, criticizing this as cruel. His answer was always the same. Normally a tiger will kill a deer on an average of once a week, so in a year's time each tiger shot saves the lives of at least fifty deer. For what better purpose could a bullock die, he argued, than to save the lives of so many of his little wild breathren?

After the kills were reported, consultations were held between Mr. Wilkinson, the Subhadar Sahib and the Jemadar Sahib, two of the Maharajah's Nepalese officers lent to the camp. After the most favorable sites had been selected, we would set out.

The elephants waited in a line by the camp. Five of them carried howdahs for the hunters to use later, seats with railings around them made of heavy caning reinforced with metal bars. When I first saw these I was delighted, as the bars across the front had notches in which to rest a rifle. This might have been a great advantage, as a rest for one's rifle means more accurate shooting, but I never saw it used. Even when an elephant is standing still it must breathe, giving just enough motion to make a rest impossible. All shooting had to be done standing to counterbalance this.

The rest of the elephants had pads on their backs, and each of us rode on one of these until we approached the kill and got into the howdahs, when I rode with Ted, and Belle with Kermit. Several baby elephants went along with their mothers, gaining experience for future training.

The elephants moved in single file at a rapid walk, mine keeping perfect time to the old football song "Harvard, Good Night!" which kept running through my head. When we drew nearer the kill the Subhadar and the Jemadar would make a rapid survey of the terrain with the local shikaris and would say, "Here is the kill. The tiger must be in that bit of jungle near the stream." As a tiger usually sleeps after making a kill, returning some hours later to finish his meal, they were selecting the most logical place for the animal to be. Only once were they mistaken and we drew a blank.

The elephants fanned out in two lines, the ends of which gradually came together and met, making a giant circle about five hundred yards in diameter. Then they closed in, trampling down vegetation, sometimes even knocking over trees by wrapping their trunks around them and kneeling on them until they crashed and fell. All this was done to drive any tiger to the center of the circle. When the ring was finally formed it usually measured a hundred-odd yards across. In most places the thick, coarse grass was incredibly tall, sometimes eight or ten feet higher than an elephant. This was carefully flattened by elephants turning around and around like dogs about to lie down, until a clear path about thirty feet wide surrounded the edge of the ring. Without this clearing, shooting would have been impossible.

The howdah elephants carrying the hunters were placed at intervals around the ring, the pad elephants between about twenty feet apart. Two veteran beasts, each carrying two men, disappeared into the high grass to stir up the tiger while excitement ran high. Every elephant knew very well what was going on, and they all made different kinds of noises. Ours trembled and sounded like a clucking hen. Others were like motors running or horses whickering while we waited. Time passed. Suddenly a roar from the tiger drove the two elephants out of the grass, trumpeting as they came. Immediately all the other mahouts laughed and jeered, offering their mounts if a really brave one was needed. After a brief pause the two veterans went back, vanishing in the high grass. Sometimes the tiger would charge out, sometimes try to slip out unseen. In any case, the shooting had to be done with the utmost speed. First you had to decide if what you saw in the lights and shadows of the grass really was a tiger. If it was, you had to make up your mind in a split second whether to fire or wait for a better shot. If you fired you might regret it. If you didn't, you might never have another chance. According to sportsmen's law, whoever puts the first shot into an animal has the right to claim it, even if someone else actually kills it. The only exception to this rule is when shooting certain kinds of buffalo, because they are so dangerous when wounded. The only really satisfactory way to kill a tiger is to be the only one to shoot at it.

Although the procedure of making the ring was always much the same, we never knew what might happen or what we would find. Once we came unexpectedly on some rare Indian rhinoceros. Belle dropped one with a very pretty shot. Ted killed another. It was the only time Ted and I were riding in separate howdahs. Someone shouted that two half-grown rhino calves were coming my way. I steadied myself, watched the waving grass, and prepared to shoot. Suddenly one of them charged my elephant, scaring it so that it rose on its hind feet, turned like a polo pony, and bolted. I was nearly thrown out of the howdah and of course could not fire. Another time Ted shot a tiger galloping past us and did not know if he had hit it. Our elephant chose that instant to run away. It always surprised me how fast those clumsy, lumbering things could go. Two other elephants were sent out to head us off, but ours stopped when we came to a swamp and submitted to the mahout's orders to return to the ring. When we got back we were afraid the tiger might have vanished forever, but it was lying dead a few feet from where Ted had shot it.

On the afternoon of our last day in Nepal we made a final ring. All four of us had shot our tigers by then and were feeling happy and relaxed, with no further effort to be made and nothing to do but enjoy ourselves.

This ring was the best of all. It was in country that combined both high grass and jungle and seemed to contain all the game in the neighborhood. First we saw a group of axis deer, then some sambar and a rhino. All these were allowed to slip out between the elephants, as we had specimens already and did not want to alert any tiger that might be there. There turned out to be five!

The circle was formed and the two veteran tuskers sent in as usual, while we sat and waited. Half an hour afterward we heard a shot from the far side. Word was passed along by the mahouts that a tiger had been killed. This meant, we thought, that the shoot was finished. As we waited for the signal to dismount, Ted and I sat talking, our rifles laid aside. Twenty minutes later we heard a fusillade from the other side of the ring but could see nothing because of the grass. Suddenly we saw a tiger coming at a dead run down the cleared path in front of us. I was too surprised to move and sat frozen, but Ted grabbed his rifle and fired almost from the hip. The tiger, still running, disappeared. "A clean miss," said Ted, "but we didn't need that one."

Some time afterward we gathered around the bodies of two magnificent tigers. Kermit had killed one, but no one knew who had fired the single shot that had brought down the other. Two of the Englishmen, using lead slugs in shotguns, had fired and each hoped he had hit. Ted did not mention having shot, as he was certain he had missed. Our host said he would dig out the bullet and see if it could be identified. He did so, and found it had come from Ted's Springfield rifle.

The other three tigers had managed to charge out of the ring, causing panic among the elephants. The total bag for the seven days' shooting was eleven killed, of which seven were ours. Of all our adventures in India, I think we enjoyed most the one in the Nepal Terai.

We were particularly anxious to get a group of gond or swamp deer for the museum. These were rare and strictly preserved in the few places where they were at all plentiful. Through Colonel J. C. Faunthorpe, the noted sportsman, we were fortunate to receive an invitation from her Highness the Maharanee Saheba to shoot in the marshes near Kheri in the Oudh as her guests.

We left Lucknow by train, alighted at Palia before sunrise, and motored to the camp prepared for us, our luggage following by bullock cart. Colonel Faunthorpe joined us, saying he had not had enough time to arrange any frills for our entertainment, just the necessities of life. What he would have done had he had more time, I cannot imagine. The camp was incredibly luxurious, with two rows of tents facing each other like a village street, an arc light on a tall pole between them. The manager of the Carlton Hotel at Lucknow, Mr. Haslam, was in charge of catering and had brought an excellent chef and assistants to look after us.

Our kit would not be there until afternoon, but we wanted to waste no time. Our rifles were always with us. Ted and Kermit were in hunting clothes, but Belle and I had only our traveling dresses, silk stockings, and high-heeled pumps. We set out right after breakfast.

The Maharanee had provided eight elephants for us, fine-looking animals with their foreheads painted black with arabesques in scarlet. Five of them carried howdahs for those who were to shoot, one was for Mr. Haslam and the lunch, and two were to carry any game we might get. We mounted, rode for half an hour, and reached the swamp, a wide expanse of grass three to five feet high cut by sluggish currents and lagoons. Here we formed a rough line, Colonel Faunthorpe directing our movements. The elephants splashed through the muddy water, testing tussocks with their trunks before stepping on them. Crossing the deeper currents where the water came up to their stomachs, they held their trunks high in the air.

Swamp deer were plentiful in these marshes. The difficulty was to make certain a stag had good antlers before it vanished into the grass. Shooting had to be done very quickly. We also wanted to collect a group of hog deer, little creatures living on the edge of the swamp where it was drier. About the size of an Airedale, they were exceedingly hard to hit as they scampered through the grass at lightning speed, their heads down. Shooting them from the back of a moving elephant was tricky, but we were lucky enough to get a good group of both species in three days.

After this we tried to pick up odds and ends of game needed to complete other groups. Ted went out early one morning in a bullock cart, hoping to get a female black buck. It is often easy to get close to game in these carts, as wild creatures do not associate them with danger. A couple of hours after he had left, word came that a leopard had been seen in the vicinity. With some excitement we prepared for a drive. A leopard would be an important addition to our collection. We hoped Ted would return in time, but we could not delay, as the animal might not stay in the neighborhood. Just as we were ready to go Ted returned. As I ran out to tell him to hurry he shouted to me: "I didn't see any black buck but I've got a fine leopard!" He had killed the very one we were going after. We never succeeded in shooting a female black buck, but later his Highness the Maharajah Jam Saheb of Nawanagar, hearing that we lacked this specimen, sent us a good skin with all necessary measurements for mounting.

It was fun riding through the jungle on elephants, our main work done. We shot a group of wild pigs, a wildcat, and several rare swamp partridges, as well as a number of peacocks which we skinned for the museum, then ate. They were delicious.

On our last morning in camp Belle and I went out together on an elephant to have a last look around. Our luggage had left, so again we wore our traveling dresses, silk stockings, and high heels. We badly needed a chital (axis) doe and fawn for our deer group. First we tried to shoot a crocodile, but both of us missed. Those great, sluggish creatures can disappear into the water with astonishing speed. On our way back to camp we caught sight of a chital doe. We fired together and both hit, killing it instantly. Belle and I slid off the elephant and after much struggling and straining managed to hand it up to the mahout, who was far more affable and co-operative than the one at Allapilli. As we climbed back he exclaimed that there was a fawn, and got off and caught it. He handed the tiny creature up to me, and I wrapped it in a silk handkerchief I wore around my neck.

When we reached the camp we caused great excitement. Colonel Faunthorpe said the fawn was indeed a prize for the museum, as a specimen as young as that was almost unobtainable. I unwrapped it and put it down on the floor of the tent. It rose to its feet, walked rather shakily over to Ted, and licked his finger. Ted patted it gently and played with it, then said firmly: "I want to say here and now that I won't be the one to kill it." None of us could bear to do so. We discussed taking it home to keep as a pet, but this was impracticable. Finally Colonel Faunthorpe took it outside and shot it behind one ear with a small .18-caliber pistol. Today the little fawn and its mother add great interest and charm to the group of axis deer in the museum.

After lunch we left the camp at Kheri and motored sixty miles in open cars through thick white dust to call on the Maharanee Saheba and to express our appreciation of her kindness and hospitality. We hoped for a chance to brush off the worst of the dust before seeing her, but she and some of her ladies met us on the front steps of her palace and took us right into the drawing room. Here her relatives were assembled, the women wearing exquisite saris in pastel colors, shimmering with gold and silver. She herself was all in flowing white. In desperation Belle and I laid our sun helmets on a chair and started to put on the hats we were carrying, when one of the princesses said, "Wouldn't you like to wash?" and took us to a tent out in the garden, where we managed to make ourselves a little less disheveled. Tea was served with innumerable dishes of cakes, pastries, and sweets of all kinds. Probably because of the caste system, none of them ate with us.

When we left the Maharanee we still had a long, chilly, dusty drive to the train. I had been fighting a cold all day, and this was no help. By evening I felt utterly miserable with a sore throat and fever. All I wanted was to get to bed. On the train our bedding rolls were spread out. I was sitting on the edge of mine, taking off my shoes, when I felt something hit my shoulder and saw a black spider as big as a mouse disappear into my blankets. After a few seconds of frantic search I gave up. The thought of taking that bedding roll apart was too much. I slid between the blankets, hoping the spider would not resent sharing them with me, forgot all about it, and slept soundly until morning.

Chapter 22

After spending a day in Lucknow we took the night train to Delhi for a visit of five days at Viceregal Lodge. Arriving at six in the morning, we were met by an A.D.C. who was surprisingly cheerful for that time of day. The Viceroy and Vicereine of India, their Excellencies the Marquess and Marchioness of Reading, lived in a large white stucco house banked with masses of pink and mauve verbena. Some of the older people at the house party stayed there; the rest of us were in tents in the garden. But what tents they were! Ted's and mine had two bedrooms with real beds, a sitting room with a fire burning in a real fireplace with a mantelpiece, and a bathroom with running water and real fixtures. The floors were covered with Indian carpets. All this was actually a temporary arrangement until the city of New Delhi should be finished, where there would be a splendid new palace for the Viceroy.

The house party consisted of Lord and Lady Devonport, Lord and Lady Lee of Fareham, the Honorable Mrs. Edwin Montagu, whose late husband had been Secretary of State for India, Lieutenant-Colonel the Honorable Sir Frank and Lady Connor, Belle, Ted, and me. Kermit was away on business and was to join us later. We were delighted to find the Lees, as they were old and dear friends. Arthur Lee had been a British observer attached to the Rough Riders, and had been made honorary member of the regiment. Since then he had held many posts of importance, including that of First Lord of the Admiralty. I had last seen him in Washington in 1922 when he was British delegate to the armament conference and had made an extremely complimentary statement to the press about the excellence of Ted's work. At a reception at the White House, in addition to the many orders and decorations on his diplomatic uniform, the little badge of the Rough Riders had a place of honor. Ruth Lee, his wife, was American, a distant cousin of my mother-in-law and a darling. It was the Lees who gave their historic country place, Chequers, to the British nation for the use of prime ministers.

At Viceregal Lodge everything was done with the greatest ceremony and pomp. The Viceroy represented the person of his Majesty George V, the King-Emperor. This governed all etiquette. The day we arrived an A.D.C. came to our tent to take us to the main house to lunch. He said their Excellencies wanted to see us and he led us to a small room, briefing us on the way. To me he said, "Please curtsy on entering the door. Halfway across the room stop and curtsy again. Curtsy again if shaken hands with. Do not sit down until invited to do so." Ted, of course, was to bow. The same routine was to be followed on the way out. We were welcomed cordially by Lord and Lady Reading. Five minutes later the A.D.C. removed us, taking us back to the others, where we all stood in a semicircle. The Readings came in, preceded by the two A.D.C.s on duty, and made the rounds. Luncheon guests were shaken hands with, the men bowing, the women curtsying. House guests merely bowed or curtsied as their Excellencies went by. Some years later when Ted and I stayed with Lord Willingdon when he was Viceroy, much of this exaggerated ceremony had all but disappeared except at state functions.

Formality reached its height at dinner parties. At the end of the meal Lady Reading would rise, walk alone to the door, turn around, curtsy to the Viceroy, and go out. Every woman in turn had to do the same. According to the fashion of the day, we were all in knee-length skirts, making it impossible to curtsy gracefully.

One evening I risked disaster. I had on a pair of silver sandals, each held on by a button on a narrow strap. Not only did they have inordinately high heels but they were lined with silver kid, slippery as ice. Halfway through the dinner the button came off one of them. The slipper would not stay on without it, and no concealment was possible under my short skirt. I had two alternatives. I could either take my slippers off and carry them in my hand while I walked out and curtsied, or I could slip under the table and hide. One of my neighbors, Sir Geoffrey de Mont-morency, K.C.V.O., C.I.E., C.B.E., I.C.S., to be precise, said he believed in being prepared for the unexpected and, bless him, took a wide elastic band from his pocket. It held my slipper on until I could get to a needle and thread.

After leaving the dining room and before the men joined us, we each had a few moments' conversation with Lady Reading, curtsying when we were taken up to her and again when we left. One evening I was sitting with Mrs. Montagu, a most attractive and chic Englishwoman. We had taken out our powder puffs when one of the staff hurried over to us. "Please put those away. Her Excellency does not permit anything of that kind in the drawing room." Surprised, we did put them away, but not before whisking them over our faces.

When the men came in it was like a well-organized game directed by the A.D.C.s. A maharajah would be brought to sit down and talk to me. Five minutes later he would be politely removed and another produced. The elderly Maharajah of Bikaner was especially delightful, with a keen sense of humor. I started to tell him about Ted and Kermit wearing tuxedos and collapsible opera hats when calling on local officials in the backwoods of western China, and he refused to be moved until he had heard the whole story. The Maharajah of Bharatpur, young and handsome, wearing cloth of gold with diamond-and-ruby buttons, said he had tried to reach us through Thomas Cook's to invite us to shoot with him, and failed because we were too deep in the jungle. He was describing his last shoot with seven leopards in one drive when his turn came to move on. I must have talked to six or eight people before the evening ended.

The next night Belle and I begged the A.D.C.s not to keep rushing people at us but to let us sit together, if necessary in another room, with a couple of pleasant ones with whom we could really talk. They agreed and gave us Sir Charles Innes, "an Ordinary Member of the Council of his Excellency the Governor General," with whom we had already made friends, and the Maharajah of Patiala, one of the most powerful and highest-ranking of the native princes. The latter talked to us on a variety of interesting subjects but never listened to a word we said. This was quite all right, as we could acquire knowledge without effort.

I had the deepest admiration for Lady Reading's courage. Three months before, she had had her seventh major operation and must have known hers was a fatal illness. She suffered constant pain, keeping up by sheer will power, yet doing the important tasks required of her. She died four years after we last saw her.

As soon as we got to Delhi I hurried to Mr. Schweiger's for my emeralds, left with him for safekeeping while we were in the jungle. They were even more beautiful than I remembered, and they reconciled me to having to wear my shabby black evening dress. Any old rag would be redeemed by this necklace. Even so, I was astonished by the interest it created in India, where so many splendid jewels were to be seen. Everyone mentioned it, everyone asked where it had come from. One maharajah wanted to know how much it had cost. I was startled and had barely enough presence of mind to bridle and answer coyly that when my husband gave me a present he usually did not tell me the price. Which Ted said later was a dirty black lie!

At tea one afternoon the Viceroy told me that an investiture, a formal bestowal of orders and decorations, would be held the night before we left. He said we would see many of the best jewels in India worn by the native princes. The treasure chambers of their palaces had been accumulating gems for countless ages. Even they themselves did not know the extent of their possessions. From the days when the only road into India was a single-file camel track through the Khyber Pass, and even after the sea route had been discovered by Vasco da Gama in 1498, the greater part of India's exports had been paid for not in goods but in cash. Much of the gold received was spent for gems, which were so well hidden that they escaped being stolen by invaders. Many of the most famous diamonds in the world came from India—the Koh-i-noor, the Orloff, the Pitt, the Great Mogul, the Darya-i-Nur, the Nizam, the Hope Diamond, to name only a few.

Lord Reading told me that the four most remarkable pearls in the world had been inherited by the Maharaj Rana of Dholpur, whose grandfather once heard that a fakir, or holy man, was being persecuted in his domain and ordained that all fakirs, and particularly this one, were to be considered under his personal protection. Thirty years passed. One day the fakir came to the palace and asked for an audience with his Highness. When he was admitted he salaamed, thanked the Maharaj for his kindness, said the time had come for him to go elsewhere, and took his leave after laying a small parcel on the floor at the feet of the Maharaj. When the parcel was opened it was found to contain the four pearls. Lord Reading told me that the Czar of Russia, Alexander II, offered the Maharaj nine million pounds ($45,000,-000) for them. His offer was refused. I said I hoped that the present Maharaj would wear them so that I could see them. The Viceroy said he would ask him to do so. Later we learned that he had not brought them with him but was sending his major-domo back to get them and hoped they would arrive in time.

The investiture was the high point of our stay in Delhi. At the end of the grand ballroom at Viceregal Lodge was a dais with a canopy of crimson velvet draped over two golden thrones. From this a wide red carpet reached to the far end of the room. On either side of the carpet were rows and rows of gilt chairs. Seated nearest the dais were the Indian princes, dazzling in their jewels and brilliant costumes. Outstanding was the Maharajah of Patiala in red and silver brocade, his red turban literally covered with diamonds. Around his neck were many ropes of large pearls, close together from his throat to his waist. He wore the pale blue satin cloak of Knight Grand Commander of the Most Eminent Order of the Indian Empire and carried a sword in a pink velvet scabbard encrusted with diamonds. His beard was wrapped in black silk according to the Sikh custom. Beside him sat the Maharaj Rana of Dholpur, in his turban a diamond ornament as large as the palm of my hand with a great panache of diamond feathers. Alas, his pearls had not come in time for him to wear, so I never saw them. Our friend of Bharatpur wore a turban ornament of emeralds and diamonds, a necklace of big square-cut emeralds set in diamonds, sparkling with green fire. One of the A.D.C.s brought us together later in the evening, saying nothing but pointing to our necklaces. I said this was an unfriendly act, as his Highness's were the only ones there that outshone mine.

As a fanfare of trumpets sounded, the company rose. The band struck up and the bodyguard marched in, Indian soldiers selected, I should say, for their height and superb physique. They were followed by all the A.D.C.s in full-dress uniform. Last came their Excellencies, who mounted the dais. The Viceroy was in robes of velvet trimmed with ermine, Lady Reading in violet and silver brocade (half mourning) with a court train of silver lamé. She wore a diamond coronet and carried a big violet feather fan. Their trains were carried by four little native princes in pale blue satin. As they sat on their golden thrones against the red velvet background, they were elegance and distinction personified.

The investiture began. Lord Reading would announce the name of a man, who rose and remained standing while the list of his previous honors was read, then walked up to the throne, received his decoration, and returned to his seat. Some were knighted and knelt while the Viceroy tapped them on the shoulder with a sword. The beauty of his voice added much to the dignity of the occasion. A few men walked well with all eyes on them, some were self-conscious, others strutted. Our friend, General Sir Andrew Skeen, Chief of the General Staff, Indian Army, did better than anyone else. Tall, with a weather-beaten face, he walked as if there were no one else in the place and as if it wouldn't have mattered to him if there had been.

I was by turns thrilled, moved, and choked with mirth. The whole proceeding was a mixture of the Arabian Nights, the Court of St. James's, the Benevolent Elks, and the Shriners.

When it was over we went into an enormous marquee for supper. It was great fun, for by then we knew so many people, and we stayed late. Next morning we rose at half-past five to take the train to Bombay.

We were on our way home. The James Simpson-Roosevelts-Field Museum Expedition to Central Asia had been a smashing success. Also, we had made a good collection of Indian fauna and had thoroughly enjoyed doing it. I don't think anyone ever had a better time. Exhausted, Belle and I undid our bedding rolls as soon as we were on the train. As I lay down, my emeralds tied around my waist, I said, "There's only one thing I'm sorry for. I wish you had let Kermit give you the other necklace as he wanted to." She answered sleepily, "He's going to give me an eighteenth-century English painting when we get to London."

Then we slept for ten hours.

When we reached home there was excitement and much publicity about the expedition, with stories on the front pages of the New York *Times, Herald Tribune,* and other newspapers as well as double-page spreads in the Sunday rotogravure sections. A Chicago paper carried a picture of Ted and his biggest *Ovis poli,* with Rahima, Khalil, and another shikari nearby. With his bushy beard and well-worn hunting clothes Ted was not recognized by the editor, whose caption read: "The *Ovis poli* with four natives." Some wag wanted to know if the *Ovis poli* was a polite egg. Will Rogers explained it in his column: "You don't know what an *Ovis poli* is? I can't stop to explain everything to you. It's a political sheep. You hunt it between elections."

Chapter 23

Here by the side of a sea that's shining
Under a sky like flame,
*   Me that was born with a taste for travel*
Give thanks because of the same.

C. FOX SMITH

What dreadful hot weather we have! It
keeps me in a continual state of inelegance.

JANE AUSTEN

The next two years, 1927 and 1928, were difficult for Ted. Although consigned to oblivion by the Old Guard and the press, he continued to receive a surprisingly large number of invitations to speak and accepted those that interested him. He established a little office at my mother's house in New York and came in from Oyster Bay on most weekdays. Miss Margaret Hensey, his invaluable secretary in the Navy Department, had come to New York in 1924 to continue working for him. During this time he dictated several short pieces to her as well as two books, *All in the Family,* describing life at Sagamore Hill, and *Rank and File,* true stories of World War I. Twenty years afterward Ted's account of Sergeant Alvin York was chosen by Ernest Hemingway for his anthology, *Men at War, Best War Stories of All Time,* which started with one by Julius Caesar.

Miss Hensey became a real member of the family, staying with us for over twenty years and going with us to Puerto Rico and the Philippines. While Ted was on his Asian expeditions he wrote articles for magazines with what the children called "Father's invisible pencil" and sent them to Miss Hensey, who alone could decipher them. She would type them and send them to me to be corrected.

Always in the back of Ted's mind was the hope of another expedition. As he wrote, "Spirits of the high places of the earth, from barren boulders and snows, hinted at days when the driving storm caked the ice on beard and face; spirits from the desert sang of blowing sand and blistering sun." When he found that Kermit was feeling the same way, that settled it. After many evenings spent examining and discussing the uncharted spaces on the map, many of which today have been explored, they decided on that part of Asia northwest of Indo-China where the Himalayas gradually descend to the tropical plains. They would push in by the old Bhamo-Talifu trail from Burma to Yunnan, which later was to become part of the Burma Road. When traveling through uncharted country, they would make a rough attempt to map it. After pressing in as far as possible, they would collect such animals as they could.

What they really wanted was to get a giant panda, but the possibility was so slight that they dared not announce it as an objective and told practically no one of their hopes. At that time no one knew where the animal might be found or indeed if it still existed. No white man had ever shot one, although sportsmen and naturalists had been trying to do so ever since its discovery in 1868 by the French missionary-scientist Père David. The noted British traveler, Brigadier General George Pereira, the first Englishman to travel from Peking to Lhasa, had hunted it for three months in the early 1920s, in vain. A few skins from animals trapped by natives existed in museums, but no specimen had ever been scientifically collected—that is, with skeleton and measurements—therefore, no one had ever been able to determine if the giant panda was a panda, a bear, a raccoon, or a new species.

Once their plans had taken shape in the summer of 1928, the question of expense arose. Again they approached the Field Museum in Chicago. Stanley Field, president of the museum, gave a dinner for them at which they met William V. Kelly, president of the Miehle Printing Press and Manufacturing Company.

Without a moment's hesitation Mr. Kelly agreed to finance the venture.

Weeks passed, during which they studied means and methods of mapping unknown country under Dr. Isaiah Bowman of the American Geographical Society, gathered equipment, and got permits from various governments to go into the Asian countries. This enterprise was called the William V. Kelly-Roosevelts Expedition to Eastern Asia for Field Museum and was in two divisions. The first, headed by Ted and Kermit, was to specialize in large mammals. The second, headed by Harold J. Coolidge, Jr., a young scientist from the Harvard Museum, was to collect birds, small mammals, and reptiles in the unknown regions of northwestern Indo-China.

Ted could not start until after election, as he was to make a nationwide tour in October for the Republican ticket during the presidential campaign. Although he was supposed to have been obliterated politically, the Speakers' Bureau of the Republican National Committee received more requests for him as a speaker than for anyone else except the candidates themselves, Herbert Hoover and Charles Curtis.

Again they asked Suydam Cutting to go with them, and on November 10, 1928, they sailed on the *Homeric*. Belle and I went with them as far as Paris. The plan was for us to join them in Indo-China the following summer, but plans do not always turn out as expected. When the time came I was to set out alone, as Kermit, because of his shipping business, had been obliged to return before the expedition was finished.

In May 1929, while Ted was away, President Hoover appointed him Governor of Puerto Rico, to take office after his return from Asia. Before sailing to meet him I talked with a number of people who had been there and knew the country, as I knew Ted would want as much information as possible. The concensus was that it would be a Herculean task, with no great credit for success but much blame for failure. The language of the people was Spanish, but no Governor had ever attempted to speak it.

It had been fairly simple for me to leave the children while they were little, but now it was far more complicated. Gracie was seventeen, Teddy fourteen, Cornelius thirteen, and Quentin nine. It was arranged for Gracie to go to France to spend the summer with a French family, then study at the Sorbonne the following winter. My mother-in-law, bless her, knowing that Teddy loved sailing, gave him an S boat and asked him to spend the summer at Sagamore Hill. The only difficulty was transportation from there to the Seawanhaka Yacht Club where his boat was kept, a long distance away. I decided to take a chance and let him have a motorcycle. My friends thought I was mad, but I knew Teddy. The plan worked to perfection. That left Cornelius and Quentin.

Signorina had left us the year before and had gone back to Italy because her father, who had always resented her working for a living, demanded it. Before leaving she had promised to come back at any time if I really needed her. I wrote her I could not go to Indo-China unless she came back to look after the two younger boys. She came, and she stayed with us for another twelve years. There was no further talk of her leaving.

I left San Francisco early in June on the *President Harrison* for Shanghai, en route to Saigon. The voyage took three weeks and was pleasant and uneventful until we ran into a typhoon, which kept the captain on the bridge all night. I was unaware of it and slept soundly until awakened by the stewardess coming in to ask if I had any white sewing silk. I had only pale pink, which she said wouldn't do, but refused to say why. Soon after I noticed a strong smell of ether. Later the captain told me there had been an attempted murder during the storm. One baker had attacked another with two knives, slashing his hand to the bone before they were separated. The ship's doctor had operated under difficulties to draw the tendons together. The sea was so rough that a boatswain had to brace himself against the wall to hold a chair against the doctor's back to steady him. The attacker was put in the brig, which was forward on deck and was hit by every wave that came over. In protest he twice set fire to his blankets. After that he was searched and his matches removed.

When I reached Shanghai I got a telegram from Ted sent out by a runner, saying he had been delayed in the jungle and would reach Saigon ten days later than had been planned. This gave me a little more time to see the country. I left the *President Harrison* and spent a few days in Shanghai before leaving for Hong Kong on the French liner *General Mentzinger*.

In Shanghai I stayed with our Consul General, Edwin Cunningham, and his wife. Rhoda Cunningham, a handsome woman of striking personality who had been born in Johannesburg, had glossy black hair long enough for her to sit on and shining white teeth which she always brushed with salt. She and I did sightseeing or poked about in little shops every day and went to parties every night. She took me twice to tea with old Mr. Tong Sha Yi, who had been China's first Premier and one of the Empress Dowager's viceroys. He had a famous collection of porcelain which he showed to his friends in characteristic Chinese fashion. After tea he seated us comfortably on a sofa in his parlor and gave us flashlights to light the beauty of a single vase, lovingly removed from its wrappings and placed on a table before us. On our next visit we were shown another piece in the same way. He gave me a tiny porcelain man down on one knee, holding a scroll. It represented the Dutch Minister presenting his credentials to the Emperor Ch'ien Lung and had long yellow hair and the big nose that Chinese think all foreigners have.

A few years later Mr. Tong was assassinated by a hatchet man.

At Hong Kong I was met by Harold Shantz, the American Vice-Consul. I told him I still had time to spare and wanted to go to Haiphong and have a day or two in Hanoi before reaching Saigon. The Standard Oil people didn't have a freighter going that way, but fortunately the Messageries Maritimes had a small coastal vessel leaving that afternoon, taking four days and stopping at ports along the south China coast. I prepared for the journey by buying some Flit, a case of soda water, and some books.

After giving me a delicious lunch on the roof of the Hong Kong Hotel, Mr. Shantz took me with my baggage in a launch out to the ship, a grimy, untidy craft. This took over an hour. When we arrived and were told she would not sail for five or six hours, he asked if I would like to go ashore again, but I thought I had given him enough trouble for one day and preferred to stay on board and get settled. It was fun watching the junks and sampans in the harbor. Just before we started, the launch came back with Mr. Shantz, who brought me a stack of letters just arrived from home, a basket of lotus flowers, and two large boxes of American candy. He was indeed a kind man. When he asked how I was making out and I said, "Very nicely, thank you," he remarked, "You're easily pleased!"

On the ship were five cabin passengers: an English manufacturer's agent, a French military official from Haiphong, two Germans from a bank in Hong Kong, and myself, the only woman. In the steerage were five hundred Chinese, who were locked behind bars at night for fear there might be pirates among them. Indeed, a companion ship to this one was so attacked a few months later. It was hot, a damp, suffocating, tropical heat. With the aid of a good tip I managed to get a cabin boy, a French-speaking Chinese, to scrub my cabin with disinfectant soap. Here I met my first giant cockroach and chased it around until I killed it with my umbrella. The food on board pretended to be French and consisted of rabbit, tripe, and brains, with a bottle of sour wine thrown in. I brushed my teeth with soda water, ate no raw fruit that I didn't peel, and got along very well.

Our first stop was at Fort Bayard, a French protectorate, where I went ashore with Mr. Pooler, the English passenger. We passed a gang of Chinese convicts working on the road, chained together and wearing huge wooden collars that came out beyond their shoulders.

Another stop was at Pakhoi, where the heat was worse than ever. This time I went ashore with Captain Henrys, the French passenger. He had looked at me with suspicion at first (why would a personable young woman be traveling on a ship like that one?), until it turned out I had been at school with his sister in Paris and probably was harmless. We called on the French Consul, a doctor who was also head of a hospital of seventy beds, did six or seven operations every day, and in his spare time collected natural history specimens for a Paris museum. He knew all about Ted's expeditions and was much interested.

I hired a rickshaw and rode around for a time to see the town, then stopped at the customs house to get some local currency. Here I was surprised to see a young American in the office. He stared at me in astonishment and said, "Just wait till I call my chief. He will be so glad to see you. We haven't had a visitor for over a year. No one *ever* comes in on this boat!" He hurried off and came back with Mr. C. G. C. Asker, the Commissioner of Customs, a Swede. I was puzzled until I learned that in those days all customs duties were collected for the Chinese Government by foreigners. Mr. Asker insisted on taking me to see his wife, saying I must lunch with them. I protested that there wasn't time. My ship sailed at noon, and I had to be aboard before then. He answered that no vessel could leave without clearance papers from him, and he would hold these up until after lunch.

The three of us walked the short distance to his house, where Mrs. Asker was sitting on the veranda, a Scandinavian snow maiden, slim, ash-blond, with sea-blue eyes and dark lashes. I have never seen people so glad to see a casual stranger, and realized what a dreary place Pakhoi must be. The two men went back to the office, to return for lunch in an hour.

After we had talked for a few minutes Mrs. Asker said, "I have been on your ship and I know what it is. Would you like a bath?" Would I! She clapped her hands, gave the necessary orders, and soon after took me up to her room and left me. The bath was ready; no running water, of course, but a big round tub painted green and white with several pitchers of cool water. On her dressing table was an old-fashioned toilet set of heavy silver, a profusion of brushes, combs, pin trays, boxes, everything imaginable, each piece engraved with a crown, the treasure of a fairy princess in exile.

When I came downstairs much refreshed, I asked her about her life. They had been five years in China and two months in Pakhoi. She was worried about her children, a little girl of three and a baby boy of nine months who had not gained an ounce since their arrival. The baby was in the amah's lap on the stairs to catch any slight draft in the hot stifling air. No fresh milk or ice was available. No fresh fruit or vegetables were to be had nearer than Hong Kong. There was nowhere to go and nothing to see. Their one recreation was playing bridge in the evening with the young American and the French Consul. Even this was difficult, as they had no common language with the Consul. The only woman with whom she could talk was the Swedish wife of the harbormaster, a woman of no education. I said the beaches were beautiful and they must enjoy swimming, but she said no. At first they had tried it with the children, but as soon as they were in the water they were surrounded by a noisy mob of curious people. "We make the best of it, hoping our next post will be more agreeable." Their next post was indeed more agreeable, as it was in Peking, but I have been told that Mrs. Asker was killed there by a fall from a horse.

They sent me down to the wharf in Mrs. Asker's chair, carried by four coolies in smart red and white livery and enormous sun hats. I swung along feeling like the Dowager Empress at least, really sorry to say good-by.

When the boat reached Haiphong I was putting the last things in my dressing case when I heard footsteps on deck and, looking out under the swinging half door of my cabin, saw a pair of unmistakable American feet. It was Austin Glass of the Standard Oil Company. He had heard I was coming and paused at my door because he caught sight of a can of Flit and was sure it must be mine.

Mr. Glass was kindness itself. He sent me to Hanoi in his car for a night and made me keep it to come back. The drive took two hours through rice fields, which were watered in a curious way. Two women would swing a basket on a rope, dipping water from large puddles and throwing it into little irrigation ditches. Sometimes four women worked together with two baskets, moving in perfect rhythm and never tangling. They were slim and straight, good-looking until they opened their mouths and showed black-lacquered teeth.

Hanoi was beautiful with its wide streets, its lake, its temples and French white stucco houses. I went around in a rickshaw and found a good curio shop where I bought some little treasures. The hotel was not bad except for the plumbing. I had asked for a room with bath and was given an enormous bedroom with a tiled dais in one corner for a shower and fixed basin. That night I decided to take advantage of the running water and wash my hair. Just as my head was covered with suds a severe thunderstorm started. Rain fell in a cloudburst. To my dismay, water backed up in both the shower and basin, bringing with it loathsome accumulations of filth. I had to sit for nearly an hour waiting for the storm to stop before I could rinse my hair.

Next day I found a French drugstore and tried to get the strongest disinfectant I could think of. I asked the proprietor, an old man with a white beard, for bichloride of mercury and was surprised by the question he asked me. Could he see my passport? What was I doing in Hanoi? Was I alone? I was going to meet my husband? Why was he not there? Why had he not arrived? How long had I been waiting? Was I afraid he would not come? What possible use could I have for such strong poison? To disinfect a bathroom? Who had ever heard of such a thing! No indeed. This shop carried nothing of the kind. People were too impulsive. Here was a small bottle of Listerine. That would have to do, and I must not lose courage. I had to get out of the store to laugh.

I returned to Haiphong and that afternoon drove with Mr. Glass and two members of his staff to his bungalow by the sea. He said I could go in swimming if I would wait until five o'clock. If I went earlier I might get a sunstroke and he would be responsible. When the time came I ran into the water, only to be disappointed. It was so hot that I had to come out to cool off, because a wide, shallow river emptied into the sea close by. The American colony came to dinner—all four of them. We ate on the veranda and amused ourselves by putting glass ash trays over the largest of the flying creatures that landed on the table. That night Mr. Glass stayed at the bungalow and generously turned his house in town over to me. Next day I sailed for Saigon on the *Compiègne*.

Chapter 24

He delighted to wander in unknown lands, to see strange rivers, his eagerness making delight of toil.

OVID

Henry S. Waterman, American Consul General, met me at the dock in Saigon and asked me to stay at the Consulate. This I was pleased to do, as a message had come from Ted saying he had been delayed again and probably would not be there for another couple of days.

That night the Watermans and I had just sat down to dinner when we heard a strange sound of howling outside. From where I was sitting I could see the figure of a man at the front door, shaking its ornamental ironwork with both hands. I jumped up from the table, crying, "It's Ted!" and ran down the hall. Mr. Waterman was close behind me, saying, "No, it isn't. It can't be! It's some sort of a crazy native. Look at that man!" But it was indeed Ted, wasted from fever and slightly delirious. He could see us at dinner with orchids on the table, a clean white cloth, and shining silver and crystal. It was all so attractive—but he couldn't quite remember how to open a door.

Never in all my life have I seen anyone who looked so sick, not even Ted when he was gassed in 1918. He had lost forty-two pounds. He came in and asked for a little brandy but would not eat. I threw my clothes into a bag and we went to the hotel where all his things were. During the night his fever broke. Next morning we sent for a doctor, a pleasant Frenchman who was unimpressed when I told him Ted's temperature had been over a hundred and five degrees. I found out later that he did not know Fahrenheit and merely thought I was demented. He diagnosed Ted's illness as malaria and dysentery, gave him some little pills, and put him on a diet.

When the William V. Kelly-Roosevelts-Field Museum Expedition to Southwest Asia entered its second stage, collecting the wild oxen of Indo-China, Kermit had to return home for business reasons. A couple of weeks after that Suydam Cutting fell ill and was forced to leave. This left the work on Ted's shoulders. With a French guide called Des Fosses, he had done it in the rainy season, when the heavy, steaming heat of the wet forest is like a Turkish bath. Not only does the vegetation become so lush that it is extremely hard to see the game, but it is infested with mosquitoes carrying many types of malaria. Collecting specimens is doubly difficult, because after the animals have been tracked down and shot they must be skinned at once and the skins stretched over a fire to dry before they start to rot. In spite of these obstacles and his illness, Ted had succeeded in obtaining a group of seladang or great gaur oxen, handsome wild creatures that often stand six feet at the shoulder and are brown with white ankles and pale bluish eyes, a group of water buffalo (one shot by Suydam), specimens of banteng, barking deer, hog deer, and an elephant.

The whole expedition had been an unqualified success. Its story has been told in two books, *Trailing the Giant Panda* by the two brothers and *Three Kingdoms of Indo-China* by Harold Coolidge and Ted. Their collections comprised more than forty big mammals, including the rarest of game—the giant panda; some two thousand small mammals, nineteen of them hitherto unknown species or subspecies, the most important a muntjak deer named by the museum *Muntiacus rooseveltorum* for the brothers; and between five and six thousand birds and reptiles. The giant panda made a sensation in the zoological world, and naturalists wrote from all over Europe requesting details. At last it could be studied and classified, and turned out to be a variety of raccoon.

Ted told me they had hunted through the country where it was thought to be if it existed at all, but never saw one. They had almost given up hope and had gone south after other game when they came across its tracks in a light fall of snow. Ted and Kermit trailed it until the snow disappeared, then took separate directions after promising that if one should find it he would signal or send a runner to overtake the other and, if humanly possible, would wait so that they could shoot together. Kermit came on it just after it had awakened from sleep. He said afterward that the short time it took to reach Ted seemed an eternity. They both fired, and the great prize was theirs.

Their discovery of its habitat near Yelhi made the capture of young ones for zoos possible until forbidden by the Chinese.

Before leaving home I had talked with Roy Chapman Andrews, famous zoologist and explorer, an old friend. He said, "I only hope Ted and Kermit won't try to go into the Lolo country. If they do, they may never get out alive. Those Lolos shoot Chinese on sight, and very probably other foreigners too. They're primitive and wild and are set on self-determination. It might be a very bad business." I was glad I hadn't known this or I would have worried, because it was in the Lolo country that they had shot the giant panda, locally called the beishung. To add to their difficulties, the beishung is sacred to the Lolos.

Believing that everything depends on how primitive people are treated, they had carefully called a halt when they met the first group of Lolos, talked affably to them through an interpreter, explained the purpose of their journey, and offered small gifts. The first group sent one of their number to introduce them to the next group they would meet. In fact, Ted and Kermit made such friends with the Lolos that when they were on their way out of the country they were assigned a bodyguard of sons of chiefs and were given a feast at the dwelling of the headman of the district on the road south from Yelhi, a road which had been closed to caravans for several years because of the savagery of these people. After they left they learned that a priest had been sent for to perform an elaborate ceremony of purification of the chief's house and compound because the sacred beishung's dead body had been there overnight. When they reached the old walled town of Tachow on the Chinese border, the magistrate wanted to know how it was that they had come unrobbed and untroubled through such hostile country. Never to his knowledge, he said, had any white man been there, and no Chinese had ventured there for many years.

In a day or two Ted's fever left him, to return shortly and at intervals for a long time until it finally disappeared altogether. We were joined by Harold Coolidge and stayed in Saigon for a few days to make certain all the specimens were in good condition and properly packed for the long voyage home. The hotel was clean and fairly comfortable. Window screens were unknown, and we slept under a heavy cotton net, a disadvantage in the heat. An electric fan in the ceiling kept the air stirred. We had running water in the bathroom but, according to local custom, no hot-water taps.

Saigon was an attractive city with its white and yellow buildings and its wide streets shaded by trees. Never have I heard such a variety of noises starting at daybreak and going on until midnight, with a slight respite about noon, when people seemed to take a rest. The main streets were choked with traffic. Automobiles, trucks, carriages drawn by tiny horses, rickshaws called *pousse-pousses*, hosts of bicycles streamed by, and through it all coolies, with long poles on their shoulders carrying a bale at either end, threaded their way at a peculiar and seemingly effortless jog trot. Everything made its own special clamor. Whether anyone was in the way or not, the car drivers kept their hands on their horns, the French kind that squawked on the intake. The horses wore bells, as did the bicycles. *Pousse-pousse* coolies and those with poles went along shouting. People on foot carried on conversations with friends by calling across the street. Sometimes two dogs would start a quarrel, to be joined by all dogs in the neighborhood galloping from every direction and fighting until beaten apart by yelling passers-by.

A parade started at seven one morning. In the crowd watching it was every shade of brown, copper, yellow, cream, and white skin. There were Annamese, Cambodians, Tonkinese, Chinese, Indians from Pondichéry, and French, as well as intermediate shades of half-castes. Many of the handsome women wore large diamonds in their ears, representing their capital.

Once we were dining in a restaurant when we heard shouts.

Two stout middle-aged Frenchmen were standing up and calling each other names. Everyone rushed to see what was going to happen. People sitting at the little tables on the street jumped up and crowded in. Then one of the men slapped the other in the face, and the other drew a revolver. In the midst of bedlam the police arrived and marched off the man with the gun. The headwaiter told me they were prominent politicians and no doubt would fight a duel. A friend dining with us was reminded of the time an American had a little disagreement here with a Frenchman and was challenged. The American promptly took off his coat, saying: "According to etiquette I believe I have the choice of weapons. We will fight this duel here and now, Kentucky style." Nothing more was said about it.

The French Governor General of Indo-China, Monsieur Pasquier, who lived in a magnificent white palace, gave a dinner party for us. I had brought my best evening dress, violet taffeta woven with pink roses. It had a full skirt and a bodice laced with jade-green velvet ribbon. As it needed pressing, I gave it to the bellboy with many warnings to be careful with it. Soon afterward I went out and was caught in a heavy shower. I was standing in a doorway out of the rain when I saw the boy go by on a bicycle, my dress rolled up under his arm. When he brought it back to me I told him just what I thought of this, but he assured me with beaming smiles that rain in Saigon never wet anything. He must have been right, for my dress was unharmed.

Although Ted was feeling better he could eat nothing but meat, bread, and tea, while the rest of us had delectable French cooking and vintage wines and ended by eating quantities of mangosteens. In the last century someone had offered two thousand pounds to anyone who succeeded in bringing a mangosteen in perfect condition to England for Queen Victoria to taste, but the prize was never claimed. I found them disappointing, as they were sweet but insipid and hard to pry loose from their outer shell. Dinner was served by Annamese boys in white with tunics of mauve and rose shot silk, the governmental insignia woven on the back. The guests were pleasant and included several Annamese ladies of extreme elegance.

Several months later Monsieur Pasquier sent me a decoration

from the Emperor of Annam, the Order of Virtuous Wives. Ted wrote him a letter of thanks in French which he showed me with great pride before mailing. Luckily I caught it in time to make a slight correction. Ted had meant to say that we had no such order in the United States. What he said was that we had no virtuous wives!

We had hoped to go to Peking on our way home, but Ted's condition made this impossible. Even he, who would never admit to being ill, said it would be no pleasure. He did insist, however, on our going to Angkor, one of the wonders of the world, which was only ten hours by automobile from Saigon.

Monsieur Pasquier with great kindness lent us a car with a driver and an extra boy. We set out at seven in the morning with Harold Coolidge and reached Pnompenh early in the afternoon. Here we spent the night with the French Resident and his wife. They too lived in a handsome white palace. Our rooms were immense, with marble floors and a bathroom with running water, but of course only cold.

We went out and roamed around the city, going first to the Royal Palace, which had a bright yellow tiled roof with blue trimmings. I rather lost interest when I was told it had been built only five years before. Inside was a combination of magnificence and tawdriness. The throne room contained beautiful paintings, carvings, and lacquer but had on the floor a cheap grade of European carpet with a design of huge cabbage roses, the middle strip not matching the sides. The Queen's golden throne behind the King's was hung with delicate silver gauze lined with harsh pink calico. We saw some of the royal jewels, including a black derby with a diamond finial on its top and a diamond cockade on its side.

We visited the Silver Pagoda, interesting because it had a vast silver floor, and walls covered with paintings showing life in Cambodia in times past. The effect was impressive until one saw the altar covered with artificial flowers and ornaments like Christmas-tree decorations. What we enjoyed most was a visit to the museum, where there was a good collection of antiques and where children were being taught the ancient arts and crafts.

Next morning we rose at five and had breakfast of mangoes, shirred eggs, hot rolls, and coffee with milk, served on the veranda.

The table was strewn with pale pink canna petals. Ted was feeling so much better that it was hard to make him skip the luscious fruit and stick to his Spartan diet.

Angkor Thom, principal city of the Khmer Empire, is believed to have been founded in the ninth century and abandoned in the fifteenth. It is said to have been the largest city in the world at the time of its prosperity, with a million inhabitants. After it was deserted it was lost in the jungle for four hundred years, its civilization forgotten. Although it was visited and described by many oriental travelers, notably Tcheou Ta-kwan in 1296, their manuscripts were unknown to the Western world and lay in the archives of Peking until discovered in 1902 and translated into French.

Tcheou wrote at length about the riches and splendor of the great city, giving a detailed description of its magnificence, its beauty, the customs of its people, and saying that everyone was freely admitted through its great gates except dogs and criminals whose big toes had been cut off. Its principal export and source of wealth, according to Tcheou, consisted of kingfishers' feathers, highly valued by the Chinese for making jewelry.

In 1860 Henri Mouhot, French naturalist who was collecting animals, came upon the temple of Angkor Wat by accident. Anxious to learn its history, he questioned the native Cambodians. Some replied that it had been erected by a race of giants, others that it had been constructed by the King of the Angels, still others that it had built itself. Because of Mouhot's discovery the boundary line of French Indo-China was moved to include Angkor. It had belonged to the Siamese, who were carting away its stones to use for building. Mouhot really was responsible for the preservation of this wonder of the world.

We stopped at the little Hôtel des Ruines near Angkor Wat. It was clean and pleasant but later was closed as a hotel because it became infested with scorpions. We walked over to the Wat, explored its courts, chambers, and galleries, climbed up to the topmost tower and sat watching the sunset, trying to imagine the place as it must have been in the days of its glory, when it was thronged with people and blazing with color. In the evening we again climbed the steep steps by the light of a full moon. Two bonzes in yellow robes were chanting antiphonally, their holy books lighted by candles. In the distance a drum throbbed.

At seven next morning Monsieur Henri Marchal, curator in charge of excavations, came for us. We explained that as our time was short we could stay only two days and so could not explore the sixty square miles of ruins but would like to see as much as possible before we had to leave. Driving in Monsieur Marchal's car over roads cut through the forest, we were able to see many wonders. Among other places, we went to the Bayon, whose outer galleries have a frieze carved in stone showing every detail of the life of the ancient people, including eating, drinking, cooking, dancing, fishing, hunting, giving birth, playing chess, fighting on foot, on water, and on elephants. Also shown are a circus, an orchestra, a cockfight, children at play, domestic and wild animals. We saw the monastery and temple of Ta Prohm in a vast compound where a tablet carved in the twelfth century gave the number of priests, deacons, assistants, and dancers as 66,625. Everywhere the jungle was creeping in. Great fromager trees grew in ruined courts and even from the tops of shrines and walls. Tropical vines and sprays of flowers hid many scars of time. Monsieur Marchal said he intended to remove only the vegetation that was doing actual damage and would leave the rest because of its beauty.

We returned to Saigon and soon after sailed for Hong Kong on a Norwegian freighter, the *Prosper,* a spruce little craft whose captain generously let Ted and me have his cabin. Harold had a smaller one nearby. He was taking back eleven wild animals, nine monkeys, and two little bears who were entertaining traveling companions. We were blithe and gay until Ted suddenly had a severe relapse. His temperature soared and he looked like death. I was frantic with worry.

The *Prosper* was a "lucky boat," and people liked to travel on her regardless of limited accommodations. For this reason seven hundred Chinese crowded her decks in space considered right for three hundred. The captain said he always made for the shore to put into port in case of storm warnings, to avoid the risk of deck passengers being washed overboard, but on this voyage we got caught without warning between two typhoons and had to run at full speed before the one from the south. The barometer fell at an alarming rate, and the sea was so rough I had to go about on all fours. In our cabin a tall cupboard with glass doors, which had been there for over twelve years, toppled over and crashed to the floor.

The captain sent for Harold and declared that if the storm became worse he would have to put the Chinese in the hold of the vessel. This would have to be done by force, for they were afraid they would die if driven below. As Ted was too ill even to be told about it, the captain would depend on his two Norwegian officers and Harold, and he distributed pistols to them. Harold came down from the bridge, made sure the animal cages were securely lashed, then sat with me while we watched the barometer. All night long we expected a call to action, but the weather gradually moderated. I was never so happy to see the sun rise as when we entered the calm waters of Hong Kong Harbor next morning.

We sent for a British doctor, but because we were to be there only one day and a night before boarding the *President Jefferson* for Shanghai, he could give Ted only palliatives.

At Shanghai, Edwin Cunningham, our Consul General, and Admiral Craven met us, both horrified at Ted's appearance. Dr. William H. Gardiner, in whom we had the utmost confidence, then took over. He said as we were to be there only a week there would be no use trying to get after the malaria, because Ted's temperature was down and blood tests must be made during a period of fever, but he could and would cure the dysentery. Among other medications, he gave Ted a German preparation called Yatren, pills the color of gun metal. If Ted would take three a day for a couple of months or until all symptoms disappeared, and stick to his diet of meat, starch, and tea, he would be well with no more relapses.

A few days later we left on the *President Grant* on our way to Tokyo, where I caved in and had to go to bed for three days with bronchitis. We went to Nikko for a day, but when we climbed the beautiful staircases we were both so weak we had to sit down every dozen steps to rest and catch our breath. Next day when we boarded the *President Lincoln* for San Francisco, Ted still weighed only a hundred and two pounds. I found out afterward that some men on board were betting even money that he would not live through the voyage.

I had complete trust in Dr. Gardiner and believed Ted was much better, when he suddenly had another severe relapse the first day out. I was terrified and wanted to call the ship's doctor. Ted protested violently and finally said, "I know why this happened. Will you promise not to get mad at me if I tell you? Promise faithfully?" I promised. "I was sick and tired of that odious diet and they had the most wonderful peaches in Japan. You were in bed and couldn't stop me, so I had a bowlful every day with sugar and thick cream. I didn't think you'd ever find out."

I could have torn him apart.

On the voyage we spent part of every day talking to a man we met who could speak Spanish, the language of Puerto Rico. Ted practically memorized his textbooks, and by the time we landed he was able to understand almost everything said to him in Spanish and to speak it a little.

Chapter 25

But first you must master their language,
their dialect, proverbs and songs. Don't trust
any clerk to interpret when they come with the
tale of their wrongs.

RUDYARD KIPLING

We arrived in San Juan, Puerto Rico, on Monday, October 7, 1929. As our ship entered the harbor we saw a great puff of white smoke from the old fort, El Morro, and heard the boom of cannon in salute. Crowds of people were waving from the ramparts. A holiday had been declared in the city, and everybody was out to see the new Governor. Our ship looked very gay with all its little flags flying. As we approached the pier the whole waterfront was jammed with people. The reception committee came on board, headed by James R. Beverley of Texas, Attorney General and acting Governor, who was to become our close friend and who later succeeded Ted as Governor. On the pier were a battalion of National Guard and a battalion of police. After we got into the waiting car the crowds broke loose and came tearing after us, cutting off the cars supposed to follow with the committee.

We drove slowly through cheering throngs (I never saw so many smiling faces) until we reached the steps of the Capitol, where a small reviewing stand had been built with a roof of fresh palm leaves. Chief Justice Emilio del Toro, another future friend, made a short address of welcome and administered the oath of office to Ted. Mr. Beverley spoke, saying the people of Puerto Rico were crying for wise and capable leadership and that the island was "important politically and economically out of all proportion to its size."

Ted then started his inaugural address. After reading the first paragraph in English, instead of having an interpreter read it over in Spanish he did it himself. When he began, *"Señores y Señoras,"* there came a great "A-a-a-a-ah!" from the crowd, then a burst of applause and cheers. No Governor had ever done this before.

A dispatch from Harwood Hull in the New York *Times* said:

> The Governor's speech was largely a discussion of the island's economic needs. It was a message to the people. By no means did he ignore the politicians, but he talked to their constituents. Immediately the people knew the new Governor had much basic information regarding them and their island. He spoke openly of handicaps and hardships which for years have been officially ignored, if not officially denied. He acknowledged and praised the many fine qualities of his island fellow citizens, and set them and himself new tasks which they know will require every ounce of energy and all the faith, optimism and courage which collectively may be summoned if they are to be performed.

Clouds had been gathering, and when Ted was halfway through his address the rain broke. Tropical rain is not a drizzle, it is more like an upset bucket. It fell in torrents through the palm-leaf shelter, drenching us. It saturated the crowds in their holiday best. Some of them ran for cover, but the majority stayed and shouted for Ted to go on, which he did, cutting slightly the remainder of his address. After he had finished, the sun came out and dried us all as we watched the parade of a battalion of the 65th U. S. Infantry, units of the National Guard, various veterans' organizations, members of the police and fire departments, delegations from public and private schools, and many bands.

When the parade was over we drove to the Government House, La Fortaleza. Half palace, half castle, this was the oldest gubernatorial residence under the American flag. It had been used for this purpose continuously since 1629, first by the Spanish and from

1898 to 1948 by the American governors. Today it is occupied by Luis Muñoz Marín, Governor of the Commonwealth of Puerto Rico. Originally its construction as a fortress was authorized in 1529. It was built a hundred feet above the water, the better to guard the harbor of one of Spain's most prized possessions in the West Indies. Its two round towers with circular staircases, its dungeon, its secret passages, and its eight-foot-thick lower walls date from this period. It has seen many invaders—English, French, Dutch—as well as many famous pirates such as Morgan and Kidd. The Dutch burned all but its walls in 1645. When it was rebuilt it was enlarged and made into a residence for the Governor, the defense of the harbor having been taken over by the fort of El Morro.

The Governor's outer office was one of the most beautiful rooms I have ever seen. It had been the throne room, where the Spanish Governor received those having business with the Crown, and was done in the manner of Robert Adam, with delicate pilasters and a wide frieze of mythological figures in high relief. Someone had painted it battleship gray, but as soon as new painting was needed we had it done in apple green with pilasters and frieze in white. Its doors were of mahogany, elaborately carved. This room, the dining room, the several drawing rooms, the music room, and the halls had tessellated floors of gray and white marble, said to have been brought from Spain as ballast in the sailing ships that were to return with cargoes of gold from Mexico.

The main section of La Fortaleza was built around a central patio. On the second floor were bedrooms, most of them without windows. Instead, they opened on galleries running around three sides of the patio which kept the heat of the sun at bay and caught every breeze. At one end of the palace was a large walled garden with tropical trees and shrubs. In front of it all ran the ancient sea wall, some thirty feet wide. The whole effect was beautiful and romantic, but the inside of the house was disappointing, as the furniture and decorations were meager. We sent home for everything we owned in the way of paintings, embroideries, brocades, and banners and soon turned it into a place of enchantment. The padre of an old church was dissatisfied with a pair of eighteenth-century crystal chandeliers he had, saying they did not give enough light, and offered them to me if I would replace them with electric fixtures, which I was glad to do. The chandeliers looked so well in the large drawing room and hall that I presented them to La Fortaleza when we left.

In the New York *Times Magazine* of March 22, 1931, Dr. Ernest Gruening, editor of the Portland (Maine) *Evening News* and *The Nation,* later Governor of Alaska and now Senator, had this to say:

> For four centuries as a colony of the Spanish crown, Porto Ricans suffered the neglect and exploitations of Spanish colonial rule—or misrule. They accepted the Stars and Stripes in gay '98 with a shout of joy. Somehow their high hopes seem to have been persistently disappointed . . . A miscellany of governors, some indifferent, others worse, succeeded one another . . . political hacks or lame ducks.

Perhaps this may have been a reason why unemployment, malnutrition, poverty, and disease had prevailed on the island, conditions greatly aggravated by the disastrous hurricane which had swept over it the year before we came. Factories, schools, even whole villages were wrecked, fruit trees uprooted, coffee and sugar crops destroyed, causing misery the extent of which people at home were unaware.

When we first arrived a delegation of country folk called on Ted and begged him not to spend all his time in La Fortaleza or, if he visited other towns, not to see only politicians and prominent citizens as other governors had done. They urged him to go out in the island and meet the people, even the *jíbaros* in the mountains, descendants of Spanish settlers who had never mixed with the aboriginal Indians or the imported Negroes and usually had light hair and blue eyes. They told him the country was superb, as indeed it was. One town, Aibonito, was said to have been given its name when the first Spaniards riding over the mountains came to a lovely valley and exclaimed, *"Ai, bonito* [oh, beautiful]!" Ted assured them that this was indeed his intention and shortly afterward started making inspection trips, visiting the seventy-odd towns, some of which had never seen a governor, and riding on horseback into the mountains where no Governor had ever been.

The people were responsive, innately courteous and hospitable. They welcomed him into their poor little houses and often tried to give him presents which to them were treasures, a couple of eggs or some oranges. They took him to their hearts and nick-named him "*el Jíbaro de La Fortaleza.*" By meeting them every-where he learned their problems at first hand, delighting them by his stumbling Spanish, which grew more fluent every day and which he used invariably except when talking to school children, whom he said must learn English.

Every night before going to bed he would memorize twenty words from the dictionary amd make a point of using them in conversation the next day so that he would remember them. Oc-casionally he used the wrong word, giving a rather different meaning from what he had intended. I went with him on several of these inspections but got so tired that I stayed home, concen-trating on hospitals, schools, and Red Cross work nearer at hand. Once when someone in the crowd asked for me Ted wished to explain my weariness. What he said was, "I brought her on other trips but she got so tiresome I left her behind today." At a large P.T.A. meeting he wanted to show off his firsthand knowledge of children, having four of his own, and made two fairly hilarious errors. First he tried to introduce Brigadier General Francis LeJ. Parker, head of the Bureau of Insular Affairs in the War Depart-ment, as "nothing but a bachelor, poor man," but by mistake called him a tapeworm (*solitaria* instead of *soltero*). Then he announced that he himself personally had given birth to four chil-dren. The audience, charmed by his speaking Spanish at all, gave no sign of amusement. It was Don Luis Sánchez Morales, Presi-dent of the Puerto Rican Senate, who pointed it out to him later with chuckles of joy, going on to remark, "But, Governor, it merely goes to show that in the tropics all things are possible!"

Few people in the continental United States, a phrase peculiar to the island, knew anything at all about Porto Rico, as it was then called. In sharp contrast to our neighbors in South America who were watching with keen eyes, many didn't even know where it was. Ted was continually getting letters from educated people addressed to "Porto Rico, Philippine Islands," "Porto Rico, Cuba," or "Porto Rico, Central America." He had a few addressed to "Ambassador Roosevelt, American Embassy, Porto Rico." Even if people knew the geographical position of the island they knew nothing about its million and a half inhabitants, American citizens since 1917. We had many requests for "Porto Rican stamps," of course no different from those in the United States.

Once a party of people we knew arrived on a yacht and came to dinner. The owner of the yacht sat next to Miss Hensey and asked her if there was a president of Porto Rico. Exasperated, she replied, "Why, yes. Didn't you know?" "What's his name?" "President Herbert Hoover!"

Ted took six weeks to make a thorough survey of conditions on the island and decided the first thing to do was to bring Puerto Rico to the attention of people at home and ask temporary help for its distress. He began by writing an article for the New York *Herald Tribune Sunday Magazine,* describing the situation as he had seen it. He said in part:

> I have stopped at farm after farm where lean, underfed women and sickly men repeated again and again the same story—too little food and no opportunity to get more. . . . Sixty-seven per cent of the children are undernourished. Many are slowly starving. On the roads time and again I have seen little groups carrying tiny, homemade coffins . . . One public school in San Juan, the capital city, has an enrollment of 710 boys and girls. Of these 223 come to school without breakfast. 278 have no lunch. We are able to provide in the school lunchroom food for just fifty-four. The rest go hungry.
>
> Our island will turn the corner in the near future. We look forward to greater prosperity for our people. But that is in the future, not the present. It will come too late to save the lives of many of our children, too late to prevent disease from permanently damaging those who will live.

The effect of this article was a storm of incredulous protest at home. Starving children under the American flag? Impossible! What Ted said was widely quoted and provoked much editorial comment. At that time Puerto Rico was under the Bureau of Insular Affairs in the War Department. The Bureau promptly cabled Ted asking that he stop all further publicity until a survey of conditions could be made. Ted wanted immediate help to feed the children. If he had stopped he would have lost the public interest, besides giving the impression he had overstated the case, which was not true. The Bureau naturally wanted no publicity because it amounted to a reflection on them that such conditions existed while they paid no attention. He replied to their cable as politely as possible, saying he had checked and rechecked his facts and did not think it advisable to stop publicity.

Things then began to move. At the request of President Hoover a commission from the American Child Health Association was sent to study the situation. They reported that matters were fully as bad as Ted had said. In addition to the appropriation made the year before for hurricane relief, which had been spent probably not too wisely, Congress provided, again at Mr. Hoover's request, two million dollars for loans to farmers and a million for road construction and repair, the basis of all rehabilitation. The latter sum served a triple purpose. It released money which otherwise must have been spent on roads and now could be used for health, sanitation, and food. It provided work for hundreds of unemployed whose families were on the edge of starvation. It was of direct permanent benefit to the financial status of Puerto Rico because the roads could be asphalt. About half the island's roads were macadam. A kilometer of macadam cost eight hundred dollars a year to maintain, while a kilometer of asphalt cost but three hundred dollars. With this appropriation almost all the roads were either built or repaved with asphalt, constituting a permanent saving in road maintenance of over $350,000 annually.

In his report to the Puerto Rican Legislature, Ted said:

> I hope and trust that, due to the work we are doing and the direct result of the savings which will ensue through these two appropriations, we will be in a position in the early future where we can carry our own burden. . . . Furthermore, the time when Porto Rico will be able to assume her proportioned responsibility in the Nation will be immeasurably accelerated by aid at just this moment.

Still our problems were not solved, for there were insufficient funds to make an adequate fight against hookworm, tuberculosis, malaria, and other diseases which were debilitating the people and depriving them of the will and the ability to work. The American Child Health Association in its report suggested that these matters be undertaken by several of the big American philanthropic organizations. Accordingly a number of them united to form the Porto Rico Child Health Committee, which announced its intention of raising $7,300,000 and worked out a five-year program dealing with health, feeding, and their kindred problems. At the end of five years this program, plus the work of the insular government, was expected to place Puerto Rico in a position to combat these evils herself.

Meanwhile the Golden Rule Foundation was campaigning to raise $50,000 for immediate use in the school lunchrooms and to establish milk stations for babies, while Ted and I were sending appeals to everyone we could think of at home. All these efforts were made doubly difficult by the 1929 crash in Wall Street and the financial panic a few weeks after we arrived in San Juan.

Puerto Rico was primarily an agricultural country, but the main diet of the people consisted of salt codfish, rice, and beans, all three imported. The principal money crops—sugar, coffee, and citrus fruits—were best suited to the large farms. Ted believed that a special effort should be made on the smaller ones to encourage truck gardening. With the advantages given by the tariff, there was no reason why Puerto Rico should not furnish the major part of the $12,000,000 worth of fresh vegetables shipped annually from the tropics to the United States markets, besides providing a food staple for the Puerto Ricans themselves. In 1928–29 Puerto Rico had shipped 368,163 pounds of vegetables to the United States. In the following year, after Ted took over, she shipped 1,678,450. It was the beginning of a new industry with far-reaching possibilities, developed by the Bureau of Commerce and Industry, of which more later. He prevailed on some of the large sugar companies to allot small plots of ground to their laborers on which to grow vegetables for their families, but he found there was an educational problem involved in this. Some of the farmers had to be persuaded to raise food for their families instead of

233

sugar cane, which they would have had to sell at a disadvantage in competition with the big companies while their children went hungry. On December 10, 1929, Ted wrote his mother:

Last week I went out visiting little farms. It was very interesting, but only increased my grasp of the difficulties of our problem. It consists in not simply changing the condition of the people, but in addition changing their attitude of mind in such fashion that they may take advantage of new opportunities. Indeed, it is the old story—we have to protect the poor not only from the oppression of the rich, but also from the equally disastrous foolishness they are guilty of themselves.

In the Boston *Evening Transcript* of June 24, 1931, Daniel Rochford, who had made a study of conditions in Puerto Rico, wrote:

Already such attention has been attracted in other tropic and semi-tropic countries by the work in eradication of tropical diseases, ignorance and unproductive agricultural methods that several Latin republics have asked for the loan of Porto Rican leaders in these fields of betterment.

Roosevelt does not claim to have started all these things. He claims nothing. But until he arrived the plans which are now raising the whole standard of life in Porto Rico were not in operation. It took his fire and enthusiasm and his leadership to get the forces in motion.

The question of education was important and difficult. The tendency had been to educate everybody for white-collar jobs, comparatively few of which existed, while there was a great shortage of carpenters, mechanics, and such. Ted started a special type of rural vocational school which taught reading, writing, arithmetic, and English, then gave the children practical grounding in elementary agriculture, modern sanitation, and vocational training.

These rural schools were built on farms of from five to fifteen acres, which were cultivated by the boys under the direction of an experienced farmer. Crops profitable in the surrounding country were raised. One third of the proceeds went to the boys themselves. The remaining two thirds were either used in the school lunchrooms or were sold for school funds. The classes in manual

training made, as Ted said, "no articles of ornate uselessness."
They made chairs, tables, beds, washboards, and other things of
practical value. In the new schools Ted established in 1931 eighty
per cent of the furniture was made by the children, also the out-
buildings for cattle. At one school a comfortable house was built
and its furniture made by the boys at a cost of $250 for materials.

Classes were held for the boys in cobbling, barbering, and a
number of similar trades. Cobbling was desirable, as the best defense against hookworm is a pair of shoes. Barbering enabled them
to make a little money after school hours.

The girls were taught home economics adapted to the conditions in which they lived. They cooked on charcoal stoves like
those in their own homes, prepared and served the meals in the
school lunchrooms, and made their own clothes. They were taught
embroidery, an economic asset.

Social workers, trained at a summer course at the university,
were provided for the rural schools. They not only cared for the
children but made the children's homes their responsibility, advising the parents on sanitation and diet.

Ted appointed a board of members of his Executive Council—
the Commissioners of Education, Agriculture, Health, and Labor
—to organize a system of lectures to be held at the schools in the
evenings for the purpose of spreading practical knowledge in
health, sanitation, agriculture, and industry in general. These lectures, primarily for adults, were carefully supervised and were
put into such form as to be easily understood. The talks on medicine, for instance, were not delivered with Latin names and technical terms but were in colloquial Spanish with illustrations from
everyday life.

Following this line, the schools were used as social centers whenever possible, with programs of music, dances, little fiestas, and
exhibitions of the children's handiwork, often providing the only
means of social contact for the *jíbaros* in the mountains.

When Ted and I received donations from our friends at home,
I kept out what was sent to me to use for something I could super-
vise myself instead of turning it into the general welfare fund.
With part of the money I bought ten cows and eighty goats with
their feed for some of the poorer rural schools, so that the children

could learn to care for the animals and have the milk to drink. It was fun to see how they cherished their "pets" and how they visibly gained weight.

An editorial in the Baltimore *Sun* in January 1930 refers to an article by Muñoz Marín, who today is Governor of the Commonwealth of Puerto Rico:

> In the *Sun* this morning Luis Muñoz Marín reported at some length on the doings of young Theodore Roosevelt in Porto Rico. When the school children at the command of the superintendent of schools each got a small American flag to wave as the American Governor passed by, Roosevelt advised them to spend their pennies on breakfast, not on flags. When he heard that efforts were being made to displace the visits of the Three Kings on January 6 with visits of Santa Claus on December 25, he promptly opposed the change and declared January 6 a public holiday. He made speeches in which he hardly mentioned Americanization at all, but urged the Porto Ricans to cherish the glories of their Hispanic traditions. He even went the length of learning Spanish and speaking it.

On Three Kings' Day, Puerto Rican children had been accustomed, for hundreds of years, to put out water and little baskets of hay for the camels of the Kings who came bearing gifts. They loved to do it, just as our children love to hang up their stockings, and there was no earthly reason to try to make them change. It merely was another small cause of friction. At the beginning of January 1930 the insular treasury was empty. Until taxes came in later in the month, no funds existed to pay government employees. This meant a sad Three Kings' Day for hundreds of people. Ted personally endorsed a note for two hundred thousand dollars so that they could be paid and buy presents for the day.

What he called his undue popularity worried him. He was afraid the people thought he could cure all their troubles overnight and was apprehensive of a bad reaction when they found this impossible. He kept telling them they must be prepared to work hard for many years to achieve noticeable improvement.

The need was so great and the money so scarce that we often longed for a government lottery, but there was no hope of that.

236

Puerto Rico was not yet a commonwealth, and Congress never would have authorized it. As it was, more than three million dollars a year, money that the people could ill afford, went out of the island to be lost in the lotteries of Spain and Santo Domingo. This sum would have made all the difference in what we were trying to do.

Realizing that Puerto Rico could not support itself on agriculture alone and that industrialization was essential, Ted removed the small Bureau of Labor from the Department of Agriculture and for the first time set up a Department of Labor with a commissioner in his Executive Council. He established the Bureau of Commerce and Industry, which was remarkably successful even though it had to be started without funds. For the first six months it operated with borrowed personnel and cost the insular government nothing. Headed by Major Cary I. Crockett, who had come to Puerto Rico to be Ted's aide, it brought more than a score of new industries to the island, besides finding and developing new markets for local products. By co-ordinating and developing local fisheries, by working with manufacturers, by organizing co-operatives, and by annulling undue restrictions, the Bureau achieved a substantial drop in the prices of fish, milk, meat, and bread. It was largely because of its work that Puerto Rico actually increased its favorable trade balance in the face of world-wide economic depression.

Tourists were a potential source of revenue, but only thirteen cruise ships had visited Puerto Rico in 1929. Because of Major Crockett's efforts more than thirty came in 1930. To help entertain the tourists so that they would make favorable comments at home and urge others to come, we invited each group to a reception at La Fortaleza. Sometimes we had as many as four hundred and fifty at a time. Ted would take time out to greet them, and Signorina and I would show them over the palace and the garden, describing in detail the charms of the island.

Major Crockett told me that, while needlework had once been second only to sugar among Puerto Rican products, very little was being sold now. He wondered if I could do something about it. It was indeed at a low ebb. The women had been so exploited and underpaid that the work was coarse and badly done on poor materials. It had a bad name. No first-class store in New York would admit that any lingerie or table linens on its counters was from Puerto Rico. Instead, the work was usually marked "Imported" and sold for the low prices it deserved. It was done piecemeal over the island, usually by farmers' wives in their spare time who were lucky if they got a few cents a day. Surrounded by misery on all sides, I felt the urgent necessity of trying to help. This feeling was shared by all of us to such an extent that when my son Teddy, aged sixteen, was given a present of a hundred dollars by his great-aunt when he was confirmed at Groton, he sent fifty to the milk-stations fund in Puerto Rico.

Ted said the government couldn't spare a penny for me to work with, but that I could have the old Manicomio or lunatic asylum for a workroom rent-free because nobody else needed it. This was a vast loft in an ancient building where convicts, the sick, and the insane were herded together in Spanish times. At first Signorina and I ran the workroom, paying twenty women a dollar a day each, riches in those days to people whose family income was between a hundred and fifty to two hundred dollars a year. We borrowed money for the wages, while I paid for all the materials—fine linen, organdy, and crepe de Chine. In the beginning our friends from New York were my prey, especially those arriving in yachts, whom I practically forced to buy their Christmas presents and to replenish their linen closets. It wasn't long before we had a hundred women, who made the finer articles and the models to be copied out on the island. A young Puerto Rican girl was put in charge of the workroom under Signorina's direction. She is now famous as Doña Felisa Rincon de Gautier, mayor of the city of San Juan.

Miss Mildred Hayes came to us from St. Andrew's Mission by permission of the Episcopal bishop and took charge of the whole project. No one was ever more delightful to work with. She traveled around the island in a Ford donated by a friend of mine, supervising the work, establishing embroidery centers in towns and villages, finding skilled workers, and keeping all accounts. I made frequent trips to New York, of course at my own expense, carrying suitcases full of samples of our work to show to heads of department stores. Most of the buyers were nice to me, especially those at B. Altman's, who encouraged us from the start.

When we began getting big orders our problem was to have them well done and finished on time. The stores always wanted them in a hurry. To our workers time meant nothing. Often things would be ready a couple of hours too late to catch the steamer. This meant a week's delay and drove us frantic. None of us knew the first thing about wholesale merchandising and naturally we made mistakes, but when we were discouraged and depressed Ted would remind us that we were feeding probably five hundred people, and we would take heart and go on.

Even my mother in New York had to work. In almost every letter I wrote her I would ask her to go to various stores to straighten out complicated situations, or to see if they had received our samples and if they liked them, or to find out if they had sent the special materials promised, or how soon they expected to pay what they owed us. Mother was a tremendous help because the mails were slow and irregular. She finally complained that I wrote about nothing but needlework. In one letter I told her I had been obliged to call in an expert to tell me how many yards of linen of what width were needed to cut out twenty dozen pillow cases of six different sizes. She was most sympathetic about our elaborately initialed chiffon handkerchiefs. Saks Fifth Avenue had given us a trial order of sixteen, all different and all in "original designs." It was as if they had said, "Let there be light." Well, there was light, for I had to sit down on a desperately busy day and draw them myself, knowing as much about it as I did about making a watch. Mother said if Saks didn't like them she would make her friends buy them for Christmas presents. Fortunately Saks did.

Several months after we started and while I was in New York the Manicomio caught fire. Considerable damage was done. Signorina and Major Crockett saw the smoke from La Fortaleza and rushed to the scene. The Major disappeared into the burning building, from which the women had fled, and succeeded in rescuing all our fabrics and our account books. Fortunately we were able to move back into the workroom in a few days.

For the sake of advertising our work I designed and had made a picture in the beautiful and unique *litografía*, on fine white organdy embroidered with number 300 cotton thread. Originally this work was done by Puerto Rican girls, who made monograms on handkerchiefs for their sweethearts, using their own black hair. It looked exactly like an etching and could be done by only a few skilled workers. The picture was about ten by twelve inches and showed the rocks and palm trees of a little harbor with Columbus's three ships coming in. We sent it to the Colonial Exposition in Paris, and to our delight it won the coveted Grand Prix for embroidery.

I couldn't bear to take any money out of our meager till to pay myself back for all the materials I had bought and so had a number of sheets and pillowcases embroidered and marked with Gracie's initials, to be given to her when she married. This gradually reduced the debt to some extent. The 1929 depression hit us hard, but in spite of it the needlework project was a success. At the end of the fiscal year 1930–31 we had an accounting made by the government auditor. We had been operating for ten months and had done $13,805 worth of business. Of this, $8,770 had gone for labor. We had orders for months ahead. We had started with $5,000 of borrowed money and had paid it all back except $1,500 which was owed to me (and still is!). By the time Ted and I left Puerto Rico we felt that several things had been accomplished. The standard of needlework had been given a push upward. An organization with several branches and many trained workers was ready to be taken over by commercial firms. The Trade Commissioner from Manila stated in his report that during the last year the sale of Puerto Rican embroidery had increased so much that it was competing seriously with that of the Philippine Islands. Best of all, first-class stores in New York were now carrying and advertising "Exquisite Porto Rican Embroidery," and many people had been given a means of making their living.

Chapter 26

My brother knows it is not easy to be a chief.
KIPLING

A former mayor of San Juan, under whose administration the city had for years run an increasing deficit until it was unable to sell its securities on the open market, was put out of office by a bill, sponsored by Ted and passed by the Legislature, placing the city under a commission government. In October 1931 this man accused Ted of using government money for his family expenses. Ted's denial was published with this attack. An editorial comment follows:

> The statement of a disgruntled former mayor of San Juan that Governor Roosevelt has been using the official funds of the island for personal and family use hardly seems worthy of denial; but the charges have been the means of revealing the fact that, far from benefiting financially from his post, it has been just the reverse. All four trips he has made to the United States on behalf of Porto Rico have been at his own expense. The one check he accepted for expenses he promptly turned over to the workshop for poor people run by the Government. He has used a Ford at the Government House bought from his own money, and most of the entertaining has been from his private purse. To sum up, he has spent for offi-

cial work or contributed to philanthropic endeavor more annually than his salary.

This is not at all surprising. It is exactly what might have been expected from a Roosevelt. Incidentally it is a reminder that a considerable number of our public men accept public position at a personal and pecuniary sacrifice. . . . In view of incidents like these the Roosevelt incident is a matter of satisfaction rather than regret. It serves as an opportunity of letting people know that there is more unselfishness in public life than many are willing to admit.

The salary of the Governor of Puerto Rico was ten thousand dollars a year, and the fund for maintaining La Fortaleza for wages and for entertaining was another ten thousand dollars. Almost three quarters of this fund had already been spent in the first three months of the fiscal year before we got there, and when the rest of the money was gone we had to pay for everything out of our own pocket until the fiscal year ended. It was indeed fortunate that we had the income from the money Ted had made, for while we were there we spent all his salary on welfare or on matters that should properly and legally have been charged to the government.

La Fortaleza needed painting. My mother-in-law, who had stayed there with my father-in-law on a visit to Puerto Rico when he was President, told me we were going to live in a pink Spanish palace. When we arrived I was disappointed to find it battleship gray, and peeling at that. I took a knife and dug through several layers of old paint until I came to the pink of twenty-five years before, a soft color so appropriate to a tropic town. This we matched, and the effect was lovely. Enough money was left in the fund for this, but none for less important work inside, such as scraping chocolate-brown varnish from the beautiful solid-mahogany doors and the staircase. We had this done a little at a time by convicts.

Considerable entertaining had to be done; first because Ted used lunch time as working time and was always inviting small groups of legislators and others with whom he wanted to discuss problems of government, and second because the Puerto Ricans liked to be entertained and loved a good party. We had dinners for ten to twenty guests every week. We gave several balls which were most successful, with one orchestra on the main floor and another in a dancing pavilion on the sea wall. Usually over a thousand people came. No caterer existed on the island, and all refreshments had to be prepared in the house. Fortunately for our bank account this was during prohibition, so no one expected anything but soft drinks.

Housekeeping at La Fortaleza was at first rather a problem. The domestic staff consisted of two cooks, four houseboys, a maid, and two laundresses. These were supplemented by eighteen convicts who were marched over from the prison every morning and did the heavy work—washing the cars, scrubbing the floors, and working in the garden. Two of them were permanent fixtures in the kitchen. I remarked to Mr. Beverley, the Attorney General, that they seemed such nice men and asked what sort of crimes they had committed. He replied, "Mostly involuntary homicide." When I wanted to know just what that meant, he said, "Oh, they say their hands slipped!" Only those with long sentences were selected, as it would not have been worth while to train anyone soon to be released.

Incidentally, Puerto Rico had under construction a new penitentiary unrivaled in magnificence. Its elaborate mosaic doors imported from Spain were said to have cost twenty thousand dollars. The running water in each commodious cell was something quite new to the convicts who were finishing the work on the building. Once some of them walked off the job, went on a spree, and got drunk. When they returned in the early hours of the morning the warden, with the wisdom of Solomon, refused to let them in. The loss of face was adequate punishment.

When I began looking into various other household matters I found much waste. Two limousines and two chauffeurs were provided. Ted immediately got rid of one of them, substituting our own model-A Ford driven by a policeman, one of the guards assigned to La Fortaleza. Ice furnished by the government was costing about $115 a month because the two large iceboxes were so old they were practically falling apart and needed ice continually. As free current was supplied by the city, we put in a big electric refrigerator which paid for itself in less than six months. Most provisions were being bought at the most expensive shop in town, which carried only imported goods. I put a stop to that and saved a good deal by dealing at the Army Commissary. Bills for nuts and olives alone averaged a dollar a day. We had no more nuts and olives. All these matters required careful watching. Because of other duties I had no time to do this myself, so when Signorina came down with Quentin I put her in complete charge of the household. We of course paid her salary. She did not only this but a hundred other tasks as well, besides acting as my secretary and aide.

Moonlight picnics were a favorite form of entertainment for our friends from the north. We used to go to El Morro, the old fort, and sit on a wide ledge high over the sea. Food would be brought in big thermos jars by a couple of the houseboys. I would hire a little orchestra to sing and play *música brava* with native instruments, which always charmed everybody.

Once we had a very special house guest, Mr. José Camprubi, editor of a newspaper in New York. Not only were we pleased to entertain him as a friend, but we hoped for his approval of what Ted was doing in Puerto Rico. We wanted him to have a pleasant time during his visit and planned a particularly nice picnic for him, inviting a number of our Puerto Rican friends to meet him. Everyone was to come to La Fortaleza at eight o'clock and then drive with us to El Morro, where we would have supper. Signorina was as usual very busy about the preparations. About half-past seven Mr. Camprubi came out of his room all ready to start. Signorina told him we would not be leaving for another half hour, and he said he would return to his room and finish a letter he was writing. When eight o'clock came, fifteen or sixteen people had gathered and we set out. The moon had not yet risen. We found our way through the old fort with flashlights and settled ourselves with cushions on the ledge. We had supper, listened to the music, talked to one another, and were having a pleasant evening when suddenly Ted came over to where I was sitting and asked where Mr. Camprubi was. We hastily looked around, as did Signorina, Miss Hensey, Major Crockett, and Lieutenant Antonio Segarra, Ted's junior aide. No one had seen him, each thinking he was with one of the others. The dreadful fact dawned on us. We had left the guest of honor at home! The picnic came to an abrupt end. We hurried back to La Fortaleza, where we found him, supperless. I told Ted we should approach him on our knees, carrying a flag of truce. There was nothing to do but tell the truth. Mr. Camprubi was sympathetic and understanding, and I think he really felt sorry for us because we had made such an appalling gaffe.

One day when Ted was off on an inspection trip, Signorina, Miss Hensey, Lieutenant Segarra, and I were finishing lunch when I heard talking in the entrance hall. With a pang I suddenly realized I had asked two women to lunch that day and had forgotten all about it. I hated myself for being such a fool and had to think fast to find a way out. Fortunately La Fortaleza had several staircases. While Signorina ran to tell the cook, I was able to get out of the dining room without being seen, come down the main stairs, and greet my guests as if nothing unusual had happened. It wasn't so easy to eat another lunch from grapefruit to coffee, but it had to be done.

Quentin, just ten years old, was the only one of our children who was in Puerto Rico for any length of time. At first we thought of putting him in an American day school in San Juan but realized he would be with American boys and would not have the best opportunity to learn Spanish. Besides, I found he was making friends with the convicts working at La Fortaleza. As this was not precisely the circle we would have chosen for him, we sent him to San Augustine at Río Piedras, a military boarding school with American teachers and Puerto Rican boys. He stayed there during the week and came home for Saturdays and Sundays. After a few months he spoke Spanish exactly like a Puerto Rican, with characteristic gestures. He had a keen interest in butterflies and already had a good collection of specimens from New York and Vermont, all well mounted and labeled with their scientific names. Puerto Rico was a new field for him. He left his net and equipment with Jiménez, one of the prisoners, to catch butterflies in the garden for him to mount over the weekends. This plan worked nicely until Jiménez was caught practicing usury and extortion and was no longer allowed the privilege of coming to La Fortaleza.

Gracie stayed with my mother in New York while she took a business course and made her debut. Occasionally she came down, bringing friends. Teddy and Cornelius were at Groton and came to Puerto Rico in the summer. They went fishing and made field trips with a naturalist friend of ours. He and Cornelius found a new subspecies of lizard on the island of Caja de Muertos off the south coast. They named it for me, *Ameiva wetmorei eleanorae.* Someone discovered a new fly and named it for Ted "because it was a good fly, it did not harm citrus fruit, and it had beautiful eyes!"

In March 1931 President Hoover came to Puerto Rico for three days. No other President had ever been there except Ted's father, and the entire island seethed with excitement. A couple of days before his arrival Colonel Edmund W. Starling of the Secret Service came down to make arrangements for the President's safety. He and I went over every inch of La Fortaleza, and he said he had never seen such a difficult house to guard. I planned to put the President in the largest bedroom, Ted's and mine, for the night he would be in San Juan. It had five swinging half doors. At first Colonel Starling said it would be impossible, but after examining all the other rooms he said they were equally bad, and the President might as well have it. He ordered a sentry at each door. Later he was horrified when he found me arranging chairs for the sentries and said of course they had to stand up all night.

We had only a few days to prepare for the President's arrival on the U.S.S. *Arizona.* He was bringing forty people in his party, including two members of his Cabinet, his military and naval aides, his secretary, newspapermen, newsreel men with sound equipment, and others. They arrived early in the morning at Ponce on the south coast, where Ted met them. He had arranged for a motorcade by borrowing open demonstration cars from General Motors to give the people a chance to see the party on its way across the island to San Juan and back by another route. He had large numbers on the cars and planned just who would go in each. They paused briefly in the principal towns while Ted introduced the President in Spanish, and drove slowly wherever school children were lined up. The President received ovations all along the way, both driving over and back.

Staying with us at La Fortaleza besides the President were Secretary of War Patrick J. Hurley; Secretary of the Interior Ray Lyman Wilbur; the President's military aide, Colonel (later Major General) Campbell B. Hodges; naval aide Captain (later Rear Admiral) C. Russell Train; White House physician Captain (later Vice-Admiral) Joel T. Boone (MC); and the President's secretary, Lawrence Richey. There were also two newspapermen, old friends of ours, Mark Sullivan, and Richard V. Oulahan of the New York *Times*. Quarters for the rest had been arranged by Ted in hotels and private houses.

After lunch I tried to persuade the President to take a siesta, but he refused. We sat around talking until four o'clock, when he had appointments to meet political, business, and labor leaders, also those interested in welfare.

The dinner of twenty-four that night was stag, as Mrs. Hoover had not come, and was followed by a reception for over two thousand people. Our two cooks were elderly women, incapable of such preparations without the two prisoners who always helped in the kitchen. When Colonel Starling asked me if the domestic staff was reliable I never mentioned these and held my breath and crossed my fingers until all was over. I had engaged a small orchestra to play *música brava* during dinner, but Colonel Starling had them sit so far away from the dining room that no one could hear them.

The reception for the officials began at nine o'clock, the public reception at half-past. In order to avoid overcrowding and traffic jams I arranged for everyone to go through the palace and out on the sea wall, where refreshments were served. Afterward they were discouraged from going back into the house. We had many local policemen on duty who were so tactful that people did not realize they were being managed.

It was interesting to see how Colonel Starling worked. We had always received opposite the head of the stairs, with the line of guests coming to us from the right. He said it was far less tiring to have the line come from the left. He was quite right. My arm and shoulder ached much less than before as we shook hands and gently moved people along from that side. He stood behind the guests, scrutinizing everyone. One man had his hand in his pocket. Colonel Starling asked him courteously to take it out. He asked another man to get rid of a lighted cigarette, telling me later this was as much a question of good manners as of security.

We shook hands without stopping until eleven o'clock, when the President went up to bed. At half-past eleven I had the band play "Home, Sweet Home," and the party gradually ended.

Next morning I let the men have breakfast by themselves and joined them in time to go to the Capitol, where the President spoke from the steps to an immense crowd. Ted made an introductory speech in Spanish without notes. The President made an excellent short talk translated by Carlos Chardon, chancellor of the university. As Richard Oulahan reported to the New York *Times:*

> The crowd became very enthusiastic when it heard the Spanish version of the President's complimentary references to Gov. Roosevelt. So prolonged was this demonstration that the Governor, sitting by Mrs. Roosevelt, was obliged to rise and bow his acknowledgments.

Which was just as it should have been.

From the Capitol we went to El Morro to show the President one of the most interesting landmarks of San Juan. Again the streets were jammed with delighted and enthusiastic people. After lunch at La Fortaleza the presidential party left for Ponce, to continue their tour on the *Arizona.*

Everything, thank goodness, had gone smoothly and everything had been on time from start to finish. One thing I was sure they enjoyed was orange juice. I knew Mr. Hoover loved it, and I had a big thermos of it in each bedroom, labeled and kept filled. Every time we came in from anything it would be brought in great pitchers and eagerly consumed. Puerto Rican oranges are among the best in the world.

Mark Ethridge, a Democrat, publisher of the Louisville *Courier-Journal,* who had covered Ted's gubernatorial campaign in 1924 for the New York *Sun* and had been with us on the special train for three weeks, wrote an editorial at this time for the Macon *Telegraph,* saying in part:

President Hoover's visit to Porto Rico has served, in addition to its other purposes, to do justice to an American citizen who has been the victim, in other days, of none too friendly criticism and much too low an estimate. That American is Theodore Roosevelt, governor of Porto Rico.

When young Teddy was defeated for the governorship of New York by Al Smith in 1924, his political career was regarded as finished. He was the victim, during that campaign, of a most vicious editorial fight by the New York *World* and other papers supporting Smith. . . .

His "crushing" defeat at the hands of Al Smith has often been referred to. The defeat was nothing of the sort. In spite of fighting the immense prestige of Smith, who was even then destined to be the Democratic nominee for the presidency, Roosevelt was defeated by only a little more than 100,000 votes. That is no majority in New York state . . . When he was defeated, however, the newspapers and politicians consigned Teddy Roosevelt to political oblivion. . . .

One of the finest tributes that has been paid him came from the Baltimore *Evening Sun*, which has ridiculed him in the past. That paper called him "one of the finest, and perhaps the finest colonial governor in our history."

This editorial was written in 1931, before Ted had an equally brilliant administration as Governor General of the Philippines and was the only man ever to govern both territories.

Ted was fortunate in his Executive Council, or cabinet, comprising both Puerto Ricans and continental Americans. Some of the members had been there previously, others he had appointed. All were patriotic citizens and men of ability, infinitely helpful in the work he was trying to do. They co-operated vigorously in his reforms, in tax collecting, and in paring down the insular budget. In this Ted was aided by a law giving the Governor power to blue-pencil any specific item in the budget without vetoing the entire measure. By this he achieved greatly reduced government spending. At the end of the fiscal year, in July 1931, Puerto Rico had realized good beginnings not only in the improvements I have described but in many others too numerous to mention, including such matters as sixteen new medical centers directly supervising the health of some eight hundred thousand people previously without medical aid. Taking all this into consideration, it was quite a triumph when Ted was able to announce that for the first time in seventeen years Puerto Rico's budget was balanced.

We always felt, Ted and I, that our life was a series of crises. This was doubly true in Puerto Rico, where we seemed to have one nearly every day. The last and worst was in November 1931. We had come north because Ted was to see the President. While we were in Washington, Ted received a cable from San Juan saying that a sudden and unexpected financial panic was starting in Puerto Rico. He left at once by air. When he arrived he found that one of the principal local banks had closed and another was in such shape that without additional funds it would be forced to close the following day. Every bank on the island was having a run. People were suffering from the same nervousness which had been evident several times that year in the United States. They were taking their money out of banks and putting it in strongboxes, stockings, holes in the ground, anywhere. The situation was critical. Ted instructed the Insular Treasurer to deposit $100,000 of government money in the threatened bank, and to secure this loan Ted handed him his personal note for that amount, about a quarter of his personal fortune. He then went on the radio telling what he had done and urging the people to have confidence. This turned the tide and is, I believe, an incident unprecedented in colonial government.

Because of kinship of common language, what was done here had, and still has, an important bearing on the attitudes of every Spanish-speaking country in the Americas toward the United States. Many of Ted's speeches were carried by newspapers such as *La Prensa* in Buenos Aires, and a keen interest was shown in what he was doing. *El Mundo*, principal paper in San Juan, had fully as large a circulation in South America as it had in Puerto Rico.

One of Ted's firmest convictions was that our relations with the countries of South and Central America were of the most vital importance and should not continue to be neglected. Sporadic efforts toward a "Good Neighbor" policy were not enough. He felt we must acquire knowledge of the people and their problems at all levels, while enlightening them as to the character and aims of the United States before a firm basis of understanding and friendship could ever be established. He saw the importance of Puerto Rico in this connection, not only for its own sake but as a link in the chain.

This idea attracted little attention at the time, but if it had been followed and developed it could have prevented a great deal of unnecessary future trouble for the United States.

Walter Lippmann, in his introduction to Ted's book, *Colonial Policies of the United States*, published in 1937, said:

> I became interested in his conception of Puerto Rico as a self-governing dominion of the future, Latin in its culture, North American in its political sympathies, which would be a meeting place for those who speak English and those who speak Spanish in this hemisphere.

When on July 25, 1952, the Commonwealth of Puerto Rico became the first autonomous dominion of the United States, Ted's foresight was justified and his original concept came true.

Chapter 27

I should like to spend the rest of my life in traveling abroad, if I could anywhere borrow another life to spend at home.

WILLIAM HAZLITT

In January 1932, President Hoover appointed Ted Governor General of the Philippines. As no air travel existed across the Pacific in those days, we crossed the continent by the New York Central to Chicago and the Northern Pacific to Seattle, where we took the S.S. *President Taft*. The ship stopped for a day or so at Yokohama, Kobe, Shanghai, and Hong Kong on its way to Manila. The journey took a month. Our party consisted of Ted, Gracie, her friend May Welldon, Signorina, Miss Hensey, Colonel (formerly Major) Crockett, and myself.

We were given quite a send-off at Grand Central Station by many personal and political friends, among them a Boy Scout color guard and several Filipinos, including Senator Sergio Osmeña, who later became President of the Philippine Commonwealth. As the *Herald Tribune* remarked: "These and a corps of newsreel and newspaper photographers were the nucleus of a group which signified to the station crowds that an event was taking place."

Although Ted had been out of the country for four years, crowds met the train and shouted for him to speak at various places all across the continent, sometimes getting him out of bed in the middle of the night.

The weather was cold, dry, and delicious, and the great pine forests we passed were covered with snow. At Victoria, British Columbia, Ted addressed the Canadian Club at a dinner of three hundred given him by the Canadian government officials.

The *President Taft* carried only eight first-class passengers besides ourselves. Japan was invading Manchukuo and fighting the Chinese in Shanghai, quite enough to stop tourist travel. We had as rough a passage as I have ever seen across the Pacific. The captain told me he had never known the barometer to be so low or the sea so high. Waves breaking over the ship cracked the heavy plate glass enclosing the bridge, but we never missed a meal. After one bad moment in the dining saloon when Ted and Gracie crashed to the floor and the captain's dinner and mine slid off the table into his lap and up his sleeves, they lashed all our chairs together.

A wireless message came from W. Cameron Forbes, American Ambassador to Japan and an old friend, asking Ted, Gracie, May, and me to stay with him the two nights we were to be in Tokyo. He said Ted, Gracie, and I were to have an audience with the Emperor and Empress. What was more, we were invited to have lunch with them, a most unusual honor. Mr. Forbes said Ted must wear a frock coat, which naturally he didn't have. The last time he had worn one was at his sister Alice's wedding twenty-six years before. It took several more messages before the Ambassador finally said he had obtained special permission for Ted to wear his cutaway.

Because of the bad weather we were twenty-four hours late in getting to Yokohama, an hour's drive from Tokyo. We reached Mr. Forbes's house at eight in the evening, just as the first guests were arriving for a large dinner party, and we had a great scramble unpacking our evening clothes and dressing. Everyone was interested in our lunching with their Imperial Majesties and said it was the first time such an invitation had been issued to foreigners. I learned afterward that Alice had been to lunch at the Imperial Palace in 1905, twenty-seven years before, but I doubt if any American had been at a meal since then. Someone wanted to know what Gracie and I were going to wear. When I said we had planned on black velvet afternoon dresses we were told this would be discourteous, for black was taboo at the Japanese court. We had left almost all our luggage on the ship at Yokohama, so this put us in a quandary. Colonel Crockett at once volunteered to go and bring us some other clothes, but no man could have picked out dresses, let alone hats and accessories. Finally Gracie, accompanied by two young men, went back to the steamer and fetched what was needed.

Next day while Ted was paying formal calls, Gracie, May, and I had the morning free. We went to the Obi Market, where I bought a lovely obi for Gracie—gold brocade with a pattern of little blue dogs and white ducks. We returned to the Embassy to change our clothes, met Ted and Mr. Forbes, and went to the palace.

First the Ambassador took Ted to be presented to the Emperor; then we all went into Phoenix Hall, where the Empress was standing on a little dais. I had hoped she would be wearing traditional Japanese dress but was told she never received foreign guests that way. Instead she had on a gown of Pompeian red velvet with wide gold lace flounces. The four of us advanced in a line; Gracie and I curtsied while Ted and the Ambassador bowed as we entered. We repeated this halfway down the room and again when we reached the dais. She said a few pleasant words interpreted by a lady-in-waiting, to which Ted replied. We then backed out according to court etiquette and were taken into a vast apartment with elaborate carvings on the walls. The Minister of the Household, Kitokuro Ichiki, said their Imperial Majesties would join us in a moment and we would go in to lunch. I asked him where we should stand and what we should do. He consulted the Grand Chamberlain, Kantaro Suzuki, then told me that, as there was no precedent for this occasion, he was unable to say. Their Royal Highnesses the Crown Prince and Crown Princess Chichibu came in. He was heir apparent to the throne, as so far the Emperor had no son. The Princess had been educated in Washington and spoke flawless English.

When their Majesties entered, the Emperor in uniform, they shook hands with us and led the way into the Homeiden banquet hall. Ted sat by the Empress, I by the Emperor, with the Foreign Minister, who interpreted for us, on my other side. It is practically impossible to carry on a conversation with spontaneity through an interpreter. Besides, I had always been told that when talking with royalty it was not considered good form to introduce new topics, so I merely answered questions, making my replies as long as possible. Things were moving rather slowly when the Minister said unexpectedly, "I shall be glad to interpret anything that you may care to say." Hastily trying to think of something to interest the Emperor, I asked if he had done any big-game shooting. He had not but was much interested in zoology. I described the *Ovis poli* and the giant panda. Ted took up the thread from across the table and told about the Lolos, of which the Emperor had not heard. When Ted said Chinese were discouraged from entering their country and risked being killed on sight, to our dismay everybody roared with laughter.

After a delicious lunch of French cooking we left the dining room. Ted and Mr. Forbes sat down with the Emperor and the other men, Gracie and I with the Empress and Princess Chichibu. A lady-in-waiting remained standing. The Princess whispered to me, "Tell her Majesty any little anecdotes you can think of. She loves funny stories." This gave us a wide range and made things easy, as the Empress was responsive and had a delightful sense of humor. An hour or so later their Majesties rose, told us they had enjoyed seeing us, wished us a pleasant voyage to Manila, and departed.

Dinner that night at the Maple Club was a Japanese meal, complete with geishas. We sat on the floor with our shoes off and ate sukiyaki and other delectable foods, with tiny cups of hot sake. At nine o'clock we went to the station to take the train for Kobe, where Signorina and Miss Hensey were to meet us before we boarded the *President Taft.* The station was jammed, but our police guard of an officer and four soldiers got us through the crowd. Quite a number of people came to see us off, some of them bringing bouquets for Gracie and me. Many of them were friends we had made ten years before at the Conference for Limitation of Armaments, where they had been young secretaries and now held important positions. While we were talking to them on the train platform we saw a detachment of several hundred sailors go through the station on the double, evidently on their way to Shanghai. Everyone scattered out of their way. They were husky and healthy, obviously elated at the prospect of a fight. To us it was rather a sinister sight.

As our train started and we waved from the windows, everyone on the platform bent double in a formal bow.

The train was clean and comfortable, with a good dining car where we had breakfast. At Kobe we were met by the American Consul, Howard Donovan, and his wife, who were friends of ours, and by another police guard. We took our luggage to the steamer, found she would not sail for several hours, then went around in rickshaws, looking at the shops, and bought some amusing wooden toys that came alive when you turned a peg. At noon we sailed for Shanghai.

The captain of the *President Taft* told me he did not know if we would be able to stop at Shanghai and was waiting for orders from his company. Active fighting had been and might still be going on there as well as on the banks of the Whangpoo. The company would certainly want to exchange cargo but would not care to have the ship damaged. The night before we were supposed to land, a radio message was delivered to the captain while we were having dinner. He read it, laughed, and handed it to me. It said: PROCEED SHANGHAI TAKING ALL POSSIBLE PRECAUTIONS. "Does this mean you are to go up the river but if a shell hits the steamer it'll be your fault?" I asked. "Just about," he answered.

We reached the mouth of the Yangtze next morning, where several Japanese destroyers and a British cruiser were anchored. We passed the fort at Woosung and proceeded up the Whangpoo. As we reached the city we saw the Chapei district entirely devastated, with many of the houses on fire. There was little or no river traffic and none of the thousands of sampans I remembered seeing when I was there before. We heard no firing except a few rifleshots in the distance, probably snipers. Luckily for us, this was a day between battles. We passed many warships of different nationalities —American, British, French, Japanese, and Portuguese. On almost all the Japanese ships men were exercising, either drilling or fencing.

It was raining when we reached Shanghai. Nelson Johnson, the American Minister, and his military attaché met us at the dock along with our friends Edwin and Rhoda Cunningham, with whom we were to spend the night. Rhoda said, "There are two teas for you this afternoon, one given by the Mayor of Shanghai, the other

by Lord Li Ching Mai. I know Ted is addressing a large gathering
of Boy Scouts as well. That gives you a couple of hours' leeway.
What would you like to do? Go shopping?" How well she knew!

Because of the drain on our finances in Puerto Rico, we had had
little money to spend preparing to go to the Philippines. Although
we really needed a variety of evening and afternoon dresses for
such an official position, Gracie and I had very few, mostly made
in the house by a seamstress from paper patterns. In Shanghai the
exchange had dropped to over four dollars Mex. for one dollar
gold and bargains were plentiful. Most of the shops were closed
behind iron gratings because of the fighting, but we found Lao
Kai Fook, the famous silk store, open and bought yards of material
there. We were overjoyed when Rhoda told us that Eleanora Gar-
nett was having a sale of evening frocks at unbelievably low prices.
A wonderful Esthonian dressmaker whose models came from Paris
over the Trans-Siberian Railroad, today she has establishments in
Rome and New York where she sells Italian-made gowns of the
most lofty *haute couture*. When we went to her and found lovely
dresses for ten American dollars, Gracie, Signorina, Miss Hensey,
and I practically cleared out the shop.

About twenty people were at dinner at the Cunninghams' that
night. As soon as we left the table Ted and Colonel Crockett went
off to visit the front lines with Colonel Gasser, commanding the
31st U. S. Infantry, and Colonel Hooker, commanding the Marines.
They refused to take me with them. I sat for a while, sad at missing
the fun, until Mr. Johnson whispered to me that if he and I could
slip out unobtrusively and leave the party we might go to one of
the press bureaus and see if anything interesting was happening.
I said I would love to, but frankness was always the best when
possible as it saved time and effort, so I announced to the company
that the Minister had invited me to go for a walk in the rain and
I didn't know when we would be back. Mr. Cunningham had
thoughtfully given me a curfew pass, allowing me to be out after
ten o'clock. I put on some walking shoes and we set out at about
eleven. Not another soul was in the streets except an occasional
sentry. We went to the United Press headquarters, where we sat
and gossiped for an hour, hoping some news dispatches would
come in, but none did. It was raining hard when we started back

to the Consulate, walking in the middle of the street because Mr. Johnson said it was safest. I never knew an evening with prospects for some excitement turn out to be such a flop.

Next day we sailed for Hong Kong, the time of our arrival uncertain. This made things difficult, as the British Governor, Sir William Peel, with whom we were to stay, had planned an elaborate schedule for us.

We arrived at 6 P.M. A launch came for us with our Consul, Douglas Jenkins, and two of the Governor's A.D.C.s, and we went right to Government House. The Peels were charming. After dressing for dinner we joined them in an upstairs sitting room, where we waited until the guests had assembled. We then went down and stood at the top of a short flight of steps, where everyone came to be introduced by an A.D.C. As the dinner was formal with orders and decorations, Ted wore his miniature medals. At the end of dinner Sir William proposed a toast to the President of the United States, and Ted responded with a toast to the King. The one thing I hadn't told Gracie and May was to wait before drinking a toast until after the band played the national anthem, and they got caught the first time.

Evett D. Hester, American Trade Commissioner in the Philippines, and Hubert C. Anderson of the U. S. Treasury Department and member of the Governor General's staff came to Hong Kong to meet Ted. This was extremely helpful, as they had both been in the islands for years and could give him much information. Ted told them he had prepared his inaugural address to be delivered in English, not in Spanish. They praised this decision, and later several other people commented on his tact in so doing. Approximately seventeen languages were spoken in the Philippines; many were not merely dialects but clearly different from one another. A senator running for office from a district in Luzon might well have to make speeches in three different tongues—Tagalog, Pampangan, and Pangasinan. When the United States took over the Philippines in 1898, English was adopted as the basic language because a common tongue was necessary at least for official use if there was to be a united people. Spanish had been spoken fairly widely but had never reached the back country or the smaller towns to any extent. In 1932 it was used by only some of the older people, while the great majority of the younger ones considered it old-fashioned and preferred English. Today Tagalog is the official language, but English is the medium of education.

Chapter 28

The sprinkled isles,
Lily on lily, that o'erlace the sea.
ROBERT BROWNING

We reached Manila on February 29, 1932, the *President Taft* stopping at quarantine. As soon as the inspection was over, the reception committee came aboard with Vice-Governor George C. Butte, Secretary of the Interior Honorio Ventura, Representative Francisco Delgado, and several others. Some Filipino ladies were there, gay as tropical butterflies in their enchanting mestiza dresses. After meeting them we went up on the bridge as the ship got under way. Three squadrons of airplanes from Nichols Field circled over the steamer in formation, one of bombers, one of observation planes, and one of pursuit planes. Thirty-five decorated motor launches carrying sightseers and even bands escorted us to the dock and many little speedboats were going round and round us. The pier, said to be longest in the world, had two levels packed with people. As soon as we were within earshot Ted shouted *"Mabuhay!"* the Tagalog word of greeting. As a Manila newspaper said, "The cheer that answered him eclipsed all others and continued until the roar of artillery sounded in the seventeen-gun salute."

We left the ship and made our way through the crowd to the street, where a guard of honor consisted of a battalion of U.S. infantry and a troop of cavalry. Ted stood at attention, taking the salute of ruffles and flourishes, then reviewed the troops. A military escort of Philippine Scouts accompanied us to the Luneta, largest public square in Manila. A grandstand had been built, and here the oath of office was administered by Chief Justice Ramon Avacena.

According to a wireless report to the New York *Times,* the crowd on the pier, on the streets, and on the Luneta was estimated between thirty and fifty thousand. I should have thought it impossible even to guess at a count. The police arrangements were excellent, but the crush was so great that one man on the pier was killed.

Ted was the youngest man to be appointed Governor General. He was also the first to take his oath of office in the Philippines instead of the United States. He did this so that the Filipinos could attend the ceremony and hear his inaugural address, the first to be broadcast throughout the islands. This, of course, cost him a month's salary, but it was much appreciated.

His speech was written while crossing the Pacific and, according to his invariable rule, was without benefit of ghost writers. It was received with enthusiasm. An editorial in the Boston *Herald* made this comment:

> The full text, only recently received here, of Roosevelt's first formal address in the Philippines is an exceptional state paper, about as impressive as anything of the kind which has come to attention in many years. It lays down an admirably phrased program of justice, health, education, business progress and development of Philippine culture. . . .

Ted told the people that his father, while Governor of New York, had written his friend Henry Cabot Lodge that he did not want to be Vice-President because his ambition was to be Governor General of the Philippines. This brought the following editorial from the New York *Times* and its amusing sequel.

> The impression given by the accounts of Governor General Roosevelt's reception in Manila is that the Filipinos would prefer his official presence among them to a status of independence that would take him away. . . .

He carries in his traveling library a copy of the poems of Theocritus and may find himself described in the twenty-fourth idyl, which tells how Amphitryon of Argos prepared young Hercules for his labors, having himself carried off a multitude of precious prizes from the swift races before Time had loosed the harness from his chariots. . . . In [Roosevelt's] "governoring" of one small island he has shown an understanding and a genius for administration that give promise of a continuance of the welcome he has received. . . .

This editorial was followed a day or two later by a comment in "The Diary of Our Own Samuel Pepys," a feature in Franklin P. Adams's column:

Monday, February 29

(Leap Year Day.) Up betimes and in good spirits, which I no more can account for than my being in low spirits, and so read that Theodore Roosevelt, who is to remain in the Philippines, always carries a copy of the poems of Theocritus about with him, which I do not believe, for one thing, and even if he does, is it the original Singer of Persephone or Andrew Lang's translation? And what I did not see printed was that Theodore Roosevelt knows, and can recite accurately, more poems than anybody else, and I have this on the word of Grantland Rice, who is no mean quoter himself, and no mean reciter of noble verse, including many of my own, thanks to Rice, deathless verse.

From the Luneta we drove to Malacañan, where we were to live, a palace of white stucco with simple and beautiful lines on the Pasig River, surrounded on three sides by wide lawns and trees. It had a tennis court and a swimming pool. A broad staircase led from the main entrance to the principal floor, on which were the great hall, dining room, several drawing rooms, ballroom, bedrooms, and a small patio with tropical shrubs, flowers, and a fountain. Over the river was a large veranda. The executive offices were in another large building connected to the palace by a passageway.

Drawn up in front of Malacañan was a guard of honor from

the famous Philippine Constabulary, which Ted reviewed before going inside to meet various officials who were waiting for him.

In the evening the Inaugural Ball was held at the Manila Hotel. Receiving with us were Vice-Governor and Mrs. Butte; Mrs. Manuel Quezon, wife of the President of the Senate; Senator Benigno Aquino, President pro-tem of the Senate; Representative de las Alas, Speaker pro-tem of the House, and his wife.

Next day Ted held his first press conference and said he intended to familiarize himself with the islands by visiting them, because personal inspection was necessary to form sound conclusions. After that was done and not before, he would take up specific problems. A reporter on a Manila paper described him in this way:

> His smile is the most attractive feature about him. The lines about his keen steel-blue eyes deepen, and those framing the corners of his mouth widen. Not only the eyes and lips but the whole expression breaks into an infectious smile that is irresistible.
>
> But there is that in those steel-blue eyes and the set of the jaw which says that the former can bore through one, and that the latter can set like a steel trap when occasion demands it.

Although I had read every book I could find on the Philippines and talked to many friends who had been there, I had no real idea what the Filipinos were like until I had been in the islands for some time. It is difficult to describe in a few words the traits of a people. If I had to do so I think I would say that the vast majority are intelligent, honest, friendly, valiant, and kind, with a most engaging sense of humor. Ted had a phrase that describes them perhaps better than anything I can say: "The Filipinos are gentlefolk." Those who were educated were intellectually equal to any people in the world, but even those in the back country, some of whom could neither read nor write, had innate dignity and poise. A year after we left the islands the AAA crop-control policy was extended to the Philippines and a bonus given to those who refrained from growing sugar cane. An elderly couple from

Pampanga who had probably never been more than ten miles away from their farm, came to Manila to find out what this meant. They were directed to Mr. Hester, who explained the plan to them. They listened intently, then retired to a corner of the office and consulted together. After a short time they came back to Mr. Hester's desk and the old man spoke. "We understand. God has given us the land on which to grow cane. The government has ordered us not to do so. We will obey, as it appears the government is stronger than God, but we refuse to accept money for such blasphemy."

The valor in arms of the Filipinos has been proved conclusively not once but many times. This was demonstrated during World War II. When other Asian colonies took the opportunity to rise in revolt and demand concessions from their mother countries, the Commonwealth of the Philippines demanded nothing and fought beside the United States with absolute loyalty. Commanded by General Emilio Aguinaldo in the Philippine insurrection of 1900, the Filipino guerrillas, short of modern weapons but adept in jungle fighting, gave our troops plenty of trouble until General Fred Funston captured Aguinaldo by a ruse. When Frederick Townsend Ward, thirty-year-old American adventurer and military genius of the 1860s, saved Shanghai and the American and British positions from the powerful Taiping rebels, his "Ever-Victorious Army" was largely composed of "Manila Men." After Ward's death in battle his army was commanded by the British General Charles G. Gordon, who as "Chinese Gordon" became a hero to every British school child. Ward had laid the foundations for Gordon's career in China but received no word of credit either from Gordon himself or his many biographers. What is even more reprehensible, Ward's name is practically unknown in his own country, although he is the only American who was ever worshiped as a god in China.

I had heard nothing much about the Filipino women and was quite unprepared to find them so attractive and so capable. In Manila and the other cities they ran the big charitable organizations and were a decided influence in politics. In the country the matriarch of the family was called *la casera*, or chatelaine. It was she who took charge of the family earnings, arranged the budget, and generally ruled the household. In a letter to his mother on June 6, 1932, Ted described one of these:

In a barrio where I stopped to greet the crowd I saw an old lady with gray hair to whom everyone was paying attention. She was lively and had a keen sense of humor. Suddenly in the middle of the road under the blazing sun she and my aide Major Abraham Garfinkel did one of the old Spanish dances with a snapping of fingers and posturing. The crowd of course was perfectly delighted. I found out that she is called "La Capitana" and owns one of the big plantations, being in fact the real leader of the community. The politicians go to her for orders. I wish you could have seen her. She would be just as self-possessed dining formally at Malacañan Palace as she was dancing a jig in the road.

One reason the Filipino ladies appeared beautiful to me was their costume. The mestiza dress, worn on all formal occasions, had come down from the Spanish days and was unique. Fragile and elaborate, it had a skirt with a long train sometimes made of embroidered satin, sometimes of brilliant-colored brocade from France or China. Over it was a shorter skirt of fine black net. The train was carried over the arm to show an inch or two of lace petticoat. The low-cut bodice and the fichu were of stiff transparent piña cloth woven from the fibers of pineapple leaves and embroidered to harmonize with the skirt. A more becoming costume cannot be imagined. My friend, Mrs. Manuel Quezon, who in later years was most foully murdered by the Huk outlaws, was popularly believed to have three hundred such dresses. A group of Filipino women, the Catholic Women's League, gave me a lovely one with a skirt of apple-green satin covered by exquisite embroidery of pink roses and gold and silver leaves, with the *camisa*, or bodice, in piña to match. They asked me to wear it at their afternoon reception to which Signorina and Miss Hensey went with me, also in mestiza dress. When we drove through the streets the policemen saluted us with beaming smiles. When I was in Manila in 1954 I was disappointed to find the mestiza costume had been greatly modified, and its morning version, the *balin-*

tawak, had practically vanished. If more changes are made I am afraid the beauties will look like anybody else.

After we left the Philippines the *barong tagalog* was made the official costume for men. I hope it remains so, for it is original, practical, and attractive. It consists of a shirt in any desired fabric, and for the sake of coolness it hangs outside the trousers. A friend gave Ted two made of the finest ecru piña stiff with embroidery in the same color. He always wore one at dinner when we were by ourselves. When Teddy and Cornelius came out to join us I had several *barong tagalogs* made for them in gay colors, which they wore for years in summer at home.

Conditions in the Philippines were good when we arrived, in spite of the world-wide economic crisis. There was no hunger such as existed in Puerto Rico, and little more than ordinary unemployment. During the thirty years of United States rule the standard of living had become higher than that of any other Asian country. Every sizable town had its hospital, dispensary, and high school, its movie theater, public playground, radios, and automobiles. Even the smaller towns had their *Puericultur* or child-care center. The work started by the early pioneers from America—doctors, nurses, schoolteachers, and engineers—has never, I think, received the credit to which it is entitled.

It is not generally realized that the Philippines are unique. They are the only Asian country that is Christian. When we were there the Filipinos were more Western in their ideas than were any other Asians. The Japanese had perhaps adopted to a greater extent the mechanization and outward semblance of the West, but the Filipinos had gone farther. Their concepts of life were closer to ours in many ways.

The American Army doctors took good care of us. They didn't like my running a stubborn low fever and made me stay in my room on a chaise longue for three weeks until it disappeared. During this time Gracie took over my most important duties. We had word shortly after reaching Manila that the Duke and Duchess of Brabant, afterward King Leopold III and Queen Astrid of Belgium, were making a tour of the Far East, including the Philippines. We invited them to stay at Malacañan, and they came bringing a lady-in-waiting, Viscountess Lantsheere; Baron Capelle, secretary and aide to the Duke; and a maid. They were traveling incognito as Count and Countess de Réthy, so many elaborate state functions were unnecessary.

I was able to be up and around by the time they arrived and made plans well in advance. Signorina and Colonel Crockett would go in a fast launch to escort them from the steamer to the Malacañan boat landing, where Ted and I would meet them with Gracie, May, and Major Garfinkel. From the landing was an iron staircase leading up to the main floor.

All went well to start with. It was a lovely, cool day. We welcomed them and started off from the landing in a little procession, first the Duke and myself, then the Duchess with Ted, followed by the others. As I had been ill, I had done no exploring of the vast basement under the palace and by bad luck went past the staircase without seeing it. Chatting pleasantly, we walked and walked, past storerooms and native servants' rooms with strange garments hanging up to dry, and general confusion. Feeling an utter fool, I didn't know whether to stop and confess I was lost or to pretend this was just what I had planned, and decided the latter was least ridiculous. We made the tour of the entire building back to the landing, found the stairs, and at last reached the main floor. I didn't tell them what had happened until days later.

Their Royal Highnesses were young, very much in love, and utterly delightful. We told them we would like to have one big dinner party for them later and asked if there was anyone they wanted to see in the meantime. They said they were tired out, having eaten their way through Siam with a banquet every single night and much preferred being alone with us for the present.

A friend had given us five pounds of the best Russian caviar, newly arrived over the Trans-Siberian Railroad. We had some of it that night, served in a bowl with little plates, and butter knives to spread it on Melba toast. I noticed that Ted and the Duke were ignoring the toast and were eating the caviar with their knives. When I sent for spoons they cheered. From then on we had caviar before lunch and dinner every day while it lasted.

After dinner the first evening we were sitting on the veranda in the moonlight when someone was thirsty. I asked Colonel Crockett to ring the bell, forgetting just how he usually rang bells. He always wanted quick service and would press the button not once but several times. A few moments later I sensed something odd and turned to see my little Filipino maid Juana in her night-gown, her long hair falling to her knees. She had been in bed and had heard the bell ring three times, her signal, and she was answering it as quickly as she could. Controlling my voice with difficulty, I thanked her quietly and told her she was not required. The Colonel, rather caught, then rang once for the number-one boy.

The Duke was at heart a naturalist and spent much time at the Bureau of Science. Baron Capelle told us that once when they were driving over the country in a motorcade with Siamese officials the Duke caught sight of a species of butterfly new to him. Stopping the car, he got out and sped after it. The officials ran to the Baron and asked him what had occurred. When he replied that his Royal Highness was chasing a butterfly they exclaimed, "A butterfly? How old *is* his Royal Highness?"

The Duchess shopped for presents for her two children left in Switzerland and went sightseeing sometimes with me, sometimes with Gracie and Signorina. Both she and her husband kept saying how pleasant it was not to be continuously entertained and obliged to make an effort all the time. At the one large dinner party we had, which included all high officials, both American and Filipino, I told the Duke I wanted to spare them both the strain of talking with people they had only just met and so had arranged some music after dinner. An excellent Filipino violinist with a good accompanist played Bach, Dvořák, and Brahms, and shortly after that the party was over. The Duke looked at his watch and said, "There was a large dinner, we had a chance to say a word to everyone, we heard delightful music, it is all over, and it is only half-past ten. What a feat!"

After five days with us in Manila and a tour through some of the southern islands they went to the Netherlands Indies, where Ted and I followed them a year later. In Bali the Dutch *comp-troleur* told us they had given him the fright of his life. Never, as long as he lived, would he forget the anguish he went through. He had turned his house over to them and at ten o'clock the first night had gone there to make certain the sentries were at their posts and all was in order. The lights were off on the ground floor but were still on upstairs. Suddenly he heard a series of piercing screams, the sound of running feet, and furniture being over-turned. He said he went up the stairs four steps at a time, his heart pounding. When he reached the landing he saw what was going on and crept downstairs as quietly as he could, still suffering from shock.

"Would you believe it?" he said. "Their Royal Highnesses were having a pillow fight!"

Housekeeping at Malacañan was easy. Everything was done by established precedent which had been made official regulation by the last administration. All the marketing was done by a vener-able Chinese paragon, Ah King, the number-one boy, who had been there for over thirty years and ruled the domestic staff. On the first of each month we paid all food bills, then handed in to the office a list of the guests we had had and were reimbursed at the rate of two pesos (one dollar) for each guest at breakfast, four for each at lunch, two for each at tea, and six for each at dinner. This covered everything, including the expense of our having to serve wines, there being no prohibition in the Philippines.

We were expected to give several balls. For our first one Major Garfinkel, who had served with previous governors general, sent invitations to everyone on the official list. Afterward he was elated because so many people had come, but I was disappointed. The vast rooms were only half full, the guests were elderly, and had all gone home by midnight. A really good ball, I told him, should be crowded with both young and old and should last until the band was stopped, no earlier than half-past two. We went to work on the list, adding many names that were not official. We got in touch with various youth organizations and asked them to recom-mend a certain number of their members to be invited. As a result our balls got better and better as time went on.

The Manila Hotel, run by Hubert C. Anderson for the U. S. Government, did the catering for the balls. It had been customary to have a real feast for supper. The first menu submitted to me called for lobsters, prawns, and other fish, young pig, cold roast beef, lamb, and chicken, four different kinds of salads, three flavors of ice cream, and cakes in abundance. The cost, not including the usual punch, was three pesos, or seventy-five cents, a head for fifteen hundred people. This was extremely reasonable, but in accordance with Ted's economy program I cut it down to a substantial salad, rolls, ice cream, and cakes, which came to very much less. We had two kinds of punch, one of fruit juices, the other slightly alcoholic, as the Filipinos drank only in moderation. Scotch and rye for older foreign guests were on a table in one of the smaller rooms.

The *rigodón de honor*, a kind of quadrille from the Spanish days, had been revived by Governor General Henry L. Stimson and was danced at most of the balls. Sixteen couples took part, chosen by custom according to rank and usually including the Governor General, the Vice-Governor, the American military and naval commanders, the President of the Senate or his deputy, the Speaker of the House, senators, representatives, Cabinet members, and of course their wives. As the dance was rather complicated because of its six figures, we always had a couple of rehearsals in advance. It was fun to do and pretty to watch because of the mestiza costumes, whose trains, two yards long on formal dresses, were allowed to fall on the floor during the dance.

When the Army Relief Ball was given at Santa Ana, said to have the largest dance floor in the world, Ted and I danced in the *rigodón*. All the women were asked to come in Filipino costume. I had worn my mestiza dress a couple of times and didn't want to wear it again, as no Filipino woman ever seemed to wear the same gown twice at parties, so I decided to go as Maria Clara, the beloved of the national hero of the Philippines, José Rizal. I had a *camisa* of the period which Mrs. John H. Holliday, wife of the Vice-Governor, had given me for Christmas. It was of fine white piña with bell-shaped sleeves and fichu. All I needed was a striped flowered skirt. I found a piece of heavy white satin brocade with a pattern of orange and yellow roses and green leaves and had a full skirt made with stripes of green velvet ribbon sewed on it. I had not realized how much sentiment was felt about Maria Clara's dress and was surprised to have groups of people applaud it as I went around the ballroom in the grand chain of the *rigodón*.

When we had our ball in honor of the Legislature I was in the middle of a migraine headache. These had bothered me for years and now were becoming frequent and severe, causing a deep, uncomfortable drowsiness and inducing a sort of coma for hours or even days on end. I wasn't sure I could get through the party but managed to do so by sleeping until people started arriving, shaking hands with them for an hour and a half, lying down again until the *rigodón* began, and after that going to bed without saying good-by. I was glad indeed when that ball was over.

Our last ball at Malacañan was in January 1933 and really was outstanding. It lasted until we stopped the music shortly before three o'clock. Part of our Asiatic Fleet, under the command of Admiral Montgomery M. Taylor, was in the harbor at the time, also the battleship *Kent* with Admiral Sir Howard Kelly of the British Asiatic Fleet, and all the officers were invited. Between three and four thousand people came, a gorgeous sight with the brilliant mestiza dresses and the different uniforms. Most of the guests were routed to the main porte-cochere, others to the side entrance, while all the naval officers were requested to come by water. A.D.C.s were at all three entrances to escort the most distinguished people. We had dancing in the ballroom, the great hall, and down by the boat landing, so that in spite of the crowd there was no crush. The palace and grounds were illuminated by floodlights. The Chief of Police made such good arrangements for traffic that there was not a moment's delay all evening although there were some fifteen hundred cars.

Next morning Mrs. Fletcher, wife of a captain in the U. S. Navy, telephoned me to say that several of the British officers had told her how impressed they were by the party. They said they had been to functions at government houses all over the world and had never seen such a "good show." Said Mrs. Fletcher, "I just swelled with pride!"

Because of the distance to the Philippines and the absence of air travel, we had few visitors from home. Teddy, aged eighteen, and Cornelius, almost seventeen, came for their summer vacation in 1932. I planned to meet them in Japan and go on to Peking, where our friend, Roy Chapman Andrews, had asked us to stay at his house for two weeks. After working out all the itineraries and making arrangements, I found this would take me away from Manila at the time of the opening of the Legislature, when we were supposed to give a ball. It would never have been understood if I had been away. If you have a job to do, you had better do it properly. My job in the Philippines was so easy compared to that in Puerto Rico that I could not side-step any part of it. Reluctantly I arranged for the boys to go to Peking without me and to stay with the Cunninghams in Shanghai on their way south.

I went to Hong Kong to meet them, arriving the day before they were due, and stayed at Flagstaff House with General James Sandilands, the General Officer Commanding. Their ship was due at quarantine at half-past seven next morning. I woke at five, dressed, and went down on the terrace, where I was joined by Captain Cameron, the General's A.D.C. We could see the ship anchored out in the harbor. When it left quarantine and started toward the pier we started too, and by the time it docked we were there. I could hear Teddy's whistle a mile off, and by our usual system of holding up an unfolded handkerchief by two corners we identified ourselves quickly. I took the boys to meet the General, then we set out by ourselves to wander along Cat Street in the Thieves' Market, and to poke about in shops on Queen's Road. We got back to Flagstaff House about half-past twelve. When we told the General we had walked for three hours he was aghast. "Wherever did you go? Why, we *never* walk here!" We went to a big lunch with the Peels at Government House, then to Shek O to swim, a little cove with a lovely beach. That night we boarded the *President Hayes*, which left early next morning for Manila. Ted met us at quarantine, and Signorina, Miss Hensey, Colonel Crockett, Major Garfinkel, and several others were waiting for us at the pier.

At noon that day Ted was having his press conference and sent for the boys to come and meet the newsmen. Although both were inches taller than I, they insisted on my coming with them, saying they were much too scared to go alone. When I firmly refused they picked me up by the elbows and carried me into Ted's office with my toes just off the ground. The reporters were delighted but tactful enough not to mention such unseemly frivolity.

Teddy and Cornelius had a good time in the Philippines. Colonel Crockett's daughter Lucy was the right age for them. Since then she has become well known as a world traveler and author of several successful books. The Chevrolet company lent them a little bright yellow roadster. I ordered white mess jackets for them which Ted had authorized as the formal dress in the islands instead of black dress suits, so they were well turned out at all the parties. They went with Signorina to see the Mountain Province, with me to shoot the rapids in canoes on the Pangsajan River; they went fishing and riding horseback with various friends. Every afternoon they played tennis or badminton and went swimming. After they left at the end of three weeks Malacañan seemed strangely quiet and lonely.

When Mr. and Mrs. George Bernard Shaw stopped at Manila on a round-the-world cruise Major Matthew B. Ridgway, Ted's aide and technical adviser, met them at the steamship and invited them to lunch with us. Years later he was famous as Supreme Commander of Allied Powers in the Far East, the same afterward in Europe, and Chief of Staff, United States Army. Newspaper reports had told of Mr. Shaw's witty and acid comments to the press at various ports, obviously meant to embarrass the British Empire. We wondered if he would make a crack at the United States, but he did not. All he said was that in the Philippines he saw the most extraordinary of all things, independence pending for a people that didn't want it.

At lunch Ted was entranced by Mrs. Shaw, who was a darling, the perfect type of old-fashioned gentlewoman with a soft voice, charm, and a will of iron. She told him that as a young girl, more years ago than she could count, she had traveled all over India alone with a maid, showing great initiative in those days of sheltered womanhood. I sat between Mr. Shaw and Roy D. Bennett, editor of the Manila *Bulletin*. The latter said he had just been reading a first draft of Ted's report to the War Department and was interested in my penciled corrections. Whereupon Mr. Shaw and I started an argument about split infinitives, misplaced prepositions, and long Germanic sentences ending with verbs, to which Ted was inclined. He said Mrs. Shaw often wanted to get her hands on his sentences. We laughed so much that Ted called down the table to know what we were talking about. From there we discussed the Revised Version of the Bible. When Mr. Shaw said he felt there was something to be said for it I asked if he approved changing the passage, "Joseph was minded to put her away privily," to "Joseph thought of breaking the engagement," which I had seen somewhere. We had a delightful time. While we were still at the table word came that a news photographer was outside to take pictures of the party. Ted said to send the man away as this wasn't an official occasion and nobody wanted to be photographed. Mr. Shaw said, "Oh, I'm afraid I do. In fact I told the man to come here. I would like to be photographed with you." Mrs. Shaw said she never allowed her picture to be taken, so Mr. Shaw and Ted went out alone and posed on the lawn.

After lunch we sent them out in Ted's car with Major Ridgway to do sightseeing or whatever else they wished for the rest of the afternoon. They went back to the steamer with a copy of *East of the Sun and West of the Moon,* which Mrs. Shaw had asked for, and some mangosteen jam for Mr. Shaw. They sent us a first edition of *The Adventures of the Black Girl in Her Search for God,* inscribed in Mr. Shaw's writing, "To Eleanor and Theodore Roosevelt, this visiting card after a memorable day at Government House, Manila, from Charlotte F. Shaw [in her hand] and G. Bernard Shaw. 9th February 1933."

Mrs. Oliver Iselin, an uncommonly attractive woman who was an old friend of ours and a neighbor on Long Island, spent the night with us. She was on the same ship as the Shaws and told me they refused to meet a soul on board. In fact, Mr. Shaw was decidedly fierce to anyone who approached them. Although they had been on the same cruise for weeks, she had met them for the first time at lunch with us.

Before I was married I had studied the violin from the time I was seven years old. In my teens I had lessons from David Mannes, founder of the Mannes School of Music, and played in an orchestra under his direction in which the forty violins and some of the other strings were amateurs. It was called the Symphony Club and was great fun because we all took it seriously and worked hard. We had rehearsals every week in the winter, and once or twice a year we gave concerts, assisted by the wind and brass from the New York Symphony Orchestra, with prominent professional soloists such as Albert Spalding, Ernest Schelling, and others.

When we came to the Philippines I hadn't touched my violin for twenty years. Ted was tone-deaf and with the best will in the world did not enjoy hearing me play. Besides, the violin is no good without an accompanist, unavailable in Oyster Bay. In Manila I found that as wife of the Governor General I could invite the best professional musicians to play with me at Malacañan, and they came with pleasure. I sent home for my fiddle, started taking lessons again, and thoroughly enjoyed myself. With a German as first violin, myself as second, a Russian cellist, and a Scottish violist, we met once a week for several months in the ballroom, where the acoustics were perfect, and played many of the eighteenth-century quartets.

In 1933, when Rudolf Friml came to Manila to stay with Joseph Stevenot, head of the Philippine Telephone Company, we asked Joe to bring him to dinner at Malacañan. Joe said he didn't think Friml could be induced to come as he was very shy, disliked meeting people, and hated making engagements. He probably would refuse to put on a dinner jacket and loathed the thought of having to be on time. I said he didn't need to dress and could be as late as he liked. I would plan a small party, and dinner would wait until he came.

When Friml arrived Ted gave him a cocktail and started talking to him about the heroes of his native Bohemia—Ottokar, the great King Charles, and Jan Hus. As we went into the dining room they were discussing the victorious march of the Bohemian Hussites through Germany to the Baltic in the fifteenth century. During the soup they described to each other the march of the Czechoslovaks across Russia and Siberia after World War I, fighting Bolsheviks and German and Hungarian ex-prisoners every step of the way. At one point Friml called across the table, "Joe! Why did you not tell me it would be like this? He knows all our history. What a man!"

I didn't dare hope that Friml would play for us and had arranged some native folk music and dancing which I was sure would interest him. After dinner we were sitting on the veranda when the sound of music drifted from the river. Friml jumped up and hung over the railing. A barge came to the landing, and several people in gay costumes got out, singing and playing guitars, and came up the stairs to where we were. Among them was the noted dancer Toy Toy, who gave an excellent performance with her partner. Friml was in raptures. After the guitars had played a rather complicated air he went to the piano and played it over with variations, to the astonishment and delight of the musicians. Then they all played together. I don't know who had the best time.

After the dancers and musicians left I told Friml I had been brought up on the classical music he wrote before doing *Rose Marie* and *The Vagabond King* and asked him to play a serenade I had studied twenty-five years before on the violin. He pretended to be appalled and explained to the company that he had written it while in short pants. I retorted that I had played it in a perambulator. He said that none of his good music had ever paid, and he had forgotten it so completely that I had to show him with one finger on the piano how it went before he would do it. After everyone else had gone home he and Joe stayed on for a couple of hours while Friml did musical stunts on the piano. When he left he embraced us, kissing Ted on both cheeks.

Chapter 29

When Tzu Lu asked about the art of gov-
erning, the Master replied: "Be in advance of
the people; show them how to work." On his
asking for something more the Master added:
"Untiringly."

CONFUCIUS

Late in March 1932 Ted started his inspection trips that were to cover forty-eight out of the forty-nine provinces in the islands, more than any previous Governor General had ever done. He began with two tours on the island of Luzon. The Army doctors refused to let me go, so Gracie, May, and Miss Hensey went with Ted, returning to Manila exhausted, as the traveling was long and hard. He visited not only the municipalities and small towns but stopped at many farms as well, where the farmers, often not knowing who he was, were apt to speak freely. At one of these in Aparri he had a good example of Philippine hospitality and kindness when he asked a woman if her hens were laying. She said she had no eggs and asked him to wait a moment. Going into her little shack, she opened a box and returned with a small coin which she gave him to spend for eggs if he wanted them. Ted, delighted, asked if she was married. She said yes, adding that her husband had gone to town to see the Governor General.

At one point Ted was invited to spend two days shooting wild carabao. His big-game record was known because a Manila paper had been publishing serially one of his books on hunting, so he couldn't very well refuse and give the impression this game was not worth shooting, but he told me it was the last thing he wanted to do. Carabao were domesticated animals in the Philippines. No truly wild ones, in the scientific sense, existed—only tame ones that generations ago had wandered into the jungle and had been living there. Few people ever molested them. The hunt was to be an elaborate affair in the nature of a drive, with so many people, including reporters, that the chances of failure were enormous. "This is going to be too conspicuous," Ted said to me. "I'd hate to shoot and miss. But it would be really disastrous if I hit a carabao and then found a brand on it. I'd never live that down!"

He killed a running one with a single shot. As the papers said, the animal was barely discernible as it bounded like a porpoise through bushes and tall grass a hundred and fifty yards away. Everyone rushed to look at it, and Ted was immensely relieved to find no sign of a brand. When I heard of it over the radio I wired him he must indeed have been wearing his shooting pants. The Filipinos were delighted and promptly nicknamed him "One-Shot Teddy."

The *Philippines Herald,* commenting on this incident, said most officials usually confined their contact with the country to formal calls, or at most to receptions and balls, ending by saying:

A Governor General who does not mind being bitten by jungle mosquitoes, who can fall into wild carabao wallows and like it, who can drink Igorot wine and lick his chops, who can be really human without losing his grin—he is some Governor General.

Some months later Ted took a couple of days off and flew for an hour and a half from Manila to the island of Mindoro after timarau, a species of small wild ox that exists nowhere else in the world—a fierce animal that will attack without provocation. This time he told no one where he was going or what he was doing until he returned after having shot two.

Colonel Louis Van Schaick, who had been many years in the Philippines, went with Ted on the Luzon tours and kept a careful diary. An extract has a good description of an incident in the province of Cavite:

> We pushed on to Tagatay ridge. A thousand mounted farmers greet us. Other thousands are gathered on the ridge a mile away. It's a thrilling sight. We mount horses and ride. It is a sight to be remembered. The Governor General and General Aguinaldo ride ahead. Crockett, Garfinkel and I ride next. The Provincial Governor was a free lance, keeping folks from riding in front of the Governor General. An old woman, sixty, with enormous hat, tucked up skirts and a cigar in her mouth, galloped on the flank along the edge of the ridge, where a false move would have dropped her in some places hundreds of feet. The great irregular mass spread out fanlike and galloped in no formation except that of not getting ahead of the Governor General. He, from his horse, made a fine speech to the united groups on the ridge. What with mares and stallions indiscriminately, the squealing, fighting, plunging horses threatened for a time the Governor General's supremacy, but his foghorn voice rang out over and above all opposition.

Ted continued to make inspections throughout the islands, traveling over ten thousand miles by boat, train, automobile, on horseback, and on foot. When it was impossible for him to leave his office in Manila during the week, he visited nearby provinces on Saturdays and Sundays. In this way he saw the people, learned their problems, talked with their leaders, and won their friendship. A few politicians criticized these trips as smacking of electioneering, but the fact that he got the people behind him was of great importance later, as will be seen, enabling him to succeed in his plan of drastically reorganizing the government to conform to its income.

I used to go with Ted after I recovered. The subsequent journeys were somewhat easier, as part of them were by sea. A yacht, the *Apo*, once the property of King Manoel of Portugal, was provided for the sole use of the Governor General. She was large, slow, and expensive to run. Her cabins were paneled in mahogany and had elaborate silver-plated lighting fixtures, also giant cockroaches in the bureau drawers. After a couple of voyages Ted got rid of her and used a smaller vessel, the new Coast Guard cutter *Arayat*, which had other duties when he was not traveling. She was faster, more economical, and much more agreeable.

In nearly every province there were large areas of public domain administered by the Philippine Government. Ted's principal study on his journeys was how to reform the complicated land administration in order to make homesteads easier to obtain. We were always accompanied by one or two members of his Cabinet, Colonel Crockett, and others, with whom he discussed this and other problems. Miss Hensey came too so that he could prepare speeches and statements and dictate letters while cruising from one island to another. We always had a member of the press chosen from the Gridiron Club of the Philippines, of which Carlos Romulo was president, a young man of whom the world was to hear in later years when he became famous as a brigadier general with MacArthur, Ambassador from the Philippines to the United Nations, and Ambassador to the United States. He became one of our closest and most valued friends. On shore we would be joined by the local officials of the province in which we were.

Russell Owen of the North American Newspaper Alliance was with us once for a brief time and described one of our typical journeys as follows:

> Campaigning is hard work, but if Colonel Theodore Roosevelt, Governor General of the Philippines, goes home in September to stump for President Hoover, he probably will look upon it almost as a vacation. For no campaigning trip ever planned could hold a candle to the recent inspection tour Colonel Roosevelt made through the Philippines during very hot weather.
>
> When he is home in Manila he works until nearly midnight. This correspondent spent less than a week with him on an inspection trip and was glad to quit. He went wearily home from the palace one hot, moist evening after dinner, leaving Col. Roosevelt just about to begin his night's dictation. . . .
>
> At one stop on the tour there was the blare of a motor horn and down the road in a smother of dust came an automobile. Out bounced a man in a Panama resembling a plainsman's

sombrero, with a broad smile beneath it. Indolence was cast off, people appeared from nowhere and banners sprang from the earth. . . .

The man in the straw sombrero was the Governor General. If he was tired he did not show it. Later it was learned that he is never tired. He weighs 145 pounds, all muscle. He is lean and hard. He waved his hat and the crowd cheered and waved. He called "Mabuhay" meaning "greeting" or "how."

The crowd swarmed around Roosevelt with the friendliness and eager hospitality so characteristic of the Filipinos. He was almost submerged until he climbed to the rear platform of the train to speak. . . .

On the train one would expect Roosevelt to drop into a chair, wilted and relaxed, but no . . . Luncheon was a peripatetic meal. When it was over the train stopped and everyone got off for another reception and another speech . . . Then into automobiles and off for a long hot ride, with frequent halts for talks and receptions.

The first halt was not more than three quarters of an hour after lunch, at a sugar mill where tables were laden with food. The warm champagne with which all Filipinos of means punctuate their welcomes was not to be refused. Not to eat, even a short time after lunch, is a reflection on Philippine hospitality. The Roosevelts ate their way around the islands. . . .

It was on the roads that the Roosevelt party was most punished. Even when the roads are smooth they are dusty, and the cars moved through blinding, sticky haze until mud formed on wet faces and chins. The cars stopped at almost every village, lest discourtesy be shown those who had erected arches and held bunches of flowers and banners.

During all these days, which lasted from early morning until ten or eleven at night, Governor General Roosevelt held conferences to which the townspeople were invited to tell their grievances and report on the state of their province. His aides went away from every place loaded with petitions from a people oppressed by some of their politicians. The Governor General appealed for co-operation and told of the necessity for economy, and was answered with the cheers of the people to whom his vigorous personality apparently makes a tremendous appeal.

Frequently a full day ended in a banquet, occasionally followed by a ball. Sometimes we stayed overnight with people, sometimes joined the yacht at a place other than where we had landed. Almost always we had to be on the road shortly after seven in the morning. From time to time Ted had to make as many as twenty-two speeches in a day. When he needed several hours for conferences in some municipality I would ask the ladies to take me to see the schools, hospitals, and prisons. A few days of this kind usually wore me out, but the sincere and friendly hospitality of the people made every effort worth while.

The trip described by Russell Owen lasted almost a month. Two or three times the yacht anchored, giving everyone else a chance to go fishing while I seized the opportunity to rest. The variety of fish in these waters was fantastic. Once when Ted had gone ashore, Miss Hensey, Colonel Crockett, and I went swimming from a tiny, uninhabited island nearby while the launch patrolled up and down to keep off predatory fish. The beach was jet-black, beautiful with blue water and white breakers against a background of green palm trees.

We spent several hours on the island of Culion inspecting the colony of six thousand lepers. Many people had advised against our stopping there, as little was known about contracting leprosy, but Ted wanted to leave nothing out, and if he went I was going too. I was thankful I had gone, for they had put up an arch with a huge sign, MABUHAY GOVERNOR GENERAL AND MRS. ROOSEVELT, and it would have been mortifying had I stayed away.

On the dock we were met by a group of people, including public-health doctors and nurses, Catholic nuns who were Belgians, and priests. In the group was a slim girl in a white sharkskin dress and a big hat, as smart as if she had stepped from the pages of *Vogue*. She was the wife of Dr. H. Windsor Wade, chief pathologist of the colony and member of the executive board of the Leonard Wood Memorial Foundation. Recently she had toured American cities to raise money for the Foundation and returned to Culion to carry on her work with the chemist, doctor, dietitian, and priest. Both she and her husband had dedicated their lives to the care of lepers. Dr. Wade was away temporarily. I tried my best to persuade her to come to Manila and stay with us for a little change, telling her she could be gay and see people or have a quiet rest, just as she liked, but she would not leave the colony. I never saw her again.

All the able-bodied people were out to see Ted. After addressing them he went to see those in the hospital. As he passed through the crowd many of them held out their hands to him. No one could have criticized him if he had failed to see the hands, but he would not risk hurting anyone's feelings and he shook every one. I think the saddest thing I ever saw was a troop of Boy Scouts, all lepers, including the leader.

At Puerto Princesa on the island of Palawan, where we arrived at five o'clock one evening, Ted addressed a large crowd from the veranda of the Provincial Governor's house, then was closeted with the local leaders while I sat with their wives and children. He had said he would not be there long, so I didn't dare go off to see anything. As time passed and we seemed on the point of exhausting topics of conversation, I asked the mothers if their children had learned any verses they could recite. The gathering was revitalized at once, and the children scrambled to perform. One mother said her children could dance. We were getting on merrily when Major George Dunham, medical and sanitation adviser on Ted's staff, came and told me we ought to be going. It was half-past eight, but Ted was still in conference. The Major insisted on my sending in a note to him suggesting that we leave. He came out at once and we returned to the yacht. Major Dunham then told me that one of the worst types of malaria was rife on that island, but the mosquitoes carrying it had never been found before nine o'clock. "Don't think it is superstition," he said. "It's true. You can set your watch by them. I think we got away in time, but I am going to make you all take a good dose of quinine." I thought of that incident during World War II when the Japanese had a prison camp on Palawan.

I loved our trips to the southern islands. We spent a day at Zamboanga, where, according to the old Army song, the monkeys have no tails. Ted was occupied seeing scores of people and had barely enough time for everything he wished to do. Someone brought me a message from the Governor of the San Ramon Penal Colony that the prisoners were lined up in the central court waiting to see the Governor General. If it was impossible for him to come it might help a little if I did. I went there, found them waiting patiently under the blazing sun, and made them a little speech, which none of them could understand but which they applauded. I thought they seemed such nice men and was touched to see them take off their straw hats when I began to speak. I inspected the prison hospital and told the Governor I would certainly inform my husband of the excellence of his work. After that Miss Hensey and I visited the General Hospital, three schools, the Pettit Barracks, and a Moro village built on stilts in the water.

While on this journey we got word that the island of Jolo had been devastated by a freak hurricane that touched nowhere else. We changed our itinerary and went there at once so that Ted could see conditions and arrange for relief. Over two hundred people had been killed and the damage was horrifying. When we arrived, his Highness Jamalul Kiram II, Sultan of Sulu, appointed Senator from the province and legal owner of hundreds of islands in the Sulu archipelago, called on us, as did his niece and adopted daughter, Princess Hadji Piandao, popularly known as the Dayang Dayang. Ted made a careful survey of the results of the disaster, going into every town and village on the island with Charles Foster of the American Red Cross, Judge Teopista Guingona, head of the Bureau for Non-Christian Tribes, Major Dunham, and the Sultan.

Jolo was in effect the headquarters of the Moros. When the United States took over the Philippines an agreement was made with the Sultan allowing him spiritual but not temporal power over his people. In America we have built a myth around the Moros. Many people believe them to be a different race from the Filipinos. Actually they are of the same blends that make up the other islanders. The difference is that they are Moslems while the others, except for certain tribes in the north, are Christians. Comparatively few in number, they live practically on the water or in inaccessible places; they are less civilized, more given to violence, and have little love for the United States. They would prefer to be independent of everyone and to have license to destroy their neighbors. They are attractive as primitive fighting men always are.

A couple of months after our visit to Jolo a Constabulary patrol was ambushed and a lieutenant and twelve men were killed by Moro outlaws. This was followed by a punitive expedition of the Constabulary. Ted received detailed reports but decided that a personal reconnaissance was necessary. Trouble of this sort can easily spread and get out of hand. Accompanied by Major Ridgway, he went at once to Jolo, conferred with officials, interviewed witnesses, and ended by going on foot through the jungle to the place of the massacre. The fact that the Governor General had come himself without delay, disregarding danger, was said to have deeply impressed the outlaws and convinced them that he would really get them in case of more trouble. To Ted this was routine, but it caused a little flurry among the people.

We left Jolo and went back to Mindanao, where we drove inland for five hours through excellent farming and cattle country with few inhabitants until we reached Malaybalay, capital of the province of Bukidnon. We went through a few villages on the way, each with its arch of welcome, and stopped to greet the people. At one point we noticed a solitary man on horseback who turned and galloped off as fast as he could go to alert a group of fifty Girl Scouts that we were coming. They had been up since long before daylight and had walked miles to reach the appointed meeting place before we did. They greeted us by singing the "Maine Stein Song." Each child had a little bunch of flowers for me.

Ted was in the first car with the Governor of the province and local leaders. I was in the second with Mr. Hester, who had been telling me that much Chinese porcelain and pottery had been shipped to the Philippines in the early days and was sometimes found when fields were plowed. As we went along I caught sight of a large blue-green jar under a little nipa-palm shack built on stilts. Stopping the car to the surprise of the following motorcade, Mr. Hester and I got out and asked the owner if he would sell it. He said he would be glad to, as he used it for water and it leaked. He could buy a nice new one for six pesos. Would we be willing to give that much? We would indeed. Later that day when ex-Governor Fordich saw it he said he had a slightly smaller one that matched it which he would be delighted to give me. Twenty years afterward when the contents of our house at Oyster Bay were appraised, I found these jars were over two hundred years old.

When the yacht anchored off Cotabato, Ted went ashore to speak to the people and inspect homesteads. He told me afterward he spoke in Spanish, as he was sure no one in the crowd of Moros knew a word of English, and he made a blunder which fortunately seemed to pass unnoticed. He quoted a Spanish proverb to the effect that he who kills no pigs eats no sausage, remembering just too late that pork is anathema to Moslems.

Later that afternoon Ted, Miss Hensey, Governor Gutierrez, Colonel Crockett, José Bautista, the press representative, and I went up the narrow river in a Chris-Craft from Cotabato to call on Datu Piang, an old Moro chieftain and a famous character. He told us he had forty-three children and his oldest son was seventy-three years old. On the dock where we landed was a seething mob of Moros, all shouting. I never saw such a variety of turbans and sarongs, and I couldn't help feeling glad they were cheering us and not yelling for our blood. The old man greeted us at his door and took us into his house, where the din was even greater. I counted twelve women beating drums at the head of the staircase. Many of the mob squeezed in with us, lining the walls at a respectful distance and never taking their eyes off us. Half a dozen other women were there, but according to Moslem custom no one spoke either to them or to Miss Hensey and me. At one point the old Datu waved his hand and all the Moro women disappeared except one, his favorite wife. We sat down at a long table while she served coffee and cakes. Ted and the Datu carried on an animated conversation translated by Governor Gutierrez.

Presents were exchanged. The old man went out and returned with two beautiful krises for Ted but apparently felt they were not enough, for after receiving Ted's gifts he went back and returned with some daggers and a cane topped with a huge crocodile's tooth set in silver. He then asked who Miss Hensey and I were, remarked that no Governor General's wife had visited him before, retired again, and returned with a gay silk sarong for me which he said belonged to his favorite wife and a cotton one for Miss Hensey.

We stayed about two hours and were halfway down the river when the Chris-Craft's engine began to skip. The mechanic looked into it, poked things at it, and had just said he thought it might hold out until it got us back to Cotabato when it gave a terrific bang and a screeching sound like a shell going through the air. Every one of the bolts holding the flywheel had broken off. There we were, in wild country with night coming on and not a soul in sight. Governor Gutierrez raised his voice and shouted. Instantly both banks of the narrow stream were lined with men. He sent two of them down the river by canoe to report our plight at Cotabato and have a launch sent for us. Another canoe towed us so that we could get steerage and not drift around and possibly get stuck. Two hours later we met the launch. Fortunately for us, the mosquitoes had not been bad.

Although the climate of Manila was agreeable for most of the year, summer was hard to take. Rain fell in torrents every morning, followed by broiling sun and clouds of steam. To help us keep cool, every room in Malacañan had a big ceiling fan. None of the beds had springs or mattresses. Instead we slept on thin cotton pads laid on caning. Electric lights and small heaters were in all the closets to keep our clothes from being ruined by mildew, but even so our shoes grew moss. When this season started the Army doctors were even more fussy about me and chided me for being anemic. People often are, in the tropics. I was made to eat a quantity of liver and raw-beef sandwiches every day. I told the doctors I would do anything they said if only they would stop my migraine headaches. I had lost ten pounds and weighed less than a hundred when they took out my tonsils, saying it probably would improve my general health. After a couple of days in the hospital I returned to Malacañan feeling a trifle battered. Ted took for granted that my health was already improved and called on me for everything as usual. Finally I asked him to look down my throat. This scared him so much that he was afraid to touch me or have me move. The doctors then ordered me to the mountains for a couple of weeks.

At Baguio was the large and comfortable Mansion House where

governors general had been in the habit of spending the summer months. The custom had been to move the entire executive personnel to Baguio with per diems for everybody. For reasons of economy and because he would have been far removed from his work Ted did not do this and never went to Baguio except for three days at Christmas. Signorina and I established ourselves in the Mansion House while Ted and the girls were on another tour of Luzon. I felt guilty at living in luxury at five thousand feet with open fires and blankets at night while the rest were working in the heat, but I had no choice and tried to atone a little by visiting schools and markets in the neighborhood and making friends. I took sun baths for the first few days until I was fooled by the cool weather and stayed out too long. My shoulders got blistered and looked, as Signorina said, like the face of a drunken man on a frosty morning.

The wife of the American Provincial Governor, Mrs. Dosser, a charming Ilocano with the prettiest hands and feet I ever saw, had a small beauty shop in Baguio. She gave me an excellent permanent wave but said a barber must cut and thin my hair, which had been short for some years. I didn't like this idea, and although dubious of what the result would be I cut it myself, removing several handfuls. It was frightening to be at my own mercy that way, but it came out so well that I went on doing it during the rest of our stay in the islands.

The Mountain Province was the country of the Igorots, a generic name for the non-Christian tribes or pagans. They came of much the same stock as other Filipinos but were to a large extent uncivilized. Their immediate ancestors had been head hunters or tree dwellers. It was sometimes surprising to meet one of them on the road near Baguio clad in a G-string and a tiny round hat in which he kept his pipe and other necessities, perhaps leading four or five dogs to be sold as food in the market, and have him greet you in friendly fashion with "Good morning, Mrs. Kelly!" Mrs. Kelly, a famous character, had been a schoolteacher in the early days who taught her pupils polite manners which they never forgot.

After a few days in Baguio I felt so much better that we went to Bontoc, a village seven hours off by car through country of indescribable beauty. The narrow road was cut in the side of a moun-

Myself in Nepal, 1926.

My barasingha, 1926.

Ted, Suydam Cutting, Kermit, 1929.

Persia, 1933.

Ted and his jaguar, Brazil, 1935.

One of my samplers.

Ted's inauguration, Puerto Rico, 1929.

La Fortaleza, San Juan, P.R.

Ball at La Fortaleza. Ted, myself, and my mother, 1930.

Ted with George Bernard Shaw, Manila, 1933.

The Maria Clara dress I wore at a ball, Manila, 1932.

Malacañan, Manila.

Same. Main Hall.

tain and had been opened two years before. Part of it lay through pine forests, part through jungle with orchids hanging on the trees and great clumps of wild azaleas. The American Mayor of Baguio, E. J. Halsema, came with us part way, saying he had inspections to make, then we were joined by the Deputy Governor of the province, who spoke English remarkably well. Governor Dosser was away but had arranged for us to stay at his house.

Here we met a man who as a Bontoc boy had been taken to the United States by an American missionary to be educated. His benefactor had given the boy his own name, Hilary Clapp. When he returned to his native village he became head of the local hospital and member of the Legislature. Dr. Clapp told me he remembered well the head-hunting days. He showed us where he was born and lived as a child, a little community built on the side of a steep slope, the thatched roofs of its tiny huts shaped like inverted cornucopias. These dwellings admit no light, but the doctor showed us the inside of one by means of a flaming pine splinter. He also pointed out the wall on which heads were hung to drip after a successful raid. Dr. Clapp said he had tried without success to induce his two sisters to leave this community and come to live in his house in Bontoc, but they always refused, saying they preferred old customs and friends to modern surroundings and strangers. We wanted to meet them, but they were too shy.

When the doctor returned to the hospital, the Deputy Governor and the *presidente* of the village showed us around, the latter a venerable Igorot in a blue shirt and trousers who spoke no English. They seemed glad to have us and appreciated our deep interest in what we saw. We came to a group of men squatting in a circle, chanting and beating gongs. They had been over the mountain and were singing to tell their ancestors about it. When they saw us watching they rose and did a dance for us, obviously pleased by our applause. Signorina was thrilled by everything. It was the first time she had seen primitive people and she wanted to know all about their life and customs. I never saw anyone have a better time. I told her she must be careful, as her snow-white hair made her head a particularly desirable trophy, and I think she was almost ready to believe me.

That night they had a series of dances, or *cañao,* in the main plaza lighted by two bonfires. All performers wore nothing but G-strings. First came a Bontoc dance, led by the elderly *presidente,* who proved both skillful and nimble. Next was a dance by members of another tribe, the Ifugao, followed by a third done by the Kalingas. This last was a rarity, and everyone crowded around to see it. After that came a free-for-all, which gave everybody a chance to dance. A dour sergeant of the Constabulary in full uniform, who had been solemnly watching from the beginning, suddenly rushed in and outdid everyone. When the dances were over, the *presidente* led five of the leaders to where I was sitting and made a little speech translated by the Deputy Governor. He said they were so pleased and honored by my presence that they wanted me to have some of their possessions, once highly valued but now of little use since their owners had become civilized. They gave me two head axes, two spears, and a shield. I told them how greatly I would prize these and asked them to accept a few small souvenirs as tokens of my deep appreciation. I had brought a number of knives from Manila in case such a situation should occur. They were overcome with rapture, and it didn't occur to me until years later that it might not have been a happy idea to introduce switch blades to the pagans!

I had also brought a quantity of candy for the children, which we distributed by having all those under a certain height come to receive it. About fifty tore up to us, were given a lollipop each and told to run off. Some candy still remained, so we told the next larger size to come forward. It was dark and hard to see them, but when we heard shouts of laughter from the crowd we realized that some of the very old men were taking advantage of the opportunity. Luckily we had enough for all.

I asked the Deputy Governor if he thought it would be possible for me to buy one of the gongs the natives had used in the dances, thinking it would be nice to call the family to meals at Oyster Bay. He picked one up and showed it to me. "I am afraid no one would be willing to sell his gong," he said. "You see, they are extremely hard to replace nowadays. Please look at the handle." It was a human jawbone.

Dr. H. Otley Beyer, the most distinguished archaeologist and anthropologist of that part of Asia, became a warm friend of ours.

When Henry Cabot Lodge, Jr., visited Manila he asked Ted to arrange a meeting for him with Dr. Beyer, saying he wanted to see the only man ever offered a full professorship at Harvard who had not even answered the letter of invitation. Ted came to the Mountain Province for Christmas and spent four delightful days on horseback and on foot in the Ifugao country with Dr. Beyer, who spoke the language perfectly because he had once lived with the Ifugao for some years. They went from community to community, climbing ladders into the single-room houses and squatting on the floor while the inhabitants described their curious customs and way of life.

Ted met me in Baguio for a Christmas so strange that I kept forgetting what day it was. A conclave of primitive chiefs assembled in the morning. They all sat around Ted on the front lawn of the Mansion House and presented petitions while he talked wisely to them. Later scores of others gathered and held a *cañao* which included a dance of triumph around an artificial head. When the dancing was over we provided a feast for them, with gigantic caldrons of rice and carabao meat cooked outdoors. Afterward Ted inspected the prison, where one of the convicts asked to speak to him, declaring that in the name of justice he should be released. The man was serving a life sentence for murdering his father. When Ted pointed out that he was guilty of a dreadful crime and must not expect to be set free, the prisoner shook his head, saying, "I cannot understand it. After all, it was my father I killed, not yours!"

Chapter 30

Who never forgot that the end of Govern-
ment is the happiness of the governed.
                                    MACAULAY

Even as far back as 1932, when comparatively few people were aware of the danger of the spread of communism, paid agitators were at work causing trouble in the Philippines. Disorder had broken out in several places, particularly among the rice farmers in central Luzon. Ted's weapon against this was the organization of community assemblies. He would send word to some place in the back country that he was coming there two weeks hence to tell the people why they were taxed, for what the tax money was used, and to explain how the government was run. He would bring with him various experts to give practical information on subjects of particular interest in the locality, such as agriculture, domestic animals, poultry, fishing, sanitation, land laws, and the acquiring of homesteads. Ted proposed eventually to have these meetings held in all the provinces in the islands, to provide the people with useful knowledge to help them form a sound and intelligent public opinion, and by means of recreational and social projects to build up community spirit.

The press hailed these assemblies with enthusiasm. The *Philippines Herald* commented editorially on the opening of the first one:

> The big way Governor General Roosevelt put over the first
> community assembly in Malabon yesterday proved the great

possibility of such public meetings in the government's effort to solve the people's needs, and in checking the nefarious designs of paid agitators in this country.

The tremendous ovation which Mr. Roosevelt received was not merely proof of his popularity; it also signaled popular rejoicing over the first concrete step the government ever took to meet the little man on his own ground. . . .

Ten thousand people gathered to acclaim a distinct landmark of civic advancement.

Knowing that "Many people read a song, Who will not read a sermon," Ted always arranged some sort of recreational feature to induce as many as possible to attend these gatherings. In a letter to his mother written on June 6, 1932, he said:

This afternoon I went out and opened the first of my community assemblies. It was a great success. In addition to the lectures we had local music. It is customary here in the small barrios too poor for bands, for some of the people to get together and form what they call a "banda de boca" (mouth band). This has no instruments and renders all the tunes vocally, various individuals taking the part of various instruments. There was also a splendid bamboo band of thirty pieces in which the instruments were made of bamboo or gourds.

After a number of these meetings Ted proposed holding one in the rice-growing region in Luzon, where agitators had been most active. Almost everyone advised him against this. So far the assemblies had been outstandingly successful. Why take a chance where the program might well be upset by unfortunate incidents, even violence? When he insisted that here was where one was most needed, he was urged to have a good detachment of Constabulary on hand and many plain-clothes men scattered through the crowd. I remember he laughed, refused to consider any such plan, and said he knew a much better way to prevent trouble. He sent word to Cabanatuan in Nueva Ecija that a meeting would be held there on a certain date, but with a difference. This time he was coming alone except for his wife.

We drove for several hours to the town, where a small bandstand stood in the middle of a large open plaza. A crowd estimated at over six thousand was waiting in silence. Here was no ovation, no welcome, no smiles. The people drew aside as we alighted, forming a narrow lane through which we walked to the bandstand. Looking at their grim faces, I felt a few little shivers up and down my back.

Ted's speech, translated by an interpreter into the local language, took almost an hour. Afterward the headmen and any others who wanted to ask questions were invited to do so. The questions and Ted's answers were relayed to the audience by a public-address system. At first a few, then gradually more and more came forward to say what was on their minds. Hours passed and it grew dark, but the great crowd stayed, listening intently without making a sound. It was not until Ted was leaving that a prolonged cheer broke out as they surged forward to shake his hand.

Ted's work in the Philippines included fighting the prevailing curse of usury, improving public health and the conservation of natural resources, dealing with difficult tax problems and the tariff, unchanged since 1909, and aiding industry. Financial affairs were bad in the Philippines. Government spending was rising every year. During the last decade the islands had grown used to an ever-increasing budget and an expanding bureaucracy. Estimates of government revenues made the year before were proving far too high. With full co-operation from the Council of State, Ted overhauled the government, consolidated bureaus, services, and activities, eliminating those not vitally needed and weeding out all unnecessary personnel. Dismissals were made so as not to cause hardship. Those let out of government service were allowed to choose between a bonus of a month's pay for each year of service or a farm of their own on government land. It was surprising how many chose the latter, showing the inherent love of the Filipino for the soil. Beginning with his own, Ted reduced government salaries from five per cent to ten per cent, the largest taking the heavier cut. While he had legal power to reduce the wages of some employees, others were regulated by statute. Even so, those whose salaries were statutory reduced them voluntarily. The Legislature followed suit in the same unselfish fashion and cut its own pay.

Ted's three major policies were:

a. To reorganize the government to conform to its income.
b. To aid the small farmer by reforming the land laws, and by executive action to place tracts of virgin territory at the disposal of homesteaders.
c. To extend and improve elementary and vocational education, and to assist institutions of higher learning eventually to be self-supporting.

His first message to the Legislature on July 16, 1932, dealt with these policies. Two days later the *Philippines Herald* reviewed it, remarked that none of them was a new objective of government, and added:

There is, however, no gainsaying the fact that the Governor General has outlined ways and means of accomplishing them so simple and so inexpensive that it would be a clear reflection on the wisdom and patriotism of the Legislature to fail to do its part in their fulfillment.

The New York *Herald Tribune* of July 18 commented editorially on the unanimously favorable reaction in the Philippines to Ted's message and wondered just how far the Legislature would support him when it came to cutting government expenses, saying in part:

His program is not only thoroughly sound, but is politically very astute. No single item on his reform agenda is conditional upon independence, autonomy or the persistence of present relations with the United States. Since the Filipinos have developed no partisan feeling on any question that is not linked up in some way with the independence issue, Mr. Roosevelt has afforded no party leader an excuse for opposing him on any familiar political score. Having completely disarmed all possible criticism by making himself the champion of the small farmers, who constitute an overwhelming majority of the electorate, Governor Roosevelt puts the professional politicians in such position that the only competition among them must now be for the distinction of giving his plans the heartiest approval.
. . . The critical test of these assurances will, of course,

come with the impending revision of the budget; for Mr. Roosevelt's plans call not only for the imposition of new tasks on many bureaus without increase of personnel, but also for a ruthless harrowing of the weed-grown bureaucracy. Since political patronage in the Philippines is largely of the Oriental variety, most of the weeds that would be uprooted are the kith and kin of the politicians whose "respect and affection" the Governor's message has elicited.

It will, therefore, be interesting to see how far a Legislature so amiably committed to the Governor's program can be persuaded to go with its detailed execution. . . .

It was indeed interesting, because when the time came for the detailed execution of Ted's program the legislators went all the way with him, passed the Reorganization Bill, and kept the 1932 deficit down to a nominal sum.

Manuel Quezon, President of the Senate and afterward first President of the Philippine Commonwealth, gave Ted full support. He said that until this year the legislative leaders had always met with the Cabinet in private caucus before the opening of the Legislature and made plans that were not told to the Governor General. This year they had abandoned the practice because they felt the sympathy and understanding between themselves and the Chief Executive rendered it unnecessary. Carlos Romulo wrote a full-page editorial published in the Manila *Tribune* on November 18, 1932, in which he said: "Theodore Roosevelt has established the first 'Era of Good Feeling' our government has ever known."

As a proof of this, the Legislature in November 1932 did something it had never done for a governor general in all the thirty years of its history. Out of a clear sky both Houses passed a joint resolution expressing "the appreciation of the Philippine Legislature of the administration of Governor General Theodore Roosevelt," and giving Ted consummate praise. This they had framed in silver and gave to him with obviously as much delight as he had in receiving it.

Vice-Governor John H. Holliday, who remained for a few months after Ted had left, wrote him as follows on November 16, 1933:

I said goodby to the Governor General [Frank Murphy] this morning, and he told me he was convinced that your Reorganization Law passed last year had saved the financial situation for the government of the Philippines.

Mr. Murphy succeeded Ted and was considered an outstanding Governor General. He enforced with an iron hand every economic policy Ted had provided in the budget, and went farther with some of his own. He reaped the harvest where Ted had broken the soil.

With regard to Ted's third major policy, he felt that education should never unfit people for making a living in the locality where they live. In one of his speeches on this subject he said:

> In an agricultural country the young people should not be taught to believe labor is undignified and overalls degrading. Anyone who feels an office is the only proper outlet for his abilities but who lives where white-collar jobs are scarce is not only of little value to his community but is doomed to personal unhappiness. That should not be the result of education.

He went on to say that, for the present, elementary education and vocational training should be made the birthright of every Filipino child, while high schools and colleges should, in the course of time, be self-supporting. Some scholarships might be necessary for gifted students without funds, but those seeking higher education should be willing to work for it. In this way professional groups would not be overcrowded and the needs of agriculture would be met. An interesting incident occurred in this connection. After leaving the Philippines in 1933 Ted addressed the Rotary Club in Singapore and described this educational plan. A year later Sir Cecil Clementi, the British Governor General, made a speech in which he quoted Ted almost verbatim and at length, ending: "Now that is precisely the policy of the Malayan Administration . . . Evidently these principles command widespread acceptance by competent authorities."

It was indeed rare for an official in the highly specialized British Colonial Service to find excellence in an American administrator and to mention it publicly.

While Ted was striving to attain these objectives he was disturbed to receive messages from Republican officials such as Patrick Hurley, Secretary of War; Everett Sanders, chairman of the Republican National Committee; Lawrence Richey, secretary to the President; Walter Brown, Postmaster General; Henry Allen, chief public relations man for the National Committee, and others, saying it was imperative for him to return to the United States and make a nationwide campaign for the re-election of Mr. Hoover. Ted was devoted to the President and eager to do all in his power to help, but he knew this would be wrong and might well have an adverse effect at home. No previous American Governor General had ever left his post to take part in partisan politics, and this might have an undesirable effect also on the relations between the United States and the Philippines. The efforts of one individual would count for little in a presidential campaign. Three months' absence from the islands at this point would mean the failure of many of Ted's plans. Hope would be lost for the passage of the all-important Reorganization Bill for which he was working night and day with the Legislature in session. Yet he could not refuse if the President really wished his help. In those days there was no telephone between the Philippines and the United States. After a futile exchange of cables he wrote Pat Hurley and Lawrence Richey explaining the situation in detail, giving all his reasons for believing his return unwise, and saying he would of course comply if the President really needed him. He begged for an immediate answer by cable after these letters were received a month later.

Despite Ted's effort to keep the matter quiet until a final decision had been reached, cables from Everett Sanders and Lawrence Richey urging his return were sent over the air in plain language, not in code, and immediately became common knowledge. Several news stories from Washington said "reliable sources" indicated that Ted was going to be drafted for the campaign. A storm of protest arose in the Philippines. Resolutions of strong disapproval were passed by the Legislature, the League of Provincial Governors, the City Council of Manila, and many from individual provincial governments. Editorials appeared in the newspapers unanimously objecting to his leaving.

All this was most embarrassing to Ted, who was unable to give a definite answer. Finally a long cable from the Secretary of War left him no choice. All his arguments had gone for nothing. He gave out a statement and prepared for departure. When this was announced in the United States an outbreak of criticism followed, just as he had predicted. The Secretary of War and Henry Allen then gave statements to the press saying that Ted had not been ordered to return but was coming of his own volition. The New York *Times* saw through this at once and published an editorial that did our hearts good, although we knew Pat Hurley was acting for the best as he saw it.

NOT SENT FOR

Secretary Hurley has been good enough to inform the country that Gov. Gen. Roosevelt's announced return from the Philippine Islands is solely the result of his own wish and will. He was not "sent for." So, in spite of his attachment to the islanders and theirs to him, his known ardent interest in his labors, the pleas of the convention of provincial governors, of the Manila City Council, of the Legislature, that he remain, the difficult problems that are still unsettled, he feels he must depart. "Circumstances," says the Governor General, "have made it necessary for me to return for a brief period to the United States."

Those circumstances, as the Secretary so plausibly tells us, must be sought in the Governor General's own mind. For some mysterious, and presumably subconscious, motive he would rather intermit the work into which he has thrown himself with so much zeal and success, and which requires so much continuity of purpose and residence, than lose the opportunity of making stump speeches in the United States . . . Such a preference in a man who has shown his administrative talent, and who holds one of the greatest administrative offices in the world, is too eccentric to be believed—otherwise than officially. The Governor General will come because he has to come.

The country is used to diplomatists who spend their "vacation" in serving their party and saving the country; but that the Governor General of the Philippines, charged with the gravest responsibilities, plunged into a continual welter of perplexities, should be taken from his post to spellbind is something new in the art of political campaigning. The Secretary's unexpressed but implicit notion of voluntary draft may be humorous enough to reconcile a little those of us who dislike to see the Governor General of the Philippines a traveling lecturer managed by the Republican National Committee.

As Ted had been away from home for months, he had no idea how the campaign was going to be conducted or what issues would be stressed. Little news from the United States reached Manila in those days, and only fragmentary bits on the political situation. He cabled repeatedly, explaining this and asking for information so he could prepare his speeches. Washington maintained a dignified and sphinx-like silence. The only replies he received said he was to start his tour of the country by speaking in San Francisco as soon as he landed.

A few days after we had faced up to the situation and a round of farewell gatherings had begun, another cable came from the Secretary of War.

AFTER FULL CONSIDERATION OF THE SITUATION AS PRESENTED BY YOU, THE PRESIDENT HAS REACHED THE CONCLUSION THAT YOU SHOULD NOT LEAVE YOUR DUTIES AS GOVERNOR GENERAL FOR THE PURPOSE OF PARTICIPATING IN THE CAMPAIGN IN THE UNITED STATES. HE HAS THEREFORE ASKED ME TO ADVISE YOU THAT UNDER ALL THE CIRCUMSTANCES HE BELIEVES IT TO BE YOUR DUTY TO REMAIN AT YOUR POST.

For a day or two there was great rejoicing as crowds of people came to Malacañan to express beaming satisfaction, then everybody buckled down to work again. On October 27, 1932, Ted made a radio address for President Hoover from Manila to the United States, the first ever to be broadcast across the Pacific. To be heard live at 6 P.M. New York time on this date Ted delivered it into the microphone of KZRM at seven the following morning, Manila time. A vice-president of R.C.A. first wired and then wrote to E. R. Riddle, superintendent of the organization in Manila, saying in part:

Congratulations again on your Roosevelt speech stunt. It was the best international broadcast ever heard in this country from any country. There is something fine and clear about the Governor's voice which came across in great shape. Many people expressed great pleasure and amazement at the opportunity of hearing the Governor from Manila.

Ted's mother came out to stay with us in January 1933 and promptly endeared herself to everyone. The Filipinos have all the oriental veneration for family elders and were constantly commenting on her charm, dignity, and grace. It was delightful for us to have her, because she was interested in everything. She had planned to stay two weeks but enjoyed the Philippines so much that she stayed a month. We had a big evening reception for her. I was afraid she would be tired if she received with Ted and me, so I arranged for an armchair between us where she could sit with a bouquet and merely smile at people as they went by. She scorned this plan, however, and stood up, shaking hands with everyone for nearly two hours.

Mrs. Roosevelt went with us on the *Arayat* for an inspection trip. If a day promised to be too long and arduous she and I stayed on board, one reading aloud while the other sewed. When we started I was recovering from a bad migraine, had eaten nothing for two days, but was determined not to be left behind. As soon as we got on the ship I went to bed and slept for several hours, still unable to think of food. My mother-in-law refused to let anyone disturb me and wouldn't allow people to bring me cups of soup, which I would have thrown at them. Late in the afternoon she judged the right moment had come, knocked at my door, and said: "How about a little crisp bacon on a piece of crisp toast?" It was exactly what I needed.

While she was with us the newspapers said that Ted's brother Kermit was off on a cruise with President Franklin Roosevelt on the *Nourmahal,* Vincent Astor's yacht. This was rather embarrassing, because people were surprised and many believed Kermit's purpose must be to try to persuade the President to leave Ted in the Philippines. One day we invited the American newspaper correspondents to lunch to meet Mrs. Roosevelt. They were naturally curious about this story. One of them asked Ted why his brother was yachting with the President. Everyone stopped to listen, because this was something everyone wanted to know. Before Ted could answer, her gentle voice came from across the table: "Because his mother was not there!"

On March 5, 1933, President Franklin Roosevelt proclaimed a bank holiday to go into effect next day in the United States, its territories and insular possessions. It included the Philippines, where it might have created conditions making the reopening of the banks impossible for months. It had taken some thirty years to instill confidence into the people's minds with regard to banks. It might take a long time to live down the arbitrary closing of the banks even for a short time. Aware of the good cash position of the Philippine banks, and believing the people would respond to leadership, Ted immediately called a meeting of all local and foreign bankers, prominent businessmen, and government officials. His plan was to deposit Philippine government funds in local banks at low interest rates, and then to have the government and all banks pool their resources. At first some of the bankers were reluctant to run the risk involved, but he so convinced them that the meeting ended without a dissenting voice. Within hours of the announcement of the holiday Ted had reported this to Secretary of War Dern, adding that the banks were agreeable to stringent temporary regulation by executive action and order and requested that they be allowed to stay open.

After his petition was granted he made several radio talks to the people asking for their confidence. The operation was completely successful. No runs were made, and all deposits were returned. The banks in the Philippines stayed open, doing business as usual, the only ones to do so under the American flag.

Of course Ted took an immense personal risk, as this was done entirely on his responsibility, but as he quoted: "One must always risk one's life, or one's soul, or one's peace—or some little thing."

Shortly before we left Manila, Ted submitted his annual report to the Secretary of War. General George C. Marshall, then Colonel, commented on it as follows:

Fort Screven, Ga.

My dear Roosevelt,

Major Ridgway sent me a copy of your annual report on the Philippines. It is one of the few reports of this nature I have ever read with such genuine interest.

I want you to accept my congratulations, my tribute of praise on a truly remarkable piece of work. It seems to me you have submitted conducive evidence of one of the most remarkable exhibitions of colonial government in history, where harmony, efficiency and patriotism prevailed throughout.

With warm regards to Mrs. Roosevelt and you,

Faithfully yours,

Mar. 30, '33   (signed) G. C. Marshall

Ted sent a copy of his report to our close friend, Edith Wharton, who, although old enough to be our mother, according to her formal custom never called us by our first names. Her comment follows:

April 13, '33

Dear Governor Roosevelt,

I am so glad to get your letter and to know that the ill-wind of party patronage may blow me the good of seeing you and Mrs. Roosevelt again.

I dash this line off in haste to say how much I hope you will both turn up in Paris during my sojourn in the "banlieus." Please note my address . . . and ring my telephone as soon as you arrive.

Thank you also for the report which I admire as a woman of letters while I am impressed as an ignoramus by your account of statistics. It is a joy to see the language we are so rapidly losing used for once as it was meant to be, and I know you will pardon my incapacity to do yr. administrative report the full justice it deserves in favour of my appreciation of the way in which it is presented.

With my best remembrances to you both and a hopeful "au revoir,"

Yours very sincerely,
Edith Wharton

The original policy of the United States regarding the Philippines was to keep partisan politics entirely separate from colonial administration. From 1898 to 1912 an unbroken line of Republican Presidents had appointed as governors general men of experience in colonial government, regardless of party. It was Woodrow Wilson who changed this policy. At first the Filipinos hoped there might be a chance of Ted remaining at his post. Many organizations passed resolutions requesting it; many newspapers carried editorials recommending it. All political parties in the Philippines resented having the governor generalship used as a political plum by the United States. At home the Scripps Howard Newspaper Alliance conducted a campaign to have him retained. William P. Sims in his column in the New York *World Telegram* on March 4, 1933, quoted Philippine public opinion as follows:

> Retention of Colonel Roosevelt is all the more important right now because the relationship between the islands and the United States is about to undergo a radical change. He or his successor seems likely to be the last American Governor General the islands will have. The American Congress has voted the independence of the Philippines, and within the next two or three years the Filipino people are scheduled first to accept or reject the independence measure, and second to frame and ratify a constitution of their own.
>
> It would seem a most inopportune time, therefore, to send out a new Governor General.

Ted had sent in the routine resignation customary on a change of national administration. When the newspapermen asked what relation he was to the new president, they shouted with delight at his answer: "Fifth cousin about to be removed." His resignation was accepted at once. On March 16, 1933, we left Manila on the *Arayat* bound for Macassar.

We had wished to leave quietly to avoid demonstrations and had tried to keep our time of departure secret, but without success.

Despedidas went on for three days, starting with a popular subscription stag dinner for Ted at the Plaza Hotel. I was told afterward it had the largest attendance of any dinner ever given in Manila, with so many people that it was held on three floors of the hotel. Even then tables had to be put in all the halls. Next night there was an official dinner given by the Council of State at the Manila Hotel, followed by a big reception.

The day before we left and the following morning Ted's office was crowded, while friends came in at ten-minute intervals to say good-by to me. Some of them brought presents. To mention only a few, Mrs. Rafael Alunan, wife of a Cabinet member, gave me a luncheon set for twelve made of piña covered with the finest embroidery. Mrs. Emilio Aguinaldo took off a beautiful gold pendant set with pearls which had belonged to her great-grandmother and tied it around my throat, tears running down her face. Dr. Beyer brought a small carved wood chest made over a hundred and fifty years ago in the hills of Cebu; Mr. Hester a large blue and white Chinese jar in perfect condition from a grave on Mindanao; the Manila Chamber of Music a brooch with the first two bars of "Aguinaldo's March" in gold with little jeweled notes. Mrs. Elpidio Quirino, whose husband afterward became President of the Philippine Commonwealth, gave me a wide gold bracelet of exquisite workmanship that had been in her family more than a hundred years. Poor woman, she and two of her children were shot during the Japanese occupation. The John Hollidays came in at noon the day we were leaving. I begged them to stay for lunch, but they refused, saying they felt so badly they doubted they would get through the day.

At three o'clock that afternoon the Cabinet and their wives assembled at Malacañan to go with us to the ship. We said good-by to Ah King and the rest of the household staff, who had served us so well, and went down the stairs to the front entrance to find three companies of Constabulary with their band. There was a catch in my throat as I heard "Hail to the Chief" for the last time. Ted took the salute and made a short speech of thanks. We drove off to the strains of "Auld Lang Syne."

Ted was met at the pier by Major General E. E. Booth, commanding the Philippine Department, and Rear Admiral Charles

E. Courtney, commanding the Naval District. At the end of the dock was a battalion of infantry and a detachment each of sailors and marines, which Ted reviewed after the salute of ruffles and flourishes. To our utter astonishment, the crowd along the great pier was even larger than it had been the day we arrived in Manila for the first time. Here was a Governor General returning to private life, with no power left to do anything more for the people, yet they turned out to give him a greater ovation than they had on his arrival. We were mobbed as we went through the throng to shouts of *"Mabuhay!"* and "God bless you!" Ted was surrounded and hemmed in by men and women trying to grasp his hand. Flowers were piled into my arms until I couldn't see over them. Some women pressed their own little fans into my hands. One hung a gold chain around my neck. Many of them were crying, and by then so was I. When we reached the *Arayat*, every member of the Cabinet broke down quite openly when saying good-by to Ted.

As we got under way Ted received his salute of seventeen guns twice, once from Fort Santiago and again when we passed the U.S.S. *Canopus*. At the breakwater the admiral's barge *Christine* was crowded with some of our best American friends, all waving. She kept beside us until finally outdistanced by the *Arayat*. From the breakwater we were escorted as far as Corregidor by four destroyers, thanks to Admiral Courtney, who had declared that this Governor General was going to leave in style surpassed by no other. By now we thought Ted had received everything possible in the way of honors, but at Corregidor that evening the guns boomed again, and every one of the giant searchlights beamed through the darkness.

Twenty-two years afterward when I visited Manila I was infinitely touched to find how profoundly and tenderly Ted's memory was still cherished. Many people came to see me. Not only did they think of him with real affection, but they remembered how hard he had worked for them. At a large gathering given for me by the Knights of Rizal, Teodoro Evangelista, supreme commander of the order and president of the Far Eastern University, made an address. He was a young man who must have been in his cradle when we were in the Philippines, yet when he enumerated the most important achievements of Ted's administration he was familiar with every one of them.

Chapter 31

When we left the Philippines in 1933 we faced a difficult financial situation. In common with most people, our income had been greatly reduced because of the depression. Ted had no job. Gracie was twenty and unmarried. While our three boys had been brought up to realize they would be on their own after graduating from college, we wanted to give them the best possible education. Teddy was a freshman at Harvard, where Cornelius would be in the autumn, while Quentin had three more years at Groton before going to college. The next few years were going to be expensive. In addition, Cornelius wanted to go to Germany in July with another boy and take a course in gliding at the famous Segelflugschule at Grünau in Riesengebirge. For some years he had been asking for cash presents from his relations for Christmas and birthdays and had saved his allowance until he had a good nest egg put away. He said he had enough money to pay his expenses, but we didn't think this possible and believed, quite wrongly as it turned out, that this would be another drain on the family purse. He wrote us asking permission, saying their plan was to hire two motorcycles after the course was over and tour Austria, Germany, Italy, and France, remarking, "I am older than I used to be." We felt that such initiative should be encouraged and cabled approval, but suggested a secondhand flivver instead of motorcycles.

What we should have done, of course, was to take the first steamer back across the Pacific with our full traveling expenses paid by the government. Instead we behaved like improvident grasshoppers and went around the world the other and longer way, paying the difference ourselves. After all our years of frugality and thrift we took a long chance, hoping the Lord would provide.

Actually the entire journey cost far less than we had feared. As the position of Governor General of the Philippines was regarded as one of the most important administrative posts in the world, doors were opened to us all along the line. The Dutch Government invited us to tour the Netherlands Indies as their guests. So did the Afghan Government when we visited their country. In India we stayed with the Viceroy and the Governor of Bombay. In Persia we stayed with the American Minister in Teheran, and in Jerusalem with the American Consul, while all our motor transport was provided by friends. For the first five months we had few expenses. The result was that we stayed longer and went farther than we had originally planned.

As I have said, we left Manila on the *Arayat* bound for Macassar, where we would take the Dutch steamer *Tjibadak* for Bali. With us were Colonel Crockett, who was going on a trade mission, and Major Ridgway, who would return on the *Arayat*. The prospect of a real holiday in strange places was thrilling.

We had several minor adventures on the way to Macassar. Late one afternoon the captain of the *Arayat* planned to go around the tiny island of Boombong in the Sulu Sea and anchor for the night. Going at full speed, he cut too close to its edge and ran us squarely on a coral reef in broad daylight, with breakers plainly visible not fifty yards away. To make things worse, it was high tide. We had to jettison thirty tons of fuel oil and goodness knows how many of water. Twenty-four hours later, by means of two kedge anchors, we managed to wriggle free. Fortunately the ship was uninjured.

Leaving Ted and Ridgway to fish from the launch, we went to Zamboanga for fuel and water. Everything went wrong. First the mooring rope of the *Arayat* got fouled with the propeller. The pipe through which the oil ran was so small that only a trickle got through, and a new one had to be installed. It took forever for the water to fill the tanks. By the time all was ready the captain remarked casually that we would of course need a bill of health, having stopped at Zamboanga. He had not thought to mention it when the health officer had been on board earlier, nor had the officer himself. Luckily the latter happened to say he was going to a regimental dinner at the Army and Navy Club, so we were able to find him and get the necessary papers. I could think of nothing but poor Ted and Ridgway being eaten by mosquitoes while they waited for us.

When we finally pulled away from the wharf it was after ten o'clock and pouring. We skirted the coast for two hours until the captain could get his bearings. At last we stopped long after midnight and played our searchlight over the waves to find the launch. After a considerable time it appeared, rolling and pitching in the tide drift. Once or twice it was almost swamped. It wasn't pleasant to watch it on that inky sea. When they came up the gangway Ridgway was first, looking like death, and was hustled into his cabin by Ted, who said Matt had had a severe attack of acute indigestion, and at one point Ted thought he was dying. They had landed on the little island of Tienga with no shelter and no resources of any kind and had gathered wood to make a fire in the rain. Then they waited for us. On the island was a small settlement of Moros who were shy and did not show themselves. The boat crew were suspicious, however, and kept their arms handy.

We decided that if Ridgway was no better in the morning we would put back at once to Zamboanga, but he made a quick recovery and ate two poached eggs for breakfast.

At Sandakan, British North Borneo, where we stopped for a few hours, we had lunch at Government House. Governor and Mrs. Richards had two engaging babies, whom we saw afterward. Although all windows were carefully screened Mrs. Richards had taken double precautions. In the middle of the night nursery was a small inner room built of fly screening with the two cribs in it. This was examined by flashlight every night and gave certain protection against any stray insect whose bite might mean malaria, dengue, or the dreaded elephantiasis. The problems and difficulties of raising a family in the tropics have to be experienced to be believed.

We were met by a representative of the Governor, L. J. J. Caron, at Macassar. Feeling it would be civil to do so, we called at Government House. Governor Caron received us politely but obviously as a matter of routine. When during the course of conversation Ted asked if he had ever shot an anoa it was amusing to watch them both, each surprised and delighted to find the other a sportsman interested in natural history. The talk shifted to colonial government. The Governor said he thought he had once met one of Ted's financial advisers. Ted remarked that he didn't count too much on advisers as they sometimes complicated things. It was better to use common sense and say, "Here is where we will cut expenses." To which Governor Caron replied, "My friend, you are right. There is only one man who can handle a colonial budget, and that is the governor." When they began talking on military matters the Governor jumped up, saying Ted must see his troops, and they disappeared together down the street.

Mrs. Caron asked if there was anything I wanted to do. I said I would love to go to a pawnshop to hunt for strange and interesting things. She said there was only one, run by the government. She had never been there and doubted if we could find anything unusual, but we could try. When we got there we went first through two enormous rooms full of bicycles in racks and even hanging from the ceiling. We reached a small inner room in which there was a large safe. The man in charge opened it, took out one of several wooden trays, and, staggering under its weight, put it on a table. I was dazzled by the incredible riches it contained. There were gold objects of exquisite workmanship and evident antiquity, necklaces, bracelets and other ornaments, belts, daggers with steel blades and gold hilts set with jewels, and boxes of every size, shape, and design. There were Chinese porcelain jars with elaborate gold mounts and covers. Although I had promised Ted I wouldn't spend an unnecessary penny on our journey I asked the man what was for sale, only to be told in a friendly but rather pitying way that nothing could be sold. Everything was pledged until the crops matured, when everything would be redeemed. I asked what happened if people did not return for their possessions.

311

What if they died? The man said their families would attend to it. Of course it is possible that specimens of this seventeenth-century gold exist in museums at home, but I have never seen any. We were told that when the United States went off the gold standard and the price of gold soared to thirty-five dollars an ounce, there was a general rush to sell these lovely things to be melted down.

In Bali we met Monsieur Jacques Hackin, noted French archae-ologist, and his attractive young wife. They had been spending their honeymoon in Afghanistan, where he was in charge of the excavations and restorations of the monastery and the colossal rock carvings of Buddha at Bamian. Madame Hackin told me her hus-band made her keep a rifle always within reach while there, al-though I should have thought a revolver would have been handier. Remembering the time we had looked across the northwestern frontier of India at that grim mountain kingdom, I started working on Ted. If Madame Hackin had been there, why couldn't I go? Ted refused to commit himself, but I noticed he was asking Monsieur Hackin about it.

The Dutch certainly treated us with kindness and hospitality. In Bali, Mr. Mörzer-Bruyns, head of the tourist bureau, went with us everywhere and showed us many things off the beaten track. We saw a spectacular cremation in the village of Panjangan and a rehearsal for a curious ceremony called a *sangyang*. In time of disaster, whether from drought, flood, pestilence, or other cause, the people assemble and sing this ritual until someone goes into a trance, speaks with the voice of the gods, and tells everyone how they have sinned and how they can avert further punishment. At the rehearsal there would, of course, be no trance. Mörzer-Bruyns said he had discovered this strange rite while he was changing a tire near a little village in the interior and had heard the sound of singing. He added that not more than a couple of dozen people, including Dutch officials, knew the ceremony ex-isted. I think he felt it was his own particular pet, to be shown to such people as he chose. The Hackins were the only other spectators.

About seven in the evening we went to the village, where

crowds were milling about. Food vendors were selling their wares by the light of coconut-oil lamps. We were taken to some chairs on a high bank overlooking a little hollow in which a torch on a high bamboo pole was surrounded by a couple of hundred men in a solid circle, all talking and laughing. Suddenly they were quiet for a moment, then the entire circle lay down to the right with a shout that ended like a sneeze. Another moment of dead silence, and everyone did the same to the left. The effect was startling. Next they sang like a Gregorian choir for a few minutes, then as if they were imitating a railway train, with extraordinary rhythm. Another silence, and the leader shouted a single syllable, "Sa!" and everyone took it up and continued indefinitely, "Sa-sa-sa-sa-sa-sa-sa-sa!" A pause, and another chant was interrupted by a thin nasal voice, answered on the other side of the circle by a deep, unctuous base, "Ho! Ho! Ho!" and words that sounded as if the voice were recounting Rabelaisian jokes. After a little they all took a short rest, then went at it again. Once they broke into a high falsetto, "R-r-r-r-r-r-r-r!" Mörzer-Bruyns said they were imitating monkeys in the forest. The village headman who ran it was a youth about twenty years of age, very smart in his sarong and batik headkerchief.

When we arrived in Soerabaja by steamer from Bali we were met by Colonel Thompson, a Dutch officer with a Scottish grandfather, who had been assigned to take us through Java. A day's banteng shooting had been arranged for us, which we planned to do until we received an invitation to a Garebeg or rice festival at the court of his Highness the Soesoehunan of Solo. Everyone told us this would be a rare example of oriental splendor well worth seeing, so we gave up the shooting.

"Soesoehunan" was a title above that of Sultan. His name was Pako Bueno, meaning "The Navel of the Universe," and he was enormously wealthy. He held his position by courtesy of the Dutch, who allowed him all the pomp he wanted without temporal power. According to etiquette meticulously followed, his Highness addressed the Dutch Governor of the province as "Grandfather," while the Governor when writing to the Soesoehunan began his letters "My Grandson."

At Soerakarta or Solo, rooms had been reserved for us in a small attractive hotel, spotlessly clean and with good food. What was more, you could drink the water from the faucet not only here but all through Java, as it was scientifically inspected several times each week. I thought this one of the crowning triumphs of the Dutch as colonizers, as it was unsafe to do so elsewhere in Asia. The Dutch Resident and his wife, Mr. and Mrs. W. H. Ockers, called on us and said they would come next morning to take us to court.

"Formal evening dress is obligatory for gentlemen attending the ceremony," said Mr. Ockers. "Also orders and decorations."

"Very well," said Ted. "I have my white mess jacket with me."

"I am afraid that won't do," replied Mr. Ockers. "His Highness is extremely particular and requires black dress suits with stiff shirts and white ties to be worn."

"What?" exclaimed Ted. "In the Philippines and even in the Malay States the white mess jacket is the correct formal evening dress for all occasions. It never occurred to me to bring a black tailed coat to wear in the tropics!"

"We can borrow one for you quite easily," said the Resident. "I will attend to it."

"But I don't want to wear a borrowed one," protested Ted. "I want to wear my own mess jacket. It's bad enough having to dress for the evening at nine in the morning anyway."

"I am really very sorry," said Mr. Ockers. "His Highness has made an adamant ruling on this subject. He insists on full dress, and we all suffer. He wouldn't know a mess jacket if he saw one."

This went on until, feeling like the mother of a small boy, I said, "You will have to wear what the others do or you can't go to the party!"

The borrowed coat did not fit. It belonged to a very tall man, and its sleeves kept coming down over Ted's hands. By this time Ted was convinced the ceremony would be tedious and tawdry and that he would have killed a record banteng if we had gone shooting instead. Next morning at nine Mr. and Mrs. Ockers came for us, the former gorgeous in a blue uniform covered with gold lace. Colonel Thompson, a white plume on his hat, and Colonel Crockett were immaculate in their white uniforms, while I was

314

cool and comfortable in a linen frock. Ted declared his feelings were too deep for words.

We set out for the palace, an immense place covering several acres. Mrs. Ockers and I went on ahead and were received by the Ratoe Alit, eldest daughter of his Highness. We watched the rest of our party arrive. Mr. Ockers, representing the Dutch Governor, who was absent, came in a magnificent coach like Cinderella's, drawn by six horses. Ted, Colonel Crockett, and Colonel Thompson were in a car just behind. A battalion of infantry in military jackets and sarongs of brilliant colors presented arms. I told the Ratoe Alit that I wanted to take pictures, and she took me to a place by the arch under which the procession would come.

The first group that appeared was so surprising that I almost dropped my camera. It was the Soesoehunan's bodyguard of a dozen women in green and gold sarongs with green silk tightly wrapped around them above the waist, leaving their arms and shoulders bare. Some carried golden animals, some birds, some little chests, caskets containing all he might need for his comfort in the field. They were followed by his concubines and dancing girls in the same green and gold, led by two little dwarfs dressed like the others. His Highness's four official wives were not in the procession, nor were any of his children, numbering seventy-nine at the last count. Mrs. Ockers told me the Golden Queen, Goesti Kandjeng Ratoe Hemas, would appear later. She was renowned throughout the Indies for her beauty.

Following the women came a group of blind men, each holding the end of another's cane. These were sent out into the market place every day to hear the news of the world and inform the Soesoehunan, who had never bothered to learn to read or write. Detachments of soldiers passed; the most striking were archers in costumes of scarlet, green, yellow, and white, with the black-and-white feathers of the arrows spread out behind one shoulder. Next came the palace servants in vivid green with orange plumes on their hats. All marched slowly to the beating of a gong, taking about one step per second.

Twenty palace dignitaries followed in black jackets embroidered in gold and brocade sarongs. When I saw a number of parasols approaching I realized his Highness was coming and got

315

set to take his picture. A short, fat man, he was leaning heavily on Mr. Ockers's arm and was covered with orders and decorations. When he saw me with my camera he stopped short, drew himself up, and posed for a photograph. Directly behind them was Ted, flanked by Colonel Crockett and Colonel Thompson.

The procession went into an enormous pavilion with a roof and polished floor but no walls. In the center was a high dais with two thrones, one for the Soesoehunan, the other for Mr. Ockers. If the Dutch Governor had been there they would have been identical, but the throne for the Resident was an inch lower and an inch narrower and was set back six inches. Rows of chairs stretched in all directions, divided by a center aisle. Ted was seated in the front row by the aisle. Mrs. Ockers and I were on the veranda of another building close by, where we had a good view of the proceedings. A gamelan orchestra played constantly, consisting of a series of gongs ranging in size from tiny ones played like a xylophone to enormous ones three feet across.

After everyone was settled the ceremonies began and went on for hours. His Highness spoke, and up the aisle marched the twenty dignitaries, headed by his Prime Minister. Halfway to the throne, they vanished from my sight. I stood up to see what had happened to them and saw that they were creeping the rest of the way in time to the music. Reaching the dais, they sat down in chairs reserved for them.

Offerings were brought in by another procession—huge decorated mounds of rice. The larger ones were supposed to be male; the smaller, female. They were carried around until everyone had seen them, then taken to the mosque for distribution to the poor.

Again the Soesoehunan spoke, and his Prime Minister rose and left the pavilion, sent out to observe the state of the world. After a few minutes he returned. Halfway to the throne, he dropped to the floor as before and crept the rest of the way to make his report. At another order from his Highness his concubines and dancing girls, who had been grouped on the floor beside the throne, crawled out in the same way, keeping time to the music.

Several toasts were then proposed, the first by the Soesoehunan to the Queen of Holland. A tall white-haired major-domo in black livery and knee breeches, with buckled shoes, aiguillettes, and a massive silver chain around his neck, brought in a large silver tray with two tiny glasses on it, one with a gold cover. Behind him walked a man in a sarong holding a parasol over the tray. They were followed by twenty or more servants carrying big trays with many little glasses. The major-domo climbed the steps of the dais, passed the tray first to his Highness, who took the glass with the gold cover, then to Mr. Ockers, and showed considerable skill in walking backward down the steps. The other trays were passed to the most important people in the audience. Everyone rose to hear and drink the toast, the band played the Netherlands national anthem, the battalion of soldiers fired a salute, and a cannon boomed. All glasses were retrieved, and the major-domo, followed by the others, left the pavilion. Fifteen minutes passed, and the entire performance was repeated. This time the toast was to the Soesoehunan and was proposed by the Resident, who had to mention every one of the former's thirty-five orders and decorations. Mrs. Ockers remarked, "When the Governor is here he recites these by heart, but my husband reads them from a paper. It would be so awful if he forgot one!"

After more toasts the gathering adjourned to a vast ballroom for speeches. Painted white, its ceiling held up by a forest of small, square gilded columns, the ballroom had three thrones on a high dais for the Soesoehunan, the Golden Queen, and their little daughter, Kandjeng Sekar Kedaton, who kept wiggling her bare toes and smiling at Ted. The Golden Queen was really lovely. Small, slim, and aristocratic, she was dressed in gay brocade and glittered with diamonds. Instead of wearing fresh flowers in her hair like the other women, she wore two tiny velvet ones over one ear. This was true chic, for the fresh flowers wilted in ten minutes.

While the proceedings were going on with great formality, his Highness suddenly sent word by his son-in-law that he wished me to take his photograph with the Golden Queen and the little Princess. I tried to explain that my film was slow and the light bad, but was merely asked to hurry. The Prince led me up the aisle between the hundreds of people, and the Soesoehunan motioned me to come to the steps of the dais. I caught sight of Ted's startled face as everything stopped while I went through the motions of taking a picture I knew would not come out, then bowed politely and hastily retired.

Two men were taking sound movies, which had never been done before, and were having a hard time. I watched them with interest as they rushed about, perspiring profusely, one wearing a white mess jacket, the other a black tuxedo. No one seemed to know their nationality until one of them leaned over Ted and said, "Colonel, it's been a long time since I took your picture!" They were from Universal Films. As soon as Ted knew they were Americans he started to help them get what they wanted. His Highness disapproved of them, thinking they were not adding to the dignity of the occasion, and had refused to co-operate. Ted told him that if he would consent to say a few words for them to record he would be heard by over a hundred million Americans. This impressed him so much that he wanted every kind of picture taken, and ended by having his Army pass in review. When it was over the photographer said, "Gee, Colonel, but you've been a godsend!"

When the ceremonies had ended and the crowd dispersed, Mrs. Ockers presented me to the Soesoehunan and the Golden Queen. He looked at me critically from head to foot and then said something. I caught a twinkle instantly suppressed in Mrs. Ockers's eye. "He asks how old you are!" I was startled into telling my correct age, adding hopefully, "I am very old," and felt rather crushed when he made no comment whatever. The Golden Queen gave me a brooch shaped like a kris in diamonds and rubies.

After leaving Soerakarta we visited the impressive Buddhist temple of Borobudur, spent the night in Semarang, and flew to Batavia next morning. Ted spent the day at the museum with Dr. Stein Callanfels, the Dutch scientist, while I went shopping with Mrs. Kenneth Patton, wife of the American Consul General, and bought a beautiful sarong woven with gold, and some elaborately carved puppets made of carabao hide and used for shadow plays. The Pattons had asked a group of people, Americans and Javanese, to meet us at lunch. We had rijsttafel, a noble dish. First a great platter of rice was passed, then some twenty other dishes, such as curried chicken, various kinds of fish and vegetables. After we had made mounds of food in our soup plates, raw eggs were served to break on the top and mix with the whole. I never saw Ted enjoy anything more.

In Batavia I was fascinated by the number of bicycles seen on the streets about five in the afternoon when schools and offices closed. They went along ten or twelve abreast, children of all ages, elderly Dutchmen, stout women sitting very straight, often with babies strapped behind the saddle, countless Javanese wearing striped pajamas. The streets were crammed with them, and as we drove along I was amazed there were not more accidents.

We spent a night at Buitenzorg with the Governor General of the Netherlands East Indies and his wife, Madame de Jonge, who were most delightful people. His Excellency took us out to show us specimens of trees on the extensive grounds of Government House, each tagged with its name and place of origin. After walking for half an hour during which time we tried to express enthusiastic interest, the Governor General stopped and said, "I wonder if this bores you as much as it does me." Ted, always frank, answered that it did. "Good! I am so glad. I have had to do it so often! Let's go back to the house and talk."

We sailed from Batavia on the S.S. *Op Den Noort* and had a large cabin, bathroom, sitting room, and private deck. Until we reached Singapore we were still guests of our wonderful hosts, the Dutch, who left nothing undone for our comfort and entertainment. Just before we got to Singapore we had a wireless message from the Governor General of the Malay States, Sir Cecil Clementi, whom we had known when he was Governor of Hong Kong, asking us to stay at Government House, where we spent forty-eight hours. As a young attaché in Japan, Sir Cecil had been in poor health and was ordered to be out of doors as much as possible. He obtained leave of absence and started on a walking tour with a small knapsack on his back and wearing a kimono, as it was inconspicuous, comfortable, and easy to replace when necessary. He traveled for months, stopping at little inns or the houses of chance acquaintances and meeting nothing but kindness and courtesy from everyone. Finally he recovered his health and had acquired an intimate knowledge of Japan possessed by few other foreigners.

Ted asked his advice about going to Afghanistan. He approved heartily of the idea, saying we might well be able to get the necessary permission. In those days it was a forbidden country, with no railroads and no planes. If travelers should be killed or captured by bandits their government would have to take steps and an international incident might occur. The British, who controlled the Khyber Pass, wanted no trouble of this kind. As the United States had no representative in Afghanistan, Ted cabled the Viceroy of India, the Earl of Willingdon, whom we had known when he was Governor General of Canada, and asked to be allowed to go through the Pass. Lord Willingdon answered at length, granting permission provided the Afghan Government made no objections, promising to help in any way he could, and inviting us to stay at Viceregal Lodge, Simla, on our way through India.

When we returned to the ship after a night at Government House in Penang we met two new passengers, young American architects William McMillan of Baltimore and Alan Stuyvesant of Allamuchy, New Jersey. They had been shooting tiger and elephant in Indo-China and were on their way home. By the time we reached Bombay we liked them so much that we asked them to go with us to Afghanistan, always supposing we would succeed in going there ourselves. They accepted at once, offering to be our A.D.C.s. I thought this a fine idea and said from then on I wouldn't write luggage labels, look through timetables, or make reservations. I wouldn't be responsible for getting to places on time; in fact, it would be up to them to see that *I* didn't miss trains. I wouldn't plan itineraries or do anything else requiring brains and concentration. It was great fun saying all this, but of course it never worked out that way.

The American Vice-Consul, Paul C. Hutton, Jr., met us at the dock in Bombay and took us to the Taj Mahal Hotel, a large dingy place where we had reserved rooms. It was pleasant being in the flamboyant city again, its ornate architecture and busy and variegated street life covered with a heavy blanket of heat. We went to lunch with the British Governor, Major General the Right Honorable Sir Frederick Sykes. Lady Sykes was in England and only his Excellency and members of his staff were there. Long ago Ted and I had found that it is possible to get a very good idea of a man from seeing his staff, and we agreed that this staff was one of the nicest we had ever met.

We returned to the hotel and had not been there more than a few minutes when the Governor's naval A.D.C. arrived with a note for me. We were invited to Government House to stay for the six days we were to be in Bombay. Ted and I were amused, for we recognized this procedure as something we had often followed ourselves. The Governor had heard we were coming and felt he must do something to be polite, so he asked us to lunch. Then, after looking us over, he had invited us to stay. It was twice as much of a compliment than if he had done so sight unseen. We joyfully packed our things and moved immediately. Bill and Alan stayed at the hotel, as the latter had a badly infected blister on his foot and was under a doctor's care.

Government House, a few miles from the city, was one of the most beautiful I have ever seen. Built of white marble on a promontory running out into the sea, it was surrounded by extensive grounds and had its own bathing beach. At the entrance, about a mile from the house, were two Sikh sentries in the smartest possible uniforms and turbans. We stayed in one of the marble guesthouses and had two big bedrooms, two dressing rooms, two bathrooms with marble tubs, a little morning room overlooking the sea where we had breakfast, and a large sitting room lined with bookcases containing an excellent library. The guesthouse was about fifty yards from the main house, yet every night before dinner a strip of red carpet was laid between the two—very good for my evening slippers.

The night after we arrived I had a migraine and was unable to think of food. I sent word by our bearer that the sahib would dine with his Excellency but I would not. This created a certain confusion. The khidmatgar came to ask if I was dining out and did I need a car. Then he asked if I wanted dinner served in the guesthouse. I said I was not feeling very well and wanted no dinner. This distressed him. He went away, only to return with a look of great concern and the dinner menu. Was there *nothing* I would eat? They were having borsch, so largely to please him I asked for a little of that, but nothing else. My tray arrived with a little porcelain one-person tureen marked with the government arms and fine linen with "G.H. Bombay 1927" woven in one corner. Next

321

morning I was sufficiently revived to eat "the brave British breakfast of bacon and eggs" that was served in the morning room.

We were busy with our preparations for the north. Ted had left our passports at the Afghanistan Consulate for visas. The Consul was hopeful that they could be given us but had to consult his government first. He said he would let us know in Simla. On the strength of this we hired a Moslem bearer, Amir, who could speak Pushtu to go with us through Afghanistan and Persia.

I spent some time trying to find a lunch basket, as I knew we would often have to take food with us to eat by the roadside. The fitted picnic baskets in the smart shops were expensive, so Julia Hutton, sister of our Vice-Consul, took me to the bazaars. I bought a large well-made empty basket, then collected tin enameled plates and cups, nickel-plated knives, forks, and spoons, a teakettle with an alcohol lamp, and some tin boxes for food. The whole outfit cost less than five dollars. I stocked the basket with malted milk powder, instant coffee, tea, sugar, dried prunes, strawberry jam, and several boxes of biscuits. These would do to start with.

Alan was still having trouble with his blistered foot, so he decided not to go with us to Simla but to join us later at Peshawar on the northwestern frontier, the jumping-off place for Afghanistan.

We were really sorry to leave Bombay and to see the last of Sir Frederick Sykes and his staff, whom we had liked so much. On the afternoon of April 25, Ted, Bill, and I took the train for the twenty-four-hour journey to Agra, where we were to stay for a day and a night on the way to Simla. We wanted to see the Taj Mahal again, to us the most beautiful building in the world, and to explore the deserted city of Fatehpur Sikri, where Akbar's magnificent palace was still in perfect condition, its great courts inhabited only by doves.

Indian trains were comfortable in winter but less so in the hot weather. Windows were fitted with shutters and blue glass against the glare, but still the heat was intense. A great cake of ice in the middle of the floor helped somewhat, but the leatherette upholstery on the couches was too hot to touch unless covered with a rug. Men came in at the stations to sweep out the appalling accumulation of dust. First-class compartments had adjoining lavatories and showers. The trains had no corridors, which sometimes led to complications. You had to get out at a station to get to the dining car, then wait for another stop to get back. Sometimes Amir came to spread out our bedding rolls and make things ready for the night and was caught for a couple of hours until the next station released him and us.

At Agra we took the train to Kalka, a twelve-hour trip. Amir brought us coffee before we arrived at half-past five in the morning. From here we traveled by "rail-motor," a little car run on rails by gasoline, through beautiful country much like the Mountain Province in the Philippines. The crisp, cold air made us hungry, and Ted wired ahead for breakfast at the first stop we made. Trays were handed in to us with boiled eggs, toast, marmalade, and coffee, which we had just eight minutes to eat. We reached Simla at half-past nine and were met by an A.D.C. on the Viceroy's staff.

This Viceregal Lodge had been built about seventy years before and was surrounded by beautiful trees with snow-capped mountains beyond. In front the ground fell away abruptly, giving a glorious view. It was large and comfortable. Lady Willingdon had arranged it inside with gay chintzes and it looked like an English country house. Others of the staff were on the steps when we drove up and asked if we would like breakfast. I answered that I had had two already but would simply love a third, so we all sat down to porridge and scrambled eggs. Ted and I were put in the "Governor's suite," where there were two large bedrooms, two bathrooms, a dressing room, a big sitting room, and a little dining room. We had been long in the tropics, where nothing but the coldest possible baths could be tolerated, so the first thing I did was to revel in a piping hot one. Afterward Ted went to talk to the Viceroy, while Bill, one of the A.D.C.s, and I went out in rickshaws to look at Simla. The hills were so steep that each rickshaw had four men instead of the usual one. No cars were allowed except for those of the Viceroy, Lady Willingdon, and the Commander in Chief of the Indian Army, Field Marshal Sir Philip Chetwode. I had never been to Simla but felt as if I knew every bit of it from Kipling.

Also staying at Viceregal Lodge were his Highness the Jam Saheb of Nawanagar and his personal assistant, Rushbrook Williams. We had known them before and were very pleased to see them. It was his Highness who in 1926 had sent us a female black buck for our group at the Field Museum. Every morning a mimeo-graphed sheet with plans for the day was sent to each of us, a great convenience. A sample follows:

VICEREGAL LODGE
SIMLA

ARRANGEMENTS
Friday, 28th April 1933

A.D.C. in Waiting . . . . .Captain Smith Bingham
A.D.C. Second in Waiting . . . . Captain Freeman Thomas
A.D.C. Third in Waiting . . . . .Fl.-Lt. MacDonald

10:30 A.M. The Viceroy will see the Hon'ble Member Rail-ways and Commerce Dept.

11:00 A.M. Colonel and Mrs. Roosevelt and Mr. McMillan will arrive at Summer Hill to stay at Viceregal Lodge.

11:00 A.M. The Viceroy will interview Mr. Venkateswaran.

11:40 A.M. Her Excellency will visit the Rippon Hospital.

12 Noon Her Excellency will visit Dr. Carlton William Smith the Dentist.

1:15 P.M. His Highness the Maharajah Jam Saheb of Na-wanagar accompanied by Mr. Rushbrook Wil-liams will lunch with the Hon. Sir George Schuster at "Peterhof."

1:15 P.M. The following have been invited to luncheon: The Revd. and Mrs. P. N. F. Young (Chaplain of Simla), and Mr. J. P. V. Weir (4/8th Punjab Regt.).

6:30 P.M. Executive Council Meeting.

6:56 P.M. SUNSET

The night after we arrived in Simla I went to bed feeling per-fectly well and awoke next morning certain that my last hour had come. I can't remember ever being so sick. Ted had to cancel all engagements for the day as far as I was concerned. Lady Willing-don came to my room, a snow-white Pekingese under her arm, in-quired exhaustively as to what was wrong, sent for the doctor, gave me a hot-water bag, shut the window, fixed the fire, picked one of

324

Ted's ties from the floor, remarked that all men were alike and all untidy, and departed, saying she would be back. The doctor told me many people were affected in the same way by the sudden change of climate, and it didn't amount to anything. Her Excellency returned to say he had told her what I was to eat, and my meals would be specially prepared and brought to me. When my dinner appeared that evening I couldn't eat it, although it was chicken mousse served by a khidmatgar gorgeous in a turban and scarlet and gold coat, but by the next morning I was entirely revived.

In the afternoon I watched tennis in an indoor court where Ted and Bill took on Lady Willingdon, who played a surprisingly good game, and the Jam Saheb. Once there was a terrific noise on the curved glass roof as if someone had lost his balance and would presently crash past the windows. An A.D.C. said, "Don't be startled. It's nothing but the monkeys running about." Which indeed it was.

Soon our passports arrived, duly visaed for Afghanistan. With them came an invitation to go through the country as guests of the Afghan Government. Everyone was interested in our plans, because no British women were allowed to go there except those married to men in the Legation. Once across the border, they were forbidden to go out without an armed guard. We went to see the American dentist, Dr. Carlton Smith, who went to Kabul often to take care of the King's teeth and who told us to expect primitive arrangements. On his last visit he had spent the night sleeping on the ground halfway to the city and had borrowed two shovels from road menders to hold up his mosquito net.

We were invited to lunch with Field Marshal Sir Philip Chetwode. Snowdon, his house, had been built by Kitchener and was delightful, with beautiful paneling, English chintzes, and open fires. For lunch we had a delicious dish of chicken creamed with lots of mustard called "White Devil." The Field Marshal told me he was a general in the Nepalese Army and showed me the hat that went with the position. It was made entirely of pearls sewed on in an intricate design, with a large flat ornament of diamonds in front. Around the edge was a fringe of uncut emeralds the size of hazelnuts. On the top was a great plume made of several birds of paradise. He said he wanted to give it to a museum when he went home, but his family objected violently.

One afternoon we had tea with Sir T. Vigyarajapacharia, a Hindu friend whom we had met at Government House in Bombay. He had three pretty teen-age daughters with enormous dark eyes. Dressed in bright-colored saris, they entertained us with poise and wanted to hear every detail of life in the United States. I heard one of them say to Bill, "Do you believe in divers?" Being used to Asian English, I knew what she meant, but Bill was puzzled. "I beg your pardon?" She repeated, "*Divers!* Do you believe in divers?" Bill was defeated. "Well, it's hard to say. I mean—well—yes *and* no." I let them go on for a moment, then came to the rescue and murmured to Bill, "Divorce, you goose!"

By the time we left Simla we were firm friends with both their Excellencies. Here there was not the rigid formality at all times that had existed at Viceregal Lodge in Delhi seven years before. Lord Willingdon had had a remarkable career as colonial administrator and pro-consul, and he told me enthralling stories of his adventures as a young man in faraway places. Once he spoke of early days in China during the Boxer Rebellion and described walking down a street where bullets were flying about. I broke in to ask if Lady Willingdon had been with him at the time and he answered, "Of course she was. I never move without the woman!"

Chapter 32

The sole relic of Timur's vast dominion was the little kingdom which an exiled prince of his own brave blood [Babar] set up among the crags and passes of the Afghan hills, whence came the "Great Moghuls" and the glories of Delhi and Agra.

STANLEY LANE-POOLE

We reached Peshawar on May 4 and stayed for two days with the Acting Governor of the North-West Province and his wife, Mr. and Mrs. George Cunningham, who were most kind and hospitable. I love Peshawar and was annoyed to have a migraine the first day, but in any case we couldn't have gone into the bazaars as we had done before. There had been underlying unrest in the city since the riots three years before. Besides this, it was a Moslem holiday, when everyone was apt to be a bit on edge. Instead of buying gold- and silver-embroidered slippers, all I could do this time was to get a little bicarbonate of soda at a drugstore.

Next day a number of people gathered for tennis at Government House. One of the members of Mr. Cunningham's staff had a little girl of three with merry blue eyes and tight yellow curls. Her mother was having a hard time, as the child had learned to imitate perfectly the unpleasant spitting noise heard all over the East and kept doing it constantly. She sat on my lap as we watched the

327

tennis and would start, "A-a-a-a-r-r-ch!" Each time her mother pounced on her in a frenzy.

Alan joined us in Peshawar, walking with a cane but determined not to be left behind. We hired a small Chevrolet touring car and a little truck for the two bearers and the luggage. Just as we were setting out early in the morning Mrs. Cunningham gave me a long pongee dust coat, saying the dust would be beyond belief.

On our way through the Khyber Pass we noticed an ingenious method of traffic control, new since our last visit. Sign posts were placed at intersections showing by means of pictures which road was for camels and donkeys and which for automobiles. We passed Landi Kotal, the last British outpost, where the railroad ended, and came to the big sign forbidding entry into Afghan territory. This time we could disregard it, as we were accredited guests of the government. We stopped to show our passports and credentials and were surprised when a guard of honor turned out for Ted.

At first the country was grim and impressive, with great barren mountains on either side, but soon after leaving the Pass we crossed a vast sun-scorched desert for hours. As noon approached we began to feel hungry but could see no spot of shade where it would be pleasant to have lunch. Finally Bill, who was hungriest, spied a cave in a cliff overhanging the road, which made a nice place for a picnic. Mrs. Cunningham had had all sorts of delicious food packed in our basket as well as a large thermos of coffee.

Much refreshed, we started off again and reached Jalalabad about four in the afternoon. Here another guard of honor turned out for Ted, and a soldier escorted us to an attractive bungalow in a large garden full of flowers. We were received by a smart, handsome young officer, Prince Mohamed Daud Khan, commandant of the East Jalalabad District and nephew of the King, with whom we sat on the veranda and chatted. He spoke beautiful French and asked us if we would have *déjeuner ou goûter*. We decided on tea. He said he had *un petit machin* which he wanted to offer me as a souvenir and gave me a large round wooden box and cover delicately incised and painted in gay colors, a nice example of native handicraft.

Late in the afternoon we arrived at the oasis at Nimlah, halfway to Kabul, where we were to spend the night. (This was where Dr.

Smith had borrowed shovels from the road menders to prop up his mosquito net.) Again a soldier met us and conducted us through a formal garden to a white stucco bungalow. We got out of the car hot and covered with desert dust and saw standing on the steps an Afghan in a perfectly tailored morning coat, striped trousers, and a cap made of the finest astrakhan. He bowed and said, "On behalf of his Royal Highness the Prime Minister I welcome you to Afghanistan and take pleasure in placing this house at your disposal."

We thanked him warmly for his courtesy and went into the house, which was furnished with everything one could possibly need. The floors were covered with soft, thick Afghan rugs; the beds had good-quality springs and mattresses and were obviously brand-new; the bathrooms had large porous jars of water. There was a general atmosphere of clean white paint.

Our host was Zul Facar, assistant to the Prime Minister, who had been assigned to look after us during our stay in Afghanistan. He spoke both English and French and had a great fund of information and stories about the country. He loved to play little jokes on us. Often he would start an anecdote and stop short at the most interesting point, saying, "That is enough for today. I will tell you the rest tomorrow!" Being a Durani, or member of the ruling race, he escaped with his life by living for months disguised as a camel driver after he had opposed Bacha-i-Saqao, who usurped the throne in the revolution of 1929.

After tea Zul Facar took us out to explore the garden laid out by Nur Jehan for his Empress in the seventeenth century. Although somewhat run down and full of weeds, it was still lovely. A high mud wall surrounded it. The central point of interest was a series of long, narrow, rectangular pools of water connected by tiny cascades at successively lower levels. Along the pools were wide paths bordered with cypresses and masses of irises. Narrow paths led into the wide ones at right angles edged with smaller trees. At each corner were orange trees in full flower. In the distance a snow-covered mountain range stretched as far as we could see. That night a full moon turned the pools and cascades to liquid silver.

We had an excellent dinner of seven courses served by half a dozen servants and went to bed early. In the cool of the morning we had breakfast on the veranda. As soon as we had finished, everything was removed from the little house. Beds were taken apart, rugs rolled up, china and kitchen utensils packed, and furniture carried out. In a short time everything was loaded into a lorry. All the servants climbed on board and set off at a brisk pace down the road toward Kabul. We had dismissed our hired car from Peshawar and now traveled in two comfortable Buicks provided by Zul Facar. He, Ted, and I went in one, Bill and Alan in the other.

After leaving Nimlah we went through miles of desert, climbed over some hills, and dropped into the desert again. We passed many little nomad camps with black tents and stopped to take pictures of the people, their camels, donkeys, sheep, and goats. When Zul Facar said we were strangers in the country—and guests—they greeted us with *"Assalam aleikum* [Peace be with you]!" To which we replied, *"Oua aleikum assalam* [And with you, peace]," as is proper. One woman was baking bread and gave me a great slab of it. The headman, an old patriarch with a white beard, told Zul Facar they would kill a goat if we stayed for a feast with them.

At noon we stopped at a small resthouse which had rugs on the floor, a table and chairs arranged, and a delicious lunch ready. The lorry with the supplies had arrived about an hour before. Some tribesmen from the mountains had assembled to greet us, tall men with aquiline features, in turbans and posteens with rifles slung on their shoulders. They gave me a sheep. I was rather dismayed at the idea of taking it in the car to Kabul, until Ted told me to pat its head and give it back with a few words of thanks. I did so and everyone was content.

As the afternoon wore on it grew colder. We climbed high on a road winding through the mountains and crossed a wide, desolate plateau with no sign of anything green. Suddenly the countryside changed and was covered with rippling wheat fields, the result of an irrigation dam built two years before.

Just at sunset Zul Facar turned to us. "There is our capital," he said.

The entrance to Kabul lay between two rugged hills with the old city wall running along their crests. From an old fort on one of them a company of Afghan infantry was marching down in a cloud of dust. It was an impressive picture, and I mourned because it was too dark for a photograph.

We drove through the city and out on the other side for four miles, then stopped at a gate in a high wall running around the foot of a small hill. A sentry opened the gate and two others presented arms as we went through. We went up the hill through a garden to a large house with another sentry on the steps. When we alighted from the car Zul Facar bowed and said, "I trust you will like this palace arranged for your accommodation by my government." It was the Chehel Sitoun, or Palace of the Forty Columns, where, we were told, no foreigners had ever lodged before, and it was furnished with every comfort, including electricity, hot and cold running water, and handsome furniture and carpets. Behind it was a crag with a monument marking the place where Alexander the Great had stood and viewed the land, and in front, beyond a valley, swept a range of snowy mountains. After seeing the house I asked to be shown the kitchen and was told it was not considered adequate for use. All our food was cooked in the city itself and delivered by truck.

We were at an altitude of six thousand feet, where the climate was ideal, hot at noon and cold at night. Great contrasts in temperature were found in the surrounding country as the altitude varied. The first of the Great Moguls, Baber, who is buried in Kabul, once said that a day's journey from the city the snow never falls, while two hours away it never melts.

Next day Zul Facar wanted us to see the modern State Department building and others in the new part of the city, but I told him we could see those in Washington, London, or Paris, and went off to the bazaars with Ted, Bill, and Alan. We needed local currency and stopped at a money-changer's. I handed over thirty Indian rupees, equal to about ten dollars, and got ninety Afghan rupees in coins, which were given to me in a bag. There was little to buy, but I liked seeing the people, hawk-featured tall "mountainy men." We met few women; practically all we saw were entirely covered from head to foot in draperies of white or light blue cotton. Over their faces were small squares of drawn-work so they could see without being seen. Often shouts of *"Khabadar!"* warned of a string of camels, donkeys, or bullocks coming down the narrow

331

street. Once an elephant passed and there was no question of who got out of the way. A young policeman went with us, but everyone was smiling and friendly. Unaccustomed to tourists, the Afghans were curious and followed us around in groups.

We had dinner once or twice with the British Minister, Sir Richard Maconachie, whose legation was a real bit of England set in the austere mountains of Asia. Lady Maconachie was away, but he and his staff were dears and very keen on trout fishing. Sir Richard offered to lend Ted tackle and told him of a stream near Bamian where only three Westerners had ever fished. Ted caught four good-sized brown trout and sent them well packed in ice to Sir Reginald Spence of the Bombay Natural History Society for study and classification. His accompanying letter went astray. Later he had an acknowledgment from a clerk at the Society's office saying the fish had arrived in good condition, but as Sir Reginald was away on vacation he had eaten them himself sooner than have them spoil.

His Excellency Feiz Mahmud Khan, Minister for Foreign Affairs, gave a tea party for us at the Foreign Office Club. We received an invitation in Persian writing with the following translation:

> The Minister for Foreign Affairs requests Colonel Theodore Roosevelt and his (their) respected wife to be kind enough to take the trouble of coming to the Club of Foreign Office at five P.M. on Wednesday the 20th Saur 1312.

> A cup of tea.   Dress.   Bon Jour.

Saur meant "The Month of the Pig" and "1312" was the Moslem year. I did not understand at first what "Bon Jour" meant and thought it was just a way of signing off, but later learned that a morning coat or cutaway was known in Afghanistan as a "Bon Jour." In reducing his wardrobe at Bombay, Ted had brought no cutaway, but fortunately Zul Facar had an extra one which fitted very well. At the Foreign Office Club, a large modern white stone building, we met the members of the Cabinet and other officials, most of whom were widely traveled and spoke English or French. No women were present either here or at any of the other parties given by Afghans, as they were Moslems and kept rigid seclusion.

The Prime Minister, his Royal Highness Mohamed Hackim Khan, brother of the King, gave a dinner for twenty of us at which we were the only foreigners. Full dress was worn with orders and decorations. As usual, I was the only woman, and all the Afghans dined wearing their astrakhan caps. The Prime Minister had traveled all over Europe and was cultivated and extremely agreeable, with a keen sense of humor. After dinner we went into a large glass-enclosed winter garden where little tables were set out for various games. Bill and Alan sat down to play with some of the party, while Ted and I talked with the others, including the Minister of War, who wore gold rings in his ears. I was interested to hear that five Durani brothers were the King, the Prime Minister, the Minister of War, and Ministers from Afghanistan to France and Germany.

On our way to and from this dinner we had an escort of bicycle policemen. Four at a time pedaled along beside the car and were relieved every few blocks by another four. I watched them for a time, then remarked to Zul Facar, "That is the smartest thing I ever saw." He replied, "We merely wish to do everything possible for your safety."

When we got back to the Chehel Sitoun we found the sentries had been doubled and all gates and doors were barred. Zul Facar drew Bill aside and said, "If you should hear shooting tonight pay no attention. It is only target practice." The idea of target practice at night was puzzling, but we naturally said nothing. Sporadic firing went on during the night. Not wishing to seem too inquisitive to our Afghan friends, we asked an Englishman next morning if he knew what it was all about. He answered, "Well, there was a bit of a dust-up last night with some mountain tribes, and the government was taking no chances of your being killed or captured."

We met all the foreign diplomats in Kabul except the Russians, who never mingled with the others but lived in a large compound with a high wall around it and kept entirely to themselves. At tea at the Italian Minister's I found myself playing poker in French, a ladies' game with the wife of the French Minister, the wife of the British doctor, the headmistress of the French School, and the wife of the Persian Minister, who, in accordance with the Moslem trend in her country, had just come out of purdah and was having a lovely time. We laughed and made so much noise that Ted finally came to see what was going on.

Ted had an audience with the King, his Majesty Nadir Shah, an elderly man wearing glasses. They discussed governmental and educational problems for an hour. Ted told me afterward that he was impressed by his Majesty's common sense in realizing to what extent modern methods in both fields should be modified to suit the needs of his people. Sad to say, the King was assassinated a few months later.

We asked Zul Facar if it would be possible to go to Bamian to see the great rock carvings of Buddha described in the seventh century by the Chinese pilgrim Hsüan Tsang. He replied that everything was possible with good will. He would send tents and equipment so that we could spend the night. From Kabul it was an all-day journey to Bamian. About halfway we ran into a severe storm with drenching rain, claps of thunder echoing through the mountains, and big hailstones rattling like machine-gun bullets on the roof of the car. We stopped for half an hour until the worst was over. After Zul Facar and the chauffeur had inspected the car, the former's smiling face appeared at the window. "All accidents are happening together," he said cheerfully. "We have three flat tires and no gasoline!" We got out to look at the tires, apparently beyond repair, knowing that we had only one spare with us. Here was a heaven-sent chance for one of Zul Facar's little pranks. "I am so sorry," he said. "I'm afraid this may mean a long delay. As there are no other automobiles in this part of the country, there is no chance of one coming along the road. The driver will have to walk back twenty miles to a village to send word to Kabul of our difficulty, but he will start at once. We might get help by morning if all goes well."

It was just noon. We concealed our dismay and watched the chauffeur start briskly down the road over which we had come. Zul Facar produced from his pocket some little puzzles to entertain us. Twenty minutes later the trucks with our camp equipment, spare tires, and a good supply of gas appeared, our chauffeur riding on top of the first one, beaming with delight and thoroughly enjoying the joke.

We drove over a pass ten thousand feet in altitude and zigzagged around the side of a mountain. The road surface was inches deep in yellow clay, made slippery as ice by the storm. Often we advanced sideways like a crab, and more than once came within a hairbreadth of plunging thousands of feet over the side. Although it had been intensely hot in the valley, much of the pass was covered with snow. On either side of it we saw nomad camps with people of Mongoloid appearance, quite different from those south of Kabul. Plump, rosy children were shy until Ted cajoled them with biscuits from our lunch basket. Each camp was guarded by a dog about the size of an Alsatian, with powerful shoulders and handsome brindle coats of thick, wavy hair about an inch long. These were "Afghani wolf-killers," entirely different from the Afghan hounds we knew at home and more interesting as a breed. Their ears and tails were cropped short so that a wolf could get no hold; they were never petted but were raised to be savage against intruders, vitally necessary in this grim, wild country.

Bamian was in a valley surrounded by the snow-capped mountains of the Hindu Kush. To the north was a cliff honeycombed by countless little cells, an ancient monastery carved from the soft rock by Buddhist monks nearly fifteen hundred years ago, when Bamian was one of the important religious shrines of the world. Thousands of monks had lived here. Their only means of protection from the cold of bitter winter, when the valley was smothered in snow and icy winds penetrated every part of their tiny cells, lay in their heavy robes and charcoal braziers.

The Great Buddha, a hundred and seventy feet high, was carved on the face of the cliff facing the valley. The Lesser Buddha was some fifty feet smaller. Both had been badly damaged by Moslem troops who had used them as targets. Only a handful of people lived in the valley, and the shrine was deserted. Buddhism had vanished from this part of the world. The old caravanserai, once used by people making the pilgrimage to acquire merit, was empty except for the two lorries that had brought our camping supplies.

Next morning Ted and Bill went off to fish while Alan and I wandered about taking photographs. Some tribesmen came, bringing a sheep for me. One of them had a great bushy beard and reminded me of "Mabub Ali the kindly." We went through the usual little ceremony of a presentation on their part and warm thanks and a return of the gift on mine.

On the way back to Kabul we had a puncture on a steep grade. The chauffeur looked for a stone to put under a wheel but could see none. A man came down the road singing loudly, and offered to help. He went into a thicket, came back panting with a large rock, and helped change the tire. When Zul Facar asked why he had been singing, he answered that he had lost his cow and had been unable to find her after searching all morning. He was singing to keep from being sad. When we were ready to go on, Ted gave him a couple of coins for his trouble, although Zul Facar said he would expect nothing and might refuse. The man accepted them but was obviously amused at the queer ways of foreigners.

We left Kabul early in the morning of May 14 on our way south to Kandahar after saying good-by to the domestic staff who had done so much for us, and mourning among ourselves because Zul Facar had firmly insisted that no tips be given. After driving all morning we stopped at the walled city of Ghazni near the ruins of the seat of Mahmud ibn Sabuktagin's tenth-century empire. Mahmud, so the story goes, retained Firdusi, the poet, to versify the old legends of Persia, promising him a gold piece for each verse. Firdusi worked for thirty-five years and at last finished the work. Meanwhile he allowed the money to accumulate without drawing it. Finally Mahmud sent an elephant laden with sixty thousand pieces of money in payment for sixty thousand verses, but they were silver pieces, not gold. Firdusi was in his bath when the money was delivered. When he found it was not gold he promptly gave one third to the messenger who brought it, one third to the bath attendant, and paid the rest for a glass of beer. Then, after writing a bitter satire on the treachery of Mahmud, he left the country. Years later Mahmud regretted what he had done and sent Firdusi camels laden with a hundred thousand pieces of gold, but too late. The camels entered one gate of the city of Tus just as Firdusi's funeral was leaving by another. We spent a couple of hours at Ghazni, but by bad luck I was having another migraine and could not explore the city with the others.

About five that afternoon we came to an astonishing sight to be found in the middle of a desert: a high, rectangular, modern building made of stucco and decorated with engaged Corinthian columns and a brilliant blue roof. It was the King's resthouse, where we spent the night most comfortably. Next day we continued south across the plain. In the afternoon we drove through a paradise of wild flowers growing in the sand—dwarf pink irises, pale yellow lupins, and poppies. We reached Kandahar about four in the afternoon and stayed at the King's palace, a vast white structure built about 1870 around a formal garden. Zul Facar said that before the revolution of 1929 its walls had been hung with tapestries and its floors carpeted with Afghan rugs, but all these had been carried away or destroyed during the sack of Kandahar. These and other furnishings had been replaced by ordinary chairs and tables and European carpets with patterns of enormous flowers on a red ground.

After tea we set out for the bazaars. Here we had a military guard, for which I was glad. As practically no one in Kandahar had ever seen a foreign woman, the curiosity of the crowds was embarrassing. My short hair added to the general interest, for it was considered a sign of disgrace. I tried to find something to use as a veil but could not.

We had tea next day with the Governor of the province, his Excellency Gholam Faruk Khan. After driving several miles over sand and rocks, we reached an oasis with a pleasant garden, surrounded as usual by a high wall. In the middle of the garden was a high, square brick tower. We entered the tower and climbed several steep flights of stairs until we came to a large room with long windows, where we were greeted by the Governor and other officials. None of them spoke English or French. When carrying on a casual conversation through an interpreter, everything you say sounds ridiculous. There were long pauses when nobody could think of anything to talk about. Ted fell back on a generally useful topic, one's children, and asked the Governor how many he had, then boasted of his own almost grown-up four. "You can see," said Ted, serenely conscious of his youthful appearance and fishing quite brazenly for a compliment, "I am a very old man." At this the Governor bowed low and declared, "In this country we have deep veneration for the aged!"

I never saw anyone out of whose sails the wind was more thoroughly taken.

For several days before we left, Zul Facar had been saying casually that the Afghan Government intended to give me a present before we left. I kept assuring him that, after all the kindness and hospitality his people had shown us, nothing further could possibly be necessary. He referred to it again and again, saying his government appreciated deeply our sympathetic interest in his people. I replied that his people had shown a sympathetic interest in us. This went on until the day we left Kandahar to drive south to Quetta in Baluchistan.

Early in the morning we said good-by to Zul Facar and tried to find words to thank him for all he had done for us. With a bow he handed me a well-made wooden box about seven inches square and said, "May I present the compliments of my government and beg on their behalf that you will kindly accept this small token of their high regard as a trifling souvenir of your stay in our country." I took the box and answered, "Please present my compliments to your government, and tell them I can never properly express our deep appreciation of all that has been done for us in Afghanistan. I shall always value this souvenir and shall treasure the memory of our visit." We both bowed.

The formalities over, I said, "Zul Facar, what is in this box?" He replied, "I must not tell you. It is to be a surprise. You are not to open it until you get back to the United States. However, I may say that this is something we have never before given to a foreigner. We hope it will give you pleasure."

By this time my curiosity was intolerable. What could it be? A small first-century B.C. Luristan bronze? A coin from the time of Alexander the Great? "Zul Facar, please! If you don't tell me what it is, you know human nature well enough to know I'll open it as soon as we're out of sight."

Zul Facar shook his head sadly. "If you force me to tell you, I will. In this box is an egg from one of our Afghani pigeons, which we prize highly. Colonel Roosevelt has remarked several times that they are an interesting species. When you get home you can have it hatched, and then you will have the only true Afghani pigeon in the United States." He beamed with pleasure.

Luckily I had had some experience in controlling my face, so I merely thanked him warmly for such an unusual and charming gift without showing how I felt about it. What on earth made them think an egg would keep until we got home? Well, there was nothing more to be said.

We set out to drive the seventy-five miles between Kandahar and Quetta over the worst road in the world. That was what they called it, and they were right. The first fifteen miles were all right, but after that it was appalling. The trip took eight hours, including the times we were stuck in the sand and bogged down in a river. We were not traveling in the comfortable Buick but in an ancient car of unrecognizable make which Zul Facar had wisely provided. If it had any springs we didn't notice them. Time and again we hit deep holes, rose as one to crack our heads on the car's roof, and fell in a heap on the floor. Twice I had the wind knocked out of me by Ted's elbow. Each time this happened someone was sure to land on a sharp corner of the box containing the pigeon's egg. Finally Ted said in desperation, "I've had enough of this damned box!" and threw it far out of the window.

Years later I told this story to a friend who had been in Afghanistan and knew the people. When I finished he said, "Mrs. Roosevelt, you don't really believe that was nothing but a pigeon's egg, do you?"

"Why not?" I asked. "That's what Zul Facar said it was."

"You said he was fond of practical jokes. Now consider this. He never would have said the present was from his government if it had not been. His government never in the world would have given you a pigeon's egg. Right there is where his little joke came in. Of course it didn't occur to him you would throw it away without looking at it. Why, it might have been a pigeon-blood ruby!"

The worst of it is that we shall never know.

Chapter 33

*The jackals prowl, the serpents hiss
In what was once Persepolis.
Proud Babylon is but a trace
Upon the desert's dusty face.
The topless towers of Ilium
Are ashes. Judah's harp is dumb.
The fleets of Nineveh and Tyre
Are down with Davy Jones, Esquire.
And all the oligarchies, kings,
And potentates who ruled these things
Are gone! But cheer up, don't be sad;
Think what a lovely time they had!*
ARTHUR GUITERMAN

The road between the Afghanistan border and Quetta wound through the mountains, and every now and then I noticed wild-looking heads in turbans watching us from behind rocks and wondered if they were bandits. Later I learned that the road was open for travel and protected for travelers only three days a week, and this was not one of them. The British Resident, Sir Norman Cator, had had special guards posted to look out for us along the way.

After the grim, rocky country of Afghanistan, Quetta was almost like heaven. Seen from a distance, the whole aspect of the city was a mass of green. Large trees shaded its streets, while smooth lawns, neatly clipped hedges, and gardens bright with flowers, so characteristic of the British, added to its beauty. We spent three days with Sir Norman at the Residency and thoroughly enjoyed ourselves. The Residency was a large, comfortable, old-fashioned house with a wide lawn and a lovely garden. Ted and I had a big bedroom, two dressing rooms, two bathrooms, and a sitting room. The whole house was full of flowers. Besides great bowls of roses on the tables, each fireplace was hidden behind masses of snapdragons, larkspur, and foxglove, and tall vases stood on the newel posts of the staircases. Everyone we met was astonished at our plan to go through Persia and Iraq in summer, saying that while we might be used to tropical heat the desert heat in these countries went far beyond it. We knew this, but we wanted to go and might never have another chance.

When we left Quetta by train for a twenty-four-hour trip to the railhead at Nok Kundi, Sir Norman came to the station to see us off and provided us with a wonderful supply of food to take with us. It included a meat pie, a roast saddle of lamb, two roast chickens, two loaves of bread, a quantity of strawberries from his garden with containers of thick cream, a bottle of claret for me, six bottles of beer and twelve of soda water. Also four bottles of whiskey to last during our stay in Persia. Besides all these, we had two large buckets of ice and our gallon thermos filled with boiled water.

The train journey through desolate country was hot but not uncomfortable. Next morning we reached Nok Kundi, where the railroad ended. No transport existed in Persia at that time except automobiles and camels. An aviation company had gone out of business the year before. We were met by Désiré Kettaneh, who had come from Teheran, a four-day trip, with practically no time taken out for sleep. He drove a new Dodge sedan and also brought a big Hudson touring car with an excellent Greek chauffeur, Stehlio. The Kettanehs are an interesting Eastern family whose ancestors migrated from Italy to Jerusalem in 1669. They control their business over a wide area by having a brother or relative living in each important city through most of the Near and Middle East. Today they represent a number of American firms, including Chrysler, du Pont de Nemours, Fairbanks Morse, Volkswagen, Michelin, and several pharmaceutical groups.

Although we had been living in the tropics for years, I never

341

knew what real heat was until that day in the Baluchistan desert. Désiré estimated the temperature at a hundred and twenty-five degrees in the shade. All metal parts of the car got so hot they burned one's fingers. The heat of the floor was such that my feet ached and next day they peeled. The air was full of fine white dust. Once we became stuck in the sand for three quarters of an hour. I got out to take a picture but was glad to get back inside the car and out of the scorching wind and the cruel glare of the sun. We had no lunch, although our basket was full of Sir Norman's provisions. Everything rotted in a few hours and had to be thrown away. As the day went on I started a bad migraine and tried to conceal it from Ted, who always worried so. I experimented by taking surreptitious sips of aromatic ammonia from time to time, but this did no good.

Late in the afternoon we came to the Persian border, where a guard of honor commanded by an officer with a long curved saber turned out for Ted. I boiled our traveling kettle and we had coffee and malted milk. At eight that evening we reached Zahedan, where we were to stay with the British Consul, Captain Galloway, whom Ted had once met on a P & O ship going to India.

Zahedan was a horrid place—flat, sandy, dreary, and frightfully hot. Every afternoon a burning wind blew, filtering dust through the house. The drinking water, even when boiled, was slightly brackish.

Captain Galloway and Ted played squash in a court he had built the year before, thinking it would provide a good way to exercise. It had never been used, as the only other people who played had moved away before it was finished. He was so glad of company that he behaved as if we were doing him a favor when Ted asked if we could stay for two nights instead of one, as I was still feeling shaky. Before we left he showed me his garden. I noticed some little green shoots about six inches high growing out of the hard bare earth and asked what they were going to be. "Going to be?" repeated Captain Galloway indignantly. "They *are!* That is my garden!"

We left Zahedan at six in the afternoon, traveling by night to avoid the heat. Soon we saw some little mountains like the pointed ones in Persian miniatures, a lovely mauve and lemon sunset behind them. Later we reached more flat, sandy country, but as it was dark the heat was not bad. Occasionally gazelles would jump up and run along beside the car—pretty, graceful creatures. At eleven that night we stopped at a little *chai-khana,* or teashop. These were scattered all over Persia, even in isolated places, and often had a caravan of camels and donkeys resting beside them. Sometimes you could get food, but usually only tea, which Persians loved and drank from glasses after adding eight or ten lumps of sugar. If there was a shortage of sugar, a Persian would put a lump in his mouth and suck the tea through it.

As we had not eaten for twelve hours, I asked for some hot water to make malted milk. An old man brought some from a steaming samovar. The jug must have burned his fingers, for he thrust it at the table and upset the boiling water over Ted's bare leg (he was wearing shorts) and down inside his shoe. In an instant we had his shoe and stocking off, but the harm had been done. It was a deep and painful burn. We covered it with Unguentine, the only thing we had, bandaged it, and considered our plight. The nearest doctor was at the American Mission in Meshed. We had to spend the next night at Birjand to rest the drivers, who were still tired from their four-day trip down from Teheran. At best it would be forty-eight hours before Ted could have medical care. I knew enough about burns to realize this might lay Ted up for weeks even if it did not get infected.

We propped a suitcase and a cushion under Ted's leg and drove for three hours until we reached Shusp, halted at a tiny resthouse, undid our bedding rolls, and lay down in our clothes for a two-hour nap. Poor Ted did not close his eyes. At five in the morning we arose. I made coffee and the bearer fried some eggs. At noon next day we arrived at the palace of Shaukat-ul-Mulk, a Persian prince who owned the countryside for miles around, including two little villages. His palace was a vast place with many buildings in an oasis about two miles from the desert town of Birjand. Here we were to stay.

We alighted from the cars, weary and thickly covered with dust, and were received by Shaukat-ul-Mulk and a number of other Persians wearing immaculate cutaway coats. After an exchange of greetings we were shown to our rooms, which were small but comfortable, with rough cement walls and tiled floors. I made Ted lie down on his bed, as he was suffering intense pain, which he bore without a word. It was heartbreaking to have nothing but aspirin to give him.

I longed for a bath, and when Ted was settled I asked Alan to find out where the bathroom was and gathered together my soap, towels, washcloth, talcum powder, and so forth. Fifteen minutes later Alan knocked at the door. He had found the bath, but it was a long distance away and he thought he had better take me there.

We set out and ran into the group of Persians who had welcomed us and who were still standing around near the main door. Slightly surprised, they drew aside politely to let us pass. We must have looked odd, as I was wearing a wrapper with a pattern of huge pink roses and Alan was holding an umbrella over my head against the hot sun. We walked the length of the palace, past numerous other buildings, down a path through a garden, across a field, and finally came to a small house where an old man with a dyed red beard opened the door and salaamed to us. This was the *hamam*, or bathhouse. There was no lock on the door. By sign language we tried to make the old man understand that no one was to come in while I was there, and although he beamed and salaamed again we had no idea that he knew what we meant. Alan went discreetly away. Inside the house were two rooms, one with a tank of hot water, the other with a tank of cold. Instead of the usual dipper there was a silver pitcher of graceful design.

After a refreshing scrub I came out to find a crowd of people gathered around the bathhouse, all chattering. As soon as I appeared there was dead silence, while everyone stared at me open-mouthed. Alan had returned and said, "I thought I had better come back, as the entire village seems to be here." We walked through the crowd, and immediately the chattering broke out again. I couldn't imagine why there was so much interest in somebody's taking a bath. We were followed by a throng until we reached the palace and again passed the group of Persians still standing by the main door. When at last I got to my room Ted told me with much amusement that the bearer said I had created excitement by going to the men's bath, where no woman had ever ventured before.

Although Shaukat-ul-Mulk had never been out of Persia he was extremely well informed and spoke perfect French. He had a sense of humor and seemed to have more progressive ideas than most Persians of high rank at that time. He told me he had three daughters and liked them to ride with him. If they had worn women's clothes they would have been the scandal of the neighborhood, so he had them dress as boys. Accompanied by the most elderly groom in his stables, they galloped together, entirely unnoticed, for miles over his domain. In this way the proprieties were observed and the girls had exercise as well as the companionship of their father. I wanted to meet them but could not, as the time was so short. Apparently Persian ladies who kept purdah as their mothers did could not be hurried into meeting a foreign visitor but needed a couple of days to get used to the idea and to make proper preparations for refreshments. Shaukat-ul-Mulk urged us to stay for a few days, but we were too anxious to get to Meshed, where Ted could see a doctor.

Without going into the *anderun,* or women's quarters, I saw the rest of the palace and was impressed by the ballroom with its polished floor and several old French crystal chandeliers. The walls and high-vaulted ceiling were entirely covered with bits of looking glass fitted together like mosaic. It must have been enchanting at night by candlelight, with the mirrors reflecting beautiful dancing girls in white ballet skirts and gay brocade jackets. This costume had been introduced into Persia in the nineteenth century by a shah who had seen and admired it in Paris.

At an elaborate dinner that night Shaukat-ul-Mulk told us that twenty years before he had heard of an excellent cellar being sold in Paris. He had negotiated for it and bought several thousand bottles, which were shipped to Bushire and then carried on camels the rest of the way, a month's journey. Among them were three hundred mysterious bottles from America. He had been keeping them ever since, hoping some Americans might visit him and tell him what this peculiar beverage was. It turned out to be Green River rye whiskey, old at the time of purchase and probably priceless. We asked him how he, a Moslem, could drink such things.

345

He answered that he obeyed the law in principle but believed in a little relaxation from time to time.

When I changed the dressing on Ted's leg that night I was appalled and frightened by the dreadful condition of the burn and was determined to drive all next day and night if necessary to get him to a doctor. The run to Meshed would take eighteen hours at least. We were supposed to start at seven in the morning, but as Ted and I were the only ones ready we did not get off until eight. A military guard of one officer and four men provided by the Persian Government joined our party at this point and stayed with us throughout our stay. Shaukat-ul-Mulk came with us to the edge of his domain, ten miles away. Here he made a speech, presented me with a bouquet, and produced two bottles of champagne for a *vin d'honneur*. Champagne before nine in the morning is wasted on me.

After crossing fifty miles of flat desert our narrow road wound through the mountains. We passed many caravans whose camels had a positive genius for doing the unexpected when meeting a car. I loved the sound of the bronze camel bells, said to be less for warning than for keeping off evil spirits. As we neared the holy city of Meshed, chief shrine of the Shiah Moslems, we noticed many little piles of stones beside the road. Each pilgrim on his first visit to the city would add a stone. After making this pilgrimage a Moslem was entitled to be called "Meshedji."

At one in the morning we reached the American Mission, where the Reverend Dr. and Mrs. D. M. Donaldson were up and waiting for us. I begged for a medical man to look at Ted's leg, and they sent for Dr. Rolla Hoffman, who got out of bed and came at once with a nurse, Miss Nelson. He confirmed my fears that it was a severe third-degree burn, washed and bound it up in clean bandages for the night. Mrs. Donaldson had hot baths for us and supper with a real American strawberry shortcake, which we certainly appreciated, not having eaten for eighteen hours.

Next morning Dr. Hoffman began the treatment of Ted's leg. He said I had done right to cover the burn to keep out the desert dust, but removing the ointment was a painful process. Then he and Miss Nelson took turns spraying the leg with tannic acid at fifteen-minute intervals all day. That hurt, too, but the result was miraculous. A few days later Ted had no pain and soon after was able to hobble around with a stick. Without this treatment the doctor said he might well have been a month in the hospital.

The day after we arrived the Governor of Meshed, his Excellency Mirza Mahmoud Kahn Djem Modir-ul-Mulk, came to call and invited us to stay at his house. He had had instructions from the Minister of Foreign Affairs in Teheran to be nice to us. We explained that we could not accept because of the medical treatment required by Ted. Besides, we would have hated to leave the Donaldsons, who were so good to us.

Dr. Donaldson was a noted Persian scholar and a mine of information on the history, manners, and customs of the country. Mrs. Donaldson spoke fluent Persian and was of invaluable help to her husband in his work. She was a delightful companion and took me all through the bazaars and to the Governor's for tea. We were received by the Governor's wife, a stout lady with shoulder-length hair who was dressed in navy-blue voile with large white polka dots. After a few minutes' talk she looked at me intently and said something in a sad voice. Mrs. Donaldson translated, "She says she admires you because you have a concave stomach. Hers, she says, is convex. The time has passed when fat women are considered beautiful in Persia. She wants to know how you keep slim." The next thing I knew, we were lying on the floor doing exercises. I was telling the Governor's wife she would have a concave stomach in a short time if she persisted, when a servant came in and whispered to her. She rose hastily and departed before the Governor appeared, followed by Bill and Alan.

In Meshed I first saw veiled Persian women. In the city streets they wore *chadars,* long capes of thin black material falling from the top of the head to the feet. Attached to these were oblong pieces of woven black horsehair supposed to cover the face. By manipulating them a Persian woman could show or hide as much of her face as she wished, often allowing a glimpse of large, lustrous eyes smudged with kohl. The shrouded black figures moving silently about the streets had an air of mystery. One always imagined them young, slender, and beautiful. One was not always right.

The Shiahs had a curious custom of temporary marriages for

pilgrims. By paying a sum of money to the mullah permission could be obtained to take a wife for any given length of time. The marriage was legal and the children legitimate. In Meshed a great number of pilgrims availed themselves of this opportunity.

The mullahs used to be the richest and most powerful class in Persia, holding control over everyone. Apparently they met their match in his Majesty Shah Pahlevi I. Not long before, we were told, the wife of the Shah journeyed to Meshed to pray at the shrine. To the disapproval of the congregation in the mosque, she was denounced publicly by the mullah because of some detail of her dress. She reported this to her husband by long-distance telephone. The Shah was furious. He rang up the Governor and ordered the mullah dismissed. The Governor, it was said, promised everything and did nothing. His Majesty, finding his orders had not been obeyed, drove from Teheran for twenty-four hours without stopping until he reached Meshed. He and his suite entered the mosque with their boots on, a deadly insult in itself, seized the mullah, confiscated his possessions, and drove him into exile.

Bill and Alan were able to go into the mosque. In order to attract no attention, they wore Pahlevi hats, at that time the new national headgear of Persia. I was disappointed that I could not go too, wearing a *chadar,* but I did not want to do anything that might embarrass the Donaldsons. The pilgrims in Meshed were then unaccustomed to foreign women, and something unfortunate might have happened. A few years before, the American Consul in Teheran, a city of far less fanaticism, had been killed by an angry mob when the lens cap of his camera fell into the pool in the courtyard of a mosque and the cry arose that he was polluting the sacred water.

When Bill and Alan returned they described the tomb of the Imam Reza, gorgeous with gold, silver, and jewels and venerated by a hundred thousand pilgrims each year. Nearby a simple slab of marble covered the mortal remains of the great Haroun-al-Raschid, neglected and unnoticed except when one of the faithful went out of his way to spit on it.

We left Meshed for Teheran before Dr. Hoffman thought Ted was fit to travel, but there was no holding him down. The journey took twenty-four hours' driving time, and here I laid down an ultimatum: I could go without sleep or food but could not go without both at the same time. If I could not sleep I must be fed, otherwise I probably would be buried in Persia. The others seemed surprised at this feminine whim but finally agreed to leave Meshed at eight in the morning, after breakfast, stop an hour for lunch, an hour for supper, and another hour in the middle of the night for tea. In this way we would arrive at Teheran, barring accidents, in time for lunch next day.

When the time came for us to start, the entire mission turned out and watched while Ted, Bill, Alan, Désiré, Stehlio, a second chauffeur, a mechanic, our bearer, Mrs. Sukias (an Armenian woman who had requested a lift), her child of six, and I, with all the luggage, were packed into the two cars. Désiré, Bill, Alan, and the two chauffeurs took turns at the wheels. Once we stopped at a village where a young gazelle was for sale, a dear little creature that Désiré wanted to buy and take with us. I was rather glad when terms could not be agreed upon.

We stopped at Nishapur to pay tribute to Omar Khayyám. His tomb was then without inscription in a tiny, shabby open cell in the side of a building erected in memory of Imamzadeh Mohamed Mahrouk. His writings were only just beginning to have the recognition in Persia that they have in the rest of the world, and there was talk of moving his tomb to a more suitable place.

The weather was cool, the food we had brought kept perfectly, and the journey was pleasant. However, after supper I was hit by another migraine, only a week since my last one. This was exasperating. I was traveling in the Dodge driven by Désiré, while Ted followed in the Hudson. Désiré had said he would stop at some place for us to have breakfast. At sunrise we came to a little village, where the others got out while I stayed in the car, asleep. When the Hudson came by twenty minutes later it passed and went on for some distance before turning back to look for us. No one had recognized our car because it was entirely covered with children. They were clambering on the hood, the running boards, the mudguards, and the roof, pushing their heads in at the windows to look gleefully at what they were calling a corpse on the back seat, where I was lying, unaware of what was going on.

At one that afternoon we reached Teheran. Ted and I stayed

about fifteen miles away at Shimran with the United States Minister and his wife, Mr. and Mrs. Charles Hart, while Bill and Alan went to the Kettanehs' house in the city.

Hospitality in Persia at that time meant something far beyond the ordinary. The prohibitive import tax on foreign articles prevented practically everything from coming into the country. The Harts could have things sent through diplomatic channels, but even this was difficult and expensive. As they expected a Democrat would shortly be given the post and they would have to leave, they had not been ordering much lately and their supplies were low. When they and the Kettanehs gave us American canned fruit, bacon, cigarettes, or even coffee, they reduced their own stock by that much. The only cheap luxury was caviar fresh from the Caspian Sea.

Ted had an audience with his Majesty the Shah, which George Wadsworth, counselor of our Legation, told me about afterward. When he and Ted arrived at the palace Ted was taken in to the audience chamber. As interviews had never been known to last more than a few minutes, George waited and chatted with the Shah's aides, whom he knew. After twenty minutes passed the Shah sent for a machine gun, which was quickly produced and taken to him. An hour went by, while the aides kept looking at their watches. Finally one of them went in to see what was happening. His Majesty and Ted were sitting on the floor examining the machine gun they had taken apart, while Ted explained it was not the best model for mountain fighting as it was heavy and bulky. Later he sent a lighter one as a present to the Shah.

We heard many stories about the Shah, all showing how well he seemed to know the psychology of his people. I have already told the one about the mullah in Meshed. Sometime before we arrived in Teheran everyone, including his Majesty, was at the races. In a certain race a Persian Army officer was riding and tried to foul another jockey. The jockey retaliated by slashing the officer across the face with his whip. As soon as the race was over, the Shah sent for the jockey and kicked him in the stomach. The foreigners, mainly diplomats, were horrified, but the Persians felt it was entirely justified. That night the jockey went around boasting he was a person of consequence because it was the Shah and no other who had kicked him.

Charles Kettaneh, Désiré's older brother, drove us to Isfahan, a ten-hour trip. We planned to leave Teheran at four in the afternoon to avoid the heat, but as usual Ted and I were the only ones ready, so we did not get started until six. At nine o'clock we stopped at a *chai-khana* for a picnic dinner. George Wadsworth had given me a large tin of caviar, which we ate with delight, forgetting it would add to our thirst. Just before we got under way, after all our paraphernalia was packed up, I felt I would die if I didn't have a drink. Stehlio brought me some water from a nearby spring, saying it was clean and safe. A moment later Alan, who had been exploring the *chai-khana*, called me to see something interesting. I went into the house, where people, dogs, and chickens were crowded on an earth floor sloping down to a small, muddy pool. "There's where your water came from," he said.

At four in the morning we reached Isfahan, a dream city under a full moon. We arrived at Mr. and Mrs. Vivian Walter's house, where Ted and I were to spend two nights, and entered a door through a high wall surrounding the garden. For the first time we were in the Persia of our imagination. The garden was flooded with moonlight, its cypresses reflected in a long pool. As it was just before dawn, a muezzin chanted from a tower close by, calling the faithful to prayer. In spite of dust and fatigue, Ted and I sat down, entranced, on the edge of the pool until he was done. The Walters were in bed, but supper and baths were waiting for us. We fell into bed and slept until nine.

Next day we wandered about Isfahan, a city of art and culture when Paris was a village. That night Mrs. Walter said I looked completely worn out and no wonder, traveling in such heat, and advised me to eat *mast,* the curdled milk the Persians depend on. She said it was sustaining and quite safe, even in a dirty dish. What was more, it could be had anywhere. It was made sometimes of cow's milk, sometimes of goat's, but the best was made of sheep's. To me the taste was utterly revolting, but that made no difference. You can eat anything if you think your life depends on it. From then on I asked for *mast* wherever we stopped, sometimes at little nomad camps, and without any rest or change of schedule I began almost at once to feel better. When *mast* got too old and too strong to eat the Persians would put some in a bottle and shake it up with water, making a thickish drink called *doogh* in which no dangerous germ was believed to survive. If the good it did was commensurate with the horror of its taste it must indeed have been the true elixir of life.

Travel on the road between Isfahan and Persepolis was prohibited after five in the afternoon because the road was infested with bandits—not ordinary robbers, but people against the government trying to make trouble for those in authority. We had our military guard as usual and planned to leave early in the morning. We were ready when the car came for us at half-past six, but when we went to the hotel for Bill, Alan, and Charles we waited an hour while they woke up, had breakfast, and packed. Ted was always far too good-natured to say anything, but I issued another ultimatum. He and I had come for them for the last time. In the future they would come for us and then wait while Ted did his usual setting-up exercises and had an extra cup of coffee and while I slept for half an hour, repacked my suitcase, changed my mind, and went back four times for things I had forgotten. I never saw people more astonished, but I can't remember that they ever improved.

When Darius built his palace, Persepolis was a large and flourishing city. Now it was a desolate and sandy waste, without trees or even water. The road wound around through the desert until it led suddenly to the ruins of the palace, which were impressive and beautiful. In spite of the fact that the palace had been burned by Alexander the Great and later rocked by earthquakes, it was astonishing how much of it was left. We were welcomed by Dr. Ernst E. Herzfeld, in charge of excavations for the University of Chicago, who showed us our rooms in the restored harem of Darius. Dr. Herzfeld said he was particularly proud of the bathroom, which had a huge sunken tub lined with blue and yellow tiles. When I started to take my bath I had trouble keeping two small dogs and a very active little pig from jumping in with me. When I asked for a glass of water Dr. Herzfeld said, "We never drink it here. We keep our health year in and year out by drinking *doogh*. Nothing in the world is so good for you." So *doogh* it was for all of us.

Dr. Herzfeld took us all over the ruins, pointing out some of the recent excavations which were so well preserved that traces of powdered stone were still visible in carving done over two thousand years ago.

We spent an afternoon in Shiraz and visited the tombs of Hafiz and Saadi. Both were dilapidated and overgrown with weeds. I wanted to buy a little something in Shiraz and asked Dr. Herzfeld what could be had. He said he had felt the same way and after spending a whole day in the bazaars had ended by buying only a piece of blotting paper. The bazaars were full of modern rubbish, but I had good luck and found two tiny silver boxes.

After two nights in Persepolis we returned to Isfahan. Poor Bill was having a fever. The rest of us wandered through narrow streets, explored little shops, climbed crooked staircases, and walked over roofs. With us was Mrs. Hermann Stier, a Frenchwoman married to a German, who knew every inch of the city. The wife of the German Minister to Persia had given me a letter to her. Ted found a large painting without perspective of a man and woman in three different poses and dressed in the old-time Persian clothes. After bargaining for twenty minutes he got it for six dollars. I bought a chandelier with places for eight candles and a hundred and forty hanging prisms. (I know just how many there were, for I had to pack them.) I paid eighteen tomans, or nine dollars, for it and was delighted when it turned out to be eighteenth-century Baccarat glass. In one of the streets in Isfahan nothing but chandeliers were sold. They had hung in all the better houses in Persia until electric lights were introduced, then they were discarded in favor of bare bulbs hanging on wires from the ceilings. The following year the Kettanehs sent me a lovely one with seventeen candles, also eighteenth-century.

As the weather had turned cool, we drove back to Teheran by day. The country was for the most part uninteresting, but with infinite resource Ted invented a kind of spelling game like "Ghost," only better, which we played for hours. As we reached the holy city of Qum our car broke a spring and we stopped for repairs. As a pilgrimage center, Qum is second only to Meshed, because

Fatima the Unstained is buried there. The sun was low as we entered the city, turning the great golden dome and the minarets of the mosque to a blaze of glory. The lieutenant of our guard sent for the Chief of Police, who asked if we would like to see the shrine. I was delighted; Ted was reluctant but made no active objections. As we walked through the streets he mentioned the fact that Qum was almost entirely a city of pilgrims and said I must be careful, for there was sure to be fanaticism. We came to the mosque, in the courtyard of which a great crowd of people were sitting on the ground. The Chief of Police stepped across the threshold of the gate and beckoned us to follow. As soon as my foot touched the ground of the courtyard a low murmur swelled into a roar from a thousand throats.

Ted barked an order at me. "Turn around slowly and walk out. Keep your head up. Don't look back. I am right behind you."

All through our life together Ted invariably got mad at me after he had been scared about me, and this time was no exception. As we reached the outside he continued, "I don't know why on earth you wanted to come here. You ought to have better sense. Someday you will get into real trouble. I expected a shower of stones which might have cut your face. *When* will you learn how to behave?" I knew from experience I had better keep quiet, but the Chief of Police trotted along, making futile apologies to which Ted paid no attention.

At lunch one day we met a particularly attractive young Persian prince who was handsome, cultivated, and a sportsman. After he left, another Persian beside whom I was sitting remarked casually, "That is a nice young man. It is a pity he killed his mother. Now he cannot go into public service." Everyone agreed and the talk turned to something else. I interrupted. "Wait a minute! What did you say about that man?"

"I said it was a pity he killed his mother."

"How did he kill her?"

"He shot her, I believe. Now, as I was saying, the Luristan bronzes——"

"Oh, please! I must know more about it. Did he shoot his mother accidentally?"

"No, of course not. In Luristan——"

"Why did he shoot her?"

"He was obliged to, I am told."

"Oh, for heaven's sake! Why was he obliged to?"

"Family reasons. His father was away, otherwise he would have attended to it. Now, if you are really interested in buying any bronzes from Luristan——"

"Never mind about bronzes. What had she done?"

"What had she done? Why, she had an affair with a mullah. She had to be shot!" After that we learned all about the bronzes of Luristan.

Chapter 34

*The world is a country which no one ever
knew by description; one must travel through
it oneself to become acquainted with it.*

LORD CHESTERFIELD

Bill had been looking peaked for some time before he finally admitted he had been running a fever for days. By then we had
been nearly three weeks in Persia and were anxious to move on,
especially Bill. Finally he said he felt well enough to travel, and
although we really did not believe him we set out on the three-
day trip to Baghdad. We spent the first night at the American
Mission at Hamadan with Dr. and Mrs. Funk in a house like my
grandfather Green's in Brick Church, New Jersey, built about
1885. Bill was worse. Next day we pushed on to Kermanshah,
where a small American mission hospital had been established by
Dr. and Mrs. Harry P. Packard. When we arrived Bill was shaking
from head to foot with a severe chill and had a temperature of
over a hundred and three. Dr. Packard said he was entirely too
ill to travel and must stay in the hospital. In time he diagnosed
Bill's troubles as paratyphoid, malaria, and sand-fly fever all at
once, and probably saved his life by untiring and skillful care for
three weeks.

We decided to split our party in order not to overtax the hospitality of the mission. Leaving Bill and Alan at Kermanshah, Ted,
Charles Kettaneh, and I made an early start next morning in order

to get through the bandit country before dusk. Our military guard went with us to the Persian frontier, but after reaching Iraq we were on our own. Not long before, two of our vice-consuls had been driving along this same road from Kermanshah to Baghdad and were held up. The robbers took everything they had, including all their clothes, then drove off in their automobile, leaving them naked in the broiling sun. By sheer good luck they were soon picked up by a passing car.

This day's travel was worse than any we had done since Baluchistan. When we left the high country and came down to sea level the July heat was incredible. Heat waves shimmering over the sand gave a perfect illusion of sheets of water in the distance. After crossing the frontier at noon we stopped at Khaniqin, at an unusually attractive resthouse with running water and clean beds. We passed several flocks of sheep and noticed a curious thing. In Persia the shepherds tended their flocks from behind. In Iraq they walked in front, followed by their sheep. No sooner were we over the frontier than the method changed.

Charles told us there had been several head-on collisions of cars crossing the desert. In spite of the great width of sand to drive over, people coming from opposite directions would run straight into each other. This was because cars passed to the right in Persia and to the left in Iraq, and after crossing the frontier the drivers got confused. Finally the British authorities in Iraq decided to change; all traffic kept to the right and accidents were avoided.

As usual when Ted was worried about me for any reason he got angry. Now he had bandits on his mind. As soon as our military guard left us he sat in the front seat beside Charles where he could watch the road, said there was a chance of real danger, and told me to sit in the back, stop asking questions, and drop to the floor on command. Luckily we had no trouble of any kind.

At five in the afternoon we reached Baghdad, where we stayed with Paul Knabenshue, American Consul General, later Minister to Iraq, who shared his attractive house with George Renshard, Sidney Lafoon, and Morris Hughes, young men attached to the Consulate. Two of them had moved out of their room for us. We felt guilty about this, but they were so emphatic in saying the pleasure of our company more than made up for it that they almost made us believe it. I went immediately to our room, as my headache was bad, fell asleep on a sofa, and did not wake until the following morning. Ted came in from time to time to make sure I was still alive, but I was unaware of this and did not hear him even when he came to dress for dinner. By the next day I had entirely recovered.

We all slept outdoors because of the heat. Two beds were in the garden in front of the house, two on the side, and two on the roof. We had extra-heavy nets over the beds to guard against sand flies as well as mosquitoes. Sand flies were the prettiest, most delicate little creatures I ever saw, but their bite carried not only fever but the infection of the "Baghdad boil," a horror that usually came on the face and always left a large, silvery scar.

Our plan was to stay three days, but in spite of the heat we stayed nine because we were having such a good time. We were very gay, met delightful people, and dined out every night but two, when Mr. Knabenshue had dinner parties in his garden. Ted, overjoyed at a chance to get hard physical exercise, played tennis every afternoon with relays of younger men. Baghdad itself, part modern, part squalid, was disappointing except at night from the river, when it became Haroun-al-Raschid's "moon city of delight." By day the air was so full of dust that the sky was the color of milky coffee.

One night we dined with Air Vice-Marshal Sir Charles Burnett and had a most entertaining evening. A young R.A.F. officer named King played the piano with marked talent. After giving us classical music for a time he took a copy of *Army Regulations* and sang the rules for treatment of sunstroke like an anthem, accompanying himself with sonorous chords. Then he sang the country-club bylaws in the same way and imitated a phonograph which had been too long in the tropics. We laughed until we ached and kept begging for more.

We went on a moonlight picnic with Ogilvie Forbes, British chargé d'affaires, going up the Tigris on a launch for a couple of hours, then stopping to swim. Supper was cooked on the river's edge. Enormous river fish, a kind of carp, were propped edgewise on the sand, and a small fire was built beside each one. They were excellent eating. We had five courses, ending in true British fashion with a savory.

Another time we dined with the Prime Minister of Iraq, his Excellency Rashid Ali al Gailani. The next evening we went to dinner in the garden of the palace with his Royal Highness the Amir of Ghazi, Prince Regent in the absence of his father King Faisal, who was in Europe. A number of government officials were there while I was the only woman. It was a real feast with many courses and different kinds of wine, but no water was provided. When I asked for some, being thirsty as usual, I didn't get it for a long time.

The Prince was nineteen years old, an attractive boy who had been educated at Harrow. He was rather shy and said little until I asked if he would like to come and stay with us in America, saying I had two sons about his age who would see that he had a good time. His eyes shone as he assured me he would love to and, after a moment's thought, asked if next October would be convenient for us. I think he might have come had not circumstances prevented this. He became King in September on the death of his father, and he himself was killed in an automobile accident in 1939.

Many of these invitations I kept and put in my scrapbook. Years afterward my son Quentin came across one from the German Minister and Frau Hilda Grobba. Surprised and interested, he told me Herr Grobba had been a famous German intelligence agent during World War I and was considered by the Allies as valuable to the enemy as two divisions of infantry.

Miss Lucy Smith, a young woman from Malta who was companion to the two young princesses, Azza and Rajiha, asked me to call on the Queen, saying it was good for her royal ladies to meet foreigners. I drove to the Queen's palace, an immense reddish building on the river where, it was said, electricity had recently been installed and was kept on day and night in all rooms, including bedrooms. The door was opened by a stout maid in a white silk dress with a pattern of red and black flowers, and a tiny beige apron, who conducted me into a large room furnished with a row of wicker chairs. The Queen was portly, with straight shoulder-length hair, and wore a white dress with big red polka dots. She spoke only Arabic, and the two young princesses acted as interpreters. The conversation was far from stilted, because when we really got going everyone but me ignored the Queen completely. Every now and then I would say firmly, "Please tell her Majesty" whatever it might be. Sometimes the girls checked themselves long enough to translate what I said, but most of the time they didn't bother about it and went on asking all kinds of questions about life in the United States. The Queen finally managed to get in a word and told me her son was planning to visit us in the autumn. She was much worried at the idea of his going so far away and dreaded the dangers he might face. I assured her that the United States was a safe country and the inhabitants peaceful.

I asked if I might photograph the princesses. The younger one, who was pretty, was dying to have this done, but the older one refused, saying their father would never allow it. They kept strict purdah and could not risk having their faces in a photograph where some man might chance to see them.

In Baghdad we met Francis Kettaneh, eldest of four brothers and head of the family, a man of wide experience and education. Although his people had been Lebanese for nearly three hundred years, it was impossible to guess his nationality, for he spoke perfect English, French, German, Italian, Turkish, Persian, and several Arabic dialects.

When Francis invited us to tour the Holy Land for three weeks as his guests Ted at first refused because he didn't think my health would stand any more driving in the heat and dust. By then my face was turned toward home and I longed for the children and Oyster Bay. However, after thinking it over and realizing that we might never have such an opportunity again, I convinced Ted that my health would easily endure it. Having conscientiously eaten *mast*, called *leban* here, I felt much better and had gained a little weight. I was rewarded by having no more migraines for a month, except for a last one on our twenty-hour bus trip from Baghdad to Damascus. If I had to have it at all, I much preferred a migraine on a journey like this than when visiting places I wanted to explore.

Ten years before, Francis Kettaneh had made the first crossing of the desert by car from Beirut to Baghdad accompanied by his father (representing Thomas Cook), a representative of the French Government, and Norman Nairn, whom they induced to establish a regular cross-desert service. This cut the traveling time between the two cities from twenty-four days via the Red Sea and the Persian Gulf to twenty-four hours across the desert.

We left Baghdad at seven in the morning, traveling by Nairn Convoy, consisting of two buses and a car with all drivers fully armed. Francis had reserved front seats for us in one of the buses. They were most comfortable, but mine happened to be by the drinking-water tank. As the day grew hot everyone became thirsty. People would lean over me and pass cups of water back to their friends. I didn't mind plain water being spilled on me, but one man dropped a cup of thick, sugary lemon syrup in my lap. We made a few short stops during the day, and in the evening spent an hour at the oasis of Rutba Wells, where there was a large establishment with bedrooms, a big dining room, a garage, and a serai for camels and donkeys. Ted and Francis had a good dinner while I slept in a clean and comfortable bed. During the night Ted didn't sleep at all, but I did and woke, feeling better, in time to see a sunrise in the desert.

Arriving at Damascus, we went to the hotel, had baths and breakfast of *leban* and coffee, an ideal combination, and left for Baalbek, the ancient Heliopolis, or City of the Sun. After lunch at a little hotel we took naps. Ted and Francis got up in an hour and tried to make me go out with them, but I said that if the ruins stayed where they belonged I could just as well see them in the morning and would sleep until then.

Next day we explored the ancient acropolis, whose grandeur and magnificence are indescribable. The main court covered three and a half acres. Of the two main temples, the greater was sacred to Jupiter, the lesser to Bacchus. In the supporting wall of the terrace were three blocks of stone measuring sixty-four feet in length and thirteen in height and breadth. They were twenty feet above the ground and were said to be the largest ever used in construction. Another such stone, even greater in size and weighing over a thousand tons, lay in a quarry almost a mile away. How these stones were moved and put in position is not known. Underground were great vaults once used as stables and vast enough, we were told, to hold ten thousand horses at a time. The architects whose brains conceived the beauty and the engineers who executed the stupendous feat of building are forgotten. According to one legend, Baalbek was founded by Cain as a protection against vengeance for the death of Abel. The Romans were, of course, a mere handful in Syria and must have pressed the entire countryside into service to erect these marvels.

Our visit to Jerusalem was highlighted by various impressions: the Church of the Holy Sepulcher, its shadowy altars dedicated to every Christian sect but the Protestants, its ancient church books with beautiful illuminations but in shabby condition, its treasure ranging from Peter the Great's sword to magnificent jeweled crosses given by some of the royal houses of Europe, and its Moslem guard to keep order among the Christians; the Orthodox Church built by Czar Nicholas II in the Garden of Gethsemane, its interior covered with tawdry stencils imitating mosaics; the Wailing Wall where Jews of every class and dress gathered while two British Tommies were on duty to keep the Pax Britannica; the Dome of the Rock, far more imposing architecturally than any of the other monuments.

In Bethlehem the lovely, flowing blue or white draperies of the women were said to have been worn by the Virgin Mary to enhance her beauty. The River Jordan was as narrow as a creek at home. We scooped up a bottleful of its water to take back with us. Although it was so full of queer little green things that we had to filter and boil it, it has been used to christen all our grandchildren except Quentin's youngest daughter, Susan, who was baptized in China.

Francis took us back to Damascus for a couple of days, stopped the car a short distance away, and told us the story of Mohammed coming across the desert. He, also, had stopped within sight of the city, gazed at its shining domes, minarets, and green trees, then turned his camel back, saying it was not given to man to enter Paradise twice. Here I understood at last that the verse in the Bible about the rich man and the eye of a needle may not have been pure parable. The houses of the well-to-do had large, heavy front doors through which anything could pass. At night or during troubled times these were locked and barred. A small door beside the big one could be opened to admit someone. These were called "eyes of needles." While it might have been difficult for a camel to go through one of them, it would not have been impossible.

We had a few days in Beirut and dined one evening with Monsieur and Madame Helleu. He was the French *haut délégué* in charge during the absence of the High Commissioner. During dinner the conversation turned on colonial administration. Everyone wanted Ted's views on Philippine independence, which he preferred not to discuss. Finally Monsieur Helleu made a significant remark. "There are three ways of running a colony," he said. "A colony is like a cow. Now, the British feed their cow and milk her. You Americans feed your cow but do not milk her. But we French have the best method. We milk our cow and make her find her own food!"

Bill and Alan joined us in Beirut, the former pale and thin. I tried my best to persuade him to eat *leban,* which had done such wonders for me, but he wouldn't touch it unless I was there and even then insisted on smothering it with sugar and thick cream, probably counteracting all its good effects. Bill was not well enough to stand the racket of further traveling with us, so he and Alan took a steamer to Italy. All through our long journey together I kept thinking that either of these two young men, especially Bill, would make a good husband for Gracie. We had seen them under all sorts of conditions of discomfort and inconvenience and had grown to know them in a way that would have been impossible at home. I was careful not to write her too much about them for fear she would fix them in her mind as "Father's and Mother's friends." The result was that six months after we reached home Gracie and Bill were married and have been truly happy ever since.

Francis Kettaneh drove Ted and me to Latakia, to Antioch, and to Aleppo, where he put us on the train for Istanbul. We were very sorry to say good-by to him and were not surprised after the train started to find that he had put on board a supply of *leban,* fruit, and Syrian honey. A more thoughtful man I never knew, nor a more delightful companion.

At Istanbul we spent most of our time at the Church of St. Sophia with Dr. Whittemore, who was restoring the mosaics painted over by Moslems. From there we took a ship to Venice, where Signorina met us and where we spent two days. Ted wanted to see everything and suggested we skip lunch every day so as not to waste time, but relented when I said I was hungry and needed time out for minestrone and spaghetti as often as possible. I had lost twelve pounds so far on our travels.

From Venice we went to Florence and Rome, where we stayed four days and had a round of gaiety. Our Ambassador, Breckinridge Long, had just arrived and gave his first dinner party for us. We also dined with Alexander Kirk, our chargé d'affaires, whose sister had once been my roommate at school. Many exiled royalties were living in Rome at the time. We had a picnic on the King's beach at Ostia with Prince and Princess Christopher of Greece and some of their friends, including the Princess's brother, the Comte de Paris, pretender to the throne of France, and the Prince's sister, Princess Marie of Greece, who spent the day playing backgammon with Miss Cornelia Armsby of San Francisco while the rest of us went swimming. Princess Christopher was young and beautiful. They were all gay and delightful.

Alan Stuyvesant's mother was away, but he had arranged for us to stay for a couple of days at her villa at St. Jean Cap Ferrat on the French Riviera, where we were to meet Cornelius and his friend, Freddy Osborn. They had finished their course in gliding at the Segelflugschule some weeks before and were now touring Europe in their somewhat battered Ford roadster. Our lines of communication failed at this point, for we found no word from them when we arrived. I told Ted we would enjoy a short stay here, as the Riviera was supposed to be glamorous, but I was wrong. It was the middle of August and must have been off season, for none of our friends were there except Somerset Maugham, of whom we were fond and whose villa was lovely. At Monte Carlo we saw nothing but fat women wearing scanty bathing suits and high heels as they walked lap dogs on leashes around the swimming pool at the Casino. Inside at the tables were frowzy old ladies bent over penciled accounts of their systems and counting money from little bags of gold.

We had the use of an old car of Alan's, a fifteen-year-old model-T Ford touring car with the bones of its top turned back because the cover had worn out and had been taken off. Neither of us had a foreign license, but we hoped our diplomatic passports would help get us out of trouble in case anything happened. I persuaded Ted to go to what was advertised as a gala at the Casino in Monte Carlo to see a ballet. When we started out that evening we found the car had no taillight. A man in a service station said it could not be fixed that night and sold us a little red paper lantern that unfolded like an accordion and had a candle in it. He said these were used by bicyclists, adding that it would be all right if we didn't go too fast. Thus equipped, we drew up in front of the Casino, where the doorman, a Senegalese over six feet tall in a plumed shako and white uniform with gold lace and many war ribbons, saluted us smartly and asked if we would mind parking just a little farther on to avoid the risk of another car coming along and perhaps damaging *la jolie voiture*. Inside the Casino the audience was sloppy, with women in slacks and men in turtle-neck sweaters. Ted said he was sick of glamour and we would leave next day. If Cornelius and Freddy had not arrived they would have to follow us.

Next morning we left to take the train to Paris. At the station I found my dressing case had been left behind at the villa and hurried back in a taxi to get it. On the way back to the station a bus stopped suddenly and unexpectedly in front of us. The taxi driver, with quick skill and a hard jerk of the wheel, managed to pass it, but a car behind us crashed into it with considerable damage. We got away before we could be delayed as witnesses. I reached the station and flung myself aboard the train as it pulled out. A few minutes later we stopped at Nice and heard Cornelius's voice. He had arrived at the villa moments after I had left for the second time. A quick decision was made. Ted remained on the train with the luggage while I seized my dressing case and got out, forgetting I had all the keys with me. Ted thrust my passport into my hands and waved good-by to us.

It took us two days to drive across the mountains and up through France to Paris. All the way, as my Scottish nurse Jane used to say, we talked nineteen to the dozen. The boys had been at Grünau for two months and had been awarded three licenses, two for gliding and one for soaring. For the latter they wore the lapel button with three white sea gulls and were amused at the number of people who noticed it while they were traveling through Germany and came up to ask when and where they had earned it. They had learned a good deal of German and had thoroughly enjoyed themselves. The cost of their tuition, board, lodging, and all expenses for two months had amounted to a hundred and twenty-five dollars each. At the time foreigners were encouraged to attend the school and were not, as Cornelius said, asked to give "that silly-looking Nazi salute"; but the following year, 1934, when he wrote to inquire if postgraduate work could be done, the answer was that no foreigners would be accepted. After the courses were over Cornelius and Freddy toured in the Ford roadster through Germany, Austria, and Italy until they met us at Nice.

Although the boys complained that the Alps got in the way—they had expected nice flat French roads—we reached Lyon without mishap and spent the night there. Next day the car's muffler broke, and flames showed close to the oil-soaked floor boards. It was a holiday and everything was closed. Finally we found a service station where the man was willing to help us. After he patched things up as best he could we continued and reached Paris at midnight. That car was really on its last legs and was not worth repairing. When the boys reached Cherbourg to take the steamer for home, they decided to give the Ford to the first man who helped them with their suitcases. It was an old porter who came out to do this. After they had unloaded, they pointed to the car and said, "It's all yours." At first the old man refused to believe it, then in a frenzy of joy hustled them to a police station to sign a deed of gift. Cornelius had borrowed fifty dollars from Ted and returned it as soon as he got the next installment of his allowance. He had paid for his entire trip himself.

We stayed in Paris a few days, then went to London for a week. One of the pleasant things we did was to spend the day with the Rudyard Kiplings at Bateman's, Burwash, Surrey. Mr. Kipling wrote us to come by car, as the trains were neolithic. When we arrived he and Mrs. Kipling were sitting under the trees on the lawn. It was a chilly day, typical of an English summer. Mr. Kipling asked if we would be warm enough outdoors and wanted to know if I wore a tummy band. When I answered that I hadn't had one on since I was a child he was dismayed. "Fresh from the tropics and without a tummy band? You are running a great risk. Promise you will get one no later than tomorrow. You can find them at Harrod's."

At lunch Mr. Kipling asked Ted if he was planning any more hunting expeditions, but when Ted outlined a journey into virtually unexplored country in Tibet he shook his head. "Aren't you getting a little too old? Really, Ted, I think you should leave that sort of thing to younger men." Ted, aged forty-five and in perfect condition, was completely silenced.

Gracie had come to England several weeks before and had been staying with Belle's sister Elizabeth, the Honorable Mrs. Mervyn Herbert, who had a lovely house in Somerset. Gracie has always been glad she had this opportunity to see English country life at its best and as it never will be again, in a house where, as she said, "attractive and distinguished people were always coming for weekends" and where Elizabeth as the landowner felt deep responsibility for the welfare of the village.

We had hoped Teddy might join us somewhere along the line, but he had been very busy that summer and had not saved enough money for the trip. Ted, Gracie, and I sailed for home together in September and were joined by Teddy, Cornelius, and Quentin at Oyster Bay, where we had a wonderful family reunion, the first in a year and nine months.

Chapter 35

The Oyster Bay or out-of-season Roosevelts . . .
FRANK SULLIVAN

Ted's first consideration on reaching home was to find a job. With his knowledge of world affairs and proven administrative ability, this was not difficult. Thanks to Winthrop W. Aldrich, chairman of the board of the Chase National Bank and later Ambassador to Britain, an old friend married to my first cousin Harriet, he was made first a director and then chairman of the board of the American Express Company.

He was distressed, as were all Republicans, at the sorry condition of the party as a result of its overwhelming rout the year before and declared we must "pick ourselves up, brush ourselves off, and start all over again." Soon after his return he was elected President of the National Republican Club, which had lost half its members and had a monthly deficit of nearly three thousand dollars. Ted started and carried through a campaign to raise funds for the club and to add younger men to its membership. Two years later it had more members than ever before, was no longer in debt, and had become a busy place humming with activity. This had not been done, however, without a few screams of protest from some Old Guard members who resented any innovations.

Ted had been on the National Council of Boy Scouts since 1919. He became vice-president in 1935 and was on nine working committees. He received the Silver Buffalo Award for distinguished service to boyhood and also the Silver Carabao in the Philippines. Shortly after coming home he was made head of the National Health Council, spearhead of a nationwide fight against disease. It co-ordinated seventeen national health-education organizations, each with thousands of local chapters throughout the country. He was a member of the National Citizens' Committee of Mobilization for Human Needs, and national chairman of the Citizenship Educational Service, whose board of directors consisted mainly of executive heads of twenty-one national organizations. He was a member of the National Civil Service Reform League and also was on the board of directors of the N.A.A.C.P., working closely with Walter White and always counseling moderation. He was director and honorary president of the National Health Circle for Colored People, a trustee of Bethune-Cookman College, and a member of the Spingarn Committee. While we lived in Washington he had been a trustee of Howard University. At the request of Newton D. Baker, Secretary of War under President Wilson, he went on the board of the National Conference of Christians and Jews. Besides these enterprises in which he took an active part, he was an honorary member of some twenty committees that changed from year to year.

After Hitler came to power in 1933 many organizations and committees were formed by liberals to protest against Nazism. Ted refused to join any that did not name communism and fascism as well, saying the Russian and Italian crimes were as reprehensible as those of the Germans and that all three ideologies were equally un-American.

When Irving Berlin turned over past, present, and future royalties from his song "God Bless America" to be used for the benefit of the Boy Scouts and Girl Scouts, he wanted the funds administered by a committee of three, a Catholic, a Jew, and a Protestant. Gene Tunney, Herbert Bayard Swope, and Ted were the ones chosen.

From 1935 until he went back into the Army in 1941, Ted was superintendent of the Christ Church Sunday school at Oyster Bay, to be succeeded after the war by Quentin. Once when our friend Victor Cazelet, English M.P., was visiting on Long Island he and Ted were eager to meet. The only time possible for both was at breakfast on Sunday morning. The night before, Victor asked his host's austerely correct English butler to arrange for a car to take him to Oyster Bay early next morning, saying he was to have breakfast with Colonel Roosevelt, who was Sunday-school superintendent and had to be at church at half-past nine. The butler's face unexpectedly wrinkled into a delighted smile. "Sunday-school superintendent, sir? How lovely! One doesn't hear too much about that sort of thing around here nowadays, does one, sir?"

Ted went to Brazil in the summer of 1935 for some big-game shooting. He wanted to get a good jaguar specimen for the American Museum of Natural History in New York and spent six weeks in the jungles of Matto Grosso with his friend Sasha Siemel, a famous athlete and sportsman who had killed these beasts with a spear. Trailing them with dogs, Ted said they had a hard time at first finding an animal large enough to be worth shooting, finally succeeding only three days before he had to leave for home. He shot an excellent specimen weighing three hundred and forty pounds and told me afterward that one of their two dogs was rightly named "Perfumado."

Ted brought back two delightful pets from Brazil, Sakiwinki monkeys from the upper reaches of the Amazon. They were about eighteen inches tall and incredibly slender, with delicate little hands and feet, and they had long black-and-gray hair and tails like silver foxes. This species' record of life in captivity was seven weeks, but we had ours for eight years before they died of old age. Balocca, a genius with animals, carefully worked out a diet for them that prolonged their life span to this astonishing extent. During the winter they lived in the basement of his cottage, but in summer they were at large on the place, seldom going far from the house and the large chicken-wire cage where they slept at night. They were gentle, had great curiosity, and loved people. On Sundays after lunch, when we often sat outdoors with friends, they would come loping across the grass to join us and amuse us by trying to remove eyeglasses as they climbed over everyone. We always had to watch for fear they would make off with little silver coffee spoons or anything else bright and shining. Once a friend of ours was reading under a tree. As no one else was around, the monkeys concentrated on him, jumping from his lap to his shoulders and from his shoulders to his head, and trying to turn the pages of his book. Finally he gave up and went away, saying he had never expected to be driven indoors by monkeys on Long Island.

I have never known anyone who read as much as Ted. When people wondered how he found time for this, he said it was merely a question of habit. "I read in bed. I read in my bath. I read in the train. I read in the subway. I would feel as desolate without a book in my pocket as I would if I had lost my trousers." For this reason he gladly accepted a chance to go into the publishing business. He resigned from his position with the American Express Company but remained a director and was invited to become a member of the executive committee of the board. In September he joined the firm of Doubleday, Doran & Company, and soon after was made vice-president.

This was a business connection he thoroughly enjoyed. When the announcement was made to the press, his old friend Nelson Doubleday, president of the firm which today is Doubleday & Company, was asked if they had any definite plans for Ted. Nelson replied that the company had realized for some time that interest in public and government matters was steadily growing among the general public and that Ted's wide experience with people and international affairs as well as his knowledge of literature would bring what was needed into the firm. When a reporter asked Ted if he would be satisfied settling down to the work of a publishing house after his life in politics, colonial administration, big-game hunting, and excitement, he laughed. "Oh yes. You forget I'm a grandfather now, and it's time I settled down. I like to work for the public, and the publishing business, after all, is a form of teaching. My belief is that there are as many good books unwritten as there are bad books written, and we'll try to get some of them done."

I had always thought of a publishing house as a dour institution whose doors were opened reluctantly to aspiring authors, but found I was quite wrong. An editor often has to conceive a book, select the right author and persuade him to write it, hold his hand while he is doing it, keep him from resenting changes and cuts, and sympathize with him if reviews are unfavorable. Ted enjoyed his work thoroughly and relished the fact that the editorial offices of Doubleday, Doran were at Garden City, only forty minutes by car from our house at Oyster Bay, making commuting pleasant.

In winter we frequently went to Bonny Hall, Nelson and Ellen Doubleday's house in South Carolina, where they spent several months every year and where members of the firm gathered from time to time to discuss books, business problems, and to enjoy themselves. Several times we went to England for a month on publishing business with the Doubledays, who were a joy as traveling companions. These trips were a real pleasure, as business was combined with seeing old friends and having fun. I kept no diary, nor did I write many letters during that time, so I have only vague memories of the whirl of gaiety we used to have in London. I remember a big dinner party in March 1936 given by Lord and Lady Astor (Nancy of Virginia) at their house in St. James's Square, where the table was set with gold plate and orchids and the footmen had knee breeches, white silk stockings, and powdered heads. Hitler had just entered the Rhineland unopposed, and things looked far from rosy, but no one would have guessed it. After dinner Lady Astor had a row of chairs placed down the middle of the ballroom and we all fell to playing "Going to Jerusalem." Toward the end I was put out and stood by Lord Salisbury, the Under Secretary of State for Foreign Affairs, who remarked, "I wish Hitler could see us now!" At table I sat by Lord Astor but cannot recall who was on my other side and can remember only two other people who were there: Enid Bagnold, who was really Lady Jones and whose novel, *National Velvet*, was a best seller, and Baroness Ravensdale.

It was during these years that Alexander Woollcott became a close friend, not only of Ted's and mine but also of Quentin's. We often went for weekends to Bomoseen, his club on a tiny island in a Vermont lake. His friends, many of whom became ours, were delightful and stimulating. Among them were Alice Duer Miller, Helen Hayes, Charlie MacArthur, the Lunts, Thornton Wilder, Grace Eustis, Gertrude Lawrence, Raoul Fleischmann, Neysa McMein, Harpo and Susan Marx. A harp was delivered to the island whenever Harpo came. I asked nothing better than to sit doing embroidery and listening to him play the most beautiful improvisations while everyone else was busy with croquet or badminton. We played "Murder," a game starting at breakfast and sometimes going on all day. Cards were drawn, and whoever got the ace of spades was the murderer, who had to say "You're dead" to someone while unobserved. The greater his ingenuity, the better his chance of fooling Aleck, who, as district attorney, questioned everyone after dinner, put clues together, and almost invariably solved the problem. The victim was supposed to drop to the ground and remain until discovered. Once a young man cheated. He was "murdered" at noon, lay in the sun for a time without being noticed, became bored, got up, went swimming, and returned to the spot an hour later. Of course this threw everything off when it came to evidence. That evening, after long fruitless questioning, he was forced to admit sheepishly what he had done. Aleck's wrath was devastating. "Do you realize what you did, you Tom Fool?" he thundered. "You selfishly spoiled the pleasure of sixteen people who were playing the game in good faith. Who do you think you are?" The young man was so overcome that he left early next morning, unregretted.

Once when we were in London, Aleck took me out to dinner and a play. Saying the restaurant was only a step from the theater, he refused to take a taxi and insisted on walking majestically down the street for half a mile, pushing through the theater crowds. He was dressed in evening clothes with a broad-brimmed black felt hat, a long black cape lined in scarlet silk, and he carried not a cane but a staff, the kind once used by Geraldine Farrar in the first act of *Tosca*. As I had inadvertently worn a white fox wrap, we were about as inconspicuous as Buckingham Palace.

Aleck was convinced that Americans liked poetry, and suggested that Ted and Alice compile an anthology of verses people had clipped from magazines and newspapers and put away in desk drawers or carried in wallets. He said he would announce this on the radio if Ted liked the idea. While we were in Europe he made a most effective broadcast on his program, "The Town Crier," asking for poems. When we returned Ted found over thirty thousand waiting for him. Going through them was a stupendous task, but the result was *The Desk Drawer Anthology,* still in print in the British edition after twenty years.

373

At this time Ted was more than ever in demand as a speaker. In the next few years his invitations from forty-three states averaged more than five a week, not counting all those received for him by the Speakers' Bureau of the Republican National Committee, which handled his political dates. Of course he could accept only a small fraction of these requests and attend to his business, but in the presidential campaigns of 1936 and 1940 he traveled over the country for three weeks before each election, often making several speeches a day. As he said, you don't stop fighting for what you think is right even though you expect to be beaten.

His purpose was to attack what he considered fundamentally wrong in the New Deal. He believed, of course, in its announced objective, "a more abundant life for all," but would have amended it to read "for all who merit it by their industry, thrift, and initiative." He held that government should serve the people by protecting their rights and opportunities but should not support them. He was convinced that government must not repress industry or limit production, which represents the wealth of the nation, but rather should work for fair distribution of that wealth. He felt that the budget should be balanced and predicted that inflation would surely result from the New Deal financial policies and our children would be saddled with a huge, permanent debt. He deplored the army of bureaucrats appointed to regulate the details of our lives, and he bitterly opposed the attempt in 1937 to pack the Supreme Court.

For over twenty years Miss Hensey had kept all letters to Ted and carbons of his answers and stored them in our attic. After his death I spent several months reading them, classifying them, and tearing up those merely asking for jobs or favors. Looking at them today, it is dismal to see how many people wrote asking for copies of his speeches to distribute, only to be told he could not afford to have them printed.

In December 1937 Ted and Martin W. Littleton, noted lawyer and former district attorney, went to a dinner and by mistake exchanged overcoats. Mr. Littleton wrote Ted as follows:

My dear Colonel,

I herewith return your coat.

Apparently through some inadvertency, the details of which I prefer not to discuss, I got your coat on Saturday night . . . Some time later when on my way home I reached into the pockets for gloves and muffler, I found three fish-hooks, two dead grasshoppers, one live cricket, a mousetrap, one sack of tobacco, and some chicken feathers (Plymouth Rock). Really, Colonel, in this cold weather you should wear gloves and a muffler. If you do not think of yourself, at least have some regard for the innocent victim who might have to wear your coat.

On further examination I found a quantity of axle-grease on the right shoulder, a torn lining and two moth holes. I immediately recognized from the equipment and ravages of political warfare so clearly manifested on the garment that the owner must be a great soldier of many battles against the New Deal forces.

I do not know where my coat is, but will describe it in case you were unlucky enough to draw it in exchange. It is of the same general breed, color and size. It is a little older and more shot, if possible. It is a double-breasted affair with eight button-holes and one button, the said one button being located on the wrong side. It has very distinctive hoof marks on the derrière.

In the pockets are an assortment of buttons, some toothpicks, one can-opener, some bolts and nuts, a notice of interest due on a mortgage, and a writ of habeas corpus. There are also a number of scattered moth holes. Wherever there is any lining it is torn, and wherever there is not any lining of course it is not torn.

My coat is a distinct liability but, I imagine, like yours it has a very distinct sentimental value, which only we can understand and appreciate.

Ted answered this letter with delight.

Dear Martin,

You are right. That is my coat. I judge from your manner

of detailing the contents of the pockets that you are rather wondering just why those articles were there. That is easy of explanation.

(a) The fish-hooks I captured from the New Deal. They had been using them to catch suckers.

(b) You speak of chicken feathers. You are evidently a poor ornithologist. Those feathers I took from the New Deal also. Some of them came from the Blue Eagle; others from geese that the New Deal had plucked.

(c) The grasshoppers again came from the same source. They represent New Dealers who skipped and hopped during the summer of idle dreams, and are going to be in bad trouble when the winter of cold facts arrives.

(d) The cricket I found myself. It was the only one that had not been plowed under by the New Deal.

As for the mousetrap, I captured that also. It was known in the public press as the Supreme Court Bill, and was baited with a bit of cheese of the variety known as "short cut regardless of cost." If people had entered the trap they would have eaten the cheese, but would never have been able to get out of the trap again.

As for the axle grease on the shoulder, as you may surmise I got that in my struggles with the New Deal. You may not know, but the New Deal has been using a lot of grease in getting its plans through.

I am returning your coat herewith.

Chapter 36

*. . . thy children like olive plants round
about thy table.*

PSALMS 128:3

A few weeks after we had returned from our journey in Asia, Ted
complained that Bill McMillan was so busy courting Gracie that
he had lost him as a friend. He never saw Bill any more if Gracie
was around. I had to explain that a good son-in-law was even more
desirable than a friend, and all we had to do was to keep quiet and
let matters take their course. Ted agreed in principle, saying he
hoped things would get back to normal someday.

Six months later, in March 1934, Gracie and Bill were married
at Christ Church, Oyster Bay. I don't know why we all looked
forward to a nice country wedding at that time of year, but we
happily made plans without thinking of the possibility of bad
weather. We were living at the time in a house close to the waters
of Oyster Bay. For two weeks before the wedding it was so cold
that the bay froze over. Two severe storms covered the ice with
inches of snow, which strong winds piled to a depth of twelve feet
in front of our house. For several days we were cut off completely.
The week before the wedding we had many things to do in New
York. After waiting in vain for the local snowplow to open the road
on which we lived, Gracie and I found some webbed snowshoes
in the attic, put on ski pants and boots, and set out. We walked a
mile to the main road, going right over the top of the police booth,

377

hitchhiked to the village, and took the only train that ran to town that day. When we reached New York we found the streets had been cleared, and people in the shops and at the dressmaker's looked at our costumes with surprise.

The wedding reception was to have been held at Sagamore Hill, but this was precluded because the place to park cars was deep in snow, so we arranged to have it in the parish house beside the church. Gracie would have to change her clothes in the real estate office of Weekes and Weekes next door. After we had settled these plans the church caught fire but luckily was not badly damaged. When I told Alice about it on the telephone she said, "Don't give up hope. Even with the church and Sagamore out you can always fall back on the Long Island Railroad station!"

Thinking I could turn the snow to some advantage, I found someone in the village who had an ancient sleigh and was willing to paint it in gay colors to give a Currier and Ives touch to the bride and groom driving away. Because of the streak of bad luck we were having I suppose I should have foreseen misfortune. The night before the wedding there was a thaw, with the temperature in the seventies. Melting snow ran in rivers down the streets, and nothing on runners could be used.

The day before the wedding someone asked me if the champagne had come. I had forgotten to keep track of it and found it had not. The liquor dealer in New York tried to reassure me. "It will surely be there tomorrow morning," he insisted. "Why, it left New York on a truck four days ago!" I started to ask why he thought it would ever come if it hadn't covered forty miles in four days, but hung up. Ted then began calling his acquaintances on the police force and among filling-station attendants and found the truck had broken down in Long Island City. We got the champagne in time.

Ted was very proud of still being able to wear the cutaway coat and striped trousers he had been married in twenty-four years before, but when the day came the trousers could not be found. Everything was dropped while everyone hunted for them. Were they at the tailor's being pressed? They were not. Or at the cleaner's? No. After searching the house we started deliberately looking in all places where they could not possibly be and found them almost at once, neatly folded on a shelf in Signorina's closet. Of course no one had put them there.

Gracie wore my wedding dress of white satin and duchesse lace with a tulle veil over her face and in a misty cloud around her. Hermann Patrick Tappé, one of the great American designers, made the bridesmaids' dresses and mine. When I asked his advice about the veil, he said if he made it and sent someone out to put it on he would have to charge me a hundred and fifty dollars. "I know you can't afford this and am sure you can manage it yourself. To look right a tulle veil must not be fussed with. I will send you the tulle you need, yards long and wide. You must pick it up in the middle with the tips of your fingers. Try to handle it as little as possible. Put it on Gracie's head, gathering it slightly, pin it firmly, then add the orange blossoms. Be sure to get it right the first time or it will look like a rumpled sheet." I did manage to get it right but was not helped by Teddy, Cornelius, and Quentin dancing around us and singing until I threatened to spank them all with a slipper and put them out of the room.

Teddy and Cornelius were ushers, but Quentin was too young. He was a little sad about this until I pointed out that he was supposed to take me to the church, and Bill gave him a pair of gold cuff links exactly like those he gave the ushers.

In spite of the condition of the roads, Christ Church was packed to the doors. The decorations were great masses of feathery green, a lovely background for the bride and the white dresses with wide green sashes and white bouquets of the bridesmaids. Duckboards had been laid between the church and the parish house so that people wouldn't have to wade through a stream of running water. The reception was gay, with music by Markel, who had conducted his orchestra at Gracie's debut and who I think plays better dance music than anyone else to this day. From time to time Quentin relieved the pianist, playing all the tunes by ear in any required key.

Gracie and Bill went to live in the country near Baltimore, where Bill designed and built an enchanting house of whitewashed stone with shutters and doors the color of the sky as reflected in its heavy slate roof. I think he intended to show what he could do as an architect and meant to sell it later, but they both loved it so much

379

that they have lived in it ever since. Bill was an enthusiastic sailor and had taken part in many ocean races in his yacht, the *Water Gipsy,* which he sold after he married, realizing that he could not maintain a wife, a house, and a yacht at the same time. He and Gracie have two children. William McMillan, Jr., today is in our Army in Germany, while Eleanor is at Radcliffe. After graduating from Princeton young Bill rowed in the Annual Regatta at Henley-on-Thames as a member of the junior varsity crew, which won all of its five races, an athletic feat unequaled by anyone else in the family.

Ted and I were living temporarily in a tiny street-level apartment in New York when Gracie's little girl was born. At three o'clock one morning in December 1937 Bill telephoned to say the baby was expected at any moment. As we were sleepily fumbling with our clothes a man sauntered past the open window singing Harry Lauder's song, "Och, it's nice to get up in the mor-r-ning when the sun begins to shine——" Ted immediately took it up and went on, "At four-r or five or six o'clock in the good auld summer-r-time." The man replied, "But when the snaw is snawing and it's mur-r-ky over-r-head," followed by Ted, "Och, it's nice to get up in the mor-r-ning, but it's nicer-r to lie in your bed!" The man tapped on the window, said, "Laddie, you've a grand sense of humor!" and went on his way.

In July 1935 we all chanced to be off on visits except Signorina and Teddy when our house caught fire and was saved by his prompt action. Early one morning the housemaid dumped a gallon of naphtha into a laundry tub in the basement. Naphtha was something I never allowed to be used. Where it came from and who bought it are unknown to this day. When the laundress switched on the electric iron the fumes were ignited. A roaring fire blazed up from the tub and mushroomed against the ceiling. Teddy was asleep in bed. Hearing screams from below, he went downstairs four steps at a time, yelled for someone to call the fire department, threw several armfuls of wet clothes on the flaming naphtha, and played an extinguisher on the ceiling to keep the fire from spreading until the engines arrived. The firemen said he had saved the house, as a delay of five minutes might well have been fatal. His hands were painfully burned, and to his disgust he was called a hero in the newspapers.

As soon as Teddy graduated from Harvard in 1936 he set about getting a job. Refusing any introductions from his father, he visited several firms and after careful thought decided he wanted to be employed by E. I. du Pont de Nemours. He went to Wilmington, Delaware, and applied to the personnel manager for a job. On his return he said everyone had been unexpectedly nice to him. He had been shown all over the place, introduced to many people, and even given lunch. He left Wilmington encouraged to believe he would be notified in a few days that a job was open for him.

Two and a half weeks passed during which he began to wonder, and then the blow fell. He received a letter from the du Pont company regretting that no position was available for him, nor would be in the foreseeable future. If a vacancy should occur, which was most unlikely, he would be notified. Meanwhile he was advised not to turn down any other acceptable offer. When I asked what he intended to do next, he said he was going back to Wilmington early the following morning.

Again he went to the personnel manager and again was taken around and introduced to several people, including William Richter, head of the Fabrics and Finishes Division. By this time Teddy felt he was being given a run-around and got mad. He told Mr. Richter it was inconceivable that no job for him could be found in a company of this size. I think Mr. Richter must have liked his persistence, for after a pause he asked him when he wanted to start work. "Right now," said Teddy. "All right. Report at our paint factory in Philadelphia tomorrow morning," he was told.

During the next year Teddy's hands looked like those of a day laborer, which indeed he was. He then was sent to the company office in Chicago, where he stayed for two years. After that he was made industrial salesman and given the territory of Kentucky, southern Illinois, and southern Indiana, with headquarters in Louisville. Here he remained for three years until the war, increasing the sales of du Pont paints and furniture finishes in his area by several hundred per cent.

Teddy came home for Christmas one year when Ted was clearing out the woods behind our house. These woods had been untouched for some thirty years and were full of poison ivy. As both of them were impervious to it, they rooted it out thoroughly. One vine had a trunk that was actually over six inches in diameter. Teddy took a piece of it to Balocca's workshop and sawed off a four-inch cross section, which he polished and covered with two coats of spar varnish. It was like no other wood we had ever seen, with a band of cream-white under the bark and a center of mottled pink. When he returned to Kentucky he took the piece with him and showed it to owners of furniture factories to whom he was selling his products. They would examine it carefully and ask what it was. When told it was poison ivy they would drop it in dismay and glare at Teddy until reassured that the varnish made it harmless. They then would be much interested and would call in others on whom to play the same trick.

Unfortunately there were sad and unexpected results of this episode. Although Teddy was immune, Signorina was extremely allergic to poison ivy, as was Balocca. When Teddy took a bath in her bathroom, enough of it clung to the tub to infect her so severely that she had to stay in bed under a tent for nearly two weeks, with a trained nurse to look after her. Although Teddy had left the workshop tidy as usual, enough poison ivy sawdust was left to give Balocca a bad attack on his hands. Teddy, of course, was both horrified and contrite but was not too popular at home for a time.

While in Louisville, Teddy once brought some friends home for a weekend, among them Anne Babcock—the daughter-in-law of my dreams. When I first met her I had to bite my tongue for fear I would spoil everything by premature enthusiasm, but Signorina had no such scruples. Taking Teddy aside, she said to him in a fierce whisper, "Don't you let that girl get away!"

When they were married we all went out to the wedding, including Cornelius, who flew up from Mexico, where he was working. Our friend, Luis de Florez, lent his small private plane to take Ted and me to Louisville with his son Peter and a pilot. When we took off from Long Island it was a beautiful day, with no reports of bad weather along the route, but we ran into a severe snowstorm over the Alleghenies. The pilot did not have a license for landing by instruments, so we were refused permission by radio to touch down at Pittsburgh and were told to go back to Altoona, where the weather was better. How to find Altoona was the question. Finally our pilot decided to make a forced landing, as the snow was getting worse. We flew around for a time looking for a good spot, avoiding great ridges of forbidding mountains. A frozen pond would have served had we been sure of the thickness of the ice. At last we came down as gently as a falling leaf in a field near a farmhouse. The farmer drove us in his car to where we could catch a bus to Altoona, where we boarded a train, changing at Pittsburgh, for Louisville.

In contrast to Gracie's wedding, this one was purely a pleasure for me because as the bridegroom's mother I went merely as a guest. The usual complicated arrangements had of course been made and the work done by the Babcocks. All I had to do was to make sure Teddy was properly turned out and the soles of his new shoes blacked so they wouldn't be conspicuous when he knelt at the altar.

Today, after nineteen years, I believe that Teddy and Anne with their son "T IV," living on their seventy-six-acre farm near Paoli, Pennsylvania, are happier even than they were then.

Teddy served in the Navy during World War II and was decorated for valor. After the war, believing that some member of the family should be in financial business in order to help the rest of us in our affairs, he went into the firm of Montgomery Scott in Philadelphia, investment brokers and successors to Montgomery, Clothier and Tyler, Ted's business association twenty-eight years before. He was given time off from his business in 1947 when he was appointed Secretary of Commerce of the state of Pennsylvania by Governor James Duff and served for two years. At the end of this time he was included by the United States Junior Chamber of Commerce in its list of the ten most outstanding young men of the nation because of his contribution to welfare and industrial development. I was not able to see him receive his award because on the same day General W. Bedell Smith came to Old Orchard to give me the Medal of Freedom for my work in England during the war. Immediately afterward, articles began to appear in newspapers and magazines calling Teddy the hidden weapon of the Republican party. One day Anne called me in distress from Paoli, saying incredible pressure was being put on Teddy to run for state office in the fall. She declared that while he had done a fine job as state Secretary of Commerce, making speeches gave him not only insomnia but ulcers. Did I think it his duty to go into politics, hating the idea? I answered that no one should ever go into politics without an overwhelming urge to do so, adding that Teddy could fulfill his duty to his country in other ways. Anne sighed with relief. Shortly afterward, at a dinner in Washington, I sat by Admiral Arthur W. Radford, whose judgment I highly respect. He asked me what Teddy intended to do, saying he had been observing him for some time and had noted his service in the Navy. When I told him of my conversation with Anne, I was dismayed to have him disagree with me emphatically and say that Teddy was needed in public life and would go far.

When Cornelius was eighteen he and a Groton classmate, Richard Cross, wanted to do archaeological work in the summer of 1934. Dr. Isaiah Bowman, head of the American Geographical Society and a friend of Ted's, suggested that they explore on foot an ancient wall in Peru running inland from the coast near Santa Clara, which had been photographed only from the air.

The boys set out in June. Reaching Peru, they called on Dr. Julio C. Tello, noted scientist and head of the museum at Lima, and found he was about to start on an expedition in the same direction. As he needed photographers and they had full photographic equipment, he asked them to go with him. They followed the wall inland for twenty miles, taking photographs of many ruins on the way, and determined it was of proto-Chimu age, or advanced pre-Inca civilization. After many minor archaeological investigations Cornelius and Dr. Tello (Cross was ill and couldn't go) crossed the Andes over a pass fourteen thousand feet high and came to a valley near the sources of the Amazon and to the village of Chavín de Huantar.

They explored the great temple complex at Chavín which was partly underground, and made maps. To investigate the underground passage and ventilation tunnels Cornelius had leather pads made for his elbows and knees and, accompanied by a little Indian boy who knew the way, he wriggled through the narrow, dark spaces for several hundred feet. He photographed the ma-

Main drawing room, La Fortaleza, San Juan.

Front Row: Mrs. T. R. III, Ted, Eleanor McMillan, Mrs. William McMillan, William McMillan, Jr., Mrs. T. R., Jr., T. R. III. Standing: William McMillan, Quentin. Inset: Cornelius, 1941.

Old Orchard, Oyster Bay.

Clockwise: Ted, Quentin, Cornelius, T. R. III, Mrs. T. R. III, 1941.

QUALIFIED RELEASE No. ....J.397....   Serial No. ......562..

Subject   AIR:)
     MIL:)   U.S. FORCES IN UNITED KINGDOM AND OVERSEAS
     SEA:)   -

Cancels and supersedes C.J.298 and all additions.

(A) U.S. MILITARY AND AIR FORCES IN U.K.

-3-

(o)   Names and identifiable photographs of officers above the rank of
Lieutenant Colonel (in the U.S.A. Air Force only above the rank of
Colonel), must be referred to U.S. Advisers unless authorised or
covered by a release (See Appendix A attached hereto).   There is a
specific stop on the following:-

    Brig. General Theodore Roosevelt and his nephew Quentin Roosevelt;
    Mr. Henry Wallace Jr., the son of the U.S. Vice-President.

(p)   All references to activities and treatment of coloured troops in Great
Britain should be referred to D.A.D. for consultation with U.S. Censors
if they fall under any of the following categories:-

   (1) any description of incidents or behaviour likely to inflame
     racial prejudice either here or in the U.S.A.
   (2) anything characterizing coloured troops as "labour" troops.
   (3) anything suggesting or giving incidents to show that a "colour
     bar" is exercised against U.S. troops in this country or in any
     way suggesting that they are treated badly or with discrimination.
   (4) anything criticising the action of U.S.A. authorities in connection
     with black troops.
   (5) anything which suggests that a "problem" has been created by the
     presence of U.S. black troops in Great Britain.

(q)   Any mention of specific operations by the USAAF, either alone or in
conjunction with the R.A.F. or of operations of any other U.S. Force
(e.g. U.S. Rangers) except when announced in communiques.

(r)   Stories about the methods or routes by which USAAF fighters come to
the U.K.,   specially that they are flown here. (But see 12 above).

(s)   Any story about the movement of any officer of the rank of Colonel
or above (in the U.S.A. Air Force only Brig. General or above), even
though the name of the officer be listed in Appendix A must be
referred to D.A.D. for U.S. Advisers.

Censorship order.

Colonel T. R., Jr., commanding 26th Infantry, welcomes a new officer to the 1st Division, 2nd Lieutenant Quentin Roosevelt, June 1941.

North Africa, 1943. Brigadier General T. R., Jr., Major General Terry Allen, Lieutenant General George S. Patton.

Colonel T. R., Jr.,C. O., 26th Infantry, 1st Division, 1941.

Ted's jeep, 1944. Note bullet hole in windshield.

sonry construction and an underground monolithic edifice ten feet tall, bearing carved heads of grotesque, tusked feline monsters with snakes for hair. This was so disposed that when a living sacrifice was made on an altar aboveground, blood ran down through a hole in the altar to a channel in the monolith and was carried into the mouth of a carved beast.

On his return Cornelius published an article in the *Geographical Review* illustrated with his maps and twenty-seven of his photographs. Sometime afterward the temple system was destroyed by an earthquake and landslide, making his photographs so important that even in 1958, twenty-four years after he had taken them, sets of them were requested by the University Museum of Archeology and Ethnology at Cambridge, England, the Museum of the National University of San Marcos at Lima, Peru, and the Smithsonian Institution at Washington, D.C. Characteristically he still had all the negatives neatly filed and put away.

The autumn after he returned from Peru, Cornelius left Harvard, where he had been for two years, and entered the Massachusetts Institute of Technology to study mining engineering. After graduating with honors in 1938 he went to Parral, Mexico, to work for the American Smelting and Refining Company. Roger W. Straus, its president and an old friend, told us the company had hoped to employ Ted's youngest brother Quentin, who fell in World War I, and was keeping a place open in his memory for a member of the family versed in engineering. Cornelius stayed there for four years, until he entered the Navy in 1942.

When World War II broke out Cornelius had difficulty getting into the Navy because he was nearsighted and, although strong and wiry, was fifteen pounds underweight. While he had normal chest expansion, when told to deflate his lungs he did so to such an extent that the medicos were surprised and not at all pleased and refused to pass him. The fact that he had taken a course in gliding in Germany and had worked for four years in Mexico after leaving M.I.T. was viewed with suspicion and required explanation. For a time he worked as a civilian contract engineer in the Special Devices Division of the Bureau of Aeronautics under Commander Luis de Florez, now Rear Admiral USNR, ret. This division today is part of the Office of Naval Research, with which Cornelius is still connected. Luis was eager to have him as one of his original engineers and pulled many wires to help him get a commission, which he finally received. His work ranged from aeronautical devices to an anti-submarine crew trainer which won him a commendation from the Secretary of the Navy. At the start he asked Luis how much he could tell his family about what he was doing. Luis's answer delighted Ted. "You may tell your mother and father anything you want to. But don't you dare say one word to either of your brothers, because they would understand!"

After the war Cornelius went to the Far East, made his headquarters in Shanghai, and traveled extensively in Asia. He became president of a company of consulting engineers with offices in China, Formosa, the Philippines, Japan, Thailand, and elsewhere in the Orient. They were agents for eighty American manufacturers of industrial equipment and installed power plants, rolling mills, spinning mills, construction and mining equipment. As vice-president of the Security Bank Note Company he produced paper currency for the Philippine Republic and later its cigarette-tax stamps after he had helped break a counterfeiting ring in Manila. When the Chinese mainland was taken over by the Communists, Cornelius returned to the United States. Today he is mainly involved in classified research and development programs for the Navy but continues as vice-president of the bank note company and in addition is co-founder and president of a small firm making electronic equipment for steel mills, whose devices are installed all over the United States and in six foreign countries.

Quentin had real musical talent and absolute pitch. When he was little he had a lovely soprano voice and took piano lessons from the age of five. When he was ten the organist and choirmaster at the Cathedral of St. John the Divine wanted him for the Choir School, saying he could make him a soloist for the cathedral in no time. While this was gratifying it would have interfered with plans for Quentin's education and could not be done.

For the next couple of years he continued his piano lessons, with Signorina supervising his practicing. By then he objected to lessons and wanted to play everything by ear. Once when Dorothy and

Richard Rodgers were spending a day with us at Oyster Bay I asked Dick's advice. After hearing Quentin play Dick told me he had had the same problem as a child when he had been made to take lessons. He said Quentin had a good grounding in music and from then on should be encouraged to play constantly and to develop his talent in his own way. The piano lessons were stopped. By his own wish Quentin studied harmony at Groton. As a result he had infinite pleasure from his music for the rest of his life and was always being asked by his friends to play.

He also had artistic ability, as shown by his many drawings of the fantastic and the grotesque. Cornelius sent some of his brother's weird, half-human little figures to Risaburo, the last of the great netsuke sculptors of Japan, who was much taken with them and carved them in ivory.

As Teddy and Cornelius had spent a summer in Wyoming some years before, Ted wanted to arrange something similar for Quentin when he was fifteen. We knew of a ranch in Sonoita, Arizona, where he could enjoy himself spending most of his time in the saddle. With him went a close friend his own age, Joseph W. Burden, Jr., one of the finest in his generation, who eleven years later, in 1945, was killed near Caen in France while serving as an officer in the British Army.

When the boys arrived at the ranch they found a long and severe drought had turned the countryside to dust. They discussed writing their families saying they would like to come home, but decided they would first explore some caves in the neighborhood. They found a narrow opening leading to a passage straight down into the earth, and by dropping a stone tied to a rope they measured its depth as fifty feet. Being slim and flexible, they decided to go down. They found a cavern thirty to fifty feet high with two entrances and the mouth of a long tunnel. The floor of the cavern was rich dark earth with fragments of rock. In its main room they found a piece of pottery and a bone crackled by fire. Although they had no means of knowing it at that time, the boys had discovered a Pleistocene cave deposit. On their way out they noticed a piece of bone embedded in rubble, dug it out, and sent it to the American Museum of Natural History in New York. Dr. Walter Granger, an old friend of ours, wrote Quentin and said it was impossible to identify one small bone and asked him to try to find a skull or at least a complete set of teeth. They worked for several days and secured two skulls, a pelvis, some vertebrae, and numerous limb bones. These they packed in a box and took to the museum when they returned to New York.

The boys had made a sensational discovery, a new species of *Antilocaprine,* the missing link in the antelope family tree. Science knew that it existed, but no specimen had ever been found. It dated from the Ice Age and was believed to have died during the greatest drought known to history lasting twenty-five years. The museum issued a pamphlet announcing the find, which was named for its discoverers, *Onusrosagris,* the Latin translation of their names. Quentin and Joe went back during their spring vacation from Groton for further exploration in the cave and found three more skulls and many bones, and a specimen was mounted for permanent exhibition in the museum.

After Quentin graduated cum laude from Harvard he received one of three commissions of second lieutenant in the Regular Army awarded in the New England area for excellence in the R.O.T.C. During the war he served in the 33rd Field Artillery, 1st Division, took part in the North Africa and Normandy invasions, was severely wounded and decorated three times for gallantry, and eventually promoted to major. Soon after taking part in the invasion of Normandy he was sent to China in the Office of Strategic Services, where he served as an American liaison officer responsible for developing good relationships between the United States Army and top-echelon members of the Chinese Government and Chinese armed forces. He was awarded a citation saying in part:

> His performance of duty was so outstanding that it is believed that no other officer could have achieved results with such a marked degree of success.

After the war Quentin worked for two years in the New York office of China National Aviation Corporation, an affiliate of Pan American World Airways, then was sent to Shanghai as its American manager with his wife and three children. In addition to operating its regular business of passenger and freight flights all over Asia and to the United States and providing maintenance for the planes of all major airlines coming into Shanghai, he organized airlifts of food to Chinese cities beleaguered by the Communists and evacuated the Nationalist wounded.

Late in December 1948 Quentin flew from Shanghai to Hong Kong on business, to be back in time for the tree and Christmas stockings he and his wife, Frances, were preparing for their little family. According to a Shanghai paper, "it was one of the most routine and least hazardous of his innumerable adventurous trips across the face of the map of China." The plane, its pilot apparently blinded by a sudden fog over Hong Kong Harbor, crashed and burned on Basalt Island. None of the thirty-five passengers and crew survived.

The following Sunday was the Feast of St. Stephen. The Scripture lesson appointed for the day was from the book of the Wisdom of Solomon and was read at Christ Church by our rector, the Reverend John N. Warren. He said, "By some strange provision —which many would call chance, but which I have faith to call the Providence of God—this lesson is meet and apt for our parish at this particular time." It was in part:

But a righteous man, though he die before his time, shall be at rest.
(For honourable old age is not that which standeth in length of
    time,
Nor is its measure given by number of years:
And an unspotted life is ripe old age.)
Being made perfect in a little while, he fulfilled long years,
For his soul was pleasing unto the Lord.
For the ungodly shall see a wise man's end,
And shall not understand what the Lord purposed concerning him.

Frances and her three little girls came home and have lived at Old Orchard ever since, an incalculable blessing to me.

Chapter 37

Hereafter you stay home!
THEODORE ROOSEVELT, JR., Cable to his wife

It had always been the family plan for Ted eventually to inherit
Sagamore Hill. In fact, when Elihu Root came to my mother-in-
law in 1920 and asked her to turn the house over to the Roosevelt
Memorial Association she refused, saying it must be kept for Ted.
From time to time she would suggest moving out and letting him
have it. Of course we could not consider that, but by 1937 we had
been married twenty-seven years and were tired of living here and
there in rented houses. Besides, Sagamore had been built at a time
when domestic help was no problem, and it was not made for easy
housekeeping. One day I told Ted that if we were to move into
Sagamore I would gladly cut out curtains, run them up on the
sewing machine, and do all the hundred-odd jobs incidental to
adapting an old house to our needs. If we were to move five years
hence I would still do all that but without pleasure. Ten years
later I wouldn't do it at all. Ted thought for a moment, then said,
"You're right. Let's build a house of our own."

We decided to have it in the old apple orchard behind Sagamore
Hill and named it "Old Orchard." Bill McMillan was the architect
and designed a house so well suited to our needs that we have
never wished anything changed.

After ground for the house was broken, the doctor found I was
badly run down and recommended a complete rest during the

summer. Ted said I would be sure later to work myself to death over the house and suggested a long sea voyage. "Why don't you go to China? A month on the sea going out, a month there, and another coming back would do you a lot of good. Take Quentin. It would be a splendid trip for him before he goes to college in the fall." I protested that we couldn't possibly afford any such thing, as every penny we could spare must be for the house. He said merely that we couldn't afford to have me die, either.

Ted was editor of a book by Madame Chiang Kai-shek. When he saw us off he gave me a package of two hundred and fifty blank pages which were to be bound with her autograph in a small de luxe edition. "Get her to sign these," he said. "I don't want to trust them to the mails. This is important. Don't you come back without them."

Quentin and I had a remarkable time in China, although it was not exactly what we had expected. We had planned to go to Peking, but when we reached Tokyo our Ambassador, Joseph Grew, an old friend, showed us a wire from our Ambassador to China, Nelson Johnson, saying we must not. Joe Grew mentioned the trouble that had broken out near Tientsin between the Chinese and Japanese and said to me, "If you went to Peking you might get into trouble, and you might get us into trouble getting you out. Now be good. Go back on your steamer and land at Shanghai." We dutifully went on to Shanghai, where we stayed with William P. Hunt, whom we had known for many years. After several pleasant days seeing old friends we flew over the Yangtze Gorges and across China to Chengtu, the great city in Szechwan. On the plane we made friends with the pilot, Frank Havelick of Montana. This was to stand us in good stead later on. While in Chengtu we thought of flying south on a Eurasia plane for a day in Kunming but found the cost of two hundred and forty American dollars too great. That plane crashed with twelve on board.

From Chengtu we flew to Chungking for a few days with Mr. and Mrs. Lester Jones of Standard Oil, who lived on the top of a mountain overlooking the city. When we left for Shanghai, Quentin was having an attack of some sort of food poisoning and had a fever of nearly a hundred and two. Two hours out of Chungking our plane turned back. Frank Havelick came out of the cockpit and said we had too much weight on board to get over the mountains. Two passengers and their luggage had to be left behind. I was afraid Quentin and I would be the ones, as General Ku Chutung and his staff of seven were the only other people on board. He was on his way to take command of the Chinese forces in and around Shanghai. Thanks to Havelick, two of the staff were put off, while Quentin and I remained. That was the last plane on which we could have left central China. The next three flights were taken over by the military, and after that all flights were stopped.

Quentin recovered so quickly that forty-eight hours later we were able to take a night train to Nanking to spend a day and have lunch with Madame Chiang Kai-shek. I still had to ask her to sign the two hundred and fifty pages for her book. W. H. Donald, the famous Australian adviser to the Generalissimo, was also at lunch. When I mentioned these pages Madame Chiang asked if I wanted them signed in English or Chinese. As I hesitated Donald said, "Why not both? That would be more interesting." I was afraid this would be a lot of work, but he went on, "Oh, Madame doesn't mind work. Just leave them with me and I'll get them back to you before you leave Shanghai."

Although there was much talk of war, no one thought anything really serious would happen until it did, suddenly and drastically. When we got back from Nanking we heard that two Japanese had been shot as alleged spies at the Hungjao Airport. This was followed by a certain amount of shooting in Hongkew, the Japanese district of Shanghai. On Friday, August 13, Bill Hunt, Dr. William H. Gardiner, and I dined at a restaurant. Between courses we kept going outdoors to see if we could hear firing, but everything was quiet. After dinner Bill and I decided to see where the fighting had been going on. Knowing that Quentin would never forgive me if I went without him, we went to Bill's house and woke him up. He pulled on trousers and a coat over his pajamas and announced he was ready. I had on my best evening dress of pale blue organza with a full skirt trimmed with black lace flounces, but they wouldn't give me time to change.

We drove to Hongkew, where the streets were practically deserted. At the street corners Japanese soldiers were standing with fixed bayonets behind sandbags. Invariably little groups of Chinese stood several yards away out of curiosity. Often we were stopped by Japanese sentries, who pointed bayonets at us and ordered us to turn back. Each time we went back a couple of blocks and tried another street until we reached the North Station, where the fighting had been that afternoon. Three blocks of buildings were on fire. Bill told me to watch for the white shirts and red armbands of *ronins,* Japanese muscle-men from Osaka who had been sent to relieve the regular police in Hongkew. These were apt to arrest people, take them to jail, and even execute them without process of law. Whenever we saw them we turned back without waiting to be challenged. I knew very well how angry Ted would be at me for going where I had no business to be and taking Quentin, but I also knew it was just what he would have done himself. An hour later we drove back to Bill's house. Along the Bund thousands of refugees were sleeping on the ground. The city was ominously still.

Next morning I received the pages signed by Madame Chiang Kai-shek, with a note from Donald. He said if I should hear a cannonade that day I must go to the roof with field glasses. From there I would see something likely to make Shanghai hum for days. He added that I must be sure to keep out of harm's way.

Bill had gone downtown after promising to let us know if anything was happening, but after Donald's note we didn't wait. Bill had left us his car and driver, so Quentin and I set out. We went to the Cathay Hotel on the Bund beside the Woosung River and established ourselves in the grille on the eighth floor, from where we had a good view. It was a gray day. The clouds matched the warships—two British, one French, one American. A short distance to the north lay the *Idzumo,* the Japanese flagship, moored beside their Consulate. This, we thought, would be the point of attack. Few river craft were out, all carrying large, conspicuous foreign flags. Two small Japanese seaplanes circled lazily overhead. The Bund was as crowded with refugees pouring into the International Settlement as Coney Island on the Fourth of July. We ordered coffee and waited.

A signal light flashed from the *Idzumo.* One of the seaplanes landed in the river; the other streaked off to the north. Suddenly the anti-aircraft guns on the *Idzumo* broke loose in a deafening racket. Quentin and I were hanging out of the window when the manager of the hotel told us he was closing the grille and made us go down to the lobby. As we could see nothing from there we decided to go to Dr. Gardiner's apartment on Canton Road, a few blocks down the Bund. I wrote a note telling Bill where we were going and gave it with a good tip to the hotel telephone boy.

We went out and found the car, but were held up for several minutes in front of the Cathay by the great throng of refugees running down Nanking Road. By the time we reached Dr. Gardiner's the whole world seemed full of shooting. We tore across the pavement into the building and went to the top floor. Dr. Gardiner's door was open. We ran through his apartment to a window just in time to see the first flight of six Chinese bombers go by. Bombs fell in the water at the edge of the Bund about a hundred and fifty feet from where we were. Great geysers of mud and water rose into the air, one of them cracking our window. Dr. Gardiner came to remonstrate with us for being there but ended by standing beside us to watch more bombs fall.

We waited for an hour or so to make sure the raid was over before starting for home. When we went downstairs at a quarter to five we couldn't find the car. The driver, far wiser than we, had gone away. A friend turned up by chance and gave us a lift. We came to several barricades and had to take a circuitous route without knowing why until later, when we learned that at one minute past five a Chinese plane, its bomb rack injured by anti-aircraft fire, had dropped a stick of bombs on the Great World Circle. Thirty-seven truckloads of dead were removed from what amounted to a concentration of refugees. Had we found our car and not been obliged to wait for those few minutes, Quentin and I would have been among them.

We did not know until afterward that another salvo of bombs intended for the *Idzumo* had landed on Nanking Road in front of the Cathay minutes after Quentin and I had sat there waiting for traffic to clear. When Bill came to the hotel to find us, the boy to whom I had given a note was dead and the manager said we had been killed. He had seen us go out immediately before the bombing and he even pointed out the car he said we had been in, a burned wreck riddled with holes like a Swiss cheese. Nanking Road was covered with mangled bodies. Bill tried to search for us among them, then left, wondering how to cable the news to Ted. Quentin and I, quite unaware of this, were startled by the unexpected enthusiasm which greeted us when we reached Bill's house.

At dinner at the country club that evening Dr. Gardiner spoke to me across the table and asked my religious belief, saying he wanted to test a theory. "I don't think," he declared, "that any woman would have stood in my office the way you did watching the bombs fall unless she had been born and raised a Presbyterian!" Which indeed I had been.

Ted had been trying frantically to reach us by telephone, but the service had been suspended. He kept sending cables, wanting to know if we were all right and when we were leaving. Navigation had been stopped on the Woosung River, so I could send no definite answer. The city was under martial law and was being shelled by Japanese warships off the mouth of the river.

On Tuesday, August 17, Quentin and I went down the Woosung with other American refugees, four hundred and ten of us, mostly women and children, in a little river tender built to carry one hundred. Some of our marines were in charge and ordered everyone to take cover in the cabin. We were jammed so tightly that we couldn't move. Quentin and I were pushed in farthest from the one door. I managed to sit down on the floor, but he, with no room to sit, remained standing. As we cast off from the dock we heard a burst of anti-aircraft fire, quite close. If a bomb had fallen near us in the river it would have meant deadly panic. I felt a pang of real terror, shut in that cabin with tiny portholes and no possible way to get out.

Until we reached the mouth of the Woosung River two hours later, firing went on over our heads. From there a heavy sea was running between us and the *President Jefferson* eight miles out in open water. We were tossed like a cork, the tender nearly turning turtle at each roll. Several times I thought we were gone. Probably our being so tightly packed prevented broken bones. Many got seasick, children screamed, some women fainted, while others had hysterics. When at last we reached the *Jefferson* the

captain refused to take us on board, insisting that it was too rough
to attempt it. The risk of losing people overboard was too great.
We must go back to smooth water and wait. The marines declared
that we could never get back, as we were too overloaded to buck
the strong ebb tide and would be swamped. I thought of Emer-
son's remark, "I confess to some pleasure from the stinging rhetoric
of a rattling oath . . . How laconic and brisk it is by the side of
a page from the North American Review."

Finally a plank was placed from the deck of the tender to a
port on the ship. The marines stood on either side of it, passing
us from hand to hand as we ran up it. The operation was successful, but the captain told me afterward he didn't think we had any
idea of the danger we were in.

As soon as we were on board I sent a wireless to Ted—ALL SAFE.
LORD LOVE A DUCK—but received no answer, although many other
messages came to us from family and friends rejoicing at our escape. "This time Father has been *really* scared about us," I told
Quentin. "Goodness only knows how mad he is at us now." Later
Signorina told me Ted had not turned off his light or his radio for
three nights, and she had been afraid he might set fire to the
house by dozing off while smoking in bed.

We were taken to Manila, where a great crowd of warmhearted
people greeted us, eager to help the refugees. I was met by Secretary George Vargas and Major Nieto of President Quezon's
bodyguard. The Filipinos have a sense of the dramatic and
stressed the fact that I had left Manila as wife of the Governor
General and returned four years later as "Refugee No. 1." On
the dock I was handed a cable from Ted. All it said was: HEREAFTER
YOU STAY HOME.

Quentin and I went to the Manila Hotel and were on the third
floor opening our suitcases when the city was hit by the worst
earthquake in fifty years. I yelled to Quentin to get into a doorway,
the best place to avoid being crushed by a falling ceiling, and as
soon as possible we made our way down the rocking staircase and
ran outdoors. As considerable damage was done, the quake was
reported over the radio at home. Ted heard it and cabled me
again: I REPEAT HEREAFTER YOU STAY HOME. He was irate indeed,
but he forgave us when we talked to him by telephone from

Manila; and by the time we reached Oyster Bay he was even proud of us for having got caught in the war.

Before leaving Shanghai I had realized we were in a rather perilous position and might well need ready money, so I cashed three hundred dollars in traveler's checks, receiving fifteen hundred Mex. As it happened, I didn't need any of it but stood to lose a good deal if I changed it back into American money. When we stopped in Kobe I could get a much better rate in Japanese money and decided to put the entire sum into goods. It was lovely being forced to spend all that money in order to save it! We bought bronzes, porcelains, scrolls, rolls of brocade, and two unusual cast-iron Lohans, Buddhist saints thirty inches tall, made on the Chinese island of Hainan in the fifteenth century. I had seen these last on our way out and wanted them, but the cost had been a hundred dollars gold for each. Now that the tourist season had been distinctly checked I got them for less than ninety for the pair. When we finally left for the steamer we were followed by a procession of coolies carrying our well-packed purchases.

In spite of everything, from a purely personal point of view our journey had achieved its purpose and more. We had come back alive. We had Madame Chiang Kai-shek's two hundred and fifty autographs in both Chinese and English. We had collected some good possessions. What was more, as a rest cure for me the trip had been an outstanding success.

When we reached home I was worried about the money we had spent, but by writing an article for a weekly magazine and giving twenty-six lectures on our adventures I made enough to cover all our expenses with a comfortable sum left over. This was fortunate, for another depression hit the country. Although we thought we had set aside enough securities to pay for our house, their value decreased so much that we had nothing for any interior decoration, wallpaper, paint, or mantelpieces. We thought of living with bare plaster walls for a time but decided to go on trying to make some extra money. Ted made the most by delivering the Watson Chair Lectures at the University of London and writing several magazine articles, while I continued my talks as far west as California, as far south as Texas and Florida, and as far north as Saginaw, Michigan, lecturing at points all along the way.

397

The Watson Chair of American History, Literature, and Institutions had been founded in 1919 and was the first chair or lectureship established on American history in any British university. It was under the auspices of the Sulgrave Manor Board, which had invited Ted to make six addresses on the United States' colonial policies. Sulgrave Manor was the original home of George Washington's family.

I was told by Mrs. Duncan-Whyte, executive secretary of the board, not to expect a large attendance at Ted's lectures and not to feel badly about it, as few people ever came to this course. There would be more at the first one than at any of the others, as invitations had been sent out to hear the address and to have tea, but this would not be done again. Also, little if anything would be said in the press. Apparently these talks were purely for prestige purposes and were not intended to create general interest, but to our surprise and delight things did not work out that way. Ted's audience grew with each lecture, and at the last one, when I came a little late, I couldn't find a single vacant seat in the large auditorium. I was so pleased that when someone put an ordinary chair in the aisle for me I made a slight fuss about feeling an imaginary draft and asked to have the chair moved about until I was sure everyone present realized no empty seats existed. Ted's addresses were carried almost in full in the London papers and were favorably editorialized. After his first talk the papers began to ask for advance releases, to the astonishment and joy of Mrs. Duncan-Whyte, who wrote him that the board was "just lyrical" about his success.

My lecture tours were hard work and took me from home for weeks on end. Usually the people who engaged me were good to me and became lasting friends, but others made me attend social functions in addition to my lectures, where I was expected to be the life of the party for a couple of hours before taking the train and moving on to my next engagement. Sometimes I would make two talks in one day, then have to wait two or three days before the next one, usually in a dull place. I never got over being so scared that my mouth was as dry as sawdust. Often the chairmen of the meeting added to my problems. One man introduced me as "a notorious public woman"—not, I thought, a happy expression. Generally introductions were flowery and flattering. I tried to make these less embarrassing by using Frank Sullivan's phrase and saying I was one of the Oyster Bay or out-of-season Roosevelts. This was a perfect opening, as it made the audience laugh. At one gathering the chairman had heard this and ended her introduction by saying, "Mrs. Roosevelt lives at Oyster Bay and says she is out of season," wrecking the remark and leaving me with nothing to say.

I was always afraid I might have a migraine and be unable to speak but luckily had this affliction only between lecture dates. Finally the headaches became so frequent as to be practically continuous, forcing me to cancel one tour entirely. At this time Mrs. Robert McLean, wife of the head of the Associated Press, heard of my plight. Although I had never met her, she was interested enough to take infinite trouble and overwhelmed me with notes and messages for eight months, saying she herself had had migraine and had been completely relieved by Dr. Harold D. Palmer of Philadelphia. By then I had given up hope and wanted to be left alone with my misery without being bothered with more doctors, but at last I consulted him. The result was nothing short of miraculous. His massive vitamin treatment was effective from the start, making me feel as if I had climbed out of the grave. He ridiculed the theory, so widely held today, that the primary cause of migraine was emotional tension, declaring that if the suffering was relieved, emotional trouble, if any, would end.

Dr. Palmer died some years ago, before he could finish a report for the New York Foundation on the first five hundred cases he had treated. His methods and the results of his research seem to have been forgotten, but I shall always remember the debt of gratitude I owe to him.

Because of the devastation and bloodshed in China caused by the Japanese war, much sympathy was felt in this country. Ted was head of the American Bureau for Medical Aid to China and in 1938 became national president of the United Council for Civilian Relief in China, comprising many organizations. He started the Bowl of Rice parties all over the country which raised a large amount of money. I tried to help in a small way by organizing the American Women's Sponsoring Committee to cooperate with the Chinese Women's Relief Association, started the year before. We had two exhibitions at the Arden Gallery on Fifty-seventh Street for the benefit of Madame Chiang Kai-shek's Fund for Chinese War Orphans, the first of ancient bronzes, the second of jade, and raised ten thousand dollars. The jade exhibit was said to be the best assortment ever assembled. It may well have been, for we borrowed not only from museums but induced private collectors to lend pieces never before shown publicly. I went to several owners of famous collections, told them they owed much to China for the pleasure they had had from their jade and asked them in return to let us borrow their pieces. They did, but it took persuasion.

Costume jewelry was coming into fashion and offered a good opportunity to make money. We had some pieces of antique jade copied in plastic and elaborately set in gilt of Chinese design, making exotic and beautiful necklaces, bracelets, and clips to sell at reasonable prices. A small costume-jewelry firm undertook the manufacture of these while I organized committees in forty-four cities to sponsor the sales.

One of the large department stores on Fifth Avenue agreed to put on a sale of the jewelry for two weeks and announced it in full-page advertisements in the papers. We had a grand opening with several prominent women to add glamour, such as Elsa Maxwell, Dorothy Thompson, Alice Longworth, Carmen Miranda, and two or three on the "best-dressed" list. By eleven o'clock that morning, when the crowds in the store were so great it was hard to reach the counters, no jewelry was left for them to buy. Every single piece had been snapped up by the salesgirls when the store first opened.

I discovered too late why the sale had been a flop. The store jewelry buyer, an old lady over whose head we had gone to arrange it, had ordered so little that it had all sold in a couple of hours. Although the manufacturer had been told well in advance to prepare for something big, he now declared himself swamped by the orders coming in from all over the country because of our publicity. His foreman almost cried as he told me of his boss's lamentable lack of foresight. It was heartbreaking to get telegrams like the one from a store in Seattle—PLEASE HOLD SAMPLE LINE. OUR BUYER LEAVING BY FIRST PLANE—or the one from Boise asking for twenty-five pounds more of the jewelry, and to be unable to comply. By the time the manufacturer came to life and started on greater production we had lost our initial publicity. I had expected to make a hundred thousand dollars for the Chinese War Orphans. Instead we made only about fifteen thousand.

After the second of Ted's Asian expeditions some years before, he had brought back a number of Nashi manuscripts and paintings he had found at Likiang in southwest China, near the border of Tibet and Burma. These he had given to various museums, with the exception of an ancient scroll forty feet long by eight inches wide with scenes and figures painted on cloth. It had been crudely repaired on the back with scraps of paper covered with Nashi pictograph writing. We decided we could not display it in our house and offered it to a museum in New York. The curator didn't want it, saying it was out of their line, besides being in bad condition and of unknown origin. Quentin, at the time a sophomore at Harvard, became interested in the scroll, so we gave it to him at Christmas.

A month later he arrived at Oyster Bay late one night with something important to discuss. A scholar in Boston had placed his scroll in the twelfth century and told him such a thing was so rare as to be fabulous. Quentin wanted to go to Likiang and search for more Nashi scrolls and manuscripts. He had been to several museums, some of whose curators had never even heard of the Nashis, but all had expressed interest and had agreed to help finance his expedition if it was successful. He had permission from Harvard to do this in order to get material for his thesis on fine arts, provided he would spend a certain time at summer school.

For the sake of form Ted and I said we would have to sleep on it and tell him our opinion in the morning, but as soon as he was out of the room we rejoiced in his interest and initiative. Next day we gladly agreed to have him go. We only hoped he would not get mixed up in the war between China and Japan as he and I had two years before.

Quentin left in February 1939 and crossed the Pacific by steamer to Japan. Operating on the family principle of "Always ask for what you want; at worst they can only say no," he got permission to fly to Shanghai on a Japanese military plane. From there he went to Hong Kong by sea, to Hanoi by narrow-gauge railway, and on to Kunming in China by Michelin, a little train with rubber tires on rails. He flew briefly to Chungking for necessary travel permits and some letters of introduction. All the way along he kept running into friends of ours who were helpful. One of them, William L. Bond, of the China National Aviation Corporation, arranged for him to fly for a couple of days to Lanchow in northwestern China, interesting because it was a center of trade with Russia. When he returned to Kunming from Chungking the seats on all planes had been booked for a month, with long waiting lists, so he was allowed to go as a steward. Everything went well until he started to serve tea to the passengers. When he loosened the cork in a big thermos it suddenly shot out and hit the ceiling of the plane, followed by a deluge of tea that drenched him and everyone nearby.

Leaving Kunming for Likiang, he traveled three days in a comfortable car with driver and interpreter kindly furnished gratis by T. L. Soong's Southwest Transport Company, arranged by W. H. Donald. When the road ended he was invited to join General Sze Hwa, Commander in Chief of the area, who was going to Likiang with a large sum of money and a guard of forty soldiers. He gave Quentin a mule to ride. They spent the first night at the house of a rich Chinese merchant, where they were served, among other things, a dish of caterpillars at dinner. The General insisted on paying Quentin's expenses. The latter wrote me that he "didn't kick any more than was necessary for politeness," but he found out what would give the General pleasure and after reaching home sent him a pistol and two hundred rounds of ammunition.

When the "bandit suppressor" of the district reported robbers active on the route, the General doubled his guard. The party was then joined by several caravans that had waited for its protection, adding to its numbers two hundred horses, twenty chairs, and several hundred coolies.

After five days on the road they reached Likiang. Here Quentin stayed at the Pentecostal Mission, "The Assembly of God in China Likiang," with the Reverend and Mrs. James H. Andrews, whom Ted had visited on his last Asian expedition ten years before. Mr. Andrews was greatly interested in Quentin's plans and went with him to little villages where treasures could be found. They rode high-strung Tibetan stallions, well gaited and sturdy, but difficult to keep from fighting one another.

As few scholars had made a serious study and collection of Nashi manuscripts and paintings, Quentin was able to secure a great number, all of which would probably have been destroyed or scattered in another year when the Burma Road went through the area. Mr. Andrews contributed what he himself had picked up during his years in Likiang, pleased at the thought of their being preserved in a museum. In all, Quentin brought back nearly three thousand items, including some artifacts and other articles of interest. These gave widespread information about the history, customs, and art of these people and also described their gods, devils, and magic. He kept a few of the things, but the majority went to the Library of Congress, the Peabody Museum and Fine Arts Museum in Boston, the Museum of Comparative Zoology in Cambridge, and the Harvard Yenchin Institute. The proceeds paid for his journey of four months and reimbursed Mr. Andrews for his share. Quentin's resulting thesis for Harvard was highly praised.

Last year the Library of Congress brought Professor Li Lin Tsang of the National Museum, Taipei, all the way from Formosa to Washington to study and translate Quentin's manuscripts.

Chapter 38

*Have I not my house, my books, my old
friends, my garden of flowers and trees?*
JAMES ELROY FLECKER

We moved into Old Orchard in April 1938, when the paint inside
was scarcely dry. Ted had always known what he wanted—a
Georgian house with high ceilings and a wide hall from front to
back. Bill McMillan worked it out to our perfect satisfaction, with
suggestions both practical and impossible from the rest of the
family.

The house was built of old brick, intended to be painted white
but left as it was because the color was so good. The shutters are
white, and so is the eighteenth-century front door with its fanlight
and two Ionic columns. We had found the door in the back yard
of a parish priest in Dublin. Father Lucey, now the great authority
on Irish antiquities, had rescued it from an old house that was
being torn down.

Inside the house was my province. I wanted color everywhere.
We had a vast number of possessions collected on our travels. Except for that day in Kobe, we never had enough money to buy
anything really good, but we had picked up many objects we
thought delightful. We had scrolls and paintings from Tibet, roof
tiles from China, primitive wood carvings from the mountains of
Luzon, stone heads from Angkor, painted wood figures from
Tonkin and Java, embroideries from Szechwan, and goodness

knows what besides. The problem was to use all these because we loved them and yet keep our house from looking like a junk shop.

The library or living room is lined to a height of over five feet with our most precious books; others have overflowed into every room in the house, both upstairs and down. The ceilings are nearly eleven feet high. The walls above the bookcases are papered in yellow, marbled like the endpapers of old books, a good background for paintings and some embroideries of mine worked on cloth of gold. An oval table eight feet long, the top made of a single piece of golden Philippine mahogany, holds books too large for the shelves and a pair of yellow Ming lamps I found at Gump's in San Francisco and bought with the fee I was getting for a lecture. In front of the hearth is a long bench of oak, solid as a rock and rubbed to a satin finish, made by Teddy while at Groton. A ten-inch carved crystal figure of Kwan-yin, the goddess of mercy, stands on a table. Crystal is hard to display effectively, and it never was noticed until Cornelius concealed a tiny light bulb under the goddess's feet, causing her to glow with diffused light. On the floor is a yellow Chinese palace carpet with a design in blue that belonged to my mother.

The dining room is paneled in white and has a powder-blue ceiling, copied shamelessly from Bill's own house in Maryland. Two open cupboards lined with Chinese tea-box paper in muted colors contain over seventy pieces of blue and white Nanking porcelain. Above the Sheraton sideboard is a large painting of the Wheel of Life given to Ted in 1929 by the King of the Mulis in southwestern China. Opposite is the biggest of the embroideries I have done, five feet by four, a scene from the Coq d'Or worked in silk, wool, and gold and silver thread with many fake jewels. The white marble mantelpiece carved with three baskets of flowers is an old Georgian one I got from a house wrecker in London. From the blue ceiling hangs the eighteenth-century Baccarat chandelier with seventeen lights and hundreds of prisms sent to us from Persia by the Kettanehs. The floor is covered with a Chinese carpet in greens, grays, and yellows on a blue ground. I bought it through a newspaper advertisement from a store in London none of my friends had ever heard of, and was delighted when it was appraised a few years later at ten times the price I had paid for it.

The drawing room is the only formal room in the house and happily combines every shade of red from deep crimson to pale rose. The walls are hung with gold Chinese tea-box paper, glazed and rubbed until it is a perfect color. Here we put our furniture that inclined to fragility, including a tall eighteenth-century cabinet made in Bath and reproductions of the "dripping water" table and some chairs, all in the Chinese Chippendale style; a carved Belter chair my mother-in-law once gave me, remarking that none of the other children had ever noticed it; a little satinwood glass-topped table, a wedding present from Senator and Mrs. Henry Cabot Lodge, containing a collection of eighteen family miniatures dating from 1730; a chinoiserie clock found in Istanbul of gilt bronze elaborately enameled in a delicate design of people, scenes, and fantastic insects, its pendulum a little lady with a flowered dress in a swing; and a pair of magnificent red and gold lacquer Chinese cabinets over six feet tall, Ch'ien Lung period, brought from Peking years before by Aunt Alice. The chandelier with thirty lights is nineteenth century and had belonged to Great-grandfather Butler. It is made of gilt bronze hung with countless glass pendants, prisms, fiddles, and stars. Originally made for gas, it is now wired for electricity with tiny bulbs. Two illuminated open cupboards hold a few old fans, Meissen groups, and bits of Chinese porcelain and pottery. Some of the latter are good; some from the Thieves' Market are merely amusing.

In a corner of the room stands a figure of Buddha in lacquer and gold leaf in a black lacquer cabinet six feet high. My mother had found it in the oriental department of the Bon Marché in Paris in 1899, but its price was more than she could afford. After it had been marked down twice she bought it. When the bill came it was listed as "un divinité en solde." On the floor is a large and ancient Aubusson carpet, predominantly in the rose-red of its period. It had belonged to a former landlady of ours who wanted to sell it and had been offered twenty-five dollars by a local undertaker. When I offered her thirty she gladly accepted it, but having the carpet repaired and lined cost a good deal more.

In some of the country houses we had visited in England the bedrooms were named. We liked the idea and named ours. Ted's and my room was named "Vermont" because of its massive iron fire frame and some furniture from an old house in that state; Cornelius's was "Manila" because of its unusual four-poster bed elaborately carved in amber wood from the Philippines; Quentin's room became "Chengtu" because of his interest in China; Signorina chose "Cuneo," her home town in Italy; and the spare rooms were named "Porto Rico" and "France." We didn't think of doing this until all the doors were in place, but Quentin painted names on them freehand without taking a single one from its hinges, and did it as accurately as if he had used a stencil.

Ted loved the house so much that he could hardly bear to leave it to go to work while we were getting settled. Every afternoon, unable to wait until he got home, he would telephone me to ask what progress I had made since morning in arranging furniture. He spent every evening for a week putting books on the shelves in the library or seizing for his study little figures of bronze, stone, or carved wood that he had called trash when I had bought them in some faraway bazaar.

As a surprise for him I finished the main hall without telling him, although we had planned it together. On the walls were family portraits of four generations. Between them stood Ted's flags, those of the Governor General of the Philippines, the Governor of Puerto Rico, the Assistant Secretary of the Navy, the colors of the 1st Battalion of the 26th Infantry, his first command, and the flag of the regiment itself, which he had commanded later. When he came home that evening everything was in place. He stopped in the doorway too astonished and pleased to speak, then dropped his brief case and hugged me until I cried for mercy.

Over the main part of the house is a vast attic measuring sixty-eight feet by thirty-four, with a fourteen-foot ceiling. Wide shelves are built around it on all sides. It has become more and more crowded as the years have passed and is famous among our friends, who often ask to see it and suggest the possibility of looting rights. Here a quantity of furniture is stored—tables, chairs, beds, desks, and cabinets inherited from my mother and aunts. Some of it is carved and gilded in the Louis XVI style, a fashion in vogue after the turn of the century. Down the center is a line of enormous trunks, the kind the British porters called "young Yankee houses" when people traveled with them. Each has three deep trays with contents carefully listed. Two of them are filled with silver, another with table linen, including monogrammed damask tablecloths big enough for a table set for twenty-four, with napkins thirty inches square to match, also handmade lace table runners, centerpieces, doilies, and teacloths. The trunk for bed linen has elaborately embroidered linen sheets, some a hundred and fifty inches long, with big square pillowcases to match, a few with places to run ribbons, all impossible to use today because of the expense of laundry. Still more trunks hold Chinese silks and brocades as well as a number of old-fashioned dresses, some of my grandmother's and some of my mother's and mine, kept through the years because they were so pretty. Furs are stored in cedar or Chinese camphorwood chests. Family Army and Navy uniforms from two wars are packed in foot lockers, including my Y.M.C.A. and Red Cross uniforms.

Beyond the trunks is well-worn camping and shikar equipment, bedding rolls, folding roorkhi chairs, copper washbasins with leather covers, skinning kits, saddles, fishing tackle, hunting clothes packed in yakdans, high Gilgit boots lined with fur, puggrees, and metal traveling cases for topees. Piles of boxes contain costumes we gathered on our travels and saved as fancy dresses for the children.

On the shelves are dozens of pictures ranging from paintings and water colors to original cartoons; also an array of china, glass, lamps, mirrors, clocks (some with wooden works), mantel ornaments, and what I can describe only as knickknacks. More china is packed in barrels.

Except for the aisles giving access to everything, the attic is crowded with a surprising variety of other things, including baby carriages, fire screens, andirons, wicker baskets from Hong Kong and Mexico, squaw-chewed buckskin, alligator hides, fabrics woven from bark, a spinet, a melodeon, music boxes, and stone crocks for salting mackerel. Hanging from the rafters are an antique Chinese bird cage with carved ivory mounts, some snowshoes, skis, a pair of crutches, and a painted wood carving of an eagle set in the center of a laurel garland ten feet long, once used to decorate the stern of a New England sailing ship.

Each of the children has his own area in which to store possessions not in use at the moment.

From time to time I make a real effort to get rid of some of these things. When Teddy and Quentin married and Cornelius moved away, a real dent was made in the attic's contents. Whenever the family gathers at Old Orchard I distribute some of the silks and brocades. Furniture has been given to Hofstra College, to the annual Christ Church fair, and sold for the benefit of the Girl Scouts. Embroidered sheets have been used as altar cloths by impoverished churches abroad. When I told John Myer, director of the Museum of the City of New York, that I was eager to clear out my old clothes, he came to Old Orchard, bringing Miss Miller, curator of costumes. They left with seventeen dresses, as well as some hats, shoes, and parasols. Another time Mr. Myer accepted with pleasure a large red leather box into which were fitted a number of elaborate articles made of tin, a necklace, bracelets, and other ornaments given to my grandmother Green on her tenth wedding anniversary in 1870. He also took some bath towels that had been in my trousseau. They were hand-knitted of linen tape, and in those days were considered unequaled for a rubdown.

Outside the house is a seventeenth-century bronze muzzle-loading swivel gun five feet long, given to Ted by Datu Piang, an old Moro chieftain. The boys mounted it so that it rotates on a concrete pillar sunk in the ground, using a ball bearing from the rear of an old Maxwell car. The gun is a favorite hiding place for eggs at Easter and has been known to contain a wasps' nest. A miniature house in red and gold lacquer from Thailand is set on a post not far from the front door and serves its original purpose, we hope, by providing a comfortable lodging for spirits so that they will not bother us. A Victorian cast-iron jardiniere filled with rocks and supplied with running water makes a popular bath for birds.

Alexander Woollcott was one of the first people to stay with us. After leaving he wrote me:

6-30-38

. . . However, what is on my mind to write you about is that lovely house of yours. My thoughts have revisited it so often that I think of many of its rooms as rooms I already know well.

At first—in telling someone about it—I tried summing it up as the final and most satisfactory answer to the whole tribe of decorators. To be any good a house must be as self-sprung as a beard. Yours, I said, was as indisputably yours as your toothbrush.

But that really doesn't tell the story. It is so clearly a part of this house's quality and secret that all the family had hands in the making of it. For instance, so much of its color and character derives from what Ted has done and is. Then Cornelius by lighting up the innards of goddesses, and Grace being at such pains to marry an architect. But you must know a hundred instances for one that I know.

An analogy haunts me. All the Du Maurier manuscripts are in the Morgan Library. Affixed to one of them—*Trilby*—is an attestation that it is all in his own handwriting except for one passage, to the transcription of which his wife and all his children lent their hands, this as a ceremony of propitiation to their household gods.

Well, there you are. I haven't really said my say because if I really set down all the elements which in my guess had blessed this work of your hands, I would have to use such words as "love" and "goodness" and our generation has lost the trick of using such words.

I declare that, from sheer force of habit, I've let this letter turn into a review of your work for all the world as though you'd written a new play. Yet why not? It's as authentic an art, and your example of it is certainly a cut above any new play I've seen in recent years except "Our Town" perhaps.

Once the inside of the house was finished, Ted turned his attention to the woods behind it which had been neglected for years. Knowing little of trees, he got books and studied until he knew the varieties and could tell the different kinds of oaks, maples, and birches and recognize a stand of beech when he saw it. On Saturdays and Sundays he spent long hours chopping down dead or undesirable trees and clearing out deadfall, helped by Balocca and also by Teddy, who got home sometimes for weekends. Guests were given overalls and urged to come out and work. For some reason Ted had marked Dan Longwell, then editor of *Life,* as a city slicker and tested him by handing him a saw and indicating a long log destined for firewood. "Will you just saw this one, Dan?" he said.

Dan, who was from Missouri, took the saw and proved himself to have been a farm boy. "Do you want it in cord length or rick?"

Henry Beston, the writer, a college classmate of Ted's, and his wife Elizabeth Coatsworth, the poet, were warm friends of ours and took a deep interest in our house. They told us the first fire should be lighted and the first bread broken with proper ceremony, and they gave us an antique bronze bell from France, to be hung outside and sounded when it was time to call Ted in from his work in the woods.

Sometimes when Ted called me to come out and admire his trees, he would be rather annoyed if I was absorbed in embroidery. I had always done a lot of sewing for the children but had never tried anything fancy until I started doing some bird pictures in petit point from plates by Louis Agassiz Fuertes, using odds and ends of wool and, as it happened, a poor quality of canvas. I became so interested in it that Ted complained, "You're always fussing with those damned little birds!"

In 1934 Mrs. William W. Hoppin organized the first of the "Amateur Needlework of Today" exhibitions for the benefit of the Lighthouse in New York. These shows are held every few years and today attract nationwide attention. I entered my birds mounted as a miniature table screen. To my surprise and delight, they won the first prize.

For the following exhibition I entered a little Russian picture done on very fine canvas, showing peasants buying at a stall outside a city gate. This also won first prize. To connect it with modern history I put across its top, "Recognition of U.S.S.R. 1933." As I didn't want anyone to think I was celebrating this event, I worked a red devil sitting in a tree and glaring at the people below with a menacing gesture. I thought I had made the matter clear, but a number of those who came to the show were critical. Half of them asked why I had honored the recognition of the Soviets; the others wanted to know why I had insulted a great nation. I gave this piece to Ellen Emmet Rand, the noted painter, who in exchange did a portrait of me in the dress I wore at Gracie's wedding. She said she was pleased. I know *I* was.

I made a sampler for Ted with little pictures of seventeen species of game he had shot. It showed him stepping across mountain peaks, with the bushy red beard he always grew on expeditions. Ted complained no longer about my spending so much time on embroidery. Every night when he came home from work he wanted to see how much I had done during the day and made various suggestions as to the drawing and coloring of the animals. I had no picture of the Himalayan bear, so I worked an ordinary black bear, adding the characteristic white crescent on its chest. Ted was very particular about this mark and made me rip it out twice to get it the right size and shape. Months later when we were at the zoo a Himalayan bear rose on its hind legs and faced us. I had made the crescent upside down. I said to Ted, "The canvas won't stand more ripping," and we walked on.

Soon I wanted to get away from the limitations of canvas and use a variety of stitches as in the old English church embroidery. This was fascinating but far more difficult. I collected books on embroidery and studied dozens of stitches, some from the old crewel designs. The work required special embroidery silk, "stout floss" which came in spools in countless filaments fine as gossamer and needed to be gently and carefully blown apart. If slightly ruffled or mussed, it could not be used. Stout floss could be found only in England in a complete range of light-fast colors. Before World War II, I laid in a supply. Now it is not made any more and my stock is low.

I became so interested in embroidery that I created a Frankenstein's monster to rule much of my life. Instead of the neat work bag usually associated with such work, I have a hoard of equipment that is staggering. Besides frames large and small I have boxes of silk, camphor chests of fine wool, a deep bureau drawer full of metal threads in different colors and weights, another full of fake jewels, drawing boards in two sizes, T squares, French curves large and small, pantographs, thumbtacks, pads of drawing paper, rolls of tracing paper, boxes of carbon paper, extra-hard pencils, extra-soft pencils, special erasers, draftsmen's pens, compasses, three kinds of "kitchen string" for lacing the fabric into the frame, and a king-size stapler. Besides all this I have yards of special linen, some of it seventy-two inches wide, brocade, silk and metal cloth, as well as more designs than anyone could use in a lifetime, taken from Chinese paintings and such ancient and modern artists as Bosch, Brueghel, Artzybasheff, and Charles Baskerville.

Before long I found myself sending embroideries to exhibitions near and far, including the Metropolitan Museum of Art, the Museum of Fine Arts in Baltimore, the World's Fairs in New York and San Francisco, and others that I can't remember. I had one-man shows in New York and Boston, two in Greenwich, Connecticut, and one in Cannes, France. Counting both needlepoint and embroidery, I have done forty-seven pieces and have kept six after giving the rest away to family and friends.

Some of my most successful embroideries were done from sketches by Quentin, who shared my taste for the unearthly and the macabre. Wheeler Williams, the noted sculptor, was impressed by his work, but after looking at several of his drawings said, "Tell me about Quentin. Is he a happy child?" When I told this to Quentin he was so delighted that he promptly drew four heads which had met death in peculiar and unpleasant ways. I surrounded these with delicate little flowers and worked them on a waistcoat for Alexander Woollcott. On the back I put a verse from the Psalms: "They are enclosed in their own fat: with their mouth they speak proudly." This was to retaliate for his calling me "the withered ingenue." Aleck declared that nothing had ever pleased him as much, except when a friend named a baby after him. The waistcoat is now in the Museum of the City of New York.

My most ambitious piece was done while I was running an unidentified low fever for three years and was unable to be active. It measures five feet wide by four feet high and is a scene from the Coq d'Or, showing the old Czar, his counselor, and the astrologer carrying the golden cock. I worked it on heavy, closely woven, natural-colored linen, which forms the background, and used silk and wool in brilliant colors as well as metal threads of gold, silver, and copper with many fake jewels. As I could find no embroidery frame big enough to hold it, Cornelius made me the best one I ever saw. It stands on the floor, adjusts to any height, and tips to any degree. Its two rollers hold the fabric not actually being worked. It is such a handsome piece of furniture that when John Koch, whose portraits and interiors I admire more than those of any other

413

contemporary artist, did a conversation piece of some of us he insisted on having it in his painting.

As Cornelius had made the frame, the embroidery had to be his, although it remains at Old Orchard until he has a place for it. He took a deep interest and wanted it done as soon as possible. To this end he cut a piece of paper seven inches square, pinned it to the material, and told me it was my daily stint. He made me consult four experts in New York and a laboratory in Philadelphia before he was convinced that the metal threads would not tarnish.

At times friends would gather around the frame to watch me sew and now and then asked silly questions. One day some of them, rather lacking in humor, noticed that I was working from the end of the picture, with the figures in a horizontal instead of a vertical position. They wanted to know why Cornelius had made the frame that way. It would have been so much better, they thought, if I had been able to start at the bottom and work up, or at the top and work down. Instead of explaining the obvious fact that this would have made the frame too long and unwieldy, Cornelius hid a wicked gleam in his eye. "We knew it would take Mother a long time to do such a big piece," he said pleasantly. "In this way, if anything should happen to her we can cut off the finished part and at least have something." A startled silence followed.

Shortly before the piece was done I had a small piece of tonsil removed, apparently left from an operation years before. The fever vanished, but it had served a purpose. By keeping me from doing much else, it had enabled me to spend nearly four thousand hours working on the Coq d'Or.

Of course my embroidery was halted by World War II, but even after that I didn't touch a needle for several years. Once when Dan Longwell was staying with us he was much interested in nine volumes of scrapbooks I had made and told me they were a unique record of an American family. With this in mind I took a good look at them, decided they were badly done, took them all apart, and started again from the beginning. Newspaper clippings had turned brown, so I had them photostated. I did considerable research at the New York Public Library to find others of interest. Old photographs had faded, so I had to learn to copy and intensify them.

I needed many more pictures of children and grandchildren and of our house, as well as of the things we had bought in strange places. Also, I wanted to be able to develop and print them myself to make certain they would be permanent and of the right size for the layout of the pages.

When our house was built the boys had asked Bill McMillan to put a darkroom in the cellar. He designed a perfect one with every possible convenience, including a light-proof entrance without a door, but it was vetoed with other unnecessary luxuries. I was to regret this later while Balocca was making me one in a small storage room in the cellar, to which Cornelius added a number of marvelous gadgets of his own invention. Our water comes from an artesian well and is so full of air that when the prints were being washed it covered them with tiny bubbles that were enough, I thought, to prevent the hypo from being eliminated. He corrected this by having the water run first through a tank of splintered glass.

Later I was so absorbed that I spent almost every day in the cellar, coming out only to put the finished prints into books with dry mounting tissue. This I did in the drawing room, turned over to the purpose and emptied of furniture except for long boards on wooden horses covered with filing cabinets, stacks of manila folders labeled with dates, a giant paper trimmer, a typewriter for captions, and two electric irons, one large, one small. At first people thought me demented, because unless I was in the drawing room I couldn't be disturbed. When friends telephoned they were apt to be told, "Mrs. Roosevelt is in a darkroom," which was surprising. Or it might be, "Mrs. Roosevelt is developing," which was worse. Finally they understood and left me alone with only mild protests against my living in the cellar. The children, after seeing me often leave the lunch table and go down into the darkroom to turn over the prints in the washer, declared that my theme song should be "Someday my Prince will come." The scrapbooks grew from nine to twenty-six volumes and at last were done.

By this time I was so interested in photography that I kept on with it, taking innumerable pictures, spending endless time finishing them, and sending fourteen-by-seventeen-inch prints to "salons," rejoicing when they were accepted for exhibition. Once when I was staying with the Doubledays in South Carolina I took some photographs of a rather weed-choked canal and made it look like the depths of the jungle. When I enlarged these I sent some of them to Somerset Maugham, who had a house on the Double-days' place. He wrote me that I had been wasting my time as a wife and mother. Instead, I should have been a great artist and led a life of sin. I sent his note to Ted, who replied, "Maybe so. But it's too late now!"

Chapter 39

Bear them we can, and if we can we must.
Shoulder the sky, my lad, and drink your ale.
                    A. E. HOUSMAN

During the years immediately before World War II Ted was troubled by the increase of anti-Semitism in the country. Believing that this could be fought more effectively by Christians than by the Jews themselves, he brought the subject up in every speech he made. In answer to a letter he received in 1941 saying it was the Jews themselves who were primarily responsible for this intolerance, he wrote:

> From the standpoint of this country the question of who is responsible in whole or in part is entirely beside the point. The fact is that we hurt ourselves—the United States—more by persecuting the Jews than we hurt the Jews. If we persecute any racial or religious group we are committing a grave offense against our concept of government.

He was on the board of directors of the National Conference of Christians and Jews, a member of Rabbi Stephen S. Wise's Committee for Zionism, and held an honorary position on several other committees for Jewish welfare.

In sharp contrast to the way we had felt at the start of World War I, when we thought it a disgrace to be neutral, we were convinced we should have a strong national defense, but equally convinced we should stay out of World War II. In one of Ted's letters in 1940 he wrote:

More than twenty years ago, with some two million other young Americans, I went to Europe to fight a war to end wars. At that time I thought I was fighting to make the world safe for democracy. Theoretically we won the war. One glance at the world today is sufficient commentary on the value of our victory.

The sober truth is that no one wins a war. The victor loses as well as the vanquished. . . . By remaining strictly neutral we can best serve not only ourselves but the other people in the world as well. Our Ark of the Covenant is our representative self-government. It was badly shaken in the last war. It might not survive another. Our primary mission is to preserve it for future generations of Americans. . . . If we preserve it, it will be a beacon towards which other nations can struggle from the mires of dictatorship. If it perishes the light will have gone out of the world.

I dislike greatly the governments of Germany, Italy and Russia and do not believe in appeasing any of them. Although the interventionists apparently do believe in appeasing Russia, I consider her crimes as equal with those of Germany and Italy.

I am convinced, in spite of my great sympathy and liking for England, that my first duty is to the United States and her citizens. For the reasons I have given I am sure they will be irrevocably damaged should we launch this country into war. As a strong neutral we would be of inestimable help at the peace table.

Because of his convictions Ted was roundly attacked and received scores of abusive letters calling him Nazi, Fascist, Communist, isolationist, white-livered coward, and traitor. In spite of this, he went on with all his might until he realized that war was inevitable. Through the years he had kept alive his reserve commission of colonel by going out as often as necessary for the dreary drudgery of peacetime training with troops in the field, which of course had meant giving up summer vacations. Early in 1941 he applied for active duty and in April, aged nearly fifty-four, he was assigned to command his old regiment, the 26th Infantry, 1st Division, then training at Fort Devens, Massachusetts.

It was indeed ironic to see how many of the people who had abused him and were younger than he had no idea of volunteering for military service to uphold the cause they had championed so frantically. Or how many of them, when they or their sons were drafted, used influence to escape the inconvenience of combat or even of overseas service.

In June, Quentin received his Regular Army commission and was assigned to the 33rd Field Artillery, 1st Division, at Fort Devens.

I moved to the Groton Inn a few miles from Devens to be near Ted and Quentin, who had Sundays off. There was little if anything to do, but we didn't care. The main thing was to be together. We used to drive slowly around the pleasant countryside, stopping to look at inscriptions on ancient tombstones, unusually big trees, or anything else of interest. I took many photographs of American Gothic houses or elaborate Victorian mansions with towers and stained-glass windows. Afterward *Life* published five pages of them. Once I left Ted and Quentin in the car while I walked around to photograph a large white house near Worcester which had been built of wood about 1875 and was covered with rococo gingerbread carving. I was standing in the middle of what had been the lawn, a tangle of tall grass and weeds. Suddenly I was knocked down by a playful St. Bernard who had come up unexpectedly from behind and put his paws on my shoulders. He was full of joy and determined to romp with me, and as I was picking myself up he laid me flat again, licking my face. Ted and Quentin, deep in talk, didn't notice at first when I yelled for help, then they got out and started toward me. The dog, delighted by all these new playmates, bounded over to them. I heard Ted call, "Good dog! Nice fellow. Gently now. Good dog! Down! . . . *Down*, you bastard!" The dog had jumped on him once too often. Quentin did nothing but laugh, and at last the owner came out and took charge.

On Decoration Day we came to the village of Townsend, Massachusetts, where the parade had just finished. The village green, surrounded by the courthouse, the church, and little white houses, was a picture by Grandma Moses. Everyone was milling about in the sunshine—the American Legion, Spanish War Veterans, G.A.R., Boy Scouts and Girl Scouts—while motherly ladies of the Legion Auxiliary in their little overseas caps were serving lemonade. Ted said, "This is America!" I felt the sting of tears as we got out and joined the crowd.

In October the Division went to North Carolina on maneuvers. I went too, taking my car and staying at Pinehurst for several weeks. Every morning I provided myself with a carton of raisin cookies, a bottle of Coke, and an apple for lunch and drove out to look for the regiment, which of course was moving around all the time. I nearly always was able to find it and could at least say hello to Ted and sometimes catch a glimpse of Quentin.

In the evening groups of men from the regiment would stroll down the road, usually to the nearest general store. I always picked up as many as could crowd into the car and led them to comment on their Colonel without letting them know I was his wife. Some of the stories they told me were fantastic, while I expressed wondering surprise. One man said the Colonel had had the legs shot from under him three times in the last war. Another declared that although one of his lungs had been totally destroyed by mustard gas he could keep up with anyone on maneuvers. A third, who had been five years with the regiment, insisted that the Old Man was the first commanding officer he had seen who believed in good food for the men. One group of eight said they were from L Company. "We're the best company in the outfit, ma'am, and gee—is the Colonel proud of us!" When I left them I would tell them I was the Colonel's wife and watch their grins as they waved me out of sight.

During the maneuvers it was once Quentin's task to lay telephone wires. Up to then the man doing this was out of communication, and no change of plan could be relayed to him until after the wire was laid. Quentin worked out an invention by which he could talk on the wire even when it was rolled up in his jeep with only one end attached at the signal post. The first time he used it was during a tank attack, as he scurried ahead talking merrily all the time and reporting on "enemy action." It made quite an impression on his superiors and was adopted by most of the Division's

420

units. When I heard of it from Ted I congratulated Quentin, who said it was as simple as a pencil. He couldn't see why no one had thought of it before, and anyhow Cornelius could have done it much better.

The people of the South opened their doors to these "Yankees" and entertained them over weekends with true hospitality. Towns and villages were asked to inform a Home Registration Bureau how many men they could care for. The response was remarkable. The little village of Pee Dee, five hundred inhabitants, offered to take a hundred soldiers over every weekend. In the large towns citizens would stop a man in uniform on the street. "Hey, soldier! Are you fixed up with a bed for the night? How would a big steak and some homemade chocolate cake look to you? Come around to my house for supper." All this was a great contrast to the people near Fort Devens, who did just about nothing for the troops.

In December, after we had returned from the South, Ted was promoted to brigadier general and was made deputy commander of the 1st Division. He was entitled to an orderly, a driver, and a small bungalow on the post at Devens with an electric stove and refrigerator. I moved in after buying a few kitchen utensils at the dime store in Lowell. I had never cooked a complete meal with everything ready at the right time but was getting on nicely when Quentin said he wanted to bring Major Walter Bride, his commanding officer, to dinner. No newlywed entertaining her husband's boss for the first time was ever more nervous than I, feeling my reputation was at stake. I planned the dinner with care and told Ted and Quentin firmly in advance that the orderly would clear away the soup plates while I fetched the next course from the kitchen. Neither of them was to move from his chair. To my dismay, when the time came it was Major Bride who jumped to his feet and helped me bring in the meat and vegetables, while Quentin looked at me in both sorrow and anger. Fortunately the dinner was good even though I burned the rice.

After the attack on Pearl Harbor—just how unforeseen we will probably never know—Teddy, Bill McMillan, and later Cornelius qualified for commissions in the Navy.

In the early spring of 1942 the 1st Division moved to Camp

Blanding in Florida for twelve weeks. Teddy was assigned to the naval base at Jacksonville, where he and Anne took a small apartment. I rented a cottage on the beach at Ponte Vedra where Ted, Teddy and his wife, and Quentin could often come for weekends. Again we took infinite pleasure in small things. Ted got some books on seashells, and he and Quentin used to go along the beach to look for specimens, which varied remarkably from week to week. Teddy and Anne went surf-riding on wooden ironing boards I bought at a department store in Jacksonville. Once in a while we drove to see the unique aquarium at Marineland, and twice we spent a day in St. Augustine. I used to start on Thursdays getting ready for the warriors to arrive on Saturday mornings, knowing they would require doughnuts and three kinds of cookies, not only to eat but to take away with them. I bought an iron kettle and made fish chowder, kept for twenty-four hours and reheated to be at its best. I learned to make Devonshire clotted cream, which they used to spoon over nearly everything. Their favorite dish was what they called my specialty, and they demanded it every Sunday. It was made of oysters, clams, shrimps, scallops, crabmeat, and lobster covered with a rich Newburg sauce and served in a ring of hominy grits. At every meal but breakfast we had those wonderful southern greens—collards, tender or mustard greens—cooked with a bit of fat salt pork. I never achieved beaten biscuit, but we did have corn bread and hush puppies, relished by everyone.

Our cottage was on a lonely part of the beach with no other house in sight. I had a little maid help me with the housework in the daytime, but at night I was by myself until Signorina came to stay with me. I used to worry for fear someone would break the flimsy lock on the tiny garage and steal my tires and rationed gasoline.

Once I awoke in the middle of the night to see a mountain of flame on the sea. It seemed close at hand but was really over two miles away. An oil tanker had been torpedoed and set on fire by an enemy submarine. The newspapers said that half the crew of twenty-five men had perished. A plane dropped flares that hung in the air for three minutes, giving a brilliant white light to help the rescue operations of the Coast Guard. When the sun rose next morning no trace of the disaster remained, but for a long time afterward the oil on the water killed the sea birds.

After we had left Ponte Vedra a group of German saboteurs were landed there by a submarine and shortly afterward were captured. From the accounts in the press I believe they used the same little path across the dunes that we did when we went swimming.

When the tour of duty at Camp Blanding was over, Ted and Quentin went with the Division to Fort Benning, Georgia, for more maneuvers, then to Hershey, Pennsylvania, the embarkation area. Signorina and I drove back from Florida to Oyster Bay and started to put Old Orchard away "for the duration." We wrapped up everything in the main part of the house and moved into the service wing which Bill McMillan, with wisdom and foresight, had designed for just such a contingency with its own water, heat, and electric power. The maids' bedrooms, dining room, and bath were more than adequate. Sadly we let most of the domestic staff go, keeping Balocca, of course, and Anita Naef, the housemaid, who was able to turn her hand to cooking, dressmaking, or anything else.

My husband had waited twenty-eight years for his dream house, and he had exactly three years in it before returning to the Army in April 1941. A chapter of our lives had ended.

Chapter 40

When the War is over and the sword at last we sheathe
I'm going to keep a jelly-fish and listen to it breathe.

A. A. MILNE

In June 1942 Ted left for England with fifteen hundred men, the advance guard of the 1st Division. The rest of the Division, some sixteen thousand, followed soon afterward on the *Queen Mary* without convoy, as she was fast enough to dodge enemy pursuit. Quentin told me later it was so crowded that they slept in three shifts.

Meanwhile I resigned from the Girl Scout Council of Greater New York, of which I had been president for five years, and applied to the American Red Cross for volunteer service overseas, believing my experience in World War I might be useful. The Red Cross was recruiting women but wanted them not over twenty-eight years old and seemed to prefer trained social service workers. I knew this was unpopular with the troops, as many of them had told me they disliked being treated as "cases" unless they actually asked for help. Thanks to Mrs. Dwight F. Davis, head of the volunteer women, I was accepted in spite of my being fifty-three. So far nothing had been said about keeping soldiers' wives at home. I spent a month in Washington taking an orientation course, then flew over by Pan American Clipper in August. As soon as I reached London I went to the U. S. General Staff Headquarters in Grosvenor Square, asked for the adjutant general, and was shown into

Colonel Thomas Jefferson Davis's office. When I asked if he would tell me where Ted was he smiled at me, bless him, picked up the telephone, and said, "How about talking to him right now?"

The Division was at Tidworth on Salisbury Plain, a lonely region, desolate even in summer. Ted said there was nothing whatever in the way of recreation for the men and told me to hurry down and start something.

I reported to William E. Stevenson, who was American Red Cross commissioner for the European theater until he left a few months later to take the same important position in North Africa. He told me a Red Cross club was badly needed for the twenty-odd thousand enlisted men at Tidworth, but so far no suitable house could be found. I might go there later, but meanwhile I was to stay in London, work at the Milestone Club established on Kensington Road, and learn how these centers were to be run.

Few American soldiers were in London as yet. One morning a group arrived at the Milestone on short leave. According to the regulations of the moment, none wore insignia to indicate their unit. Unexpectedly they gathered around me. "Hi, Mrs. Roosevelt! Remember us? We're from K Company, 26th Infantry. Last time we saw you was when you gave us a lift in your car at Hemp, North Carolina!" It was like meeting old friends. That afternoon three of them shared a taxi with me, and when I tried to pay my share they wouldn't allow it. Said one, "You're not going to pay a cent, and if anybody says different I'll break his arm!"

A day or two later another group from the Division boasted to the club director that they had the only general who hiked with them on maneuvers. Once five men came into the club and looked around. One of the Red Cross women asked if they wanted beds for the night or something to eat. They said no. When she asked what she could do for them they answered, "We heard that Teddy's wife is here, ma'am, and we just wanted to see what she looks like."

I stopped again at G.H.Q. to say hello to General Eisenhower, who said emphatically, "I'm glad to see you in uniform. I hope you're going to work for the enlisted men. If my officers can't look after themselves they're not fit to be my officers." I agreed heartily and told the general such was my firm intention. Working for enlisted men is the most rewarding of tasks, because they are so responsive and appreciate with enthusiasm anything you try to do for them.

After four days in London I decided to go to Tidworth myself and try to find a place for a Red Cross club. Ted met me at the train in Salisbury and suggested that I look at Tidworth House, which turned out to be perfect for the purpose. It was a huge old-fashioned country house with over a hundred rooms, built in the eighteenth century, and remodeled at great expense in the nineteenth. The vast rooms on the ground floor would provide an ideal place for a club, while the many bedrooms upstairs could be used for office space and living quarters for the Red Cross workers. It had been used for a British officers' club and later for the Nursing Sisters, but it was now empty except for a small detachment of the Royal Artillery Medical Corps who were occupying the flagstone kitchen and a few rooms near it in the basement but were due to move out. The question was whether we could get permission to use the house, as the British Commander in Chief of the area, Major General Pakenham Walsh, was thought to want it again for an officers' club. Ted knew and liked the General, with whom he had been trout fishing, but refused to take the matter up with him, saying I must do it because if *I* were turned down it wouldn't matter.

I went to see General Walsh and began by telling him I had come to request a very great favor which I feared he would not grant. We needed a place for a soldiers' club. Only one building in the neighborhood was suitable, but I was certain it was one that he wouldn't want to give us. The only reason I ventured to ask for it was that the large number of combat troops in training at Tidworth had no place to go for recreation. Every evening after maneuvers long lines of them waited at the bus stops to go to Salisbury or Andover, towns about fifteen miles away. Arriving at either place, they would overcrowd the local pubs and the few movie theaters, or else mill sadly around the streets to find something to do. We had to have a place where they could feel at home and have a canteen, games, and general cheerfulness. We had found just the building for this, but I hardly dared tell him which it was.

The General looked slightly alarmed and sent for his Chief of

Staff. Again I hesitated until I think they almost expected me to ask for Salisbury Cathedral. When I finally let them worm out of me that I wanted Tidworth House, the General laughed. "Tidworth House? Come, that's not so bad. Why, yes! We can let you have it."

I took the next train back to London to report my triumph to Mr. Stevenson but was rather crestfallen when he said that things were not done that way. We must deal correctly with the British authorities. I could not barge ahead making arrangements without having things go through the proper channels. He would take the matter up with the British Army and would let me know the eventual outcome.

That evening I was dining at the Ritz with John Wheeler-Bennett, the English historian, when Ronald Tree came across the room to our table. With him was Brendan Bracken, Minister of Information in the British Cabinet, who said, "You are interested in Tidworth House, aren't you?" Surprised, I answered hastily that the American Red Cross had asked for it but of course the application must go through channels. I didn't know if we were to have it or not. He replied, "It went through channels this afternoon and is all settled. You *are* to have it." I never knew red tape to be cut so quickly.

Next day I returned to Tidworth. Driving from the railroad station, I passed a detachment of the Division hiking in the rain with Ted at the head of the column.

For the next couple of nights I slept at the American Army hospital nearby while I was cleaning out a room to live in, then moved into Tidworth House. The wife of the cricket professional, who lived in the lodge and was in charge of the playing fields, agreed to feed me in return for my ration coupons until we were settled. Domestic help could not be found. A corporal and nineteen men from the Division were detailed to come every day and help clean the house. At first I was afraid these crack combat troops would resent being made to do housework, but they didn't, because they missed morning inspection and many training hikes. They worked like beavers, scrubbing, dusting, waxing floors, and washing windows. One morning we were cleaning upstairs when suddenly every mop was dropped as they ran gleefully to the windows to watch their company going by under full packs. They brought their own rations for lunch, but at ten o'clock each morning and three each afternoon I gave them mugs of tea and buns from the local bakery and we all sat down to gossip and talk of home.

On the main landing of the wide staircase leading from the great hall stood a white marble group of the Three Graces, life size and nude. The day the fireplaces were being cleared of soot one of the detail, with jet-black hands, made telling prints on the figures. I was coming around the corner but stopped short when I heard the corporal. "Look what you've done! You're a disgrace, that's what you are. If Mrs. Roosevelt was to see that you'd be in the guardhouse, and a good thing too. Quick now! Get a rag and wash them dames off!"

While we were getting the club ready I went every evening to Ted's quarters, where it was warm and comfortable with an open fire, a luxury in the chill of an English summer. We played Monopoly with his two aides, William Gordon and Robert Emery, who three months later was killed at the Oran landing. Sometimes Quentin joined us. Those precious family interludes when we could forget briefly that we were at war were soon over, for two weeks after we opened the club the 1st Division went to Scotland. Shortly afterward the 29th Division, under the command of Major General Leonard T. Gerow, moved to Tidworth.

Our Red Cross clubs were supposed to be run by an American staff with many British volunteers. Some of the clubs in London were to have as many as three hundred women who came for certain days every week. At Tidworth this was impossible. Few women were available in the depths of the country, the distances were great and no one had enough gasoline. Because the Red Cross was still short-handed, instead of a full staff we had three: Jean Daugherty as assistant program director, who planned and ran programs as well as any full-fledged director could have done; Mary Frazier as first-aid nurse, who doubled wherever necessary; and myself as club director and general wheel horse. More of us were vitally needed, considering the size of the garrison we had to serve.

A British Army hospital in the neighborhood had been turned

over for our troops, and its ninety Voluntary Aid Detachment girls were being transferred and scattered after having worked together for three years. I met several of them, liked them, and wondered if I could possibly get some of them instead of volunteers. I asked their leader, Miss Beryl Duncombe, an older woman known to everyone as "Madam," if she would be willing to choose eight of the best workers and come with them to help at Tidworth House. She was enthusiastic over the plan, as were the girls, who hated being separated, but she said they belonged to the British Army and probably would not be released.

Ted had arranged for me to meet Major General Richard H. Dewing, then senior British representative on General Eisenhower's staff, saying he might be a useful friend. He certainly was. I went to see him in London and asked if he would conspire with me in a revolutionary plan. He said he had nothing to do with V.A.D.s, but he went himself to the War Office and then explained to me what steps I should take. The result was that the War Office was surprised into letting us have the girls for three months. This period was renewed until the war's end because of the influence of Brendan Bracken, who took an interest, as the club was in his home district. He declared it could not be run without help, and he did not propose that a man from Texas, say, should go to the club and then write home that a decent cup of coffee was not to be had in England.

Indeed we never could have operated the club without these girls. Coming as they did from different backgrounds, they were equally dedicated to hard work. One had been on the stage, one came from a family so poor that while she had seen nylon stockings she had never owned a pair, and one was the daughter of a baronet and later married the Duke of Sutherland's heir. They took entire charge of the canteen, and for the first four months before we had any equipment they made over eighty gallons of coffee a night in open pots on the kitchen stove, carried it sixty yards to the counter, and served it in earthenware pitchers and mugs discarded because of chips and cracks and left behind when the R.A.M.C. moved out. They cooked over thirty dozen hamburgers a night in two small frying pans, all we had. They washed the dishes in fire buckets behind the canteen. They acted as cashiers, checked and listed supplies, worked in the garden, and did a hundred other jobs willingly and cheerfully. Never did I have to criticize their conduct or get after them in any way except to shoo them out of the house on their days off to prevent them from staying around to lend a hand where it might be needed. In describing Tidworth House to a friend one of them remarked, "It's just wonderful. A cross between Bedlam and the Ritz!"

As soon as the troops heard of the club they started pouring in. In the beginning we sometimes ran out of everything and would have to tell the long line of waiting men how sorry we were. The response was always immediate: "Now don't you worry, ma'am. We can see you're trying your hardest, and that's what a soldier appreciates."

Close by the club was an enormous indoor tennis court with a glass roof. When I proposed using it for movies and theatrical performances everyone was discouraging, saying it would take at least six weeks to paint the glass for an adequate blackout against German bombers. We got it done in two after I heard that Al Jolson, Patricia Morison, Frank McHugh, and Al Jenkins had arrived in England as a USO troupe and would visit Tidworth. We borrowed a stage that was found unexpectedly in the neighborhood, some mess benches from the Division, installed temporary footlights, and by working day and night got the place ready for a grand opening of the club early in September. When the actors got there we had managed to squeeze fourteen hundred wildly enthusiastic men into the theater, as big an audience as they had anywhere in England. Even so, the clubrooms were filled with an overflow of nearly eight hundred. After the performance the troupe came over and gave a short additional show for them.

At this official opening I did a dreadful thing. I suppose my brain was paralyzed by all the details, including one or two unexpected mishaps, such as the players arriving three hours later than Special Service had told me. I forgot to ask the London office for Red Cross banners and posters to hang in the theater and in the club, which no one had thought of sending me. This was bad enough, but worse was to follow. When Mr. Stevenson came all the way from London for the opening, bringing his wife, who was one of the best Red Cross girls, it never occurred to me to ask him to speak. I greeted them when they arrived and said good-by when they left, nothing more. Mr. Stevenson never mentioned my lack of ordinary politeness, but he did point out that because of the absence of banners and posters the soldiers had no means of knowing the whole thing had been organized by the Red Cross.

Bebe Daniels came shortly afterward with her own excellent company and was received with rapture by the troops. When she saw our chipped earthenware she sent us a whole set of cups and plates, "for the use of the workers."

All equipment came under reverse Lend-Lease and was issued by the British Ministry of Works and Planning at the request of American Red Cross headquarters. For weeks I tried to convince them of our desperate needs. A representative from the Ministry came to see us from time to time, but he always arrived in the morning when things were slow, as the majority of the troops were in combat training and comparatively few could come to the club before evening. He was obviously skeptical when I described the crowds that jammed the immense rooms until midnight. One evening I was astonished to find him behind the canteen counter busily helping the V.A.D.s serve coffee. He looked a bit caught and told me he had come "to observe conditions." When I asked if the Ministry and Red Cross headquarters realized the work we were doing and how many things we needed he said, "Mrs. Roosevelt, they do not. They have no earthly idea. Nor had I until now!"

Perhaps we were wrong to open the club as early as we did, but the sight of the men waiting drearily at the bus stops spurred us on. We felt they had to have some place of their own. The result was that we and the Red Cross came in for a certain amount of criticism. Before we had succeeded in getting any equipment Henry Morgenthau, Jr., Secretary of the Treasury, came with Mr. Bracken to see the club. I hastily assembled the American staff, all three of us, in my office upstairs, while a V.A.D. fetched coffee and doughnuts. Mr. Morgenthau sat down and proceeded to take the Red Cross apart, saying he had visited many centers in England and had seen none that was doing proper "social service" work for the troops. He declared that Tidworth House was a good example of wasted effort. It was typical of the Red Cross and was a disgrace to the United States. What on earth did we want with such a great barnlike place? No wonder so few soldiers used it, when there was nothing in it to make it attractive. I begged him to return in the evening and see the club filled, but he refused. Jean and Mary were on the verge of tears. He then told us he had just had an extraordinary experience downstairs, which I think may have affected his point of view. When he came into the club he saw a dozen soldiers sitting around reading magazines. He said to them, "Men, I am your Secretary of the Treasury." One of them looked up and said, "Oh yeah?" Rather taken aback, the Secretary continued: "I am Mr. Henry Morgenthau, Jr." Dead silence. "Did you never hear of me?" By then the group was listening and several answered, "No, sir." He took out his passport, opened it to his signature, unfolded a dollar bill, and went on, "Look, men. If you examine these two signatures you will find them to be identical." The soldiers crowded around, ready for any diversion on a rainy day, and looked intently at the signatures. One of them remarked, "Sez you!" and they returned to their magazines. Mr. Morgenthau finished the story by saying incredulously, "Not one had ever heard of me!"

Little by little we began to get our much-needed equipment. Six months after we opened we had a Jackson boiler for coffee, a grill for hamburgers, a doughnut machine that turned out several hundred dozen doughnuts a day, easy chairs and sofas, radios, phonographs, two pianos, billiard and ping-pong tables, books for a small library, magazines, American newspapers, running water laid in behind the canteen for dishwashing, hot showers for the soldiers, and finally a barber and a tailor.

One of the most popular features of the club was the weekly dance. We used to shut off three of the large rooms and invite a number of British girls in uniform, ATS, WAAFs, and the like. Jean devised an excellent scheme to prevent overcrowding. Tickets were sent to various Army units in turn, and admission was by ticket only. The units receiving tickets furnished transport for the girls. Men not admitted to the dances had the rest of the rooms and another canteen for their use. A house committee of soldiers, with its chairman as m.c., worked hard to keep things going and to make sure there were no wallflowers. Once we had a group of Wrens, but although they were the most popular of all we could not have them again, as they were stationed too far away and too much gas was needed to fetch them. When they arrived a great shout went up, "Here comes the British Navy!" and they were snapped up instantly as partners. Another time we had the Land Army girls, but although they were pretty and nice the soldiers protested afterward that they didn't like dancing with girls in pants. I was sorry about this, as those girls had tough jobs and needed diversion more than the others.

Jean also worked out a most successful plan by which as many as five hundred men visited English families over every weekend. The soldiers were those recommended by their C.O.s. They took rations with them and established cordial relations all over the district.

On Sundays the men brought in children from the village, scrubbed until they shone, gave them Cokes and doughnuts, and played games with them. They also brought in all the dogs in the neighborhood and usually forgot to take them out. Once several were overlooked as they slept under the sofas. The resulting fight woke us all up at three in the morning. After that we had dog patrol at closing time.

The Army considered the club essential for morale and co-operated with us fully. They gave us fat for frying doughnuts. Five hundred 1st Division replacements spent a day in nearby woods gathering and sawing up deadfall for our fires, for which we had to get permission from the local authorities. They came back with pigeons' feathers in their caps and had specially reserved seats at the movie that night. Many individual soldiers spent their free time doing odd jobs in the club. We were given a permanent detail of six men who came early every morning to sweep out the clubrooms, supervised by a V.A.D. American medical officers looked after us when we were ill, as we often were. At least one of us was always laid up with what was called upper respiratory infection, meaning everything from a head cold to bronchopneumonia, and once when we had a full staff seven of us were in the Army hospital at the same time. It was probably due to the bleak, damp climate and also to our diet of British civilian rations, which had no fruit or fruit juices, little meat, few vegetables, and practically no eggs. The saying was, "One egg per man per month, perhaps." How the British endured it so bravely for years is to me almost incredible.

We had to work so hard that we had no time or energy to cook our own food, make our beds, or clean our rooms. Fortunately we were able eventually to find a cook and also an elderly maid who came part time. Her name was Emily and she told me proudly that before her marriage she had seen service in great houses. Once she said I reminded her of Queen Mary. "It's because your room is always so neat, madam. When I was with the Earl of Warwick, her Majesty used to visit Warwick Castle. Her room was always tidy, with nothing left lying about, just as yours is. The true aristocracy is always just so." "That may be, Emily," I said. "But you must admit that Queen Mary had plenty of people to pick up after her, while I have to do my own picking up. I think I deserve much more credit than she does!" Emily bridled. "Oh, madam! You will have your little joke, won't you?"

We had a day and a half off every week. I usually went to London and stayed at the Savoy for a brief taste of utter luxury, where I could summon a valet and say, "Please press my uniform and have the boots clean my shoes!" Twice I spent weekends with friends, once with Lord and Lady Cranborne, now Lord and Lady Salisbury, at their house in Cranborne, part of which dated from King John. Another time I stayed with William Waldorf Astor and his wife, Lady Violet, now Lord and Lady Astor of Hever at Hever Castle, where the topiary art was remarkable and included an elaborate maze and a set of chessmen taller than I. Here I had inadvertently left my suitcase unlocked and when I went to my room after tea was dismayed to find everything had been unpacked. My toilet preparations were in containers from Woolworth's, with which I had replaced the heavy silver fittings of my dressing case for the transatlantic flight. Some of them were black celluloid, as modern plastics were as yet unknown. These unsightly objects were all carefully spread out on the dressing table and did not add to the beauty of the original Queen Anne embroidery with which it was covered.

As time went on our staff was gradually increased until we numbered twenty-six in all. Among our new American Red Cross personnel were an assistant club director, a program director, and several staff assistants. Of these, the two most outstanding were Wilma Clizbe from Michigan and Dorothy Chandler from California. Among the British employees engaged and sent to us from headquarters were a club manager and his assistant, an accountant and his wife who lent a hand where needed, a movie operator, and a Western Union man to take cables from the troops. With one or two exceptions they were excellent, but even so it was not always smooth going in the beginning. Our first manager was accused by the accountant of robbing the till and had several other serious drawbacks as well. I explained the matter at headquarters, asked for his removal, and was surprised when he was made head of a department in the London office, from where he sent me directives. The accountant was then found unable to keep accounts, so he had to be changed. One of our most efficient individuals later went to jail, alleged to have been the smartest black-market operator with whom the Red Cross had to cope.

Because we lived far from the village, usually surrounded by a sea of mud and without gasoline, we found it hard to get out. As a result people sometimes got on each other's nerves. Part of my job was to calm them down and try to make them see the funny side of things. We had several rows among Americans and among British, which would have been worse if they had crossed international lines. Two of our Englishmen refused to speak to one another for days, the first driving the second wild by whistling gaily whenever they chanced to meet. At staff meetings in my office it was awkward to have them willing to communicate only through me.

These troubles, however, were small and easily dealt with compared to what happened when a certain American Red Cross man infuriated everyone to such a degree that we were threatened with wholesale resignations. Even the movie operator and the Western Union man, over whom he had no vestige of authority, said they wanted to leave because of his insulting way of telling them, quite unnecessarily, how to conduct their business. The American girls nicknamed him "Fiend"; the V.A.D.s for the first time lost their spirits and went around looking sad; and the cook gave notice. I was ready to fight for my staff but tried at first to make friends with him to see if I could persuade him to change. I got nowhere. He merely pointed out my own failings and recommended esoteric yoga exercises. Finally headquarters notified him at my frantic plea that his transfer was pending but didn't send his orders until three days later. During this time he ate alone in a corner of the dining room to avoid having to speak to anyone.

After he left, the staff drew a long breath of relief, laughed at the episode, and settled down again to work as a team. Some months later a visiting inspector stayed with us for a few days and reported that no other club in England had a happier atmosphere or a more congenial and efficient staff.

When the American Red Cross was recruiting great numbers of personnel in 1942, the WPA was disbanded. Many of its members joined the Red Cross and were given positions of authority. Those to whom I was responsible were dictatorial and arrogant, making things difficult, until Harvey D. Gibson, president of the Manufacturers Trust Company, came over to take charge and assigned his friends and business associates as zone executives. These men of wide experience were highly efficient and understanding and brought an end to most of our troubles. The work of Harvey and his wife Helen has never received enough credit and applause. They were in the Red Cross as a team, a shining example to other older couples who could have done the same thing. Helen had a full-time job running Rainbow Corner, the biggest Red Cross club in London, and did it and several other things supremely well.

I always kept in mind the great number of small contributors to the Red Cross, whose donations meant sacrifice, and was determined that no money should be wasted at Tidworth House, so I asked the accountant to figure out exactly what our running expenses were, including the salaries paid from headquarters which did not appear on our own books. According to regulations, no food or refreshments were given away but were sold at cost. Two movies a night, with a change of program twice a week, the theatrical performances, and everything else were free. The cost to the Red Cross was four and a half cents a night per man using the club. Albert Gregg, our zone director, was so impressed that he told me he was sending the figures home to be used in the next campaign for funds. I was surprised myself and went out and hired another piano.

During the ten months I was at Tidworth and the club was

thronged with thousands of enlisted men, we never had a single unpleasant incident caused by any of them.

Immediately after the invasion of North Africa I applied to the Red Cross to be sent there, as I was used to living under primitive conditions and could speak French, but was told that no soldier's wife could be assigned to his area.

Chapter 41

He has never felt so lively since he got his first
command (which was rather more than forty
years ago).

C. FOX SMITH

A mystery that to this day has never been solved was the issue in
November 1942 of a censorship order by the British Ministry of
Information by authority "U. S. Advisers," who were unidentified.
It was marked: CONFIDENTIAL. FOR OFFICIAL USE OF CENSORS ONLY.
I have one of these original documents, a photostat of which is now
on exhibition in the museum at Sagamore Hill.

This order directed that no names or identifiable photographs
of officers above the rank of lieutenant colonel were to be mentioned in press dispatches without permission of the "U. S. Advisers" except for a list of some sixty names in an appendix. These
included Generals Dwight D. Eisenhower, Mark W. Clark, J. Lawton Collins, Ira C. Eaker, and Carl Spaatz. In other words, all the
most important officers then in the European and African theaters
could be freely publicized.

Only three names could never be mentioned. A paragraph in
the order read:

> There is a specific stop on the following: Brig. General
> Theodore Roosevelt and his nephew [error for son] Quentin
> Roosevelt; Mr. Henry Wallace Jr., the son of the U. S. Vice-
> President.

When Ted led his combat team at Oran, newspapers both in the United States and in England gave high praise for valor to a General whose name was withheld, but as some of the accounts said his aide was Lieutenant William T. Gordon we knew who the unnamed General was. Sometime afterward an article by John Bell in the New York *World-Telegram* described twenty-eight generals in all theaters of war who were distinguished in various ways. The lead paragraph told of Ted at Oran, but he was the only one of the twenty-eight whose name was not given.

John Lardner in March 1943 wrote a delightful column which was published in the *Herald Tribune* about a tour he had made of the battle lines in Tunisia with a Brigadier General who recited poetry all the way. When interrupted by a Stuka raid the General went to one side of the road, Lardner and the driver to the other. After they had reassembled in the jeep a few minutes later, the General went on with the poem he had been repeating. It was easy to recognize Ted even though his name was omitted.

Sometime after the war H. R. Knickerbocker, chief of the Chicago *Sun* foreign service, told me he had written two stories about Ted in Sicily, only to have both canceled by the censor.

Nothing was allowed to be printed about what he did in Sardinia, or of the part he played in the capture of Cherbourg, where he was Military Governor until order was established. Few people were to know that in two wars he was awarded all combat medals given by the United States Army Ground Forces, the French Legion of Honor twice, and had the right to wear five palms on his Croix de Guerre.

In 1943 the ban seems to have been lifted on Quentin's name so that the account of his wedding could be told, but Ted's name was deleted from the stories until published in a London gossip column. Consequently the Associated Press dispatch was allowed through, adding that Ted had been in London for some time recovering from a severe illness.

The mystery was deepened in that this order applied purely to dispatches from overseas. Occasionally wounded soldiers returning home gave interviews in which they mentioned Ted to the press. Nor did the edict apply to news given out by the War Department in Washington. At times something would transpire from there. When Ted and Quentin were awarded medals in Africa a month apart and in separate engagements, no correspondent could mention either of them. Sometime afterward this was announced by the War Department in such dramatic fashion that father and son appeared to have been decorated together, and it was carried all over the country by the news services. When Quentin was wounded nothing could be said until the War Department reported it several days later, adding for good measure that Ted also was serving in Africa, up to then a secret. Whereupon several editors cabled their representatives asking why they had not reported Quentin's wounds.

Who was responsible for this strange edict and what was behind it will probably never be known. It was effective in keeping people at home from knowing the full story of Ted's war record. Because of it Ted has been called "the hero America kept hidden."

The invasion of North Africa took place on November 8, 1942. Ted led a combat team at the landing at Oran in Tunisia. Sometime afterward a group of wounded soldiers from the 1st Division arrived at the American hospital at Salisbury. They told me that after the heights above Oran had been captured the city still held out. The question was whether to bombard it into submission. Ted ordered that nothing be done for the moment and drove into the town to give it a chance to surrender, his jeep flying a somewhat dirty white undershirt. "If I'm not back in two hours, give it all you've got!" Oran capitulated, and much bloodshed was averted.

I was inclined to think that this story was merely one of the legends growing up about Ted, because every one of the men swore he had seen it happen. This was obviously impossible, as they all came from different units. After the war I asked Bill Gordon, his aide, about it. He replied, "They only got one detail wrong. It wasn't a jeep, it was a half-track. I know, because I drove it!"

After the landings and during the first months of fighting in Tunisia the 1st Division was taken apart and spread across the front like a film of oil on water. With a French officer as his Chief of Staff Ted was put in command of a heterogeneous gathering called the "Groupement Roosevelt." It consisted of three battalions from the 26th Infantry, a company of American light tanks, extemporized American, British, and French artillery units, and six thousand Goums or Arab Irregulars with French officers. These were given a section of the front and forced to operate without reserves.

The confusion resulting from this disintegration of our forces can be imagined. "To split and mix units to such an extent is a military crime of the gravest order." Things were to go almost disastrously until our high command was reorganized early in March.

At Kasserine, Quentin was shot from a strafing Messerschmitt plane. The ambulance that picked him up with other wounded drove to three field hospitals before finding one that was not in the process of evacuation before the German drive. A piece of shell had pierced his lung and lodged in his liver. A surgical unit tried to remove it, then decided to let it remain. As this happened during a battle, Ted could not take time out to go and see him. For two days Quentin was said to be doing well, but on the third day the doctors sent word that his temperature was over one hundred and four degrees and they thought he was dying. Providentially the fighting had subsided. That night Ted drove sixty miles, fearing the worst, and found Quentin asleep on a cot in a tent with a dirt floor. His fever had dropped and he was thought to have taken a turn for the better. Even this field hospital was now ordered to move eighty miles and to evacuate its patients. Because of Quentin's critical condition he was flown to the base hospital at Oran, where he stayed for twelve weeks after developing a lung infection. He had already received the Silver Star at Ousseltia. Now he was awarded the Croix de Guerre and was amused to have his citation dated "Forces Terrestres," saying this pleasing term suggested the possibility of celestial forces as well.

Quentin, still with the piece of shell in his liver, was sent home in June 1943, and Ted wrote me to go back and look after him. I had been in the hospital for ten days with a fever and was unable to start for another week but finally reached Oyster Bay, expecting to have Quentin home for a year. When he said he was pleased to have me back and that we would have a lovely few weeks before he returned to the 1st Division I did not discourage him, but he was right. His recovery was so rapid that eight weeks later he returned to command his battery in the 33rd Field Artillery, rejoining them in Sicily.

Ted was always convinced of the vital importance of seeing and talking to the troops not only in the tedious, morale-sapping intervals between battles but also in the front lines during combat. He never believed in so-called pep talks to a captive audience. He and his aide, Lieutenant Marcus O. Stevenson from Texas, known to everyone as "Stevie," used to drive around in his jeep making inspections, stopping to ask a captain how things were going, or listening sympathetically while a mess sergeant complained about supplies. "General, sir, we ain't got no cooks. We just got ration destroyers!" In Africa when it was cold and rainy he would ask if they were obeying the official instructions on wearing sun helmets and making sure that roofs were adequate against sunstroke. Or he would say, "Soldier, I suppose you're planning to settle down here when the war's over." The windshield of his jeep had a star-shaped bullet hole right in the middle and another patched up in its radiator. When asked about them he would say, "Stevie was trying to commit suicide but didn't know how!" None of it was brilliant, none of it was even very funny, but it served its purpose. The men almost invariably saluted him with a grin. One private said, "The Old Man isn't just cheerful. He exudes cheer."

He was sharply criticized by the high brass for visiting the front during combat. The front was no place for a general officer, and a deputy division commander was supposed to stay in his command post. Gault MacGowan, correspondent for the New York *Sun*, told me Ted was the first to break this unwritten law but said he had personally observed that afterward nearly every deputy commander followed his example. When after his death Ted was awarded the Congressional Medal of Honor, it was for doing this very thing on D-Day on Utah Beach, Normandy, this time with official sanction.

Ted wrote me almost every day, always reiterating his loathing of the painful discomforts of war and his longing to be at home. No ordinary APO mail went between Africa and England, so all our letters to each other went via the United States, taking three months on the way. At Christmas, Ted wrote me that he had received two packages, one from Signorina, the other from the Parish Aid of Christ Church, but he had no letters except one "from an unknown idiot in California asking for an autographed photograph." In February 1943 he wrote:

When I'm riding in my jeep or rolled up in my blankets I plan what we'll do after the war. Here's my plan for our first day, God willing.

The arrival in the morning. A visit to Christiansen to get gadgets for my uniform, a new overseas cap, etc. Then, a very good barber for a short haircut, a manicure, shampoo and so forth. Squash-racquets at the River Club for a big sweat and a salt rub-down. Then upstairs to your room in the Club where we doze and read, the children popping in and out.

Meanwhile my uniform has been cleaned and pressed, my shoes polished until they're brown mirrors, and clean—spotlessly clean—linen has been laid out. Then we get dressed, you and I. Here comes a hitch. I can't decide what you ought to wear, your Red Cross uniform or your best clothes. I'm inclined to think your best clothes.

The children have been all doing the same and we meet in the bar, ostensible purpose to have a cocktail, real purpose to have friends admire us—three Navy blue or white uniforms, two Army.

Next dinner. Here again I'm not sure. The dinner must be good, but obviously there must be people to look at us, and some will get up to greet us. We'll be very nice to them! After dinner—Madison Square Garden or a play. Probably a play, though Madison Square would provide more people to look! Then 21 or the Stork Club. More people of a different kind would be the reason for the Stork Club (I've been there only once).

Finally, all into the cars and out to Oyster Bay, where next day we'll all revert to type.

The campaign in Tunisia was long and hard, lasting several months. Toward its end Ted was awakened one night by the sound of German machine guns closer than they should have been. He rolled out of his blankets, lost no time in dressing as he had not taken off even his shoes, and drove with Stevie to a forward observation post at Djebel el Kaddab. The 10th Panzer Division was counterattacking. Communications with the 1st Division command post had been torn out by shells and bombs, so Ted stayed all day and the next night on the highest point of the ridge occupied by our forces. From there he saw the battle spread out like a game of chess and was able to command by field telephone as he saw the developments before his eyes. According to his citation, "he constantly exposed himself to intensive shell-fire and repeated air attacks while supervising the forward elements of the Division. His timely decisions calling for artillery fire resulted in the virtual annihilation of the advancing enemy infantry" and also of their tanks. Thus the battle of El Guettar was won.

A few weeks after the Tunisian campaign was ended the 1st Division invaded Sicily in July 1943. Stevie later wrote me describing the landing at Gela.

> For the second time the General hit a beach at H-Hour and established the advanced Division Command Post. The operation went well until afternoon when the Germans attempted to split our landing forces with a tank attack before our anti-tank equipment had been put ashore. The General saw it coming, huge clouds of dust from oncoming tanks. He rushed in his jeep on a parallel road back to the C.P. and gave the alarm. On his way back he met the 18th Infantry cannon company, put them into position and personally directed our counterattack. This saved the landing from being pushed back into the sea.

Needless to say, Stevie drove the jeep and was with Ted while this went on.

By the time Ted reached Sicily he was using a cane. In 1941, before he returned to the Army, he had mentioned a pain in his hip. With some difficulty I persuaded him to go to the hospital for X rays and a checkup. The doctors found him in splendid shape generally but said he had marked traces of arthritis around an old injury that had been aggravated by his playing squash rackets for years on hard courts, and they advised him to stop all strenuous physical exercise. When he asked if his hip would get well if he did so, they were vague, saying they could promise nothing. Even with rest it might keep on getting worse. One doctor told him that wild horses had been known to go through their life span with such conditions without becoming crippled. This was enough for Ted, who refused to give up the exercise that kept him in good shape. The result was that as time went on he suffered increasingly from nagging pain.

After twenty-three days of hard fighting in Sicily, where he had two teeth broken by a spent fragment of mortar, Ted was transferred from the 1st Division and made Chief Liaison Officer between our Fifth Army under General Mark W. Clark and the French Expeditionary Corps under General Alphonse Juin. While the corps was still in Africa preparing to go into battle against the German forces in Italy, he was temporarily removed from this duty and sent to Sardinia to straighten out a critical situation which had developed after the surrender of Italy.

In Sardinia there were some German and a considerable number of Italian troops. All the latter had capitulated except the Nembo Airborne Division. Most of them had been with the Fulgare Division, a crack unit of professional soldiers who had been fighting side by side with the Germans in Africa and were in no mood to yield. One of their battalions had mutinied and gone off with the Germans. The rest of them had been put in camp and were carefully watched. Ted's mission was to establish contact with General Antonio Basso, commanding the 13th Italian Army Corps, in order that the Allied plans to drive the Germans from Italian soil might be co-ordinated, and to win the Nembo Division over to our side.

When he arrived in a little P.T. boat with two aides and a radio operator Ted found his friend, Lieutenant Colonel Serge Obolensky of the O.S.S., who although fifty years of age was engaged in training our military personnel in parachuting behind enemy lines and had taken part in commando raids in Africa and later in Italy. Serge had parachuted into Sardinia to deliver messages to General Basso from the King of Italy and from General Eisenhower and to prepare for Ted's coming. He already had matters well under way except for the Nembo Division, which Ted proposed to review next morning. The Division Commander protested vehemently, saying he could not be sure of controlling his men. If such a thing were attempted it would be touch and go as to whether Ted and Serge would be welcomed as new allies or shot as former enemies.

The review was held. Ted wrote me that the paratroopers were "good, plug-ugly rough-necks." Many had beards from the African campaign; all were hard as nails and surly. Ted strode forward, his chin thrust out, his step cocky, his cane tapping the ground. He and Serge had purposely removed their guns and were unarmed. At the first battalion he stopped in front of a giant with a chestful of ribbons and spoke to him in broken Italian. "Sergeant, where'd you get those medals?" "In North Africa." "Fighting against me! I remember your outfit. I wish I'd had you on my side!" The sergeant started to smile. Ted felt his biceps. "You must be a boxer." "Yes, sir." "Any other boxers here?" The Italian general ordered all boxers to come forward on the double. Ted asked if any had been to the United States. Several had, and said so with grins.

At the second battalion he asked to have the wounded step forward and spoke to them. Then he went around talking to the others and ended by telling them all that he knew them to be good fighters and said if they would stick by him he would see they got all the fighting anyone could desire.

Afterward Serge said in a talk at the Adventurers' Club, "By the sheer force and charm of his personality and an exhibition of the coolest gallantry he won the wavering troops to a wild personal ovation."

In Serge's memoirs, *One Man in His Time,* he tells a sequel to this story:

Ten years later a Captain Minietto, now the purser of an Italian Line ship, came to see me at the Sherry-Netherland. He had been one of the Nembo paratroopers. He told me that he and five others had been designated to kill us when we came to review the division. The plans were all set. When

Ted and I arrived they were so impressed by his manner and the fact that we were alone and unarmed that they were delighted to become our allies.

From Sardinia, Ted, following his orders, went with Serge to make sure all was well in Corsica, where it was said Mussolini had never ventured for fear of being shot, then returned to North Africa. Shortly before Christmas he went with the French Expeditionary Corps into the line in Italy near Cassino.

A liaison job is what you make it. Ted followed his usual custom of visiting the troops in the rear and at the front, which was also the habit of the French generals, many of whom had been privates or company officers in combat and so had exactly the right touch when talking with the men. A French general will go into a café, sit down with a group of enlisted men, and chat for a time, calling them *"mes enfants"* without the slightest relaxation of discipline or loss of prestige.

The story of the heroism and endurance of the French Expeditionary Corps under the command of General (now Marshal) Alphonse Juin during those months in Italy was never fully told by newspapers in this country. Ted's letters to me gave them the highest praise as a corps and as individuals for their fighting over frightful terrain.

I'm just back from the front and I think the battle for this end of the Gustave Line is won. It has been bitter, with every foot of ground paid for in blood. Attack and counter attack have succeeded one another in unending sequence. Day has merged into night and night into day until time seemed to have no periods. I've been at the front every day, usually with Juin—he's a front-fighting general—often alone. My memory of this part of Italy will always be a series of rugged hills, the valleys between filled with smoke and echoing with the rumble of artillery and the rattle of small-arms.

The French Corps has covered itself with glory. It pushed out and cracked the first hole in the Gustave Line, and for four long days and nights it held while the Germans attacked on its front and flanks. Those Frenchmen need to take no second place to anyone when it's a question of gallant fighting. Of course they've paid dearly, especially with their young officers. At one post four artillery observers were killed, one after another. The last one gave the order to lengthen fire three hundred yards. Then, back at the battery, they heard on the telephone the roar of bursting shells and the voice of the mortally-wounded Lieutenant, "You are on the target!"

Yesterday a company attacked a German-held hill. On the first assault they were beaten back by murderous machine-gun and mortar fire. Most of the French officers and N.C.O.s were killed or wounded. Again they attacked and again were beaten off, losing the rest of their French officers and N.C.O.s. The senior Moroccan N.C.O. gathered the remnants of the company together, had them fix bayonets, then charged the hill, took it and bayoneted all the German defenders.

The country we're fighting through has to be seen to be believed. It is a jumble of sheer rocky hills and mountains so steep that they seem about to tumble down on you when you get among them. The soldiers assault them in the face of hostile fire, often climbing hand over hand in rain or snow. Roads either do not exist or have been destroyed. Every mile or so a road or bridge has been blown out, and the Germans are covering the gap with fire. The infantry has to drive them from the heights before the engineers can start repair work. And always after days of battle the weariness—the desperate weariness. Sometimes you'd rather take a chance of being hit than throw yourself down and have to get up again.

And this was part of "the soft under-belly of Europe"!

Ted's little mobile unit was as compact as a pocket tool kit. He, Stevie, and Kurt Show, his driver, had a jeep on which Show had painted "Rough Rider." Ted did not care much for this, fearing people would think he was aping his father, but did not want to discourage Show, of whom he was very fond and who had done it as a surprise. Behind the jeep was a half-ton trailer containing all their belongings—tent, luggage, clothes, and rations. Ted said it proved how little one needed to live outdoors in bitter winter weather in the mountains, but even when he had a bad cold and admitted he had never felt as utterly frozen as in "sunny Italy" he did not regard these conditions as hardships for a man of fifty-five with arthritis. He merely said that in times like these one did not want to be living soft. In one letter he wrote:

> The longer I live the more I think of the quality of fortitude —men who fall—pick themselves up and stumble on—fall again —and are trying to get up when they die.

General Juin declared that Ted was far more than a liaison officer, he was one of his own generals. The French corps took him to its heart. Their little newspaper, *La Patrie,* referred to him as "Général Roosevelt, Soldat de France." The 8ᵉ Régiment des Tirailleurs Marocains made him honorary corporal, complete with insignia. I had no idea what this really meant until Colonel Jacques Balsan explained later that it dated back to Napoleon, "The Little Corporal," and was an honor rarely given to foreigners. When General Henri Giraud visited the French Expeditionary Corps, Ted went with him and General Juin to inspect the front lines. When they came to this regiment half a dozen men were drawn up to receive decorations. Unexpectedly General Giraud said to Ted, "Please take your place at the right of the line." Ted peeled off his muddy trench coat, handed his cane to Stevie, and received the medal of Officer of the Legion of Honor from Giraud, who afterward tapped him on each shoulder with a bayonet and, according to custom, kissed him on both cheeks.

When Ted left Italy at the end of February 1944, General Juin wrote him in part:

> There is no one in the Corps from the lowliest private to the most be-starred general who does not know and love you. At our most exposed places, such as the front line of battle, you appeared every day at one point or another with your great calm, your wide smile and your good words, to see that all was going well and to attend to necessary liaison.
>
> It is with profound distress [*déchirement*] that I see you go.

Chapter 42

Lest the young soldiers be strange in heaven,
God bids the old soldier they all adored,
Come to Him and wait for them, clean, new-shriven,
A happy doorkeeper in the House of the Lord.

KATHARINE TYNAN

All during Ted's tour of duty in Italy he kept writing to General Omar Bradley and General Bedell Smith that his proper place was in command of combat troops and asked to be so assigned. He even made me go to Washington and petition General George C. Marshall, telling me it was all right to try to pull strings and ask favors if what you wanted was a more dangerous job than the one you had. Finally, in late February 1944, he was overjoyed to receive orders to report at once to General Headquarters in London.

His trip by air took four days and four nights, including endless exasperating delays, and was a nightmare, for he had started running a high fever. At one point an Army doctor examined him, found his temperature well over one hundred and three degrees, diagnosed his condition as pneumonia, and tried to take him to a hospital. Ted refused flatly, determined at all costs to get to England lest there be some slip-up in whatever assignment was planned for him. He wrote me that all along the way everyone took care of him, including a young Mormon lieutenant who looked after him as if he were his child. A colonel on the train from the northern airport wired ahead, without telling him, for an ambulance. At the station in London, Ted thanked the men with it, asked them to go back and reserve a room at the hospital, took a taxi to G.H.Q., and reported to General Bedell Smith, who assured him he would be placed with troops as soon as he was well.

Ted was three weeks in the hospital with what the doctors called the worst type of pneumococcus. At first he reveled in being able to rest in a clean, warm place and have time to read with nothing else on his mind. I sent him pictures I had taken of every tree and shrub at Old Orchard, which he showed to everyone. "Whether people want to see them or not, it gives me pleasure." As time went on and he began to feel better he became nervous and fidgety and must have been a trying patient. He wrote me that the nurses irritated him.

> They are kittenish and arch, and always say brightly, "Well, how are we today?" One has patted me three times on the head. I suppose it's what elderly generals usually like, but it shrivels me up inside. If she does it again I'm going to pat her hard, not on the head. I know I'm being unfair. Some nurses are different. I've seen them just behind the front, living in tents in a sea of mud—cold, slimy, all-pervading mud —with rain slashing down. I've seen them in dirty slacks, their hair mussed, their faces drawn with fatigue, worn to the bone caring for an endless stream of wounded coming from battered, mud-caked ambulances. Five of our Roosevelt Hospital nurses were killed by a bomb in Italy.

At last Ted was released from the hospital. Ten days later he wrote me he had been out on maneuvers and had spent all day in a small boat, shivering-cold. The weather was raw and bleak with a sharp wind. His clothes were drenched several times and he wore them until they dried. He said, "I knew I was all well and now I've proved it!" This was, of course, amphibious training for the invasion of Normandy.

He was assigned to the 4th Division, commanded by Major General Raymond O. Barton, and was deeply content with his lot. The Division, Ted said, was a good one, with spirit and dash. The men came from all over the United States and were physically tough. The officers were confident and alert, with good basic military knowledge. Of General Barton he wrote me, "He's a very fine character of a real American type. His nickname is 'Tubby.' I look forward to your meeting him some day. You will like him, he's so square. Not only is he sound on military tactics but he's a real leader. I've seen so much of generals who were neither that it's a joy to be with him."

Meanwhile Quentin had met and become engaged to Frances Webb from Kansas City, who was working in the American Red Cross Clubmobile. Ted wrote me full details in March, adding, "Don't worry over Quentin. Just feel happy about him. All is well." He said the engagement was still a secret, but they were to be married on April 12. I heard nothing from Quentin himself and did not know until later that he and Frances had both written, but he had kept the letters in his pocket for a week until all mail in the area was impounded because of the coming invasion. By April 8 I felt that, as the bridegroom's mother, I must communicate with the bride's family if merely out of politeness, so I telephoned Mrs. Watt Webb in Kansas City, to find she had had no word from Frances. As they had never heard of Quentin, both Mr. and Mrs. Webb were fairly stunned by the news. As we talked she was interrupted by tears and gave the telephone to her husband, whose reaction was one of disapproval. I found myself rather in the position of the traditional French mother approaching the family of a desirable match for her son, and described Quentin's life from babyhood. That afternoon I wrote it all out and mailed it with photographs. In reply Mrs. Webb sent me a most amiable letter, blaming herself for being selfish when I must be anxious too, and accepting the situation gracefully. Afterward I learned that at first she had thought her daughter was engaged to Elliott Roosevelt.

Quentin and Frances were married at the little Church of St. Peter and St. Paul in Blandford, England. Quentin had his father as best man. Ted wrote me:

Thank God I was here at this time, but I miss you something awful. I am not used to being two mothers and two fathers all at the same time. I feel as if I should flit from

452

place to place dressing first the bride, then the groom, then giving the bride away and acting as best man. With all the work I must do I have so little time to help them.

The wedding breakfast was given by the 33rd Field Artillery, Quentin's old unit, at its headquarters, and was described by Ted:

It was very touching, for everyone from the battalion C.O. to the junior cook had done their best. At home perhaps it wouldn't have seemed much, a shabby barracks, deal tables and chairs, coarse food, bad punch, harsh coffee in thick cups, heavy cake—but no one thought this, least of all the bride and groom. To them and to all it was wonderful—a breakfast arranged with every effort possible and with respect and affection.

We sang songs—we had the 26th Infantry orchestra—and Q played his accordion. We drank toasts to the bride and groom, to the two mothers, the two fathers and the best man, and finally I proposed a toast to the absent wives. After that I kissed them both goodby, and to the rattle of tin cans they drove away.

They've gone for their honeymoon to a seaside resort for five days, and Frances has an evening dress! And, bless their hearts, they're very happy. There are shadows when they stop to think, but Frances believes God could not be so cruel.

Shortly before D-Day, General Bradley held a conference of officers who were to take part in the invasion. During the course of his address he said that those present would have ringside seats at the greatest fight in history. I don't suppose he realized why a sudden and hastily suppressed burst of laughter swept part of his audience when Ted said in a hoarse whisper, "Ringside, hell! We'll be in the arena!"

On June 5, 1944, he wrote in a letter to me:

We are starting on the great venture of the war, and by the time you get this, for better or for worse, it will be history.

We are attacking by daylight the most heavily fortified coast in history, a shore held by excellent troops. We are throwing excellent troops against it, well armed and backed by good air and naval support.

We are on our transports, buttoned up, our next stop France. The Germans know we are coming, for the harbors of southern England have been crowded with our shipping and the roads choked with our convoys.

I don't think I've written you that I go in with the assault wave and hit the beach at H-Hour. I'm doing it because it's the way I can contribute most. It steadies the young men to know that I am with them, to see me plodding along with my cane. We've got to break the crust with the first wave or we're sunk, for the following groups won't get in. At first Tubby Barton did not want me to do this, but eventually he agreed after I'd written a formal letter stating my reasons.

Quentin goes in, I believe, at H plus 60. That's bad enough. Frankly, it may be worse than when I go in.

We've had a grand life and I hope there'll be more. Should it chance that there's not, at least we can say that in our years together we've packed enough for ten ordinary lives. We've known joy and sorrow, triumph and disaster, all that goes to fill the pattern of human existence. Our children are grown and our grandchildren are here. We have been very happy. I pray we may be together again.

This will be the last for the present. The ship is dark, the men are going to their assembly stations. Before going on deck they sit in darkened corridors to adjust their eyes. Soon the boats will be lowered. Then we'll be off.

At H-hour on D-Day two battalions of the 8th Infantry, 4th Division, under fire for the first time, landed on Utah Beach in Normandy. The boat carrying Ted was the first to touch down. The moment he arrived he knew something was wrong, for he saw a house by the sea wall where none should have been. Scrambling up on the dunes, he recognized a ruined windmill and realized the troops had been put ashore three quarters of a mile too far to the south.

454

By now the beach was under intensive enemy artillery—machine-gun, mortar, and small-arms fire at point-blank range from little over a hundred yards away. Swiftly Ted improvised a new plan of attack necessitated by the unforeseen position, found the commanding officers and gave them this vital information. With Stevie beside him he went from place to place, rallied groups of men, urged them to go forward and not "turn into a target," led them over the sea wall, established them inland, and returned for more. Under the grueling fire he remained on the beach for hours, going back and forth to redirect succeeding waves of troops until the last assault forces had been cleared.

For this day's work Ted was recommended for the Congressional Medal of Honor by the Division commander, General Barton; a regimental commander, Colonel James A. Van Fleet, afterward famous as Commander in Chief of the United Nations forces in Korea; and a battalion commander, Lieutenant Colonel Carlton O. MacNeely. The award was made posthumously a year later. His long citation referred to "his seasoned, calm, precise, unfaltering leadership" and ended, "He thus contributed substantially to the successful establishment of the beachhead in France."

Some years after the war, when General Bradley, then Chief of Staff, was asked by a magazine syndicate for a statement on the bravest act he had ever known, he described Ted's conduct on the Normandy beach on D-Day.

Quentin had landed with the 1st Division on Omaha Beach, some miles east of Utah. Ted knew they had faced stiff opposition, especially Quentin's unit, as a German Panzer division chanced to be on maneuvers in the vicinity. He was deeply worried about Quentin and was unable to get news of him for over a week. One afternoon as he lay on a blanket in the sun, resting, just before an attack, Quentin appeared, to his great joy. He wrote me that the latter was filthy, having lost all his equipment in the landing, but looked better than ever. Ted said Quentin had had hair-raising escapes and adventures but promised to try to take care of himself from then on. I believe these two were the only father and son in the invasion.

Late in June an incident occurred, described by the New York *Times* as one of the strangest battlefield scenes in the invasion of

France. A group of elderly German nurses who had been captured were returned to the enemy lines. Our forces saw no reason why they should be detained. A brief truce was arranged by radio. For thirty minutes all firing stopped on both sides while two American captains, Quentin and Fred Ghercke, walked down the road between the lines. They were met by a German major, a captain, and eight enlisted men. Having made contact, they radioed back that the way was clear for the ambulance, which arrived with the nurses. Salutes were exchanged, polite comments were made on the weather, the women were released, while Quentin had the major sign a receipt. After that everyone returned to where he belonged. A few days later a second group of nurses was sent back the same way. This time the radio communication failed after the Germans had been notified but before they had a chance to promise a truce. Ted heartily disliked the idea of Quentin taking this risk, but all went well. Later Quentin told me that the nurses greeted the German officers with vigorous Nazi salutes, which the officers, poker-faced, returned in the ordinary military way.

Tough fighting went on for weeks. Although the Germans were gradually being driven back, the ubiquitous hedgerows were proving more formidable obstacles than anticipated. Cherbourg fell. Ted served briefly as Military Governor until order had been established in the great port. Show was with him at his headquarters, a cellar lit by a single oil lamp, and said afterward that the Old Man was bone-tired and must have been thinking more than ever of home when he gave out the password for the night, "Wandering Father."

The last letter he wrote me was dated July 10, 1944.

Well, now I've got a little home in a truck. It was captured from the Germans by one of our units and given to me by them. The ordnance has done it over and I've got a desk and a bed in it. The inside is painted white. Show is having a time fixing it up. He's put a headboard on the bed, made from the back of an old French chair. He's found a place for my footlocker and bag. He's put in an electric light. I feel positively a softie.

The truck arrived yesterday at a most opportune moment, for the old chassis had begun to feel the strain of these last few years of combat. I was a pretty sick rabbit, and it had been raining for God knows how long. It still is, for that matter. I got in and was dry after I'd screwed up energy to take off my drenched clothes. The Doc came and said with a little embarrassment that my troubles were primarily from having put an inhuman strain on a machine that was not exactly new. Anyhow, he gave me something to make me sleep, and this morning I was almost as good as new.

It's getting late and tomorrow we attack again—as we will day after tomorrow. Artillery is firing nearby—the heavies—and every salvo shakes this paper. I'm glad you've liked my letters.

For the next two days he made the rounds of the front and on the night of July 12 he died in his little truck. Orders giving him command of the 90th Division and recommending him for promotion to major general were on General Eisenhower's desk to be signed next day. This he never knew.

July 14, 1944

Dear Ma,

The Lion is dead—you've already heard, of course, and I hope you got the message I sent back through press channels telling a few details.

It was like the magnificent climax of a great play. There is no one today, there probably has been no one, who had so full a life. He had great material successes, but the part that really counted was the unfailing, complete loyalty which was felt for him by the people that he felt counted. To him, and to me, that counted a thousand times more than any further gain or advancement.

To me he was much more than simply a father, he was an amazing combination of father, brother, friend and comrade in battle. Thank God I had an urge to go and see him on the night it happened. I dropped in at seven-thirty and stayed having a wonderful time until after ten o'clock. We talked about everything—home, the family, my plans, the war—having a swell time. He hadn't expected me to drop in and was terribly happy when I left him, as I was.

Ma, it was better, much better, that he die that way than that he die in battle. He had the thoughts in his mind of all the things he loved. It was almost as if he had died at home.

He told me for the first time that night that he had been having heart attacks, and I naturally asked him a lot of things about it and told him to lay low. Right after that I had an opportunity to see the doctor, and I told Steve to hold him down the next time he was sick. I told Pa too, but you know how much effect that had. Apparently after 2 years of steady combat under terrible conditions and after a serious illness, he had begun to get "very tired" as he put it to me that night.

I heard about it when I got back to the Division at 2 A.M., and I turned right around and went back. The entire 4th Division staff was waiting for me. They took care of me at 4th and 1st HQs, giving me sedatives, all the help they could give, etc., etc. All of them were absolutely swell. They certainly loved him.

The funeral was in the official cemetery at Ste. Mère Eglise. As you may already have seen in the newspapers, Gen. Bradley, Gen. Patton, Gen. Collins, Gen. Huebner, Gen. Barton, Gen. Hodges and others were his honorary pall-bearers. The band came first, playing Chopin's Funeral March, followed by a division half-track bearing the flag-draped casket, followed by the sgt. and seven men that were supposed to actually carry the coffin. Then the family (Steve and I and Show), then the Generals, then the Honor Company (a man from each unit in the division, all old timers). A great many others were there, many from the Old Outfit.

I can never tell you how terribly impressive it was, a warrior's funeral in every sense of the word—the other great leaders paying homage, and his followers. Nothing else, no matter where or when, could have fitted in so wonderfully, so perfectly with what he wanted and what he was. The band, which by the way was very good, played "The Son of God Goes Forth to War" as the hymn. The sound of battle rumbled and surged in the distance. The chaplain described him as a great statesman and soldier. He was more than that. He was truly a great leader.

Steve and I and Show stood at attention closest to the grave, the Generals off to one side. The firing-squad fired three volleys, followed by two bugles playing Taps, echo fashion. The colors were behind, and at one end of the cemetery the flag was at half-mast.

General Barton and General Collins have both told me that he was very largely responsible for the success of the Peninsula Campaign, which is true. He landed with the assault as usual and led his men up into Cherbourg. The day he died he spent with his front-line battalions. He came as close to dying in battle without actually doing so as is possible. It happened very close to the front lines, within earshot of small-arms fire. As you know he got a very strong recommendation for the Congressional Medal of Honor from a battalion commander, a regimental commander and also the Division Commander.

Above all, remember that he was happy, especially that last evening—with family and friends around him. Also, remember the ceremony was perfect.

I know you're feeling right now that there isn't any incentive left for working on the place and Old Orchard. That's utterly wrong. He really lives to us through all that. It was something he loved with all of us, and should go on in exactly the same way and never change.

Remember all these things, Ma—especially that he was happy and had had everything.

Much, much love. I'll see you soon.

Quentin

INDEX

476